Online a Lot of the Time

Online a Lot
of the Time

RITUAL, FETISH, SIGN

Ken Hillis

DUKE
UNIVERSITY
PRESS

*Durham
&
London*
2009

© 2009 Duke University Press

All rights reserved
Printed in the
United States of America
on acid-free paper ♾
Designed by Jennifer Hill
Typeset in Chaparral Pro by
Tseng Information Systems, Inc.

*Library of Congress Cataloging-in-Publication data
and republication acknowledgments appear
on the last printed pages of this book.*

For Winnie

>>> Contents

>>> Acknowledgments

A sketch of this project first took shape in a paper I was fortunate enough to present in 1999 at the Knowing Mass Culture/Mediating Knowledge Conference hosted by the Center for Twentieth Century Studies in Milwaukee, Wisconsin. In the intervening years, the research for this book has been supported by my home institution, the University of North Carolina at Chapel Hill. My work was greatly advanced by a research and development leave from teaching as well as by a Spray-Randleigh Research Fellowship, both from UNC. A separate fellowship at UNC's Institute for the Arts and Humanities allowed me time to revise the manuscript.

This book is an outcome of my decade-long research adventure into the various complex intersections among ritual, fetishism, signification, and Web-based identity practices and techniques. Many individuals supported me during this time. At UNC, my department chairs, Bill Balthrop and Dennis Mumby, were strongly supportive of my endeavors. My sincere thanks to the individuals at Duke University Press who helped marshal this book toward publication, particularly Ken Wissoker and Courtney Berger. I am grateful to the three readers who provided both pointed critique and helpful commentary during the process of anonymous review.

No book is written in isolation, and my friends and colleagues provided many different forms of kindness and assistance. In particular, I wish to thank Ricky Barnes, John Beauchamp, Lisa Bloom, Wendy Chun, Paul Couillard, Lauren Cruickshank, Mary Ann Doane, Nathan Epley, Philip Hartwick, Jeremy Hunsinger, Martin Jay, Lynne Joyrich, Jon Lillie, Liz McKenzie, Susanna Paasonen, John Durham Peters, Rob Shields, Jon Simons, Jonathan Sterne, T. L. Taylor, Carol Vernallis, Nina Wakeford, Michele White, and Aylish Wood. I owe a special debt to Michael Petit, whose critique, editorial commentary, and partnership sustained me throughout the book's production and were pivotal to its completion.

Portions of this book began as papers and presentations at Brown University, University of Surrey, University of Wisconsin, Milwaukee, North Carolina State University, Northwestern University, the Crossroads in Cultural Studies Conference in Tampere, Finland, and the Console-ing Passions Conference in New Orleans, Louisiana. I further benefited from presenting parts of chapters at conferences organized by the Association of Internet Researchers, the National Communication Association, the International Communication Association, and the Association of American Geographers. I extend my sincere appreciation to all concerned.

It was as a graduate student in geography at the University of Wisconsin, Madison, that I first encountered James Carey's pivotal arguments from the 1970s on communication as ritual and communication as transmission. While I argue for the subsequent emergence of Web-based rituals of transmission, Carey's work formed an early matrix within and through which I was able to identify and develop arguments for the synthesis of transmission and ritual at the heart of many contemporary internet practices. It was John Fiske, then a faculty member at Madison's Department of Communication Arts, who introduced me to Carey's thought and who encouraged me to think critically about how the divide between the disciplines of communication and geography might be bridged. John made no claim to foretell the future, but I remain hopeful that his 1996 prediction about the present work proves true.

Rituals of Transmission,
Fetishizing the Trace

World Wide Web: Diogenes's ancient spirit infuses the name. When asked from whence he came, the cynic is said to have replied *Kosmopolites* — I am cosmopolitan: a citizen of the world, without country, society, place. The "cosmos" in cosmopolitan once referred to adornment and ordered arrangement; we see this etymological linkage in the word "cosmetics." In the same way that cosmetics and cosmetic surgery refer to what is visible on the surface or the skin of a body, both cosmopolitanism and the Web organize an experience of what is visible — a mobile worldview that articulates to cosmopolitanism's related meaning of "rising to the top." By offering a view from the top, the Web contributes to the production of value driven by desire — for the Web, like a cosmetic, never fully takes leave of the bodies and cultures it simultaneously appears to adorn, mask, and alter. Its qualities of virtual space promise the cosmopolitan virtual pilgrim or wanderer the penthouse view, and offer the detached cosmopolitical power of the mind's eye to see the world, including oneself, as a picture. The Web, therefore, like the ideal of cosmopolitanism, is an intersection-cum-fusion of art and life; it remains profoundly ambivalent to modern sensibility.

Subject formations most consonant with such hybrid or in-between qualities of ambivalence are those comfortable with a self-alienating and cosmopolitan placelessness that offers them the (utopic) possibility of transcending the restrictions of dominant sociocultural norms rooted in tradition, place, embodied locality, and the state.[1]

This is the cosmopolitan Web dynamic: A culture of networks and a culture of individualism linked by endless electronic nodes implicitly promoted as an ordered and harmonious system; everyday manifestations of a desire for a worldwide *oikos* or *ecumene*; networked assemblages of digital information machines "wherein" it is imagined that a global and capitalized sensibility might find a mobile and universal home away from home. Cosmopolitics. Fabrication of flexibility, flow, modularity, displacement, simulation, and ephemerality. Visual assemblages of graphic traces. Sign machines. Moving images of exchange value. World as theater. Search as map. Link as road. Network as territory. Monad as nomad. Spectacle as destiny. Anywhere, everywhere, and nowhere but always on the move.

A mobile focus on the visible organizes the cosmopolitan Web dynamic; yet in never fully detaching from the Web user's body, the visible also authorizes understanding the sign world of the Web as constituting a psychic or even material extension or indexical trace of this individual. Materially, Web participants remain "here" in front of the screen's display; experientially they are also *telepresent* (literally "distant presence") "there."[2] To the extent that networked information machines enable individuals to transmit or move a sensory experience of self-presence "elsewhere" across virtual space, the ground is set for the creation of human rituals in networked environments.[3] Traditional rituals set in situated places have been adapted to online settings; at the same time, these settings facilitate new possibilities for ritual that wouldn't otherwise exist. Renovated practices and new techniques of ritual, fetishism, and signification have emerged. Web participants, as connected cosmopolitans, are forming part of a utopic move into a graphical world in which communicability—the state of communication and the means to communicate—becomes a cosmopolitical end in itself.

Second Life is one example among many of a Web-based virtual world that allows individuals to create animated identities depicted onscreen as moving icons called avatars. It exemplifies the vanguard aspirations surrounding the experientially immersive "3D Internet." The popularization and hype surrounding the introduction of concepts such as the 3D Internet and "Web 2.0" reflect, in part, the desire to position the internet as more a social creation than a technical one. Here we can identify how hype works to culturally embed new technologies. In certain ways Web 2.0 operates as a branding strategy: it asserts that new forms of social networking applications are better able to facilitate new forms of online commerce than are the established "1.0" utilities with proven commercial potential, including voice over internet protocol (VOIP) and giant American firms such as Comcast, Yahoo! and MSN.

At the time of this writing, Second Life enjoys its status as the premier and most technically sophisticated multi-user virtual environment (MUVE) 3D Internet graphical chat site.[4] On the Second Life site, corporations such as Toyota, Sears, IBM, American Apparel, and Circuit City have opened virtual offices for disseminating information, academics hold virtual conferences and use the site to recruit and teach students, politicians provide interviews, therapists assist autistic children.[5] In September 2007 the Royal Liverpool Philharmonic performed works by Rachmaninov and Ravel in a replica of its concert hall fabricated on the site.[6] As of October 2007, the Second Life site simulated 375 square miles of land,[7] and after spending time there it is easy to imagine a Guggenheim Second Life by Frank Gehry — the rendering of the museum as pure sign.

A crucial reason for Second Life's vault to prominence is that in November 2003 its developer, Linden Lab (owned by Linden Research, Inc.), allowed Second Life "residents" to fully own what they "build" on the site. In early 2007, the company further announced that it would make available to developers the software blueprint of its PC program. Developers are free to modify it for personal use and share it with others.[8] Residents of Second Life negotiate, through their avatars' moving performances, the increasing expectation that they take their places as traveling signs within a networked world based on communicability and flow. Residents design and set up their own site-compatible virtual spaces (sometimes referred to as "persistent environments"), and they design avatar forms according to their own skills, preferences, requirements, and desires.

Figure 1 is a still image from a video capture of a wedding ceremony conducted in Second Life in early 2006. The wedding took place in the "Secret Garden," a personal iconographic environment designed specifically for the occasion by code-savvy site participants. The avatar named River Donovan officiated the exchange of vows between the avatars Merwan Marker and

1   Second Life Wedding, 2006. Courtesy Jeremy Hunsinger.

Mercurious Monde. Not all Second Life activities mirror traditional ritual practices, but the wedding ceremony is respectful, thoughtful, even conventional—and it is as fetishistically executed as any ceremony on this side of the screen, down to the bride's dress, the elaborate floral arrangements, and the release of virtual doves. The ceremony relies on the agreed-upon standards expected of any social ceremony focused on individuals who intend to publicly proclaim their commitment to one another. It is a ritualized form of storytelling that, as Nick Yee argues, gives heft to the virtual, avatar identities of the residents taking part.[9] It is also something more: in the replacement of the perceptible world by a set of images (Debord 1994:26), a Web experience such as Second Life's virtual wedding constitutes a learning experience pointing directly to the image as an iconographic sign/body, a formerly mechanical bride on its way to cosmopolitan mobility and seemingly conscious independence.

>>> Rituals of Transmission

Web-based rituals such as the wedding on Second Life depend on the merger in practice of two ideas of communication often held distinct by communication scholars: communication as the use of a device or mechanism such as the postal system, telephone, or radio to *transmit* messages between people across space; and communication as a *ritual* gathering, often of a religious nature, of people coming together in the same place for the performance of activities intended to generate, maintain, repair, and renew social meanings and relations. Transmitting information across space is centrifugal—messages move outward and away from the sender centered in the here and the now. Such messages, composed of words and images, are fully distinct from the sending bodies. In contrast, physically gathering together to "hear the good news" or bear witness to a testimony of action is centripetal—the gathering place is the productive center where communication is produced; it constitutes a middle ground that draws together various individuals into a group, the members of which enter into communication with one another. Members perceive what gets said or shown as directly emanating from the body of the teller or actor. The networked transmission of digital information collapses this binary understanding of communication and blurs distinctions between these processes. Each individual who "enters" the sites discussed in this volume in the digital form of what I will call the "sign/body," though remaining geographically separate from other "visitors," can experience a sense of joining with them in a form of virtual gathering place. A variety of ritualized activities may then take place virtually in these settings that fuse and modulate the centrifugal and the centripetal, and therefore may seem to do the same for human bodies.

Common sense and traditional Western understandings associate rituals with embodied *rites of passage* set off from daily routines; they are extraordinary events distinct from yet lodged within the everyday: individuals gathering together to solemnize, mark, or celebrate birth, marriage and civil unions, death, healing ceremonies, coronations, graduations, and trials. The practices traditionally associated with bounded ritual performances situated in a physical space remain strong. The specific forms of language, habitual social interactions, and relationships between bodies and the codes of communication they entail, however, are inflected in new ways (at times renovated, at other times made superfluous) by information machines and the virtual spaces they render graphically possible.

Strayer University, headquartered in Arlington, Virginia, launched its Web-based "virtual commencement" on June 27, 2006 (figure 2).[10] Graduates and others opened the original commencement website to attend a graduation ceremony complete with a keynote address, names and degrees in di-

2   Virtual commencement ceremony for Strayer University, 2006.

ploma format, and a rendition of Edward Elgar's *Pomp and Circumstance*. The setting of the ceremony positions the viewer at the rear of an auditorium behind rows of mortarboard-clad graduates facing the stage. The valedictorian or master of ceremonies stands behind an on-stage lectern as curtains open and a screen descends to project, at appropriate points in the ceremony, viewer-activated videoclips of inspirational speakers who address "the leaders of tomorrow." The ceremony includes a keynote address by Susan LaChance, a U.S. Postal Service vice president for employee development and diversity. In her speech, LaChance departs from conventional boilerplate to promote the neoliberal value of flexibility built into the ceremony itself: "Not only did Strayer University give its graduates the option of deciding when they could take classes, but it has given them the option of deciding the day of their graduation ceremony. The life of an online student comes down to balancing many responsibilities . . . so it's only fitting that online graduates experience a ceremony that helps strike a balance in their lives."[11]

The "balance" achieved through Strayer's virtual ceremony lies at the intersection of a produced opposition between culture and economy. We live in a period when "the basic unit of economic organization is . . . the network . . . relentlessly modified . . . to . . . market structures" (Castells 2000:214). The development of digital rituals such as Strayer's virtual commencement indicates that the participants require that traditional rituals shed specific associations with actual places and adopt greater flexibility of form. Such a requirement means that the image of the graduation must be divorced from its original discursive and bricks-and-mortar settings. The ideology of convenience (a necessity for individuals who must be flexible, that is, customizable as employees) requires simulating a gathering place. This supersedes the older cultural meaning of a ritual as bringing people together in the same place to produce meaning, and the virtual ceremony that "strikes a balance" reveals the logic of capital colonizing an older collective form of producing meaning and order through ritual action.

We generally understand a ritual as an event constituted in a set of activities that induces a change or shift in people's perceptions and interpretations: when the officiator announces that the couple is married, they really are. This constitutes a change in circumstances. Rituals such as marriages, funerals, and trials are "framed" or positioned as differing or standing out from everyday life. But rituals also confer order on and an understanding of everyday life; their form signifies meanings that extend beyond the actual ritual activity. And while rituals entail customary and formal qualities, this need not preclude their also being small, personal, and informal performances.

Consider, for example, the emergence of dozens of online memorials and virtual gravesites to commemorate the dead (figure 3). With names like Virtual Memorial Gardens, World Wide Cemetery, DearlyDeparted.net, ForeverStudios.com, ToLive4ever.com, and MyDeadSpace.com, these websites allow individuals to upload personal details about the deceased, including biographies, photographs, and digital videos. Depending upon the application, the bereaved and other visitors can leave personal notes, present virtual flowers, and light virtual candles. The listings, according to the memorial site Memory-of.com, "have become a way to speak to the departed by writing them letters, for friends to exchange memories, and for strangers as well as distant relatives to send condolences to the family. In this way these rituals take a traditionally private ceremony and render it public."[12] According to the online *Encyclopedia of Death and Dying*, digital cemeteries first appeared in the mid-1990s, and most "evoke images of traditional cemeteries, with

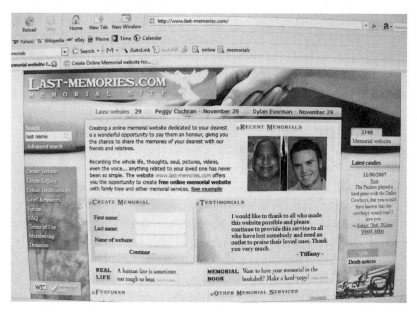

3   A screen display from Last-Memories.com virtual memorial site.

pictures of cemetery gates or gardens on their opening pages. Opening pages often invite visitors to 'enter' their cemetery, and once inside, web cemeteries ... [provide] a sense of place and to many, a feeling of community; as with traditional cemeteries, other losses and the people who mourn them are nearby."[13]

Figure 4 illustrates a more personalized ritual indicative of the growing use of personal webcams for audio/video chat and PC-to-PC phone calls. Webcams are cameras attached to networked computers that over the Web transmit images that are continuously refreshed. I live in North Carolina, and for the past year I have had coffee every week or so with close friends who live in Toronto. We do so through webcam technologies supported either by Skype or Yahoo! Messenger. We prefer Skype because the webcam image can be expanded to fill most of the laptop's screen or display, thereby enhancing the experience of meeting together in virtual space. On both ends of the wire a small webcam placed somewhere close to where we are seated transmits our images in real time to one another; microphones do the same for our voices. We exchange personal information — something we could also do on the telephone or by email. The exchange of visual images coupled to

4 A screen display of friends during a virtual coffee klatch.

audio information, however, heightens and makes more direct my friends' experiential presence to me. We see each others' faces move in response to what we are saying and seeing, and the time we allot to each coffee klatch— no more than half an hour—marks an informal, performative ceremony set off from the day's demands yet part of the everyday. It is both transmission as a ritual and a ritual transmitted or communicated (see Carey 1975; Rothenbuhler 1998:5). At times these encounters induce feelings of absence and "wish you were here," yet mostly they have the opposite effect: everyone feels that they are somewhat in each others' presence.

These examples of networked rituals are, in part, contingent—the Second Life wedding relies on code-savvy participants who cannot all be in the same material place at the same time; the spatiotemporal and economic demands placed on Strayer's graduates mesh with the "convenience" of online convocation; online memorials spatially relocate gravesites and make private mourning public; my virtual coffee klatch meshes available technology and the group's desire to maintain regular and friendly contact. What is contingent, moreover, becomes historical when it gains meaning through human interpretation such as our collectively produced understanding that we all benefit from meeting this way online. Virtual weddings, funerals, graduations, and coffee klatches are "localized" examples and personal actions that take on positional value as part of a broader cultural dynamic (Sahlins 1985:109).

Whatever their material or virtual forms, rituals are communicatory activities variously intended to generate, maintain, repair, and renew as well as to contest or resist relationships among people; relationships between people and the natural world; and relationships between people and the supernatural world. Though the technologies supporting digital ritualizations are commodity forms, they also articulate in the public imaginary to a belief in progress and, by inference, technology and science and the latter's disinterested, cosmopolitan view from above that is afforded by the former. The ritualized uses of these devices, however, also serve as contemporary talismans. In a circular fashion that conforms to cosmopolitanism's deeply ambivalent dynamic, the talismanic, fetishistic body-referencing practices that Web settings increasingly situate also point to the ideal of science. They confirm allegorically for those using the Web that such practices in themselves constitute a form of applied knowledge as well as a kind of vanguard practice.

Few of the website participants I discuss conceive of their practices as ritual per se. They would not describe their use of information technology as ritualistically enacting, rehearsing, or enabling a virtual future that could actually come to pass, or evaluating how things should be—each a component of the ritual function of negotiating the order of the world. Instead, they would variously say they are having fun, killing time, honing web-based skill sets, teaching a class, making friends after a particularly nasty breakup with a boyfriend, or opening themselves to new ways of meeting people for friendship or sex or a relationship and so forth. Ritual theorists identify many of these activities as rites of passage that serve to provide one of ritual's benefits—the induction of a semblance of order during difficult or even chaotic periods of change that might otherwise prove too destabilizing to individual or group social relations. Rituals, as modes of social action, give shape to the everyday organization of time and space. For networked individuals, such chaotic periods include the contemporary conjuncture, a part of which is the virtual dictate to circumnavigate the "flow" of the ongoing computerization of everyday life.[14] For such individuals, networked digital settings may be used as ways of performatively taking control over, or at least modulating, significant changes that otherwise threaten to overtake the already over-individuated and disintermediated neo-monad. In this way virtual space, as a setting or ground for online ritualizations, accrues increasing importance as the stage on which individuals donning the form of the networked sign performatively give some order to their chaotic experiences of time and space. Ritual, then, like ideology, is an interpolating dynamic. Its nature has been theorized as essentially conservative (Bourdieu 1991; Couldry 2003). A ritual works to incorporate participants into certain forms of order. Some support dominant social forces; others may operate at askance purposes. Yet all rituals offer participants a way of making sense of an at times radically unstable world.

My examples of Web-based rituals, therefore, illustrate more than the useful application of a utilitarian tool. Ritual is foremost an activity. It does not take place in a vacuum. It is never pure or detached from culture, consequences, power, and desire. Its practices range from the strategic (those intended to influence future outcomes through calculated combinations of timing and gestures that make means visible) to the tactical (such as my having coffee with friends) that introduce a quality of order and help getting through the day. The forms that rituals take matter, and their forms are contingent on the places, both real and virtual, where they take place. People develop and perform rituals across a wide range of flexible, individuated practices. In this volume I direct my assessment of ritual practices to those developed and emerging within and across two broadly based online settings that feature moving images of bodies. The first is avatar-driven graphical chat (MUVEs such as Second Life), also known as 3D Chat and, less frequently, as a multi-object virtual environment (MOVE). Graphical chat settings rely on animated graphical illustration to render MUVE participants as sign/bodies that move within virtual environments.[15] The second setting is that of personal webcam sites, specifically those mounted by gay/queer men,[16] in which webcam operators stream live video images of themselves on a regular basis. These two foci of analysis indicate that geographically dispersed individuals are using online settings as a virtual surrogate for the gathering space necessary for a ritual's participants to come together. Such individuals, therefore, are also ritualizing the idea of virtual space. These two foci thus support a divergent range of participant techniques and practices;

considered in tandem, they indicate the complex dynamics and modalities by which individuals produce meaning through their networked transmission of information across material space.

>>> Fetishizing the Trace: The Sign/Body

Media rituals "re-create the illusion of bodily presence, the most basic of all ritual gestures" (Marvin and Ingle 1999:140). Human perception accords to movement the quality of liveliness, and becoming an iconographic sign/body in the form of an avatar or a moving webcam image erases *experiential* distinctions between the psychic reality of an image representing an individual and transmitted through Web networks, and the physical reality of the individual's moving, active body. Recent empirical research using immersive virtual reality (VR) technology confirms that individuals lose track of their body locations in virtual settings. H. Henrik Ehrsson reports that it is possible to determine the experience of embodiment through "visual perspective in conjunction with correlated multi-sensory information from the body" (2007:1048). To induce the sensation of out-of-body experience in subjects, Ehrsson had them wear VR head-mounted displays that transmitted images of the subjects recorded from behind. The display prevented them from seeing any other spatial representation or image of the self in virtual space. Ehrsson then used the end of a rod to press on the subjects' chests while at the same time he held a different rod in front of the camera behind them that made it seem as if the virtual individual viewed from behind was also being poked in the chest. Subjects reported perceiving their chests being probed, yet they also sensed that it was the virtual individual lodged within the display (in other words, a moving image or sign) that was also being touched by the rod. In a second experiment Bigna Lenggenhager et al. (2007) demonstrated that the sight of a humanlike figure, such as an avatar in virtual space, combined with the actual stroking of the subject's body can induce an experience of relocating the subject's sense of self away from his or her body's location in actual space. As Ehrsson comments, "We feel that our self is located where the eyes are" (2007:1048).

Gesture and movement are crucial to any success at communicating and inducing belief on the part of these sign/bodies. Gilles Deleuze (1986:56–61) identifies the rise of cinema as pivotal in revealing the previously naturalized binary placing images in the qualitative realm of consciousness and movement in that of quantifiable space. Such a binary between idealism and materialism, interior and exterior, divorces consciousness from the thing itself.[17] Deleuze identifies how viewers bridge this gap between perception and ideology through his concept of *l'image-mouvement*, which is translated into English as "movement-image" (56). Cinema, a technology that renders image equal to movement, erases the psychological distinctions between the image as a psychic or experiential reality and movement as a physical reality. In cinema, there are no actual moving bodies distinct from spectators' perception of movement. The image's ability to move confers on it a quality of immanence: "The image exists in itself. . . . The identity of the image and movement leads us to conclude immediately that the movement-image and matter are identical" (59).

Both l'image-mouvement and movement-image signify the interpenetration of interior image-generating consciousness and external movement in space. To my thinking, however, the French term somewhat better conveys the truthful ambiguity of cinema as the realm of images — images of moving bodies and objects in space. My use of the hybrid term sign/body attempts a similar strategy: I understand the online moving image of a body or object as a special kind of sign. The sign/body points to those online forms of signification mounted by Web participants and users whose practices and techniques reveal the broader project of using the Web to collapse the binary that Deleuze identifies; that is, to render the Web as both the realm of the image and consciousness and that of space and movement, thereby to reconnect consciousness to the thing.

Not coincidentally, assertions and implicit beliefs that the Web constitutes a form of space multiply in tandem with the growing ability of the Web to support images that move. Moreover, the moving images of graphical avatars and personal webcam operators allow viewers to experience these moving images as indexical traces of actual human beings. The sign/body is indexical; it points back to the operator's body on this side of the screen or display. At the same time, as the philosopher Deleuze and the scientists Ehrsson and Lenggenhager et al. confirm in different ways, moving images hail perception autonomically, and the viewing of a moving image of an object, thing, or event has the potential to authorize the perceptual sense of experiential access to a trace of the referent. The dynamics of signification further suggest to human perception that the moving image/icon articulates metonymically and allegorically to the thing it stands for and points toward:

the human body of its operator or referent. This point about the indexical trace, with its implication of cause and effect, is crucial to the arguments I develop in this volume. While the indexical sign/body is clearly a representation, I am arguing that it is not perceived, autonomically or psychically, as such by those who consume it in the kinds of online settings I examine. The autonomic reception of the moving image operating as if it were a trace of an actual human being located elsewhere parallels the psychic desire made into the need to receive this image in the same way—that is, as if it were a transmogrification that can render actually present the distant individual it represents. In such a way does communicability become an end in itself.

A concrete example will serve to further clarify this point. I recently attended a seminar devoted to the relationships between ethics and research focused on Second Life and its resident avatars. Many participants engage in virtual ethnography on the site; others use the site to teach. Several participants stated their concern as to how best to protect the privacy of the person to whom each avatar is directly linked. In American contexts, the general consensus is that private space and private life on this side of the screen are protected by the privacy provisions contained within the guidelines of the academic Institutional Review Board (IRB). But Second Life is a media form, and what gets represented "there" could be argued to take the form of a public transmission of information. Certainly the technology itself readily facilitates the ability of an individual to archive what happens in the setting for her or his subsequent transcription and review. The seminar members' concern to protect the privacy of Second Life participants was paralleled by the members' very real concern also to protect the privacy of the individuals' avatars. The logic of such an articulation seems to me to inhere in the assumption that 3D Internet sites such as Second Life are no longer only forms of media per se; rather, because they allow for indexical experiences of traces of actual human beings they are now experienced as actual spaces "in" which aspects of actual human beings have come to reside and are publicly and privately addressed. Such a development far exceeds the powers of modern representation or even postmodern simulation; indeed, it depicts and insinuates the evolution of the machine world of images as an abstract, sovereign postrepresentational force into which, nevertheless, aspects or traces of human beings can (re)locate. Such a development was anticipated by Guy Debord who argues that "for one to whom the real world becomes real images, mere images are transformed into real beings" (1994:17). Within this machine-dependent virtual world the appearance—the image—takes command as it stands in for presence itself. And the forms of public discourse that this world enables lend support to the seminar members' concern to obtain IRB approval. The success of public discourse "depends on the recognition of participants . . . people do not commonly recognize themselves as virtual projections. They recognize themselves only as being already the persons they are addressed as being" (Warner 1990:114). In such combinatory ways the contemporary moving image has become a form of social relation with which we must all now increasingly reckon. And we will perform this reckoning within social contexts increasingly embedded in spectacular technological systems that can distance us from the adequate recognition, let alone consideration, of crucial life-threatening issues on this side of the screen. The lack of adequate recognition here points to an underlying difficulty in imagining different futures and therefore different politics than those currently beckoning from a purportedly postrepresentational virtual space.

The networked ritualized activities I examine depend for their efficacy on an underlying cultural fetishization of information machines and the global practices of transmission they enable and propel. To varying degrees, networked individuals fetishize not only information machines as the economic and social actualization of the progress myth but also an experience that such machines support—of the postrepresentational trace, transmitted to them in the form of an indexical sign/body, of geographically distant individuals who pique their interest for any number of reasons. Fetishizing this experience reflects, in part, an underlying recognition that experiences that can be transmitted are also enduring—memorable. Each setting allows for a semiotic interplay of symbols (words), icons (images), and indices (traces of the referent), though semiotic strategies vary in accordance with the form of the virtual environment and the expectations it excites. Most theories of fetishism posit that a distance or a space must separate or divide a desired material object (the fetish) from the person who desires it, and that this object must be visible to the eye. While the absent/present binary this entails is part of Web dynamics, there are no material objects on the Web but rather only signs and, at the level of viewer experience, sign/objects and sign/bodies. Nevertheless, the implicit desire remains that one might use the Web as an ersatz space to reach out, touch, and fetishize not only a (virtual) object but also other individuals. This desire is fueled by at least two factors.

The first factor is lodged in the ways that cosmopolitan networked individuals are encouraged to identify as mobile, flexible, and engaged in on-the-go yet customized and interpenetrating forms of consumption and production. Community-based rituals of association designed to induce support for place-based community increasingly compete for the time and attention of such individuals with the demands of the neoliberal work world, the time spent commuting between exurban homes and distant employment centers, and the related requirement, marketed as a choice, convenience, or even destiny, to assume ever-greater self-responsibility for all aspects of one's daily life. Booking hotel or airline reservations or maintaining one's own retirement account online are small examples of the move away from an earlier form of service economy based on employing specialists trained in such practices. These newer online activities may offer a form of consumer empowerment; they certainly indicate the cultural fetishization of information machines. Despite the hype that promotes such activities as requiring little more than "point and click," the time and labor required to perform them is considerable and might once have been expended on place-based community activities. I am not suggesting, however, that the latter activities are inherently more desirable. For some, they may be; for others, they may constitute oppressive social demands happily abandoned. Yet the underlying human need for some form of social cohesion with others that ritual practices support has not abated, and as Mark Andrejevic (2004:29) argues, the kinds of customized production and consumption inhering in the promise of flexibility promote nostalgic associations with purportedly more communitarian, premodern forms of social relations. The desire for at least the possibility of community continues. In a cosmopolitan and customized fashion, one may continue chatting with one's virtual friend at the same time that Expedia.com furnishes a list of flights to the next city that one's job requires one to visit.

The Web's pervasive and persistent applications that feature aesthetic appeals to viewer sensation is the second, intersecting factor fueling the desire, or even the need, to connect through networks. This hegemonic redirection of activity is rendered more appealing by the graphical quality of many Web-based transmissions. As I elaborate in chapter 3, to graph something is to make a record of its material presence. Graphing is a recording practice, but not of a preexisting symbolic code. Rather, it is a *tracing* or an index *of the real*. As John Peters notes, "Tracing implies recording . . . Recording implies transmission" (2006:144). This quality of graphing as the transmission of a trace—in *graph*ical chat; in webcam video transmissions of people's moving images, the precursors of which lie in the cinemato*graph*; in the extensive use of photo*graph*y by fans of webcam operators—is central to the appeal of the potential for networked personal experiences of traces of embodied human referents that always reside somewhere else. Though the transmission of a trace through online digital settings depends on the ephemeral, modular nature of Web connections, the graphical and therefore implicitly recordable nature of such a transmission also suggests its durability and hence contributes to experiencing it as psychically real and, by inference, somehow possibly material.

Transmitting images of bodies in the form of moving, graphically inflected signs that are experienced as psychically (but not actually) real introduces the possibility for an individual to be experienced phenomenologically as a *telefetish* both by others and by the individual himself or herself. He or she can fetishize the trace of others. The differing forms that individuals adopt to represent themselves in these online settings point back indexically—like pointing fingers—to themselves. Why is this important? All individuals engaging the Web remain on this side of the interface. But as chat and webcam participants they can experience seeing themselves as a networked sign/body; in cosmopolitan fashion, they experience becoming an image with exchange value courtesy of an assemblage of information machines that maintain separation between people even as they transmit a virtual experience of coming together. As Giorgio Agamben (2000) notes, this separation allows for language and communication practices to gain autonomy from actual bodies—a separation, again, of the practices of consciousness from the thing itself, of conception from the perceptive faculties that first inform it. *Cogito ergo sum.* Like a ghost within the machine, the networked digital image acquires a quality of semi-independent liveliness seemingly worthy of fetishization in its own right. With this status the image can then also be imagined as itself a social relation in itself. Yet to the degree that, for example, an individual participating in graphical chat comes to understand his or her avatar as an extension of himself or herself, he or she also understands that the avatars of others also point back to the individuals they represent. The avatar image is both sufficient in itself and serves as the instantiation of desire for spatially distant others.

The avatar of a webcam operator, as a visible and fetishizable sign/body, is a "virtual object" that can become as desirable to viewers as its embodied referent who can also see herself or himself transmitting as a sign/body to other participants. Seeing oneself seeing oneself—a graphical chat participant manipulating her avatar so that it turns toward her on the screen, waves, and says "hi"; a webcam operator watching his digital image update in real time—can induce an experience of awe. Each individual witnesses a self-produced self-representation as transmitting back to himself or herself the potential of his or her multiplicity within a sign system—including all the things he or she is not yet, or might desire to become. A crucial use value of the avatar or the image of the webcam operator for their owners and operators, therefore, lies in the degree to which viewers (including owners and operators) experience these iconographic images as psychically equivalent to their embodied referents and, therefore, as a means to signal their collective desire to bridge the gap between consciousness and movement, inside and outside, body and sign. This implies either that a part (the avatar) can stand in for its whole (the assemblage of the human operator and the avatar sign) or, more perversely perhaps, that they are equivalent in that the avatar signifies one aspect of an embodied human entity constituted in a plurality of meanings. In these virtual settings such signs can accrue a value equal to that of their owners or operators. In this way, MUVEs and personal webcam sites serve as ritualized forms of learning. In these "progressive" settings, virtual forms of exchange value between bodies and signs can come to seem at least equal in importance to use value to the point where exchange value itself develops a form of autonomous power (Debord 1994:31). The online rituals I examine perform this set of exchange relations.

>>> Transcendent Desires, Information Machines,
and the Society of the Spectacle

The West turns its philosophical assumptions, its ideas, into technologies.[18] As semioticians would argue, all humans think in signs. We also build the signs we think. These signs, like ideas, generate or gestate from within material and historical realities. Neil Postman observed that "we are surrounded by the wondrous effects of machines and we are encouraged to ignore the ideas embedded in them" (1992:94). But when we build the signs we think, while the resulting technology reflects the idea or sign embedded in it, it also comments on the earlier material world that it now enters, in part to also alter through new forms of mediation. The information machines upon which sites such as Second Life and Strayer's "virtual commencement" ceremony rely participate within an ongoing history of naturalized yet contradictory assumptions about vision and sight, including metaphysical, empiricist, and positivist epistemological assumptions. Such assumptions manifest age-old desires that symbolic expressions of material reality can be adequately communicated in images and related optical effects. More recent cultural instructions encourage people to identify both with and as commodities, images, and simulations. Debord argues that the spectacle is the "material reconstruction of the religious illusion" (1994:18). Within a Marxian framework Debord's analysis seems complete. But if I were to agree with the nature of this illusion I would also think something more is at stake, and it would be both an individual and a collective need to confer meaning on an otherwise disenchanted world. The development of programmable software agents and electronic avatars doing one's bidding within electronic networks indicates a cultural revival of Neoplatonically inflected belief systems that for their cultural salience rely, in part, on fetishized uses of allegory and emblems, as forms of "visual language," to accord aspects of personal control to exterior forces such as divine symbols, magical signs, and inanimate forms perceived as occupied by living spirits. This revival also depends on a Cartesian and Gnostic inflected belief that the self, like a kind of spirit, is in possession of a body but is not the same as this body it controls.

The issue of the body double, in the form of the online avatar but also the doll, the puppet, and the automaton, expresses a set of desires that has a long history in the West. This history is freighted with underacknowledged issues of transcendence, magical affect, mimesis, and an ongoing Neoplatonic desire to synthesize the empirically verifiable sense world in which we live to that "other," more ideal world of forms of which we are purportedly aware, and which surrounds us, but which we remain incapable of fully perceiving (Nelson 2001). These issues, moreover, are not the exclusive purview of metaphysics—they parallel and implicitly inform capital's focus on abstraction as seen, for example, in its use of data collected about workers as part of rationalizing production and making workers conform to principles of "scientific management" (see Andrejevic 2004:33). The idea of the body

double suggests the redoubling of the subject through forms of exteriorization, whether in data banks or mechanical devices. With respect to doubles
and information technologies, Andrejevic explains that "Deleuze coined the
term 'dividual' to refer to the no longer discrete (in)dividual, who finds him-
or herself multiplied in myriad databanks. Similarly, Mark Poster describes
the data image of the subject as a 'second self,' and Phil Agre calls it a 'digital
shadow'" (2004:33). While Neoplatonic ideas about transcendence through
forms of doubling are coolly received in the academy, except perhaps within
the history of philosophy and certain departments of theology and religious
studies, their circulation nonetheless proliferates through popular culture
"entertainments" including digital variations. Graphical chat MUVEs illustrate how the Web has infused new meaning into the role of puppets trans-
mographied into digital avatars. In updating a number of the sociocultural
functions of puppets, online avatars take the form of moving images discursively rendered as desirable virtual objects endowed with godlike, quasi-
independent powers. Like puppets, avatars are positioned as having inner
spirits that participants unleash. The Web, along with video gaming, is arguably the site where these shamanistic ideas about the animation of inanimate forms enjoy a popular resurgence even if their complex history remains little known or a subject of indifference to most gamers, Web users,
and participants.

The possibility of a body double as a form of second self, moreover, articulates to a different set of more recent discourses of inscription and automation. Readers may recall an earlier cultural anxiety that humans were soon
to be replaced by robotics and other forms of mechanized, industrial automation as exemplified by the very models of automatons—Disney World's
animatronic laborers. If this specific form of fear of replacement by commodified devices has receded, the digital avatar is a different, equally metaphysical vision of replacing the human with an automated machine—an information machine rendered as a screen image and fabricated according to
ideological and contingent assumptions about actual bodies. The idea of a
digital avatar replete with a quality of "digital humanity" trades in supernatural associations; even the name of the ersatz space where avatars "reside"—Second Life—connotes religious associations with rebirth and renewal. (Some Second Life residents now refer to the world on this side of
the screen as "First Life.") These supernatural overtones intersect with the
commodification of reality that the site proposes. The site's name also recalls

Karl Marx's discussion, filtered through religious analogy, of commodities that come to be seen as "independent beings endowed with life" (1952:31). One might say that in Second Life the commodity is born anew, constituted as a haunted technological vision "of the exiling of human powers in a 'world beyond'" (Debord 1994:18).

Thomas Hobbes also contributes to the Western history of the double. By 1651 Hobbes, in *Leviathan*, as part of his theory of the modern social contract, already could theorize the multiple "actors" who would do the bidding of a central "author" on the various stages of early modern life. The materialist Hobbes did not intend to promote a mind/body dualism—that would be a principal legacy of René Descartes, Hobbes's contemporary and philosophical adversary. However, actors who do the bidding of someone more sovereign than they concord with the notion that the actor is a laboring body that may speak ventriloquistically for the central author who controls the scripts. Equally, a central author organizing and controlling the actions and speech of the actors concords with the idea of a central, unitary, and interior core self that may have multiple exterior "cosmetic" personae or masks performing strategic gestures. It is thus possible to locate Hobbes's author-actor binary within the Neoplatonic tradition of inscribing human bodies as sets of texts and other representations. Here, Neoplatonism meshes with Cartesian dualism contained in the idea that the self possesses a body that remains distinct from the self. Hobbes's binary is grounded in this immanent metaphysics of an exterior body "ornamented" by a set of implicitly cosmopolitan personalities distinct from the interior self. Hobbes was clear that the author would control the "scripts" that actors would perform. The current transfer of activities and power to "actors" taking the form not of human bodies but of designed electronic devices, virtual objects such as avatars, and other software agents simulating and standing in, indexically, for human bodies indicates the seldom acknowledged trend in popular and commercial practices to disavow or at least renegotiate the status of a fully autonomous self based on universal principles. At the same time, for those who are online a lot of the time, spheres of communicability such as the Web are increasingly perceived as spaces where quasi-autonomous sign/bodies (the descendants of Hobbes's actors) perform their coming to life.

The websites and practices I examine in this volume suggest that the implicit qualities of transcendence once thought to imbue the unitary self are being transferred to networked information machines. As quasi-autonomous beings, the digital actors or sign/bodies in such virtual spaces seem increasingly lively and in sufficient control of their own "scripts" so that one might postulate that the embodied operator on this side of the interface is in the process of trading places, of becoming something of an actor himself or herself. The human activity in such settings is a form of networked ritual that serves as a teaching text to instruct Web participants in new ways of relating to the inanimate but animated world and new ways of coping with or transcending the social disaggregation of everyday life. Individuals negotiate the threat of images through their engagement with sign/bodies; in increasingly mediated social relations on both sides of the interface, images pose the threat of acquiring greater power than that held by many of the individuals they mediate. Images, moreover, resist complete definition and therefore never fully fall under human control. In relying on networked settings for performing disavowals of the unitary self—disavow-als of the transcendental unity of individual perception—such individuals also treat the Web as a set of possibility spaces. They render visible and ritu-alize a theory of the neoliberal postsubject constituted through the act of transmission. In cosmopolitan fashion these individuals surf capital forma-tions and the bifurcated, ephemeral, flexible, yet extensible sign and body politics that draw together political economy and metaphysics.

A related issue in the accelerating engagement with Web-based rituals is manifested in the ways that networked individuals negotiate the tensions between the Enlightenment's privileging of abstraction—of the semiotic symbol—and the contemporary move to abandon modernity's suspicion of iconographics. The culture of networked individualism is, in part, con-ceived and fabricated through digital imagery and visual technologies. This culture portends a quasi exteriorization of consciousness not unlike an elec-tronic exhumation of a medieval form of allegorically inflected conscious-ness. Though the medieval and Renaissance eras may have lacked today's information machines, theorizing such links remains productive. As Walter Benjamin (1968) reminds us, images from the past that we are able to relate to our own past and present can provoke critical insight. The Renaissance's philosophical interests in such issues as hieroglyphs, allegory, and emblems were esoteric yet practical, and a similar metaphysics of presence, coupled to a "seeing is believing" empirical pragmatism based on the visible, fuels contemporary interest in visual virtual environments as "immediate" yet intensely mediated communication spaces *and* practices. In the digital settings I examine, ritual, fetish, and signification operate synergistically, *synchistically*, and in relationships of *continuity* among one another (to introduce terminology coined by Charles Sanders Peirce, a figure at the center of chapter 3).

Debord's identification of a society of the spectacle is key: "The spectacle is not a collection of images; rather, it is a social relationship between people that is mediated by images" (1994:12). To what degree, however, might humans accord to these mediating images a quality of independent agency? In *Capital*, Marx engages in a thought experiment that asks what commodities would say if they could speak (1952:37). His question privileges speech and the word as the logical axis of truth, but Marx is aware of the magical power of a commodity object's image. Debord's identification of social relationship as a spectacle points to the ways that commodities move beyond speech to display—from truth claims based on memory, narrative, and history to those based on visible presence, emotional response, and occupation of space. My research, I hope, contributes to answering a set of questions that any study of a "society of the spectacle" arguably would raise: If images mediate social relationships among people and thereby also potentially disarticulate us from each other, what does the practice of contemporary visual culture seek from images and the technologies that manifest them? Do we want images, particularly those that move, to get together to perform a digital version of the public sphere? Do we seek from images modes of self-depiction denied to us or made difficult through speech? How do we negotiate and enter into the complex, overdetermined relationship among images, words, and desire, between the icon and the symbol? Does a society of the spectacle induce a culture of display? More specifically, does the online moving image of an avatar or webcam operator do double duty as both the mediating image between communicants and as the surrogate individual or body double of one, both, or all communicant(s)?

The moving image's increasing liveliness hails viewers' latent understanding that the movement of any human representation is indexical to movements and gestures of actual human bodies. Yet the specific ways that a thought or idea is communicated organize human experience, and my ability to arrive at any meaningful answers to the questions stated above means proposing refinements to existing theorizations of ritual and fetish activities. Because the dynamic of presence/absence is always at hand in virtual settings, answering these questions calls for examining the relationship among the changing significance of networked signs, the ways they are displayed and interpreted, and how we conceive of the location of human beings across material space in relationship to the sign world of networked virtual space.

The relationship of virtual space, perception, and display, and the degree to which sensory perception is subject to a cultural history increasingly inscribed by technological processes, is also an issue I pursue in the chapters following. Given the conjuncture of space, perception, and interpellating spectacle, I question the political and experiential possibilities raised when individuals tactically, if not strategically, agree or consent to the implicit expectation that they *should* increasingly display themselves principally through networked information machines that serve to conjoin them more firmly to the economic interests standing behind such assemblages (Baudrillard 1997:22). This expectation, however, moves further toward becoming "only natural" when the images transmitted through such machines begin to move. The moving, animated sign/body displays depth and liveliness. This expectation also implies that individuals should organize themselves in ways that closely adhere to how rituals organize individuals into groups: as active *participants* within a broader technological assemblage and not as instrumental *users*.[19] One may, in the idea of the participant, identify a preexisting commonality between ritual and contemporary networked practices. In a ritual, all of those present participate even if they do so differently and with different degrees of activity. Similarly, the Web is now positioned as a series of networks mixing practices of communication, creativity, consumption, and telepresence. Such multimodal practices suggest engagement by participants who are more than just "users" and certainly more than audiences. The needs of networked individuals, many of whom adhere to plural identity formations and are members of multicultural societies, recommend incorporating into ritual theory interpretations of how networked individuals engage the Web to perform new ways of redefining and renewing themselves consonant with their broader participation in the neoliberal society of the spectacle.

My use of the term information machine acknowledges that new media are constituted through intricate assemblages of networked social and technical practices and devices drawing together the technological and the social, the material and the ideal. The first machines were entirely human in their composition—for example, the organization of laborers into the mega machines needed to build the Pyramids at Giza and the Great Wall of China (Mumford 1934). Humans, however, also have long imagined autonomous machines as instruments and tools that could imitate human action or reproduce the way the world operates. The ability of information technology and so-called autonomous systems to offer "feedback" builds on this imagining and renders it more intense. The utopian dream for such automata is one of machine independence. Yet most machines are not automatic in this sense. Rather, they are mechanisms that depend on external energy sources (Beaune 1989:431–32). The concept of the information machine relaxes this asymmetry between automata (which are a subset of machines) and the broader world of machines. The information machine also conforms to the reality that technology and the culture of which it forms a part operate in tandem, synchronistically. In the Heideggerian sense, technology is a general condition of action, and the term information machine captures the ways that networked individuals and automated digital technologies mutually engage as parts of a wider environmental, infrastructural people/machine assemblage.

The term is also useful to the degree it helps span generational barriers. Most of us who learned to use computers even as early as young adults likely harbor the belief that they fall under the rubric of technology. But younger individuals for whom an increasing panoply of digital devices has formed part of their lived worlds almost from their beginnings understand their relationship to these machines in a more hybridized, less binary fashion. What was once technology per se now seems more a cross between everyday social infrastructure and everyday social environment or ecology; culture and technology mutually inform one another on a continual basis. The idea of information machines points to the ways that humans are more easily hailed by and buy into the logic of digital infrastructures and environments of which, the idea implies and confirms, we already and always form a part.

Networked information machines operate across increasingly interface-based cultures.[20] Interfaces abound—for example, those of cinema, television, computers, mobile phones, and PDA and GPS devices. Screen and display sizes range from that of IMAX cinema to hand-held camera phones or readouts on microwave ovens. First-world interfaces are ubiquitous: in airports and on airplanes; in bars, restaurants, student unions, shopping malls, and other commercial environments; at ATM machines, self-serve gasoline stations, and automated supermarket checkout stands; on overhead and curbside traffic information screens on freeways; and on medical devices and consumer appliances, including one's watch. The interface fits the palm of your hand. The technology exists to turn regular eyeglasses into a personal video display.[21] What the networked computer screen displays at any one moment constitutes an interface to different virtual worlds and forms of representation and information; the practices that the interface organizes refract off one another. People with access to digital virtual environments spend increasing amounts of time in front of and in them.[22]

>>> Premises

MAGICAL EMPIRICISM

One premise subtending my approach to the themes organizing this volume is the operation in high-speed Web settings of "magical empiricism," a term I deploy within a longer history of communication research theorizing the desire for codeless communication through modern technologies. The hybridity of such a belief emerges at the ironic intersection of the supposedly empirical veracity of the image coupled to the prestige of science and digital technologies, and a revived Neoplatonic belief, partly rooted in autonomic body responses to movement, crystallized in notions of the movement-image and the sign/body, that text/image, symbolic/iconic sign combinations actually convey a perceptual trace of the real. This hybrid of verifiability and belief is also manifest in the idea that networked iconographic representations and allegorical simulations of embodiment have moved communication practices to the point where any one viewer might rely on forms of depiction in order to directly *see* what other viewers mean. (Recall the earlier discussion of a similar ambivalent dynamic at work in the Web as cosmopolitanism: a never quite fully disembodied subjectivity retains both a detached, scientific "objective" view "from above" *and* sufficient embodied experience to support the fetishization of virtual sign/bodies on the Web that point directly to fleshy human bodies.) Magical empiricism reveals itself in the desire for codeless communication—for escaping the communicatory bounds of representation and even simulation but especially those of words. Academic and corporate promotional materials together encourage the belief that advanced information machines constitute proof of the continuing supremacy of the ideology of progress. From this flows an increasingly widespread, underacknowledged, and deterministic belief that an independent and therefore sociomagical power resides in these machines that render possible, as displays of applied knowledge, these hybrid sign/ bodies and other sign/objects of human design and manufacture. If only we try hard enough, so the drill goes, we can finally escape the "limits" of representation and join as if one in an ideal sphere of communicability and unity—the technical construction of the *oikos* or *ecumene*—wherein each of us will "truly see" the inner meaning we each struggle in vain to express. In such a magically empirical virtual landscape, the problems of Plato's cave and the Tower of Babel—and (by inference) all other inequalities based on symbolic difference—would finally be laid to rest.

THE WEB IS NEITHER TEXT NOR SPACE, BUT . . .

Though the internet is dependent on computer code (a form of writing) and therefore is text dependent, I resist thinking of it as a "text." This is the case even more so for the Web. The naturalized academic metaphor "to read" points to the word, printed page, book, and political economy of text-based modes of production and distribution. More importantly perhaps, in logocentric fashion, it subsumes the unruly image under the rational sign of the text. Formally, however, the moving image is not a text; the sign/ body moving on the interface is not decoded by viewers in the same way as readers decode a novel or a newspaper article. Metaphorically positioning the Web as a text reproduces modernity's iconoclastic bias and, more importantly, deflects consideration of the ways that images, in an interfaced culture focused on display, communicate differently to viewers than texts do to readers, and how emblematic text/image combinations might operate synergistically to produce hybrid forms of "viewing-reading."

If the Web is not a text then neither is it a space, though discursive strategies coupled to the eye's perceptive faculties of engagement with movement encourage the desire to naturalize the belief that it is. Understanding the internet as a space blurs distinctions between activities undertaken through the technology and the "action of human actors in social space" (Bassett and O'Riordan 2002:2). There are, moreover, broader experiential, perceptual, and socioeconomic factors at play here. While the earlier text-based internet and newer multimedia Web applications both require individuals to look into a screen or display, the Web's image-driven graphical user interfaces (GUIs) often provide representations of landscapes in which humans take on a variety of activities. Such imagistic spatial metaphors operate in ways that allow the virtual places they display to act as experiential interfaces that bridge the scale and distance between the individual seated in front of the display and the ubiquitous networks "standing behind" such interfaces. A program such as Google Earth directly trains individuals to experience the Web as a form of space that equates to a view they may also enter and control. It is possible, for example, to experience a sense of flying over Google Earth's virtual landscapes and then of navigating one's way down to move between city-center buildings in "places" like Sydney, Chicago, and London. Deploying similar spatial and cosmopolitan logics, individuals using chat sites frequently construct Web profiles that include images of themselves set against picturesque backdrops such as city skylines and mountain vistas. Or they may be photographed in everyday, familiar settings such as living rooms, lounges, or dens, where they are often seated in front of the computer interface, or changing clothing in a fetishized space. In graphical chat MUVEs one's avatar is always embedded in an animated virtual landscape. It is easy to understand why people might perceive the Web as ersatz space: they see simulations of 3-D space displayed on the screen and despite any instruction (scant at best) to resist understanding the Web as a space, phenomenologically it is difficult to avoid experiencing as anything but spatial the images depicted (whether cartoonish, videotic, or photographic) and the physical sensations to which they give rise.

The experience of the "world as display" gains further verisimilitude the broader the bandwidth, the faster the transmission speed, and the more the Web is always on. To such factors should be appended an overall political and ontological reliance on spatial metaphors — also forms of spatialization. The idea that one visits a website, for example, forms part of understanding, personalizing, and coming to terms with how an individual can meaningfully "interface" with ubiquitous networks operating largely according to the logic of the black box. Such strategies are understandable given the circumstances within which they arise. But they are actions reliant on various forms of representation: they do not in themselves constitute space. Why individuals would desire admission to settings they cannot materially enter is a broad theme engaged by this volume in each chapter. Belief that the Web might constitute a space resonates with the adaptation of ritual practices to its settings. Some rituals take place in settings clearly marked as distinct from everyday places. Others take place in special settings linked in various ways to the wider geography of which they form a part. Belief that the Web constitutes a space for performance different from yet linked to material space allows a ritual's participants to confer on virtual space the necessary qualities for an adequate ritual gathering space.

NATURALIZED IDEOLOGIES AND THE LARGER WORLD
Consider the pull-down menu. Its taxonometric logic is the norm for simplifying choices on the Web, whether selecting a flight, the material for a countertop, a yogurt maker, or one's race. In 2006 subscribers on the American MUVE site There! initially could compose their avatar from a limited number of choices. After choosing between "male" or "female," a prospective subscriber "selected" his or her avatar's race based on three skin tone choices: "vanilla," "caramel," or "chocolate."[23] Selecting "female" resulted in a prompt to choose from "Blonde Dancer," "Cocoa Bob," or "Espresso Halle." Those selecting "male" next chose from "David Ash Blonde," "Joey Cocoa," and "V. Espresso." The near universality of pull-down menus as a feature of graphical software has the tendency to organize the thinking of those selecting race in this way as a function of "software options." Equally at issue is the way that selecting race from a pull-down menu renders it *cosmetic*, something visible on the skin of a body as a superficial, depending overlay but not actually a part of that body. Choosing race (or any identity marker) in this way depicts everything as skin deep—a cosmetic or an ornament, detachable and changeable at will.[24] Jennifer Gonzáles (2000:27) argues that such avatars operate as digital appendages and are received as "integral to the object" of which they are also additions. Gonzáles raises issues of identification between avatars and their embodied referents, and her argument articulates to my own: a performative networked identity composed of bodily assemblages reinforces conceiving of embodied identity as changeable, flexible, and skin deep.

Positioning race as a set of simple design choices, as a skin game with rules that are changeable at will, conforms to the logic of magical empiricism built into pull-down menus and avoids the nuanced history of race and its complex social constructions. Depicting race as a *persona* or skin (and therefore a theatrical mask) that one dons, performs, or *selects* at will as one would any ornamenting commodity reveals the capitalized (and implicitly white) desire *to see* the seemingly intractable myriad issues organized around race as skin deep, as cosmetic, and therefore amenable to "friction-free" market solutions of flexibility and free choice. Such "solutions" flow from the neoliberal doctrine that market exchange is an ethic itself under which all human actions are best governed (Harvey 2005:3). The pull-down menu theorizes in visual form that this has already come to pass. It also reflects a deeper ontological assumption, coded into the technology's form, that all the world is not only a display but also a performative process of selecting goods fully amenable to a hierarchical yet modular taxonomy.

A consonance links the logic of free choice when one depicts oneself as an avatar, and the avatar's above-noted relationships to the doll, the puppet, and other earlier mechanical forms. We do not hold dolls and avatars to the same visual standards of truth as photography. We tend to see them as designed and therefore as subservient to what they represent, for, so the logic goes, how could a designed object be equal to the real? Dolls and puppets, therefore, are conceived as amenable to the selective logic of menu formats and quick changes rooted in desire: they highlight certain features while leaving others out. We tend, however, not to apply this selective logic to photography as it violates cultural beliefs that photographs, constituted in light, capture the real. Cocoa Bob and Espresso Halle are not alone. The American Girl company sells dolls directly to purchasers from the Web. The company website depicts race as a modular choice; purchasers select from thumbnail illustrations of dolls made up of various mix-and-match racially inflected features. Which is closest to you? On one page, twenty-five doll images run from "light skin, dark brown hair, brown eyes" to "medium skin, textured dark hair, dark brown eyes" to "light skin, black hair, brown eyes." The majority of darker-skinned dolls lie below the bottom of the page; viewing them requires scrolling down in a way that confirms the naturalized hierarchy of race.[25]

Ironically, these sites also depict the progressive idea that race is a social construction. At the scale of the minority individual in most national societies, however, including many promoting multicultural inclusiveness, race is not a choice. Individuals most often find this "choice" has been made for them in advance. Depicting race as a product, as an appearance one selects, evokes the desire for skin-deep design solutions to complex social problems. In addition, it relies on a coupling of empiricism and commodity fetishism to produce a use value in that it suggests that everything is interchangeable, disposable, modular (see Haug 1986:42). The skin of the avatar or the doll reflects something more. Appearance, and therefore representation, replaces actual presence. At the International Consumer Electronics Show held in

Las Vegas in 2007, IBM promoted the virtual stores it is building in Second Life for the Sears department store chain. Future visitors will "swap cabinets and counter tops to determine which combination they most like . . . configure couches and flat-screen televisions to see what might look best in their real-world living room."[26] Those who interpret such developments within a framework that technology is but a tool, and that clients and applications, therefore, are only using the technology's inherent powers the best ways they can, miss the broader point that the idea of the world as a pull-down menu, of the world as flexonomy and appearance as ultimate reality is built into the technology. Race, countertops, depression, gender, a mountaintop, financial statements . . . at base are all rendered as "the same"—as indexical to one another at the level of the sign. Peel one off, paste another on . . . the social and natural worlds transmogrified to the implicitly metaphysical utility of exchange values.

>>> Methodological Principles and Themes

Within the humanities, unevenness pervades recognition of the importance of critically theorizing the issues raised by information machines and the practices they engender. Scholars need to rethink how they perform internet studies and how internet studies intersect other forms of media studies. They need to consider more centrally the relationships between the historical and contemporary force-flows at work in information machines.[27] Media studies and internet scholarship need to bridge binaries erected between approaches that are object oriented and those that are theoretical. One goal of this volume is to help shift the emphasis in internet studies (and related fields interested in digital humanities) toward research organized around objects but also more centered in critical, philosophical, and theoretical engagements. Assessing the kinds of virtual objects manifested through Web technologies offers a means (at times ironic) to reconsider the binary between object-oriented and theoretical or conceptual approaches. As a methodological principle, I attempt this through grounding the volume's critical, philosophical, and theoretical arguments in objects—both virtual and material—articulated to interrelated themes. My examination proceeds from the understanding that innovations in technology always articulate to reconfigurations of the social. As such it can be read as a form of political theory. Langdon Winner argues, "any society that hopes to control its own structural evolution must confront each significant set of technological pos-sibilities with scrupulous care" (1986:54), and it is my hope that this project forms part of this kind of careful confrontation.

My methods are interdisciplinary, synthetic, and on occasion eclectic. Because the internet is *multi*-media I approach it *multi*-methodologically. I appreciate Benjamin's approach, as noted by Hannah Arendt, to "force insights" through "tearing fragments out of their context and arranging them afresh in such a way they illustrated one another" (1968:47–48). Once-distinguishable borders between disciplines and their "proper" objects and boundaries of studies have become more porous. To induce new understand-ings for new media and their shifting virtual landscapes, I work across disci-plines and combine elements of diverse theories, practices, and techniques. I draw on media theory and literary studies; geographic, anthropological, and psychoanalytic thought; theories of ritual, fetishism, and signification; reli-gious, cultural, and visual studies; and histories of art, philosophy, and tech-nology. My methods are subjunctive, recursive, and askance: subjunctive in theorizing specific objects and accounting for the settings within which they take place and form parts; recursive in applying specific theoretical insights across a range of objects, nonlinear events, and modular processes and tai-loring this application to the object, event, grouping, or algorithmic pro-cess interpreted; askance in offering side glances intended to get at indirect meanings lodged between and among this porous range of objects, events, and processes.

The volume interrogates specific forms and practices of visual culture, and I ground my discussions of internet practices and the social capital they entail through examples drawn from the Renaissance to contemporary postmodernism, from the hieroglyph, novel, and telegraph to print, film, and television, including mass media advertising campaigns. This is not an ethnographic user study in any strict sense, though I have been a participant in and an observer of the practices I examine; instead, it is more a medium study or a study of techniques and practices. I focus on techniques and prac-tices because power flows through the Web detached from individuals and at times even institutions (Foucault 1977). Power takes form in practices that in certain ways precede yet also anchor and help authorize contemporary subject formation (Feenberg 1999:110). Increasingly it is the practices and the techniques upon which they rely that organize the formation of those subjects who submit or are submitted to them. Yet at the same time technique itself also organizes an inherent and potentially productive contradiction that draws together practical mastery of an activity with the ability to regulate, as Randy Martin states, "what is considered appropriate to that activity. Mastering a technique develops the fluency in practice that loosens the fixed hold on the body initially commanded by that very technique" (1998:20). Practices (such as rituals and fetishism) that rely on technique's productive yet contradictory dynamics help render individuals and groups as productive agents who gain what (surplus) power they can through repetition, punishment, or reward.

I have noted ritual's potentially conservative operation in maintaining dominant forms of social relations, and I indicated that performers gain stability through participating in a ritual's ordering dynamic. Aspects of graphical chat and webcam operations are potentially liberatory. Others are regressive and I interpret these sites as both models and cautionaries. For example, by allowing gay/queer men to transmit claims to exist based on their display of online visibility, a webcam—in a society of the spectacle equating seeing with believing—can advance their claim to be part of the body politic. This claim, however, is cosmopolitical; it is constituted in virtual space and moving images and may also reflect desires for an impossible utopia. Mounting it, therefore, as a spectacle inadvertently indicative of the commodity form having completed "its colonization of social life" (Debord 1994:29) does not mean that the webcam site through which the claim transmits necessarily contributes to producing or sustaining a counterpublic that always opposes the relentless commodification of the lived world. Rather, such sites may constitute a tactic or even strategy for negotiating what it is to be perceived by others as primarily an image or a commodity form that may or may not be associated by viewers with the labor involved in transmitting the image in the first place. These sites are ambivalent forms of making do coupled to the *potential* for forms of action that resist identification as only conservative, only liberatory, only about commodification, or only about resistance to it.

I have just raised the issue of perception. Both cultural studies and political economy approaches would be enriched by greater acknowledgment of the role of perception in relation to experience. The reticence of these approaches to do so at times amounts to an academic Achilles heel. Accounts of perception are always inflected by conceptions of perception, and an individual's communication of his or her perception itself is necessarily dependent on historicized and culturally specific concepts necessary to the success of the communication. This need not preclude the recognition, however, that the faculty of human perception, as an embodied process influenced by emotional states, past experiences, and location, nonetheless precedes and continues to run parallel to its historicization and politicization. In making this assertion I am positioning perception as a subjective human faculty of sense. I understand human beings as forming parts of both the arbitrary world of culture and the differences it produces, and the natural world. For quite a while such a claim was difficult to make under the signs of postmodern and constructionist orthodoxies insistent that all the world is a social construction; all forms of representation, images included, are texts; and any theoretical recourse to processes inflected by biology or evolution deterministic *tout court*. I appreciate the politics behind this—postmodernism's rejection of master narratives indicates its broader understanding that assertions based on essential "first principles" somehow always seem to hold greater metaphysical and political sway when advanced by those with the bigger microphones, the deeper pockets. Questions about identity and change, however, are also questions of first principle and these questions subtend the issues I pursue in this volume. Humanities researchers need to remain vigilant to not articulate naturalized cultural biases to first principle concerns; such articulations promote reactionary assertions, stated as facts, about, for example, the superiority of a race, a gender, or a sexual orientation. Such vigilance, however, does not mean that questions of first principle, and therefore metaphysics, can be avoided if research is to arrive at more coherent explanations (and thereby contribute to potentially more persuasive political programs) for why things are as they are in the mixed-mediated lived world around us. On its own, critique is not enough and to avoid first principle questions risks handing them over to reactionary forces always ready to moralize them in ways that best suit their purposes. In a study of what images do on the Web, to ignore perception and its presumption of a *contingent* human universal inflecting experience is scholarship poorly fleshed out. Including perception in the matrix scarcely means I avoid treating the ways that humans make meaning out of the always historicized and therefore politicized circumstances in which they find themselves and under which they labor. Quite the opposite: including perception sheds additional light on the subject.

>>>

MUVE graphical chat and personal webcams showcase what the image can and cannot do. I have organized this project around these sites as dual foci of study for the following reasons.

Social Facilitation. The practices I examine are popular with many individuals because they support ways of engaging with the world with which people are already somewhat familiar or conversant. Second Life participants may already have naturalized cosmopolitan associations before having discovered the site, which may facilitate their further mining of these associations. Men using personal webcams to transmit images of sexual desire and identity claims may seek new forms of sexual equality online that build on preexisting and somewhat naturalized assumptions about gay/queer socialities and sexualities and the goals, desires, and practices organized around them.

Historical Richness. Although my arguments about ritualized Web practices are applicable to Web 2.0 social computing applications such as Flickr and YouTube that also allow for a phenomenological experience of a trace of the referent, one of my goals is to historicize Web practices and techniques. By internet standards, graphical chat MUVEs and webcam applications have lengthy histories; examining them as indicative of how the Web has changed over time provides historical depth to this project.

It is part of internet lore that webcams started with the Cambridge University computer scientists Quentin Stafford-Fraser and Paul Jardetzky, who in 1991 wrote software that would allow them to watch, via a local area network, the collective coffee pot located elsewhere in the building where they worked. The coffeecam was connected to the internet in 1993 as the first live, twenty-four-hour webcam site, and when it was taken down in 2001 it had amassed more than 2.4 million visitors.[28] Webcams are popular for watching busy highway intersections, prisons, airports, "people places," famous monuments, and aspiring international tourist destinations. Commercial webcam sites offering pay-per-view action are a staple of Web pornography. Yet like Jardetzky and Stafford-Fraser's watched pot, the majority of the personal webcam sites mounted by the "early adopters" I examine in chapter 5 are "history." These sites form part of a history of claims to visibility made by gay/queer men understanding themselves as very much part of an emergent and cosmopolitan digital visual culture. Google these sites today and find next to nothing. One may think of the Web as a "great records machine" but it also accelerates the ephemeral logic of the commodity fetish that weeds out and deletes those parts of the past no longer adjudicated as having sufficient display and exchange value. Accordingly, part of my account of these earlier webcam practices forms part of a gay/queer history that otherwise would be lost.

Graphical chat has a lengthier history than do webcam applications. It spans the mid-1990s transition from the text-based internet to the multimedia Web. Graphical chat's immediate ancestors date from the Dungeon & Dragons role-play board games that were introduced in 1974 (and influenced by J. R. R. Tolkein's 1965 *Lord of the Rings* trilogy). During the 1980s these board games evolved into computer games such as Zork and text-based internet MUDs (multi-user dungeons/domains) such as Scepter of Goth, Swords of Chaos, and Mordor for which players wrote visually resonant descriptions of the virtual worlds they also built, navigated, and populated. The internet program IRC (Internet Relay Chat), which allows those with a modicum of UNIX-based programming skills to open channels of communication and chat by typing messages to each other in real time, is another important precursor technology. The ways that specific chat techniques facilitate certain forms of communication, as I discuss in chapter 4, also have antecedents in the development of the nineteenth-century bourgeois novel and the Renaissance and Baroque reliance on the emblem.

Emblematics. Earlier I posed the question of how we can negotiate and enter into the complex, overdetermined relationship between images and words, between the icon and the symbol. Any answer to this question has several components, and graphical chat MUVEs and personal webcams point to one: the centrality of emblematics. Emblems are text-image combinations in which the text (composed of words that, in general, have broadly based and conventionally accepted meanings) works to clarify or secure the preferred meanings for the images that, on their own, could be interpreted in any number of ways. While the image component suggests ideas more immediate to sensation than to text alone, the text acts to police the image's

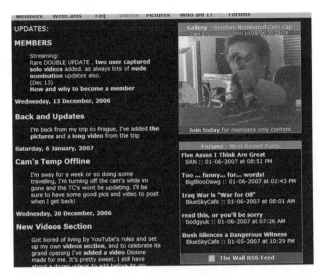

5   A typical configuration of a webcam image displayed within the overall webpage setting.

inevitable polyvalency of meaning. Three forms of iconographics are used in the settings I examine: video (either real time or rebroadcast on demand), graphic illustration, and photography. The intent is to best convey something personal and specific about the individual or "sender" who remains on this side of the interface. Though the quantitative relationship between text and image in graphical chat differs from that in personal webcams, each setting's textual components influence how viewers interpret and focus on the visuals; the logic of the emblem is on display in graphical chat MUVEs. The avatar "speaks" by means of text lodged within speech balloons that refresh as the avatar's owner types new "speech" for her or his avatar engaged in conversation or announcing its presence or intentions to other residents of the virtual world. I have noted the indexical quality of moving images, and the moving components of an overall image "attract and direct the eye, *much as a pointing finger would do*" (Fagerjord 2003:209; emphasis added). While a personal webcam's principal attraction is its indexical, real-time (often scheduled) video appearances of its operator, site visitors would know little about any other desirable qualities of the operator were it not for textual commentary provided on the larger website that also includes the webcam screen (see figure 5).

Issues of Space. I enrich my historicization of the settings, techniques, and practices I examine by taking into account the differing ways they interweave their use of the actual 2-D space of the screen display with a variety of visual spatial metaphors. Any form of materiality that is not understood as an extension in space is very difficult to imagine or write about. In order to live, human beings need to interpret the world reductively through a series of fixed objects. We see the material before we see the cultural. This is reflected in the excessive reliance on spatial metaphors to situate Web practices — "sites," "under construction," "browsing," "visit," Active *Worlds*, My*Space*, Net*scape*. These spatial metaphors and the sense of affective materiality to which they point also speak to a new discursive positioning of active digital subjectivity connected to a 3-D spatialized sense of *doing* resonant with, while also repositioning, Arendt's concept of *homo faber*. Graphical chat, in particular, is about the building of virtual worlds — virtual architects, planners, and builders abound.

Implicit concepts of space, place, and landscape inform website design and subtend this dynamic of fabrication. All landscapes are framed. Their content is representations of what once were nature's "wide open spaces." Landscapes are enclosed and commodified, whether by the ha-ha (an invisible trench) or fenced enclosure of a bucolic pastoral setting framed by vegetation and designed to be seen, or by the frame of a painting, or the framed screen display. The landscape tradition in the West emphasizes horizontality, and the side-to-side dimensions of most Western landscape representations exceed those of the vertical or top-to-bottom ones. This is consonant with the human eye's horizontal span of 180 degrees and vertical span of 150 degrees. While the vertical dimension of the Apple Macintosh PC screen exceeded its horizontal dimension to produce a "portrait" or pagelike effect, most earlier cathode-ray tube (CRT) computer displays, long predating the Web's popularity and still in use on many desktop systems, had slightly larger horizontal than vertical dimensions. Contemporary LED displays, moreover, concord ever more with the Western landscape tradition and most now exceed in horizontal dimension the 18–15 aspect ratio of human sight that favors horizontal views of space. While text displays as easily as ever on such interfaces, the image of virtual space that the Web permits is more consonant with how human sight is bounded not only by convention but also by its perceptual limits (the original frame, perhaps). As spatial metaphors colonize Web practices, their psychic or experiential realism is supported by having adjusted the screen or display ratios to better conform to the Western landscape tradition operating in concert with how we have been trained to conceive natural space in accord with sight's physical limits.

A graphical chat participant can expand the landscape to occupy the entire computer screen. Its edge forms the landscape's frame, suggesting the landscape's fullness and accessibility (avatars' moving bodies included) on the other side of the interface. The position of one's avatar in the virtual space at any given time determines how the program continually refreshes the surrounding landscape to agree with the changing coordinates of the avatar moving through the landscape. Personal webcam sites, however, by incorporating screen within screen and frame within frame techniques, display the landscape concept differently. The framing of the operator within the larger frame of the website within the larger frame of the computer screen suggests the packaging of a commodity—a sign/body available for exchange within the larger mise-en-scène. Because the moving image and the sense of depth it creates relative to the overall frame transmit to viewers as real-time video, the landscape's ambivalent qualities of framed fullness made available to viewer perception intersect with the display of the operator's body as a tableau vivant.

>>> Organization of Volume

This volume is organized in two parts. The first part sets out and frames key theories of ritual, fetish, and signification central to my project. As such these theories are its central objects. The second part presents two monograph-length studies, each of which interprets an online object—graphical chat MUVEs and personal webcams—and examines the different and interpenetrating ways that user/participants combine practices and performances of ritual, fetishism, and signification. Dividing the book in this manner reflects two interlocking goals: to interrogate Web practices in light of the theories discussed in the first part, and, in turn, to interrogate these theories of ritual, fetishism, and signification through an assessment of the Web-based techniques and practices constituting the objects in the second part. Some readers who may be less interested in theory will find that the chapters constituting the volume's second part stand on their own. Even without recourse to the more detailed explications of theories of ritual, fetishism, and signification provided in the first part, these chapters should make sense, and each offers its own detailed set of interpretations and conclusions. Those reading the book sequentially, however, will see that I draw on theory for its explanatory power, and that I also extend its applications in order to reveal the need and propose some new ways to renovate these same theories.

My meta-analysis is an effort to understand the overarching or higher-level sense of why participants engage in these practices in the ways that they do, but I also use "meta" in its related meaning of raising questions about the assumed nature of the original subject or concept and the methods and theories that flow, in part, from naturalized assumptions about this original subject or concept. On its own, theory cannot tell us what is actually happening in the world. I am guided by Catherine Bell's (1992) cogent observation that just as modern theories of ritual have had powerful influences on ritual practices, the ways that people ritualize deeply influence the formation of ritual theory. Therefore, while I have identified continuities between traditional wedding practices and their online adaptations, I do so largely as a bridging mechanism for readers needing to think through the very possibility of online rituals before they are able to think through forms of online ritual that depart from those practices, such as weddings, traditionally associated with ritual. More to the point, however, if the ways that people ritualize influences ritual theory, even a ritual clearly inflected with traditional or religious meaning, once located online, demands theorization not just at the conscious level of its participants' intentions but also as a metaritual. Even the religious rituals in Second Life (there are, at the time of this writing, more than a dozen traditional churches, mosques, and synagogues conducting scheduled services through the setting) reveal the overarching desire based on the need to somehow be in two places at once, to be flexible, and to be part of telemediation, transmission, and communicability through the magic of one's second self online avatar.

The three chapters in the first part of the book form a compendium that takes into account theories of ritual, fetishism, and signification and discusses these theories in light of one another. Chapter 1 situates (the history of) theories of ritual and ritualization, while chapters 2 and 3 perform similar work for theories of the fetish and fetishism and theories of signification, respectively. Because internet studies as a research field brings together scholars from different disciplines to produce interdisciplinary outcomes, it requires theories to define itself. All theories are grounded in the structures of feeling within which they gestate. Some stand the test of time better than others and have been and can be adapted to interpret circumstances that were not anticipated by the original theorists. Theories of ritual and fetishism originated as components of and responses to the colonial encounter between incipient European empires and those who were to become these empires' colonized "dark others." The situation does not apply to Web-based settings, but aspects of these theories, which have undergone continual renovation over the past century, retain value in assessing networked digital practices and techniques. I endeavor, therefore, to apply theories in ways appropriate to the techniques, practices, and themes I assess. These practices and techniques, however, suggest the importance of an intertextual rethinking of parts of these theories so that they do not inadvertently work to keep us from recognizing new issues. This includes those parts of ritual held to be invariant by theorists due to a combination of their inadequate consideration of how a specific technology might have contributed to the organization of a specific ritual coupled to the heavy hand of binary logic that continues to inflect many theories' legacies. The latter can produce an unfortunate politics — an aesthetically tinged policing or gate keeping as to which new findings will be allowed to fit within a specific theory's invented traditions and which will not.

Many theorists, for example, point to the invariance of ritual practices. Many ritual practices, however, despite ritual's naturalized association with tradition, do not remain fixed. They are not invariant but are adapted by practitioners who comprehend in varying ways that reflection and experience are "interconnected moments of the same activity" (Martin 1998:5) and who, therefore, are able to understand that new settings and social circumstances at times require new forms of ritual. Otherwise, like dead metaphors rituals would (and do) fade away. While ritual is frequently associated with "tradition," ritual theory has little to say about how necessity coupled to mutability might influence the establishment of new traditions. Likewise, theories of fetishisms posit that fetishes are material objects. The fetish is understood as an object, not an ideology (McCallum 1999:135). Yet the online images of avatars and operators I examine are increasingly positioned as virtual objects, a discursive ploy that works to deflect not only a fuller acknowledgment of the ideological work performed by these images but also one that calls on meanings of the object not tethered to material forms.

Examining online ritual and fetish practices reveals certain limitations of existing ritual and fetish theory. Any social theory with explicatory power is based on an assessment of actual practices and, as such, remains most powerful when theorists take into account ongoing changes to the relevant practices theorized. Therefore I also examine how viewers, contrary to many extant theories of the fetish, fetishize online virtual objects. The networked intersection of online forms of ritual and fetishism draws together the ideological components inherent in ritual and fetish practices focused on virtual objects. This intersection is a powerful one. It draws together ideology and actual practice, signification and an *experience* of desire for a moving image serving as a body double that points to the actual body to which it is closely articulated — to the point of psychic appendage. New media thus offer a way to shed light on intellectual issues with which researchers have long struggled.

The second part of the book offers two extended studies of specific Web-based settings. It weaves together historical accounts, the application and expansion of theoretical arguments introduced earlier in the book, and analytic, political, and subjunctive interpretations of user/participant practices. This organization should help readers to grasp the specifics of the websites in question — and their antecedents in philosophical texts, cultural practices, literatures, and precursive text and image technologies — and, therefore, to better access what kind of future to which these technologies and practices may be pointing. I trace associative networks among these objects, settings, and themes across the entire volume and within the more specific formats developed in each chapter. Each chapter therefore contains an extended set of meditations on the ways that individuals engage these technologies as practices in themselves. As an evolving set of technological and social assemblages already imbued with sedimented meanings, the internet demands this approach of its scholars. This volume, therefore, is something of a methods experiment — because the practices and techniques I examine are in many ways waiting to be better understood as part of an emergent future already upon us, in attempting to provide better understandings this volume is, in places, a variant of speculative philosophy that hints at something beyond itself (Deleuze and Guattari 1994). It is also, to paraphrase Michel Foucault (1985:9), an exercise of myself in the activity of thought — in reflecting the complexity and intricacy of the Web's panoply of diverse users, participants, and competing yet overlapping uses and desires.

For some, popular internet practices such as participating in Second Life or mounting a personal webcam are derided practices and degraded experiences; however, I hope to engage the high theoretical and political stakes at play precisely through their assessment.

Chapter 4 interprets the development of avatar-driven graphical chat MUVEs, such as Second Life, as a current manifestation of a longstanding sociocultural and political set of dynamics whereby the use of indirect forms of discourse and self-presentation allow for the thinking through or utterance of ideas more difficult to express, give voice to, or depict through direct and embodied forms of address. Lev Manovich (2001:9) notes that "the computerization of culture" not only generates new cultural forms but redefines existing ones, and I historicize contemporary MUVEs by comparing their rise with that of free indirect discourse. Free indirect discourse is a discursive technique, developed during the nineteenth century, that is specific to the modern bourgeois novel and the author standing "behind" it whose voice, nonetheless, emanates from within its pages. I also access the rise of MUVEs by providing a series of discussions of text-based forms of first-generation internet chat such as MUDs and IRC.

Expression organizes experience (Vološinov 1986). Thought and its means of expression are consubstantial. But experience and reflection also organize expression. Assessing the differing yet overlapping social circumstances of free indirect discourse in the novel and digital avatar images online reveals the complex disjunctures and continuities between and among the uses, experiences, presentations, and representations of texts and images. Free indirect discourse and the digital avatar each operate as a techno-cultural strategy devised in response to specific social, cultural, political, and economic expectations placed on individuals. Certain similarities in the logics of deployment of these different modalities allow for the production of politically useful, strategically ambivalent, and at times ironic and distanced representations of self and others. Whereas free indirect discourse does so by recourse to a technique sometimes termed "middle *voice*," graphical chat does so via a "middle *ground*" of virtual space onto which one transmits a moving image of oneself. Avatars and the virtual landscapes they inhabit synthesize fantasy and mimesis, the event itself and its representation. The websites discussed in chapters 4 and 5 are representations, yet the experience of moving images they organize is a kind of event that frequently exceeds the logic of representation. Following on Alain Badiou's (2005) discussion of the event, the avatar as a new form of expression may allow otherwise unspoken, unseen, or absent points of view or truths to present themselves, or to emerge. These truths have the potential to unsettle naturalized ways of thinking. The avatar is also an allegorical form of relation that indicates a change in circumstances of the relationship between images of human bodies and actual human bodies. In literary terms, allegory is a form of extended metaphor through which materiality, in the form of objects, actions, and individuals, is rendered equivalent with meanings lying beyond the narrative itself (Holman and Harmon 1992:11). In online MUVEs, the avatar is an allegorical figure. It expresses an avant-garde yet very ancient desire for unity between the ideal (and virtual) realm of meaning and the materiality of the object or human for which it stands. Extending Geertz (1961:153–54), the avatar indicates *and* epitomizes the actualization of a more general cultural phenomenon — the networked desire for a form of virtual embodiment that could somehow still retain and transmit qualities of the animated material referent. In specific ways graphical chat is where the everyday meets the avant-garde: an increasingly commercialized intersection of mundane individual action and out-of-this-world collective display (see Sahlins 1985:108).

To further historicize the uneasy ways that graphical chat draws together image and text, virtual and material, I draw on art historical and textual analyses of uses of the emblem — a synthesis of the written and the depicted — by the Italian Renaissance and the Baroque period. I assess the ambivalent and seemingly magical possibilities that attend to a renovated politics of the contemporary emblem. I also examine the ways that such politics intersect with a capitalized and inherently metaphysical discourse of mobility and ubiquity that promotes the Web as a set of networked spaces into which we can seemingly and productively relocate aspects of ourselves. To cement the chapter's relationship to networked ritual practices and Neoplatonic thought I conclude by assessing the United Kingdom Methodist Church's graphical chat experiment called Church of Fools — its attempt to attract new members through the establishment of a sacred virtual space.

Chapter 5 examines the relationship between personal webcam sites and the networked forms of digital identity expressions they allow. In particular, it assesses gay/queer male webcam use in the second half of the 1990s and into the early 2000s as a vanguard indicator of the West's ongoing projection of utopian aspirations onto the latest, at times uncharted, technologies. These men display an "ambivalent mastery" of the webcam as a technology that combines the logics of tantalization, futurity, spectacular self-authorship, and the utopian idea of living in art in the here and now of virtual space. Historically shaped modes of conceiving and perceiving space, the self, and the other combine in gay/queer webcam cultures with well-defined aesthetics of the virtual, the lived realities of these men's lives, and consumer culture more broadly to commodify and brand experience so that the image of the webcam operator and indexical access to it come to constitute a crucial component of experience itself.

The theoretical framework I develop to interpret this webcam culture extends and complicates Marx's notion of the commodity fetish and proposes that certain networked practices ritualistically update archaic understandings of the fetish to produce the telefetish. Like the archaic fetish, the telefetish, in taking the form of an operator's refreshing webcam image, garners unto itself an ironic power: skillfully contrived, made by art, animated by spirit, and at times worshiped in its own character. Yet when an operator or his fans judge the telefetish inoperative or exhausted, like the fetish object it is discarded. I intend the theory of the telefetish to contribute to a renovation of theories that focus solely on fetishes as material, visible objects. I also question the politics underlying how and when the fetishist comes to understand that the formerly powerful fetish is now exhausted.

Chapter 5 also examines the potential for a politics of visibility established through webcam practices. Operators and fans who engage in networked displays of desire within the neither fully public nor fully private yet both at once spatial quality of personal webcam settings call into question the heteronormative standards of "good taste." Such standards have worked to marginalize "unacceptable" (read visible) same-sex presence and activity in heterosexually coded public spaces and same-sex representations in older broadcast media. They join with these men's experience of the HIV/AIDS crisis to produce a sense of history as an apocalyptic narrative.

The webcam is a commodity form. The production of images on webcam sites conforms to the commodity's logic, but these vanguard webcam operators also used their online images to establish an ontological claim to exist through a politics of virtual visibility and networked display. Through taking the form of webcam niche celebrities with appreciative publics, they became less "silent" and, in cosmopolitan fashion, more "everywhere." While it is ironic and, arguably, politically untenable to base such a claim on the utopics of representation alone, such a strategy of the interface is tactically justifiable when framed within the broader ongoing violence against too visible actual same-sex bodies such as those of the now-departed Matthew Shepards of this world. To paraphrase Antonio Gramsci, for these men the old heteronormative assumptions may live on in parts of the broader culture, but they are long dead for them. New modes of being, however, are not yet fully capable of being born or spoken. In the interregnum, the webcam provides a tantalizing glimpse of what the new might look like. New art suggests new thought, but this image is as much a "morbid symptom" as it is an effort to rescue or sustain these men's utopian imagination. No one can remain a fetish image for long without becoming exhausted of broader purpose. The history of these webcams suggests that the word and the image still have much to say to and show each other.

Rituals

In reading the literature on ritual one is struck by the ongoing, evolving sets of disputes among researchers, often anthropologists, over the definitions, meanings, and purported utilities of the idea of ritual. "There is the widest possible disagreement as to how the word ritual should be understood" (Leach 1968:526).[1] Ritual is a Western academic invention (Bell 1992:ch.1; 1997:253) that "will not stay neutral" but can be made to conform to whatever purposes the researcher intends her or his analysis to serve (Bell 1992:14). Ritual is a slippery concept, variable in its meanings, mechanisms, and dynamics. Many activities are considered rituals and many perspectives of analysis compete, contradict, and inform one another. Ritual is less a formal category of human behavior than a historical and cultural invention to distinguish various modes of religiosity, cultural determinisms, and rationality (Bell 1992:14; 1997:ix-xi). Nevertheless, the idea of ritual has been widely popularized and taken up by all manner of cultural actors. Ritual has real affect, and individuals, consciously or not, are inventing new forms of public and private ritual practices. This chapter discusses the concept of ritual as articulated by various theorists in order to provide a multilayered definition of the term, its disjunctures, and its applicability to online settings.

In their traditional and commonsense understandings rituals are associated with ceremonial performances that signal an exceptional event or transition in status in the life of a community, social group, family, or individual. Rituals may be state sanctioned, as in the funeral of a sovereign or head of state, or more localized, such as the baptism of a child. They are understood as rites of passage set off from daily routines. They may signal, for example, the importance of birth, marriage, and death—events a newspaper editor once referred to as "the hatched, the matched and the dispatched." Rituals work to induce qualities of social coherence and order among participants. This is why they are often understood as stabilizing and containing social relations that favor the maintenance of elite or dominant powers. In a ritual, everyone participates; there are no observers. At a funeral, for example, everyone is expected to pay respect to the deceased; it would be taboo to denounce the dearly departed during the ritual. Such rituals, we are given to understand, have invariant rules of conduct rooted in hierarchy governing how people should (and should not) act during what is positioned as a sacred moment.

Traditionally, people associate the idea of the sacred with religion, and many commonsense understandings of ritual draw from religiously inflected practices. Religion is constituted in a set of ideas and practices by which "people sacralize the social structure and bonds of community" (Bell 1997:24). Religion, like ritual, works to ensure the primacy of group or communal identification. At base, however, this traditional understanding of ritual assumes that rituals are only performed to induce a sense of unity or collective social cohesion among people—as noted above, to stabilize and contain. Such naturalized and commonsense understandings of ritual bear a considerable debt to the ongoing influence of Émile Durkheim (1857–1917), a founding figure of sociology. Durkheim developed his theories of ritual in part by reading the published ethnographies of nineteenth-century anthropologists. When early anthropologists, as part of the colonial encounter, first observed the indigenous practices they would identify as rituals, they were studying premodern cultures organized according to highly developed and hierarchical understandings of group identity. The ceremonies they observed frequently engaged the *entire* society or a significant number of its members so as to constitute a noteworthy subgrouping within the society. This reportage and Durkheim's analysis of it focused on ritual as a group process and associated it with the maintenance of tradition that, in turn, has been associated by many subsequent ritual theorists with the idea that a ritual is invariant. Tradition is always a social force, so it is not hard to understand how rituals have come to be associated in theory with the production of group cohesion through traditional, invariant practices. As a consequence, however, we are left with overly narrow popular understandings of what qualifies as a ritual and what does not, including ideas about the "proper" social scale at which a ritual occurs. That is, we generally equate ritual with a group and with an assembly of this group in the same place.

It is important to note that the indigenous cultures observed by early anthropologists were not yet unduly inflected by modern capitalized social relations marked by the privileging of the individual and practices of individuation. They were positioned geopolitically as static, without a modern sense of progress and therefore of mobility. Protestant-inflected, on-the-go Western modernity defined itself in opposition to this purported stasis, and it is interesting to consider the relationship between this created opposition and a Protestant deemphasis on most forms of ritual, as in "they have rituals, we don't." Protestant and, more generally, Western privileging of the individual has difficulty fitting into these theories except insofar as they position individualism as a problem that ritual might help solve (for example, Durkheim 1965 [1912]).

Today it would be difficult to find a culture uninflected in some way by capitalized social relations and modern forms of individualism. Would this mean that ritual no longer exists—that it has been completely dismissed as atavistic, given capitalism's interest in continually transforming the status quo and upending tradition in favor of mobility, flexibility, and flow? Scarcely. Not surprisingly, in an increasingly networked and individuated world rituals also operate in more complex, hybrid, potentially messy, contradictory, and less binary-dependent ways. There is no compelling reason why a ritual need always be religious in nature. Neither are there compelling explanations, for example, for why a ritual cannot be an individual public or private act, or why rituals cannot be mobile. There is no inherent reason why mobility itself cannot be ritualized, particularly given its (ironic) centrality to contemporary social order, or why rituals cannot be performed electronically among individuals who remain geographically distant from one another but nevertheless have some common desire or need to commingle through online settings.

One issue for which ritual theory applied to contemporary circumstances must account is the ways that capitalism and Protestantism have worked to naturalize social arrangements based on an ideology that individuals, not the collective, are discrete entities responsible for their own self-determination. A "tradition" in the West at least two centuries old holds the purportedly autonomous individual as responsible for determining his or her own roles. As part of capitalized and increasingly technicized social relations, individuals enter into an order composed of myriad forms of contractual and economic relationships with other individuals and organizations. Self-determination is a contract with oneself and it, too, can be ritualized in many ways as part of making sense of one's place in this larger order of individuals. Moreover, a contractual, economically oriented worldview devalues (but does not dispense with) traditional forms of group relationships. At a metalevel—in terms of a capitalized structure of feeling—the West's longstanding emphasis on individualism forms the trajectory of a tradition that earlier ritual theorists such as Durkheim were not prevented from considering yet for the most part overlooked.[2] The emphasis on individualism is not the only unrecognized tradition worth noting. Paralleling it is the by now naturalized tradition of commodification of the individuated self on the part of those born modern—a tradition empowering those who seek to transmit traces or doubles of themselves through online settings.

Durkheim, in *The Elementary Forms of the Religious Life* (1912), argued that rituals enact or perform ideas of the sacred. Periodic in nature, rituals allow participants to identify with a larger reality than themselves—such as venerated ancestors or a god figure, which, Durkheim argued, is really the collective in a disguised form. "God," he is attributed as having said, "is society, writ large." Durkheim believed that individuals, as part of the social collective, need some form of faith in order to bear their own mortality. He turned to the possibility that rituals, repeated over time, could serve as a principal *functional* means for inducing and maintaining group cohesion and social comity. In certain ways, this understanding can apply to the Web settings described in the introduction. The wedding in Second Life clearly fits within these parameters. A university graduation ceremony, though secular in nature, does as well. It marks a sacred or consecrating and collective moment in the lives of the (largely) young adults ready to embark on the next phase of life's journey. Visitors to online memorials who leave comments often indicate that they did not know the deceased, yet they also believe they are participating in a collective or public sense of mourning. The fourth example of having coffee with distant friends with the help of a personal webcam might seem less like a ritual to those adhering strictly to the traditional associations just noted, but it too reinforces our collective sense of remaining a group.

Durkheim understood religion as "the medium through which shared social life was experienced, expressed, and legitimated" (quoted in Bell 1997:25). Religious phenomena, he observed, occur when everyday activities (the profane) are separated from the extraordinary and the transcendent (the sacred). All religions, he believed, organize the world into the sacred and the profane. Insisting on a strict sacred/profane binary is also an insistence, however implicit, on holding apart the social and the political. Nevertheless, this binary is at the center of Durkheim's theory of ritual even though he favored a secular, rational form of life. Durkheim examined ritual from a positivist perspective. He believed that science was asserting itself over religion as the basic means by which people make sense of everyday life; over time, he suggested, religion would take on ever more secular forms.

Yet in contrast to the ritually induced social cohesiveness Durkheim identified as a feature of "primitive" or "mechanical" societies, he "was struck by what he saw as the pathological state of his own society, signified, as he saw it, by the lack of public rituals. He saw this lack as an index of social pathology, of a transitional state of 'uncertainty and confused agitation'" (Lukes 1975:291). This lack, I suggest, also reflected the increasing secularization and individuation of late-nineteenth-century French society. Durkheim's theories, then, constituted a form of cultural intervention on his part—an attempt to mediate his own historical moment. In writing about the Zeitgeist within which Durkheim labored, Jacques Rancière points to the connections among the "haunting" of the nineteenth century by the perceived "democratic dissolution of the social body, by the fanciful correlation between democracy/individualism/Protestantism/revolution/the disintegration of the social bond," and the rise of "sociology as a science . . . born from this obsession with the lost social bond" (2004:57).

Durkheim's articulation of ritual to induced social cohesion remains valuable in thinking through how rituals operate, but it is not the whole story.

His metaphysically inflected idea of a "collective consciousness" holds that the totality of a society's shared social norms and values constitutes its common ground of meaning and ensures that everyone acts in agreed-upon ways. Saluting the flag, covering one's mouth when one coughs, and driving on either the right or left are examples of such norms.

Durkheim's conception of how ideas (or morality) influence material reality (and the aesthetic of the surface appearance of rituals) is an early form of ideology theory apposite to his theory of ritual. Connecting the dots linking ritual to ideology is productive. It allows for identifying the ways that religious institutions organize the performance of ritual practices as meaningful forms of "lived hegemony" (Williams 1977:112); it positions ritual as a model for understanding and for constructing ideological practices based on hybrids of persuasion and coercion; and it facilitates looking at ideology promoted through forms of lived hegemony as a contemporary, secular form of ritualization. Capitalist consumption practices, for example, are forms of lived hegemony that provide consumers with something of value in exchange for their consent to be governed by the logic of capitalist ideology. Thus shopping, as an outcome of capitalist belief, itself constitutes a secular ritual practice, promoted as invariant, that promises qualities of transcendence associated with traditional religious experience. Shopping as ritual both confers order and allows for certain expressions of self within a system of mass individuation. To refuse to see how contemporary forms of capitalized expressions (including my virtual coffee klatch) constitute rituals because they do not conform to the idea that rituals are invariably associated with tradition and religion is to have bought into a specific form of ideology that gains power precisely in separating itself from ritual. It works to suggest that contemporary forms of consumer expression are all about individual freedom and never about producing social conformity in the same way that ritual does. A refusal to see how ritual practices evolve in tandem with broader forms of political and social organization is, in terms of capitalism, a refusal to see that capitalism—its logics and techniques of greed and accumulation unable to mount convincing moral arguments that would cause individuals to cohere sufficiently so as to preserve the capitalist system—itself relies on traditional ideas and practices productive of social cohesion that it absorbed from the earlier patriarchal and noblesse oblige social systems it has also progressively moved to undermine.

The South African-born British anthropologist Max Gluckman observed that Durkheim failed to adequately consider the internal tensions inherent to any society. The social unity that Durkheim desired is always difficult to achieve, and Gluckman (who was openly anticolonialist) by identifying rituals of rebellion argued that rituals also express the complexity of social tensions, upheavals, and struggle rather than only affirming social unity as a totality. Here he points to the ways that change, or at least its possibility, arises from conflict and disagreement that frequently do not get expressed in words but instead are enacted ritualistically. Gluckman accounts for the actions of those not included in a social center in ways that avoid producing the binary "other" as a marginalized outcome that is somehow surplus to (and therefore potentially productive to the forces claiming) the social center. And yet, if binary logic is central to Durkheimian ritual theory, binaries also remain central to many successful ritual practices. If a ritual activity is to succeed as a way of negotiating power in social relationships, it will first have naturalized the arbitrary difference between those performing the ritual and those not involved. It will have separated certain people from one another at the same time it will have successfully promoted cohesion within the "in group" (Bourdieu 1991:118–19). Rituals can operate to stabilize and contain or they can be part of contestation and struggle. All operations, however, are parts of the discursive and material practices of community. Within modern capitalized social relations, moreover, the discourse of community legitimates the proliferation of social hierarchies upon which advanced capitalism depends (Joseph 2002:viii). Binaries constitute mutually imbricating concepts and, in circular fashion, by promoting sacred group cohesion the ritual performs an experience of community. This experience, however, remains inherently unstable because its production depends on the continued existence of the community's profane, exteriorized other. Hence, given this instability, the need arises for rituals (like practices of fetishism) to be repeated at somewhat regular intervals. Constructing a center (a key assumption of Durkheim's theory) induces "in group" cohesion, thereby legitimizing the socially constructed center as true and ideal even as it necessarily means the exclusion and repression of others (Derrida 1976). Rituals both distinguish and articulate center and periphery; these operations stand in contrast to one another but need not be contradictory (Rappaport 1999:101). Bourdieu further identifies how elites seeking to naturalize dominant understandings deploy rituals to police their own members who, fearing to be excluded from the circle and thereby rendered profane and low-status, conform their activities to group norms (Bourdieu 1991:119). Rituals may sanction or deny a sacrilege even through the very act of committing the sacrilege itself (Bourdieu 1991:136–37).

Although understandings of ritual owe a great debt to Durkheim's thinking, we have not previously faced a conjuncture demanding assessment of networked digital settings as virtual locations for ritual, and there may remain a tendency to erect a sacred/profane binary that certain settings are apposite to ritual while others remain profane. Based on this logic, for some an initial response to the proposal that ritual performances increasingly take place on the Web may be to refuse it as profane. From a neo-Durkheimian perspective, some might allow that my examples of traditional formats relocated to digital settings are rituals, whereas others would refuse them as "just metaphors." The contributions of the German-born French ritual theorist Arnold van Gennep help to counter neo-Durkheimian binaries. Van Gennep, who was never admitted to Durkheim's circle, coined the term "rites of passage" in 1909. Differing from Durkheim, he argued that the sacred is always a mutable concept—what gets defined as sacred changes according to circumstances, the nature of the specific ritual, and what it is intended to accomplish (Bell 1997:36). Just as we have come to understand that there is no one general audience for any message, Gluckman and van Gennep realized that there is no one center around which all members of any society cohere.[3] Instead, a ritual itself can define what becomes "sacred."

The sacred versus profane binary achieves a sovereign quality in certain theories of ritual. Yet when the temple and the stock market imbricate one another in American cultural and political values—or when formerly "sacred" distinctions between priest and politician; Wall Street and the state; the shopping mall and the shrine begin to dissolve so that these opposites seem to trade places, coalesce, and interdepend in ways that once would have been positioned as taboo or obscene—then the parallel, inherently depoliticizing assumption that ritual activities *only* organize sacred (and therefore preferred) understandings needs rethinking. Contemporary ritual practices "encode very different ways of being in the world" (Bell 1997:191). The disaggregated culture of networked individualism suggests that members of this culture who also share citizenship in the same state no longer need identify in the same universal way with that state, or with a unitary identity formation that reinforces that state's official values or the values of a dominant religion. This in no way precludes such individuals from identifying variously, even at the same time, with different groupings, some of which they may see as sacred, others as profane or even taboo, and some as "secular sacred" admixtures of the two. An individual who participates in more than one ritual practice will have the inherently political opportunity to perform "very different ways of being in the world." Some of these ways remain material. Others are virtual, yet they also contribute to the actualization of material practices on this side of the interface.

Theorists with a broader variety of emphases than Durkheim's have investigated a wide range of circumstances within which rituals are invented and take place. Victor Turner (1982, 1995 [1969]) describes rituals as essential "social dramas" that "depict, act out, or otherwise give form to conflicts and the dominant values holding the group together" (Bell 1997:40). Specific aspects of online rituals do facilitate the maintenance and repair of certain forms of social cohesion; however, at times they also allow for alternative expression and formation of new, potentially resistant, or at least askance social orders. Equally, however, they may serve as a means to let off steam. Like carnival, they help maintain a dominant social order while also allowing for entertaining performances of a variety of different standpoints or subject positions. In this way they are hegemonic *and* they conform to Turner's thesis. As social dramas, aspects of the ritualizations enacted in graphical chat environments and personal webcam sites can induce cohesion and meaningful experiences of virtual community, but they are equally about negotiating the spatiotemporal and identity shoals of neoliberal global capital. As social dramas, they are performances of what it might be for a virtual commodity to "speak" through the moving images it produces. They also enact and thereby negotiate the tensions produced as a result of embodied human participants having to negotiate a networked culture's increasing emphasis on an image of the body seemingly elsewhere than the place of its referent (see Gabildano 1995; Gonzáles 2000).

It is equally the case today, moreover, that in networked digital settings individuals, those marginalized and those merely negotiating their places in the world, craft ritualized performances (some of which would be identified as profane by dominant discourses) specifically *not* intended to appeal to dominant understandings. Networked rituals signify and render sensible performers' own experiences both to themselves and others with whom they may form common cause, if only for a time. Turner notes that through performances of rituals "groups become adjusted to internal changes

. . . and adapted to the external environment" (1982:21), and Roy Rappaport (1979:29) argues that rituals help regulate relationships between people and their natural resources, including the world around them. Ritual allows participants to performatively enact or rehearse strategies to cope with the crucial changes they may undergo. Through such enactments rituals also regulate and help organize aspects of participants' interactions with the world around them. Though the forms of regulation may differ from those imposed on rituals taking place on this side of the interface, if networked virtual environments increasingly allow users to experience such technological assemblages as ecologies or infrastructures in themselves, then rituals taking place "therein" are equally capable of transmitting ordering strategies of accommodation to the progressive inclusion of these virtual ecologies as part of everyday life. Further, apart from negotiating the meanings of virtual worlds for everyday life, networked rituals give order to a wider range of material experiences. Graphical chat participants, for example, have indicated their turn to these environments of signification as part of negotiating the loss of a loved one, and personal gay/queer webcam operators engage in ritualized displays of visibility intended to make a claim that through the transmission of their image they form part of an actual community taking place in the material here and the now.

>>> Media Rituals, Distributed Social Centers

Web settings portend the rise of new forms of media rituals.[4] The presence of information machines in Western daily lives has achieved the quality of a virtuous circle in which the expectations placed on these machines grow ever larger. As they meet certain of these expectations, their convergence with daily life practices further expands. The growing number of mobile devices — BlackBerrys, iPhones, GPS technologies such as General Motors' On-Star, camera phones, Radio Frequency Identification (RFID) tags — confirm that the updating of digital technologies and their interfaces continues to allow for ever more varied forms of access to modes of transmission among individuals and between individuals and machines, including access to new forms of knowledge. Michael Hardt and Antonio Negri go so far as to state, "Interactive and cybernetic machines become a new prosthesis integrated into our bodies and minds and a lens through which to redefine our bodies and minds themselves. The anthropology of cyberspace is really a recognition of the new human condition" (2000:291). This "new human condition," moreover, arises within a culture of technique (Ellul 1964; Marcuse 1964; Winner 1986). Within such a culture "social cohesion depends on technical prescriptions since traditions, laws, and verbal agreements are insufficient by themselves to hold together a complex society. Thus the social bond is mediated by technical objects as well as by human communication, and that mediation supports a *sui generis* form of normativity" (Feenberg 1999:102). Within a culture based on technique, increasing access to information transmission introduces possibilities for new forms of power relations exercised and negotiated among the Web's myriad users, the technology itself, and capitalized and institutional media forces jockeying for influence and control related to the production of social cohesion. The contemporary transmission of information through networked digital technologies is a key communication process that, in its apprehension, is subject to new forms of ritualization by individuals frequently termed "users" but whose quality of hegemonized engagement with the kinds of Web practices assessed in this volume recommends identifying them as "participants." These participants may not use the term "ritual," but in effectively renovating ritual forms and techniques of signification to better concord with the constraints and opportunities of virtual settings, and the expectations associated with mobility placed upon these settings, they indicate the need to augment aspects of ritual theory to better concord with the intersection of IT-dependent practices and contemporary forms of making meaning and producing order and new forms of mediated social cohesion.

An array of new media, the Web included, now contests the dominance of older media forms such as television, an apparatus of transmission that in continually claiming to constitute the social center of industrial society has managed to convince many viewers of the natural truth of the claim. Nick Couldry, in his study of media rituals, focuses on ways that "the media" claim to be the social *center* that "helps states and societies hold together" (2003:10); an ideology of (mass) media power has naturalized the assumption that media should centralize access to contemporary social reality (12).

The ongoing claims by TV to social centrality (think Edward R. Murrow's "You are there" or Walter Cronkite's "And that's the way it is") depend on the human face of, say, a Katie Couric, a Peter Mansbridge, a Sophie Raworth, a Maxine McKew, an Oprah Winfrey, or a Jay Leno to "anchor," enliven, and legitimate these claims. The Web does not depend for its legitimacy on the authority of comforting human anchors. Yet for increasingly networked individuals the Web occupies a position of *distributed* social centrality equally as powerful as older broadcast media. This is indicated by the rapid social diffusion and exponentially increasing popularity of Web 2.0 social networking sites. Witness the popularity of MySpace, and its purchase, in 2005, by Rupert Murdoch, for US$580 million. Or the rapid rise of the video-sharing service YouTube, which was quickly sold to Google by its creators for US$1.65 billion in October 2006. Many formerly "stand alone" PC-based services and applications such as data storage, word processing, and spreadsheets have migrated to the so-called cloud of networked internet settings. This distributed social centrality is further apparent in the building of the 3D Internet.[5] Google Earth, a networked mapping application that has logged tens of millions of downloads since 2005, increasingly reorganizes the look of many television broadcasts. The success of 3D MUVEs such as Second Life, which at any one time may have between 15,000 and 22,000 participants logged on to its site, confirms this shift. So, too, does the rise of eBay, which in 2005 facilitated intentional gross sales of US$40 billion and claimed 157.3 million registered users worldwide of whom it counted 64.6 million as "active"—those having bid on, bought, or listed an item within the previous twelve-month period (Hillis, Petit, and Epley 2006:1).

The media claims to occupy a social center trade on naturalized Durkheimian assumptions that mass social coherence is a necessary good. Older media, however, must now share the limelight with networked digital information machines; at a metalevel the Web is a networked constellation of many social centers. It does not produce mass coherence organized around one universal center. Given the widespread fetishization of efficiency and new technology, however, the Web does work to induce acceptance that communicability itself and the information machines on which it depends should be the virtual ecumene—the central object of our affection and attention. Yet it is not germane to my argument whether we might or might not wish that the ideology of the social center were not so powerful, that less mediated forms of a social center or social cohesiveness were ready to take center stage, or to dismiss the idea of a social center as authoritarian or only as administered. For how does any individual or group in an industrialized society acquire the majority of their information today? Do they talk with their neighbors? Do they stand at their door and look out? Do they travel to distant places to see for themselves firsthand? Or do they turn to the page, the speaker, and the screen? Whether critics approve or not, a culture of net-worked individualism increasingly thinks of information machines as con-stituted in networks of networks—dispersed versions of the idea of a social center that can accommodate as many subcenters, and therefore messages, as desired. It is, therefore, more technology per se and less media (in the latter term's hybrid meaning of both the humans who produce the content and the technologies that broadcast it) that becomes the new social center that simultaneously allows for the organization of distributed, plural, social centers "within" itself.

With respect to national cultures, broadcast media arrogating to them-selves a position of social centrality arguably have been more successful in in-dustrialized societies where identity as a mode of self-identification coupled to identity politics rose to prominence earlier than in other countries. I am thinking particularly of the United States, a multicultural, multiracial, multiethnic series of social admixtures where a variety of identity politics of ethnicity, gender, and sexuality established themselves considerably earlier than, say, England or France—countries that for many generations orga-nized social distinctions principally along class lines. In France, parts of the Left still decry efforts to establish a gay/queer progressive identity politics as inimical to what it is to be "French" (Eribon 2004). In mediated North American realities, broadcast media's social centrality and purportedly "big tent" approach earlier on not only allowed for an image of social cohesion but also provided the beginnings of a voice, however truncated and distorted, for identity movements unwelcome at most other tables. Such distortion is a feature of American broadcast media in particular, whose fetish for "objectivity" and "balance" often produces a flattening or even exclusion of messages that challenge the status of the center. As indicated in the media-savvy politics of ACT-UP (AIDS Coalition to Unleash Power), media are im-plicitly understood as the central revolving door through which most mes-sages now travel. Minorities must develop strategies of address that ensure that their messages get through this door—typically highly truncated but at least through the door. A legacy of relying on broadcast media as a form of social center, with all the possibilities for mass media rituals they hold on offer (Couldry 2003; Rothenbuhler 1998), coupled to the difficulty of mi-norities in particular to fully access this social center or to find nondistorted representations of themselves within it, has made it easier for networked individuals to imagine and then build the Web as the "natural" center to organize the culture to which they belong or aspire. Media encouragement of the myth of social centrality is based in self-interest only made stronger when media agents themselves buy into the myth. Media come to be understood as socially central and talismans of progress. The two myths imbricate, feed off, reinforce, and in essence administer one another. The ritualization of aspects of networked digital performances is one way of enacting the two myths at once, and at the same time it is a way of "trying them on" to see how they work and thereby, perhaps, to discover or invent askance ways of imagining a future different from the present.

Dedicated internet settings such as Internet Relay Chat (IRC) channels intended to facilitate new forms of group communication and virtual communities conform to the identification by longstanding theories of ritual of ritual's requirement for special places where group rites are performed (Danet 2005). But understanding media rituals in neo-Durkheimian terms as only about connection, coupled to an ongoing emphasis within communications research to focus on broadcast media rituals inducing consensus such as Princess Diana's funeral or the aftermath of 9/11, deflects consideration of the many other roles played by media (Couldry 2003). It also minimizes consideration of different forms of media rituals now taking place on the Web that may bring together certain individuals for periods of time but are not about producing a unitary center and are not invariant in their formal practices. Turner's identification of rituals as social dramas, a reworking of van Gennep's idea of rites of passage, argues that rituals work to transform the individual by elevating or diminishing her or his status. A site such as Second Life has a steep initial learning curve. One must concentrate carefully on how to negotiate one's way through a practice island landscape that is strange and new before "graduating" to Second Life proper. Mastering the necessary skills, initially a solo performance, elevates the status of the participants, interpellates them psychically, and confers on them the discursive status of *residents* of the social center called Second Life.

>>> Ritual and Transmission

In 1975, the communications theorist James Carey published a now canonical essay, "A Cultural Approach to Communication," that challenged the study of communication as then conceived by most American communications scholars. Carey's essay, influenced by Durkheim, identified a binary mode of thinking, longstanding in American thought, about the meaning of communication: a dominant, naturalized meaning of communication as the transmission of information, through the use of a communications medium or technology, between or among individuals, across *space*; and a second, "archaic," culturally inflected meaning of communication as ritual, as the maintenance of society in *time* through the performance of shared beliefs among people gathered in the same place. If communication as *transmission* across space refers to, for example, postal services, telegraphy, telephone calls, or television broadcasting and reception, *ritual* communication practices, Carey argued, gather people together for the collective performance of rites and ceremonies intended to facilitate and confirm the invention, maintenance, and ongoing repair and renewal of social relations. In a subsequent elaboration of his thesis, Carey argued that "if a transmission view of communication centers on the extension of messages across geography for purposes of control, a ritual view centers on the sacred ceremony that draws persons together in fellowship and commonality" (1989:43). Carey saw that transmission models dismiss the cultural dimensions of communication. He opposed what he identified as the spatial bias of the transmission model, with its presumed emphasis on control and its effacing of the sociocultural, material geographies lying between (or separating, depending on one's perspective) senders and receivers. His turn to the ritual model, with its emphasis on time and therefore history's unfolding, was a strategy to reframe communication as a research object amenable to cultural analysis.

The physical space of a religious service grounds Carey's neo-Durkheimian discussion of ritual communication. He traces the considerable zeal with which the telegraph, successfully demonstrated by Samuel Morse and Albert Vail in 1838, was, after 1844, seen by American religious leaders as manifesting a divinely inspired "electrical sublime," which they seized upon as particularly appropriate for spreading Christianity. One may read Carey's discussion of religion's early adoption of telegraphy as confirming that ritual and transmission modes of communication rarely have been fully held apart; he understood that neither the ritual nor the transmission model of communication "necessarily denies what the other affirms" (1975:9). Nevertheless, a binary mode of thinking that separated ritual and transmission, arguably, precluded anticipating that transmission and ritual practices would find ways to converge through new forms of communication techniques and practices. Recent assessments of Carey's influence on communications theory argue that this binary also prevents adequately thinking through the ritual model's relationships to power and control (see Hay 2006:41). Carey may also have inadequately assessed the various ways that control might be a state or experience, however transitory, actively sought by disadvantaged or marginalized agents and not just by dominant forces. Communications as transmission of a signal across space and time might actually offer cultural groupings something more than just their own hegemonization; it might, in ritual fashion, offer them ways of reimagining or making more visible their place in the world.

Telegraphy, Carey argues, deeply influenced the reorganization of important aspects of nineteenth-century corporate, spiritual, and social life. The crucial role of information machines such as the Web (in a world where the binary of wired and wireless is rapidly yielding to a panoply of information machines always on, always available, and ever present) is fundamentally more "central" still to first world, twenty-first-century quasi-networked, quasi-rhizomatic, quasi-ritualized, quasi-transmissive sensibilities, structures of feeling, and the social relations they inform. Bell notes that the majority of older theories of ritual rely on classificatory systems that, in circular fashion, support the theory being proposed. Such mutual imbrication naturalizes assumptions about the nature of ritual (1997:93). Binaries beget binaries. Counterposing transmission and ritual allows for extracting from the resulting binary parallel counterposings of economy and culture, culture and space, sacred and profane, insiders and others, and history and transmission—dead-end theoretical outcomes that Carey argued against throughout his career (Hay 2006:44). Carey's contribution to my project is apparent in the title of this volume's introduction. But understanding the Web's flexible and networked practices in relation to the kinds of ritualized activities taking place "there" on the part of communities constituted more in mutual interests and less in geography or place requires moving beyond binary modes to understand how ritual and transmission might actually inform rather than oppose one another.

Carey revisited his theory frequently, and in a 1997 article he stated that "to reconceive *transmission as ritual* is to reveal communications not as a means of sending messages but as the constitution of a form of life" (11;

emphasis added). Here Carey explicitly argues against "anti-democratic tendencies" that allowed representations of communications to be understood "both as a model *of* and a model *for* reality . . . a model for a social practice — this is how you do it" (10). In coming to see that transmission might constitute a ritual, Carey modulated part of the theoretical difficulties raised by setting transmission against ritual, yet in so doing he also set the idea of a form of life against the sending of a message. This newer binary may be ethically and politically defensible, but it is theoretically unhelpful in assessing Web-based practices as rituals and cultures of transmission, however unsavory, depoliticized, mistaken, or power-ridden some theorists may hold specific forms of such practices to be. For it is precisely the sending of messages — many signs circulating within a vast and increasingly animated sign system — that Web practices instantiate as part of a networked culture. This culture does constitute a "form of life," and it is one in which people are online a lot of the time. Rituals performed through networked digital settings are indices pointing to the assumptions undergirding sociocultural institutions and political economies within which a ritual's performers find and locate themselves ideologically and as embodied human beings. These rituals, together with the technologies that transmit them, are constitutive of the culture of networked individualism's formation and reproduction.

Participants of graphical chat MUVEs and personal webcam sites understand these settings as virtual environments that allow for experiencing specific kinds of movement within and through them. Not only are participants shaped by the sociohistorical and sociotechnical moment in which they live, they are also shaped by their experiences of communication as articulated to space and place together with their awareness of how space and place are socially and geographically constituted. Such awareness includes knowledge, experience, and meanings ascribed to places as well as the embodied sociospatial relations and political economies that constitute any place. Experiencing the online settings of communication as forms of virtual space influences participants' geographical imaginations (Harvey 1973). In turn, such experiences inform how participants come to understand and relate to the concrete places of the world, the ever more mutable and slippery interface between the virtual and the actual, interior and exterior, and any possibilities (including for a secular sacred) that might ferment at or be fomented through this interface.

The sacred is a mutable ideal, as indicated by the resurgence of Neoplatonic beliefs that subtend the popular reception of information machines. These beliefs presuppose that the ideal, in contrast to "this earthly plane," is where the real (action) is to be found. Yet the otherworldly realm of the Platonic ideal bears strong consonance not only with the sacred but also with the virtual realm of the profane space of networked communication technologies. Certain academics (Pierre Lévy [1997, 1998, 2001]; Marvin Minsky [1986, 2006]; and Hans Moravec [1988, 1999], for example) as well as corporate hypesters (Kevin Kelly's Hive Mind [1994] and the neoliberal, transcendental "California ideology" featured in the pages of *Wired* magazine) propose that such technologies will evolve to become, in essence, transcendence machines for realizing a future variation of Plotinus's World Soul or Teilhard de Chardin's noosphere (1964).[6] It does not hurt these various metaphysical proposals — some of which are religiously inflected — that they trade on the sacred-secular equation of progress equals advanced technologies equals tomorrow rendered today. Here one can identify how the virtual has come to stand in for the future. Technology itself, for these individuals, approaches a material actualization of the ideal and performs sacred, even spiritual, operations similar to those once reserved for the sphere of religious practice. Moreover, many networked settings occupy a place in the social imaginary somewhat akin to utopian, sacred disembodied spaces such as the Christian idea of "the promised land." These are set in contrast to the mundane, profane, and messy world on this side of the interface in which we actually reside. While I do not wish to perpetuate binaries between the virtual and the actual or the virtual and the real, I do note that they remain alive and well in such theories and help motorize the movement toward ritualizing and fetishizing virtual space and the experiences for which it allows. In the closing pages of *The Elementary Forms of the Religious Life*, Durkheim lamented that "the great things of the past that filled our fathers with enthusiasm do not excite the same ardour in us . . . but as yet there is nothing to replace them . . . we desire another [means of religious passion] which would be more practicable; but as yet we cannot clearly see what it should be nor how it could be realized in facts. In a word, the old gods are growing old or already dead, and others are not yet born" (1965 [1912]:475). Durkheim could not predict the future, though one new god had already been born in the elementary forms of communication technologies of his era. Today that god is mature. Many participants and users of networked sites, while using the sites for purposes that some might consider profane, do so in ways that accord *to the technology* a status akin to the divine. The difficulty here is that in making the virtual stand in for the future, other possibilities or ways of imagining the future get foreclosed. Implicitly positioning the virtual as the "new" future forgets that this virtual is actually taking place right now.

No ritual is guaranteed success. Ritual practices constituted through information machines, however, are forms of applied knowledge taking place in settings already associated with the successful outcome of science and technology. The genealogy of information machines is understood as secular. As fetishized talismans of the new they are increasingly appreciated in their own right: that is, as material proof that progress remains a viable concept. Information machines acquire a patina of the sacred as they shift in the popular imaginary from the means to an end to an end in themselves— medial zones of pure communicability (Agamben 2000). The conjuncture of a scientifically inflected and capitalized fetishization of information machines with ritual practices commonsensically associated with the sacred and the ideal of community is a powerful ideological combination. It is also, with respect to Web practices featuring images of human bodies, an indication of the mostly unspoken though accelerating cultural desire to accord these images a status equivalent to our own, and in so doing to produce a shift in the meaning of the real.

The widespread conceptualization of the Web as a form of space is a profoundly ambivalent move based on a return to or renovation of the pre-Enlightenment belief (never fully extinguished) that visual allegories are not lifeless but instead are simulations that might allow direct contact with something like the postmodern divine. Of course the majority of the participants and operators of these settings do not see themselves as communing with the divine any more than they identify as fetishists or as engaged in ritual activities. This concords with Rappaport's (1999:24) observation that ritual participants are never fully in command of the cultural codes upon which rituals rely. If they were, if they understood themselves as the center of agency and as participants engaged with a larger set of internalized ritual practices and techniques, the resulting self-reflexivity would defeat the ritual's intent. Rooted in magical empiricism, the desire for a supernatural force suggests that something is missing—a lack that is not only politically and culturally difficult or impossible to acknowledge but also possibly not yet fully able to be thought. The desire points to the ineffable. Discursively positioned as a problem of representation or of simulation, the desire for a spirit world (capitalized exchanges included) manifests itself through digital allegory. This is a world where explanation is more visible and direct, where difficulties and tensions associated with embodied misrecognitions and failures of communication cede to the "friction free" sphere of the Neoplatonic and neoliberal ideal. The Web understood as a visual allegory, moving pictures included, animates the longstanding desire of allegorists to have the material world resonate with its equivalent in the insensible world (Nelson 2001). This insensible world, rendered graphic on the Web, has become, for those participating seekers, quite experientially real.

I have raised the notion of the seemingly self-contradicting hybrid of magical empiricism. A number of ritual theorists maintain that ritual is nonutilitarian in the sense that it does not directly seek practical results. Magic, understood as a technique for producing practical outcomes — revenge, healing, love potions, good crops — is held distinct from ritual. Some theorists have contrasted science — rational actions seeking practical outcomes — to both ritual and magic (Bell 1997:46–47). Durkheim strongly articulated religion to ritual and the moral collective and he opposed ritual to magic — which he held as a selfish, private action. Van Gennep, on the other hand, was inclined to understand magic as a practical religious activity. The noted Polish field anthropologist Bronislaw Malinowski, who is credited with inventing participant-observation and who rejected Durkheim's "armchair anthropology," found that magical rites enhanced the self-confidence necessary for group effectiveness. "The logic of magical rituals lay in how they were used — primarily to alleviate anxiety" (quoted in Bell 1997:48).

A serviceable definition of magic is "action at a distance." While I do not hold that magical outcomes are possible on this side of the interface, I do identify in Web practices an unarticulated set of spatialized desires for magical outcomes relocated to virtual worlds. The relationship among doubt, belief, desire, hope, and ritual is crucial. One can, through the exercise of doubt, dismiss magic's immaterial promises yet at the same time wish that they might be so. As children of the Enlightenment, we identify the latter as magical thinking and dismiss it by associating it with childishness. The interface of ritual practices and networked information machines, however, suggests the value of refocusing attention onto these desires. In many ways the Web is the building of what once would have been called a magic act. The idea of telepresence — "[The] experience of presence in an environment by means of a communications medium" (Steuer 1992:76) — attempts to fuse appearance with presence. Its postrepresentational claim resonates with the definition of magic as action at a distance.[7] While telephony allows for an auditory experience of telepresence, popularization of telepresence as a real-izable idea grew in tandem with the Web's increasing geographical and social diffusion. Telepresence connects directly to the increasing ability of moving images in virtual environments to transmit an experiential sense of a trace of the referent — that I can, for example, remain materially "here" yet also be present, through processes of transmission, to you, located at a distance. The idea of online telepresence strongly articulates to my argument that online moving images transmit to perception an experiential trace of the actual individuals they represent. There is, in the perception that the Web-based trace carries something essential about the individual, the implicit understanding that the Web also carries us, that we are more present on the Web *through* the form of our own animated sign/bodies than the instrumental understandings of telepresence-as-efficient would suggest. The idea of telepresence, at least, retains the suffix *tele* as part of its explanatory power. Underacknowledged perceptual dynamics strongly inflected by capitalized desires, however, increasingly dispense with the idea of the *tele* to move directly to implicit assumptions grounded in indexicality about actual spaces peopled by "something" resembling actual human bodies.

The power of the Web as an outcome of scientific research coupled to its ability to induce a sense of presence, recommends it as an empirically in-flected setting to which ritual, and its recursive set of associations with tran-scendence located in the immanence of ritual practices, can profitably locate. In many ways, this relocation seems "only natural," empirically evident, and makes "perfect magical sense." Though the transmission of moving pictures that seem experientially real through telepresence is an outcome of science, in general, science's explanations of phenomena have become too complex and too abstract for most people to grasp. Few people fully comprehend how the Web works. Most just know that it does. We have, to borrow a phrase from Malinowski (1961:83), no knowledge of its "total outline."[8] For many, it functions as a personal transformer, a magical black box. Durkheim's Vic-torian belief that all things would be understood through science has not come to pass in the way imagined by that era's elite. Ironically, science's increasing detachment from the everyday coupled to its increased importance to everyday industrialized and networked lives lends science something of a mystical character. Though different in setting, the dynamic is uncannily similar to the accordance, by colonial anthropologists, of mystical character to tribal elders charged with guarding ritual's mysteries.

>>> Ritual Play, Ritual Performance

The Web rituals I examine accord with most ritual theorists' understanding that rituals are media that concretize or embody assumptions about their performers' place in a larger order of things (Bell 1997:ix). In the absence of censorship, any group or individual can craft a networked performance pointing toward a potential future, desirable or otherwise; a nostalgic regret for a loss or the past; a problem in need of a solution; a tragedy; an exceptional set of circumstances referencing the unknown, experienced as a puzzle or riddle not yet fully understood. The "playful" use of avatars in graphical chat, for example, can be seen as a defensive procedure, a way of taming the psychic effects of the computerization of life, coupled to a productive attempt to give "voice" to and learn from this complex conjuncture. A performance is one way of seeming to take control over the monumental changes these effects portend that might otherwise threaten to overwhelm some participants. Such "playfulness" does not challenge the forces underwriting the networked society. Quite the opposite. Such a ritual might implicitly sanction them even while allowing participants a chance to try on for size new forms of self-definitions and social practices within the set-off ritual space located "within" the larger luminous, and increasingly everyday, virtual world.

PLAY

In Western societies where forms of ritual are conceived to be relatively weak, it is easy to deny that one takes part in a ritual and insist instead that it is play. How then do play and ritual intersect theoretically and practically? In 1938, the Dutch cultural historian Johan Huizinga published his now classic study of play, *Homo Ludens*. In it he identified the element of play as a necessary, though not sufficient, condition for the generation of culture. Huizinga also identified what has come to be known as play's "magic circle"—a temporarily sacred space, not unlike Second Life's virtual wedding, the spatial dimensions of which may vary according to the cultural game played, and within which players remain until the obligations of the play in question are discharged (1955 [1938]:57). Huizinga identifies what he calls "the play of culture" as a form of ritual, and he argues that it is "precisely the play-character [of various forms of gaming] that gives [them] so important a place in ritual" (58). Serious forms of adult play raise the individual or the collective to a "higher power" (61), and Huizinga observes that all ritual is rooted in the primeval soil of play (5). A more common-sense understanding of play is as "a free and voluntary activity" and "a source of joy and amusement" (Caillois 1961 [1958]:6). And while we may not usually think of play spaces as "magic circles," we have only to consider the arena, racetrack, sandbox, schoolyard, stage, bridge table, chessboard, or the liminal spaces of the movie or computer screen on which photoplays and videogames materialize to recognize that play spaces are bounded. Like ritual, play encompasses a range of activities set off in time and space from other everyday practices. And while we often consider play relaxing, the cry of "play fair" reveals how serious, even transfixed, players may become. Play is often contrasted against work, but as Mark Twain observed at the beginning of the twentieth century, "work and play are used to describe the same thing under differing conditions" (1989:106)—an observation anticipating and consonant with participants' activities in MUVEs such as Second Life. "Playful" Second Life activities such as regularly enhancing the look of one's avatar or the rapid shifting of the perspective from which one views the setting either through the eyes of one's avatar or from a distance so as to include the avatar within one's view of the larger setting can be understood as forms of free labor through which participants add value to the site through "learning how to learn," a core neoliberal skill that, together with "lifelong learning" "is the requisite for the adaptability and opportunism demanded in the dauntingly flexible world of informational capitalism" (Robins and Webster 1999:203). Like ritual, play serves as an activity for rehearsing life's events, and this observation does not conflict with the fact that play's associative meanings run from innocence to manipulation and deceit.

PERFORMANCE

Performance is central to ritual practices, yet the academic linking of performance and ritual only achieved full ideation in the 1970s, a period during which a number of concepts mutually informed one another to produce a performance approach to the study of ritual (Bell 1997:72–73). The performative turn in ritual studies emphasizes participants as active and questions how the symbolic components of ritual activities allow individuals and groups to change, refashion, reinterpret, appropriate, or discard certain sociocultural values, beliefs, and ideals (73). Bell identifies four defining characteristics of performance approaches to ritual: first, ritual is an event—a set of activities that actually effects changes in people's perceptions and interpretations (physical and sensual activities of the rituals are stressed); second, rituals are "framed" or discursively positioned in advance as at least somewhat differing or set apart from everyday life; third, during ritual performances, participants may possibly achieve some quality of transformation (a point germane to my interest in identifying the ways by which individuals transmit an experiential trace of themselves through digital networks); and fourth, ritual does what it does by virtue of its formal characteristics (74).[9]

If ritual as performance emphasizes active participants, how central does the human body need to be in any one ritual performance? The discursive positioning of networked settings asks us to focus on the representations lodged within the screen or display to the virtual exclusion or at least marginalization of actual bodies. However, the human bodies that look into the computer interface are never divorced from these practices. Indeed, the power of these settings depends, in part, on the indexical relationships (discussed more fully in chapter 3) established between digital sign/bodies and the human bodies to which they point. The performances of virtual bodies and objects that move within digital networks have the potential to provide those looking on with an *experience* of a trace of actual bodies residing elsewhere. They situate or ground a performance of virtual objects that can sometimes seem alive and independent in their own right even as the performance is produced and directed by humans who, in circular fashion, may also experience a sense of greater liveliness through interacting with the performing virtual bodies and objects displayed on their screens. Van Gennep identified human bodies moving through space as crucial to ritual practices; movement such as passing through a portal can signify changes in status and situation (Bell 1997:36). Like Huizinga's identification of play's "magic circle," ritual space, van Gennep argued, is specially constructed space that allows bodies to move through it in ways that allow for the simultaneous definition and experience of the special environment (82). Rappaport (1999:50) confirms this point, noting that designating special times and places for ritual performances not only congregates "senders and receivers" of messages together but also specifies what it is that they are gathered to communicate about: "Unless there is a performance there is no ritual" (27).

>>> Ritualizing Hegemony

All rituals are marked (in different ways) by performances, the possibility of their taking place on some kind of regularized basis, and the production of a sense of individual or group coherence for those participating in a particular ritual. I have noted that performance signifies assumptions about participants' place in the larger order of things. Ritual can be thought of as performing one's place within hegemony, including contemporary forms of hegemony organized through media and popular culture with their coercive insistence on flexibility and ambivalent reliance on fleeting, ephemeral, and commodified productions of subjectivity. However embodied a ritual performance might be, it also *signifies* assumptions about its performers' place in a larger order of things. Order, Michel Foucault observes, is "that which is given in things as their inner law, the hidden network that determines the way they confront one another, and also that which has no existence except in the grid created by a glance, an examination, a language; and it is only in the blank spaces of this grid that order manifests itself in depth as though already there, waiting in silence for the moment of its expression" (1994:xx). Rituals, like naturalized ideologies, are regular social processes that may allow participants to identify and therefore produce order, to allow participants to interpret and create meaningful order through signifying performances, however compromised or pure, that, like narrative, help stave off the Void and the meaninglessness of existence it portends. In this way, rituals produce and move energy toward needed goals.

Rappaport observes that ritual performances are "not entirely encoded by the performers" [who are following] "orders established or taken to have been established by others" (1999:24, 32). While individuals engage in networked ritualizations as potentially strategic and certainly tactical ways of acting,[10] they need not fully organize, control, or craft every aspect of their performances. In this way, the logic of rituals is also somewhat akin to the hidden logic of the black box. Participants in the MUVEs Virtual Laguna Beach, Rose, and Church of Fools do not design the program software or the representational avatars through which they represent themselves online. In Second Life, which does encourage participants to engage in quasi-immaterial forms of free labor by developing open-source software to fabricate their own customized avatars and virtual environments, the design of all such virtual personae and settings is necessarily compatible with overall site operation. Personal webcam operators customize their websites and modus operandi, yet all conform to certain predetermined spatial logics of screen display; rely on cinematic close-ups; and offer ways for fans to incorporate commentary.

Rituals of transmission are hegemonic in that participants enact and seemingly buy into certain dominant assumptions or cultural perspectives. One assumption is the idea that information machines, as an increasingly central aspect of everyday life, coupled to the social, cultural, and economic associations constellated around them, are fundamental to how such ritual actions *should* operate, take place, and transmit. A second assumption is the desirability of conceiving oneself as an image flexible enough to be located in multiple locations different from one's embodied location. A third assumption would be that there is no inherent contradiction between the importation of existing ideologies, structures of feeling, and social expectations into networked setting and the constant promotion that such settings are entirely new. Such assumptions are built into these programs and rely on users and participants buying into concepts of identity based on informational, neoliberal, and commodified yet malleable and even ephemeral "skin-deep" understandings. Participants negotiate these assumptions even as these sites variously allow for tactical and affective uses unanticipated by designers. In all of this, participants "live in an order in which all aspects of life—work, communication, leisure, consumption, education—are increasingly subordinated to the logic of the Information Society" (Robins and Webster 1999:129). As Marx argued, a person makes her own history but never in situations fully of her own choosing.

Consider, for example, personal webcam operators who actively participate in a ratings game whereby fans and other site visitors evaluate and rank them as more or less valuable screen- or display-based commodities. The actions of such individuals conform to Gramscian hegemony theory to the extent that forms of social control, including the naturalization of dominant ideas of competition and self-commodification, are achieved and maintained not through coercion but by gaining consent through such mechanisms that are overt and subtle at the same time. Yet the actions of these individuals indicate not only their interpellation into dominant ideologies or discourses but also that they are consenting for reasons of their own. Ritual entails performing hegemony, yet a "lived hegemony" is always changing and never complete (Williams 1977:112). Power operates at two levels in ritual: at the level of the participants and in the structuration of the ritual itself. Understanding that an individual might consent to be rated for reasons other than those promoted by dominant elites allows one to better identify why ritualized Web practices may be strategic as well as tactical. They certainly evidence contradictory tensions. One may play the competitive ratings game as part of building long-term strategic alliances with other peers. Understanding timing and gesture is central: what one does today, one hopes will pay off tomorrow. Yet the ratings game may end, terminated by site operators' fatigue; desire for change, novelty, and refreshment; or discouragement flowing from complaints expressed through a tally of too many negative votes. If this happens, a certain comfort is available in the knowledge that one was operating tactically—holding one's own, making do for the time being.

My examples illustrate Raymond Williams's discussion of hegemony as "not just passively exist[ing] as a form of dominance. It has continually to be renewed, recreated, defended, and modified. It is also continually resisted, limited, altered, challenged by pressures not all its own" (1977:112). Like Alain Badiou (2005 [1988]), Williams retains a place for agency and free will. The ability of certain networked settings to provide participants with opportunities for ritualizing experiences, therefore, is likely to be greatest when it operates at the intersection of corporate hegemony and the ironic or networked "public interest" of a culture of networked individualism. Such a culture in many ways enacts the intersection of Williams's (2003[1974]) concept of mobile privatization and Anne Friedberg's (1993) notion of the mobilized virtual gaze: ever more private living practices that do not interfere with capital's impersonal and cosmopolitan requirement for unprecedented mobility and flexibility. But while such practices form part of dominant strategies of social containment they are also unacknowledged rites of passage. They support an alienated form of freedom experienced as lived isolation in metrical space that, perhaps ironically, conforms to Turner's understanding of rituals as transforming the individual through a change in status. In circular fashion, such practices lead to a mobilized visually based subjectivity reliant on indexical and virtual information machines as seeming "solutions" to the "problem" of alienated, capitalized social geographies.

More is at stake here, however, than the hegemonic fine tuning of economic and social subordination and dominance. Marshall McLuhan points to new media as potential forms of lived hegemony when he writes: "Experience translated into a new medium literally bestows a *delightful* playback of earlier awareness" (1964:211; emphasis added). The desire McLuhan implicitly identifies explains, in part, the hegemonic logic identified by Stewart Hoover: "In both scholarly and popular discourse, the media seem . . . to be somehow always 'new'" (2006:31). Information machines such as Second Life are the collective contemporary site where "the future" retains a transcendent, frequently pleasurable and playful, point of purchase. They are experienced as the collective site where "the future is now." At a time when for many the future, like nature, seems to have receded from view or is spun by mass media as a fearful dystopia, the possibility of such an experience itself is enough to recommend participating in networked rituals of transmission. In all of this, however, information machines organize, situate, and also distort the necessary utopian aspirations that counterbalance the already ideologized social and geographical material spaces and their constraining empirical "realities." Theodor Adorno would understand. In a world reduced to factual explanations rendered in words that often mask the big lie, the Web, positioned as a space into and through which one might transmit an indexical trace of oneself as a moving image—as if one were "living in art"—animates the promise of getting beyond the potential for lies that always attend textual representation—"mere words." Such a positioning, therefore, implicitly promises the Neoplatonic ideal of "communication without codes." This is a promise of aesthetic refuge similar in affect to art's transcendent powers. These powers are located in art's ability to suggest to hegemonized subjects alternative future possibilities to a status quo deceitfully naturalized by dominant forces as the totality of reality, "the facts of life," and "just the way it is." Such seemingly magical qualities as telepresence therefore seem to allow the imagination to conceive of new ways of becoming that exceed a dominant, positivist constraint on thinking outside the empirical box of "facts . . . nothing but the facts." At the same time, however, networked individuals are capable of seeing for themselves that they have something to gain from buying into the equation that technology equals progress equals the future, and something to lose in not so doing.

While ritual entails nonverbal communication, the signs it deploys only have meaning in relationship to other signs from which they differ but with which they also form part of a larger set of signifiers (see Bell 1997:44–46; Derrida 1976:27–73). Rituals allow for an experience of transforming one category (for example, an unhappy marriage recently ended, or the experience of others' loathing of one's gay/queer body) into another (the chance to view today as the beginning of the rest of one's life, or the opportunity to experience an image of one's embodiment as desire incarnate). At the same time, they maintain the integrity of the categories and the belief systems that produce the categories (romantic love, the institutions of marriage and divorce, heteronormativity, and so forth). Rituals participate in making something present by making something else absent. At the same time, they work to efface from participants' direct consciousness an awareness of any potential metaphysics. Additionally, whether one approaches networked settings tactically to gain a moment's respite from everyday demands, or strategically to negotiate new ways of becoming, categories of the real and the virtual can be made to merge. Networked performances enact the possible. They allow for an experiential suturing of the real to the virtual, the referent to the sign. Temporarily and at the level of experience, distinctions yield to hybridized continuities. Web-based ritualizations are always "lived hegemony" in their ability to offer meaningful experiences of freedom and self-redefinition even while they work to not overly destabilize dominant social orders.

>>> Ritual and Form

In the overall estimation of the theorists I have discussed, form, more so than content, is the nexus of ritual's power. If overt expression of ideas is less central in ritual practices than performing or acting them out, then the potential for the mystification of these ideas through their performative symbolization looms large. Rituals, however, while repeated with regularity or at least occurring at somewhat regular intervals, are exceptional activities. They may take place everyday but we cannot ritualize every waking moment any more than remain constantly attentive to all of the material qualities of the places we inhabit. Networked ritualizations, extending Turner's (1982) proposal, are liminal—that is, out of the ordinary without being fully "other than." Rituals are Janus-faced, "virtually real" performances allowing for various forms of synthesis among "the ideal and the material, the general and the particular, the cosmic and the ordinary, the past and the future, the structures of history and the happenings of individual lives" (Shields 2003:64). While one of the intents of any ritual, therefore, may be to actualize the virtual, rituals also remain in dialectical relationship to the restoration of the ordinary and the social orders it entails. While participating in Second Life or some other MUVE remains a distinct practice from the rest of one's everyday life, this participation also constitutes part of everyday life. Some participants indicate a reluctance to disengage the setting. Others turn to it as a form of mediated self-disclosure to negotiate life transitions ranging from the banal to the tragic to the transcendent: "In all rituals private psychophysical processes and public orders are at once articulated to each other and buffered against each other" (Rappaport 1999:105). Participating in Second Life's ritualized performances conforms to the idea that in ritual one lives through the event (see Couldry 2003:55; Turner 1982:86). Participants face both ways, neither fully private nor public, separated *but* connected, symbolic *and* embodied, indicative of the virtual and the real, and joined in a high-speed, fiber optical state of sacred and profane potentiality. Participation allows for certain forms of temporary suspensions of everyday social orders. One may don a virtual identity intended to reproduce one's everyday existence. Given the ongoing expectation, however, that the central Hobbesian author interiorized in each of us remains conceptually stable and self-responsible, one may also approach a MUVE identity as one of the many Hobbesian actors or personae and then craft it in a fluid fashion appropriate to what one desires to obtain from the setting. One may do so, for example, in how one wishes to appear or not appear to others, and in how one transmits a sense of one's "inner" state to others through an exterior, quasi-automated manifestation of the actor/avatar.

Networked ritualized performances both depart from and extend older ritualized practices, and changing forms of Web technologies also allow for changes in the ways that individuals perform. Couldry reminds readers that whatever their centrifugal potential, "new media . . . are not disconnected from the material processes by which society's symbolic resources are centralised" (2003:53). However, while identifying unequal power relationships in mediated formats is crucial to understanding the meanings of Web practices, it is also the case that "the moral portrait of the world most citizens share comes from the media" (Marvin and Ingle 1999:146) and that new forms of networked digital cultures can indicate the emergence of new forms of mystification *and* new forms of social change. Couldry's is an admirable project to identify how media mystify the ways they assert their purported social centrality and thereby their ongoing cultural and political dominance. However, the ritualization of transmission might not be so ironically central today if, in turn, media weren't so central (and effective) in connecting all the spatially isolated latter-day monads.

Couldry does not closely examine *why* media gets to naturalize its claim to social centrality, or, equally important, any potential relationships between productions of social centers (in the plural) and satisfaction of basic human needs. It is not his project to historicize the idea of a transmitted or virtual center, or of how its ancient connections to the ideal world of Platonic forms and truth remain culturally available for economic mining by media moguls such as Rupert Murdoch or the Google triumvirate of Sergey Brin, Larry Page, and Eric Schmidt. Armand Mattelart, however, has linked communication's association with social harmony. He identifies "the idea of communication as the regulatory principle counteracting the disequilibria of the social order" (1994:36); rituals of transmission are a principal contemporary means by which the ends of social order and control are achieved. Networked settings often reflect and promote the Western idea that the self is a mutable, interior creature that seeks to communicate its carapaced quality of existence within a long-standing and now resurgent set of Cartesian and Neoplatonically inflected premises: representing is better than presenting; the ideal is morally superior to the real, the mind to the body, the imaginary to the material. Therefore, these premises imply, one *should* buy into a metaphysics of virtual "presence" to communicate one's "ideal essence," come out of one's shell as much as possible, and render oneself as a visible image in the virtual commons. These settings are virtual centers for those seeking cosmopolitan exchanges of "points of view" with others. Signs created by body movements are important to transmitting a ritual's meaning. When "'virtualities' are enacted . . . they are usually buffered with ritual" (Shields 2003:210). Bodies are important in ritual, but if the signs that their movements produce are also central to the transmission of a ritual's meaning, then the sign-world of the Web is a "perfectly natural," even ideal, vision machine and location for the kinds of ritual performance of interest to a society of the networked spectacle.

>>>

Durkheim left his mark on how we understand ritual. In developing his theory, he did not turn to traditional French customs, religious practices, and folkways as available to him for ethnographic enquiry as they were to van Gennep, who made their study a hallmark of his research. Instead, Durkheim looked "elsewhere," finding what he sought in the text. The texts that pleased him pointed to a further elsewhere — to the non-Western exotic locales of "natural men" where Durkheim, inflected by a kind of Rousseauian spirit seeking freedom from existing social restrictions, would identify an uncontaminated set of collective practices amenable to the needs of his theory. The individuals whose practices and techniques I examine also look elsewhere, not to the text but to the digital interface and the 3D internet. They fetishize the Web as a realization of the progress myth and as a more pristine, "friction free" setting conducive to the solitary yet networked meaningful practices such individuals have need to ritualize "all alone together."

I am reminded of two passages that, read together, reveal something of the complexity of assessing networked ritualizations and their digital forms. For John Dewey, "society not only continues to exist *by* transmission, *by* communication, but it may fairly be said to exist *in* transmission, *in* communication" (1916:5). For Frances Barker, society is "the associative name we give to lived isolation" (1984:52). Whereas Dewey's assertion relates to his belief that language is required for the formation of thought, Barker's focus is the self-regulation of the body as an anxious performance that proclaims its vigorous dedication to productive ends. Coupling these ideas captures something of the ambivalent realities that attend the adaptation of social practices to digital environments. Society as existing *in* transmission's increasingly digital milieus is consonant with the idea of society as the name we give to everyday associative or connected isolation. And yet, hegemony is never complete. As part of a cosmopolitan networked society engaged in the play of a democracy of moving images, individuals need online ritualizations that help them make sense of, resist, and accommodate the digital move to all things virtual.

Fetishes

How websites reveal the ways that rituals are adapting
to networked settings is a central theme of this volume. As a concept, however, ritual is overarching and
on its own does not fully capture the complexities of
the social, political, cultural, and economic work that
websites and related practices are expected to (and do)
carry out. In this chapter I turn to fetish theory for its
applicability to contemporary Web-based practices and
techniques, including models of viewing, eroticism,
and self-commodification. I account for and interpret
how and why individuals craft themselves as digital
fetishes — what I term the telefetish. As a term, fetish
is already inhabited by a set of psychoanalytic, Marxian, and anthropological discourses, and much of this
theorization posits fetishes as only material objects. I
provide a selective account of these at times competing
theories, some of which I employ and also extend, in
order to argue that fetishes can also be virtual objects.
Examining the possibility that people fetishize virtual
objects is necessary if we are to make sense of the ways
the Web has become a setting for fetish practices. These
practices are distinct from yet organized by and through
already widely fetishized information machines.

In making these arguments I am cognizant of the difficulties in applying older theories to contemporary situations. Eric Rothenbuhler, for example, asserts that all claims about media rituals are debatable "because anthropological ideas developed in the study of small-scale, nonindustrial societies are being applied to the production and consumption of modern, commercial media" (1998:78). Fetish theory also developed from the contact by early anthropologists with premodern societies, and Catherine Bell's (1997:xi) observation that ritual is less a formal category than a contingent, historicized academic construct equally applies to fetish theory. Moreover, some theories, or parts of them, simply do not "time travel" well. Fetish theory, like ritual theory, is shaded by colonial legacies and cultural assumptions about "dark others" that were naturalized as theories.

Amy Villarejo argues that "the politics of fetish discourse require investigation for their historical underpinnings" (2003:27). While I identify how components of early anthropological theories of the fetish, with their focus on the interpretation of objects, might still pertain to thinking through online fetish practices, I also need to state my opposition to the assumptions of European white cultural superiority that attended the bestowal of the term "fetishists" on non-Western peoples encountered by colonial traders and missionaries first in Africa and then elsewhere. The concept of the fetish, arising from this cross-cultural encounter, was used to denigrate Africans as dupes in their purported inability to distinguish the exchange value of things. The fetish was also used to demonize an alien set of ritual practices deemed inferior to Protestant ceremony and belief. Georg Hegel, in the introduction to *The Philosophy of History*, summarily dismisses Africa in a few pages in which he links its people's alleged inability to conceive of a proper Spirit and sense of History to their blockage and subsequent need to produce the Fetish: "Africa proper, as far as History goes back, has remained . . . the land of childhood . . . enveloped in the dark mantle of Night . . . the second element in their religion, consists in their giving an outward form to supernatural power—projecting their hidden might into the world of phenomena by means of images. What they conceive of as the power in question, is therefore nothing really objective, . . . but the first thing that comes their way. This . . . they exalt to the dignity of a 'Genius'; it may be an animal, a tree, a stone, or a wooden figure. This is their Fetich" (1956:91–94). A certain irony inheres in Hegel's assertion that the fetish originates in the "dark mantle of Night" given that most fetish theories focus on vision and the fetish as a visible material object. Peter Stallybrass notes that "what was demonized [by Europeans] in the concept of the fetish was the possibility that history, memory, and desire might be materialized in objects that are touched and loved and worn" (1998:186). Networked information machines operationalize this possibility and allow the fetishist to accrue value in part from new forms of exchange specific to the moving digital image.

I assume no exact correspondence between non-Western situational exigencies important to the development of the fetish object and its practices, and the virtual realities of digital lived worlds. I wish to avoid one of structuralism's problems, by which underlying structures are always deferred from their actual presence. And while I aim for a materialist and critical phenomenological account of Web-based practices and techniques, the telefetish I examine is never fully material and is frequently allegorical. It is, as I detail below, a networked hybrid of persona and practice, a virtual object operating as a digital trace that exceeds the meaning of representation yet nonetheless remains wholly reliant on pixelation and the codes that underlie it. Its efficacy depends on a technologically induced metaphysics of telepresence (which literally means distant presence, but in the present instance means the experience of presence and the simulation of immediacy by means of a digital, networked communication technology). And like the position in which networked cosmopolitan individuals find themselves, a virtual object in the form of a digital trace is "as though displaced while still in place . . . virtual objects exist only as fragments of themselves" (Deleuze 1994:135).[1] Such consonance between the fractured kinds of territorial practices demanded of networked individuals and that of virtual objects supports the former's fetishization of the latter.

Although ritual theory and fetish theory both developed within similar colonial circumstances, updated versions of fetish theory enjoy considerably greater application across a range of contemporary academic formations and humanities enquiries than is the case for ritual. In understanding why this might be so, I note the attention paid to the fetish by Karl Marx and Marxist theorists and by psychoanalytic theorists, including Sigmund Freud and Jacques Lacan. These theorists contributed to revitalizing fetish theories in ways that have allowed contemporary scholars to engage critically with the concept and extend its meanings and applications in ways that acknowledge forms of hybridity less apparent or even denied during the colonial period. The fetish, then, has evolved into an acceptable and even lustrous psychologically inflected academic object and concept. While Bell (1997) notes that ritual studies have grown exponentially, the literature suggests that ritual, as an academic heuristic, remains more centrally anchored to religious studies and anthropology (and to a lesser extent communication studies) than does the fetish. Ritual's theorists too often relied on binaries in developing their theories. This led to modes of analysis inimical to articulating ritual to hybridity. Unlike the fetish (an inanimate object animated by "spirit," associated with personal desire and therefore individual psychology, and frequently crafted as a means of asserting temporary psychic control over complex situations), ritual—long associated with collective interests and therefore with sociology, but, like the fetish, also crafted and requiring a performative element as a means of making meaning—has not enjoyed sustained attention on the part of Marxist or psychoanalytic scholars outside of the disciplines noted above. Nevertheless, because both ritual and fetishes are used by individuals and groups to create meaningful order in their lives, where apposite to my arguments I note their intersections.

Since the early 1980s there has been an upsurge of interest in fetishism on the part of academic criticism and aesthetics (Apter 1993). Much of this work is psychoanalytic, semiological, or poststructural in approach; it extends the insights of Freud and Lacan and often is organized around an interest in eroticism and the sexual practices of sexual subgroups (see, for example, Clark 1991; Krips 1999). Broadly stated, psychoanalytic theorizations position the fetish as a substitution mechanism for displacing psychic distress or *lack* through projecting certain attributes or desires onto a particular external object. Marx's (1952) writings on commodity fetishism continue to inform recent Marxian-inflected research. I introduced his theory of the commodity fetish in the introduction. It borrows from yet is critical of an already established European positioning of fetishism as the practice of racialized others, a cross-cultural positioning undertaken not only to confirm the Enlightenment premise of the unitary rational subject but also the "natural" superiority of Christian abstraction and generalizability and the attendant capitalist values of exchange and economy. Anthropology's long history of interest in the fetish practices of aboriginal peoples has yielded a third set of texts available for current research on fetishes and fetishism, and also on the relationship between people and objects constituting the core of the fetishist-fetish relationship.

The *OED* notes the etymological connection of the term fetish to the Latin *facticius*, as in "made by art, artificial, [and] skillfully contrived" and to the modern English "factitious," as in arising from custom or habit and not natural or spontaneous. A subsequent entry highlights the work of Charles de Brosses (1709–1777), who is credited with first theorizing the term: "By writers on anthropology (following C. de Brosses, *Le Culte des Dieux Fétiches*, 1760) used in wider sense: An inanimate object worshiped by primitive peoples on account of its supposed inherent magical powers, or as being animated by a spirit." In part because Marx drew from de Brosses's account in formulating his theory of commodity fetishism, William Pietz pays close attention to the circumstances surrounding de Brosses's crucial formulations of the fetish. With respect to his actual circumstances Pietz writes: "The methodological force of the theory of fetishism formulated at this time by . . . Charles de Brosses is found in his insistence that philosophy and social theory could no longer be based on the unexamined presuppositions of the intellectual tradition of Western Christendom, but must more radically derive its authority from what might be called a method of 'ethnographic materialism,' of cultural interpretation based on the 'direct observation' of contemporary peoples, including those outside Europe and its traditions. De Brosses' . . . own world had been changed in its substance by the new global economy: the monetary value of the landed estates that were his ancestral inheritance . . . had plummeted as the overseas war went badly for France. . . . For de Brosses there could be no doubt that the non-European world was part of his world" (1998:249).

With respect to the Neoplatonically inflected Christian beliefs of de Brosses's period that reduced ancient myths and cult beliefs to New Testament allegories, Pietz has written: "Rejecting the adequacy of Euhemerist explanations . . . de Brosses identified a savage 'manner of thinking,' . . . which located divine power in terrestrial, material entities . . . and which was purely contingent and particularistic. *Fétichisme* was the term de Brosses used for the cults and superstitions formed from this 'natural propensity' toward the nonallegorical personification of material powers (which is what de Brosses means when he defines fetishism as a 'direct' cult of terrestrial things 'sans figure')" (1993:138). Pietz's observations offer readers a glimpse of the enlightened, contingent empiricism informing de Brosses's thought. Nevertheless, as Henry Krips (1999:3) observes, the way that fetishism has been theorized assigns it an essentially conservative function, and contemporary popular meanings widely presuppose psychological or social deficiency, sexual pathology, or deviancy sometimes articulated to modes of fashion, other forms of "arrested development," or obsessional "behaviors."

Certainly such psychoanalytically inflected conservative understandings of the fetish bear a trace of Freud's notion of blockage. On the first page of *Totem and Taboo* (1950) he equates "the psychology of primitive peoples" and "the psychology of neurotics." For Freud, the primitive peoples are "infantile" and neurotics are hobbled by "blocked" development. This idea of blockage or obstruction (akin to the idea of lack of progress), whether or not retaining its association with the infantile and the neurotic, informs the concept of displacement—an unconscious transfer of an intense emotion from one object (generally assumed to be human in form) to another (assumed to be inanimate) so that one is "blocked" from a direct relationship with the original object. In referring to *Totem and Taboo*, Bell has argued that Freud also constructs a related theory of ritual as "an obsessive mechanism that attempts to appease repressed and tabooed desires by trying to solve the internal psychic conflicts that these desires cause" (1997:14).

Theorists have scant control over how their ideas will be taken up and promulgated. Though de Brosses (and later, Marx and Freud) points to the need for enlightened European thinking to address the ways by which human beings may learn more about themselves through investigating the other, and to the extent he is arguing that at one time or another we are all fetishists in some way, the broad reception of his ideas has been marred by the refusal or inability to acknowledge that the "natural propensity" toward "nonallegorical personification of material powers" might equally apply to European subjects as to racialized others. This need not have been the case. De Brosses's contemporary, David Hume, can be read as suggesting that a tendency to fetishize objects is an innate human condition. In *Natural History of Religion* (section 3) he writes, "There is a universal tendency among mankind to conceive all beings like themselves, and to transfer to every object those qualities with which they are familiarly acquainted, and of which they are intimately conscious" (cited in Freud 1950:77). Hegel, despite his dismissal of Africa and his theorization of fetishism as grounded in profound ignorance of spirit, sees fetish practices as the first spiritual expression of subjectivity (noted in Pietz 1993:124, n.14). A narrow reading of fetish practices that did not admit Western fetish forms served to justify a sociopolitically regressive and economically instrumental understanding of those profaning others about to be colonized in the sacred names of Christendom, empire, resource extraction, and exchange value—including the trade in human beings.

The *OED* further supplements de Brosses's definition in noting that the fetish, with respect to his theorization of the term, "differs from an *idol* in that it is worshiped in its own character, not as an image, symbol, or occasional residence of a deity." A premodern fetish is a "visible object," the power of which "resides in its own right as a dwelling for a deity," yet early modern observers such as Portuguese traders noted that the fetish was "thrown away as useless when the consecrating nostrum is discovered to be inoperative." In these definitions one may also grasp something of the ambivalent complexity behind Marx's decision to choose the term "fetishism" to name the process by which the mystical character of the commodity form always works to disguise the commodity's origins. Marx arguably draws from not only a mid-Victorian scientific rejection of fetish practices, but also from the root similarity between *facti*tious and *fact*ory and his grasp that something in the potentially transcendent nature of a work of art and its reception inheres in the aesthetics of the commodity form. Participants within graphical chat environments and personal webcam operators and their fans—*homos faber* all—ritualistically enact similar sets of understandings when using information technologies to fabricate online personae experienced both as a component of personal identity and as a set of discrete animated images that move or refresh.

Pietz argues that for Marx fetishism was the "religion of sensuous desire" (1993:140), a submission of intellect and moral will to libidinal aesthetics. He further proposes that Marx turned to the idea of the fetish in his discussion of the commodity because, he asserts (echoing de Brosses's finding that a fetish is "direct" and "sans figure"), a fetish is not a representation. Turning to this way of theorizing the fetish allowed Marx to argue that the logic of the fetish resides beyond that of capitalism, with its strong emphasis on representation. In so doing Marx hoped to point out that the proletariat was also "other" to bourgeois society in that it was largely in possession of only its own sensuous embodiment. As Stallybrass notes, "In attributing the notion of the fetish to the commodity, Marx ridiculed a society that thought it had surpassed 'mere' worship of objects supposedly characteristic of 'primitive religions.' For Marx, the fetishism of the commodity was a regression from the materialism (however distorted) that fetishized the object" (1998:186). An adherence to the logic subtending Marx's attribution, however, creates impediments to theorizing virtual fetishes. Marx translates or inverts what can be termed as indigenous fetishism's dialectics of the positive into a negative dialectics of the Western fetish as commodity in order to expose and critique exchange value. Yet Marx himself, in noting that the "mystical character" of the commodity abounds "in metaphysical subtleties and theological niceties" (1952:31), admits a role for allegory in its formulation.

Pietz's argument proceeds from the assertion that fetishes must be non-representing material objects, but before I continue with my argument that fetishes can also be virtual objects, I want to note the understandings of fetishism that raise issues of space and sight. Peter Brooks raises the idea of the role of space when arguing that fetishism is "the insistence that the missing object of the investigatory glance is present elsewhere" (1993:101). He also foregrounds the relationship between sight and not seeing—"the missing object of the investigatory glance"—along with the material quality of the fetish *object* onto which the fetishist supposedly displaces desire. Pietz, writing with Emily Apter, notes fetishism's "profound" link to scopophilia, the love of looking: "Fetishism works to obstruct, displace, or refocus the scopophilic gaze rather than facilitate its attachment to the longed-for object" (1993:x). In interpreting Lacanian theories of fetishism, Krips offers a definition of fetishism as "a paradoxical refusal to follow up on one's desire" (1999:29)—again, the object, whatever it may be, is physically (and psychically) elsewhere.

>>> Fetish as Virtual Object and Utility

My discussion in the preceding section of the various accounts of the fetish and fetishism indicates that three ideas are central to most theories: first, spatial distance *separates* or blocks (yet articulates through a relationship mediated by distance itself) the object of desire from the desiring individual; second, people fetishize material objects; and third, the fetish object must be visible to the eye (the most space-sensing of our perceptive organs). The meaning of the term "object" is complicated, but it refers, generally, to a spectrum of senses. Fetish theories holding that the fetish is a visible, material object implicitly rely on a modern definition of an object as "a material thing that can be seen and touched" (*OED*)—a definition implicit in Stallybrass's conferral on the fetish of qualities of touchability and wearability. However, the *OED* also provides an earlier definition dating from the Renaissance as "something placed before or presented to the eyes or other senses." Both meanings privilege sight but the second, earlier meaning, with its use of "something" instead of "a material thing," does not preclude inclusion of a virtual object within its definitional purview. The idea of a digital virtual object breathes new life into this premodern meaning in that "something" can mean anything apprehended intellectually but also anything visible or tangible and relatively stable in form. A separate meaning of the object is as an end or goal, a telos in itself that also calls forth the concept or intellection that fuels the drive to realize the end or goal.

Following from these definitions, then, the word "object" can reference both a material thing and a concept or idea. I articulate this polyvalency of definition to the possibility that viewers experience an individual's online moving image not only as a representation but also as an animated trace of this embodied individual. The Web-based virtual object depicts and ritualizes the desire to bridge the modern gaps between objects and concepts, the material and the ideal, and the present from both the past and the future. The possibility that viewers experience the virtual object/avatar/telefetish as a visible trace of something material cannot be acknowledged by those theories of the fetish that implicitly rely on the modern definition of the object as material. Such reliance renders these theories unable to account for a viewer's experience of an online allegorical personification as achieving telefetish powers precisely because this image can be experienced by the viewer as transmitting a trace of its referent. While theories such as Pietz's correctly identify the nonallegorical quality of the material fetish, in so doing they foreclose due consideration of the ways that allegory might actually be an essential component of emergent fetish practices based on digital indexicality.

Solely focusing on fetish *objects*, moreover, is insufficient to fully account for the possibility that in a society of the spectacle people might fetishize non-material representations. This possibility contradicts Pietz's assertion that the fetish is not a representation only if one fails to account for the ways that the index or trace, as a sign, exceeds the powers commonly accorded to representation. Further, fetishizing certain kinds of animated signs actually concords with the fetish's connections with artifice and contrivance. While I am wholly sympathetic to Pietz's interest in salvaging the fetish from capitalism and its focus on representation, he articulates his assertion too closely to Marx's mid-nineteenth-century concerns. For better or worse, like capitalism itself the contemporary world of images, in their number, variation, and modes of circulation, exerts far greater power than did images in the years leading up to the 1867 publication of *Das Kapital*. Within the capitalized and commoditized logic of a society of the spectacle, predicated on the bedazzlement of images and where "the spectacle is *capital* accumulated to the point it becomes image" (Debord 1994:24), representations have come to be fetishes, and allegorical moving images accrue increasing power. Material objects are still fetishized but so too are hybrid sign/bodies in virtual worlds. And so too are the interactive techniques and practices of digital technologies that are fetishized as ends in themselves.

Restricting the definition of fetish to visible objects also works to deflect consideration of the ways that people fetishize the iterative or repetitive nature of experience itself. This can be understood, for example, by reference to addiction, where the individual is less in thrall of a drug's ability to provide a novel experience than of its utility as a recurrent experience that, more likely than not, will be roughly the same each time the drug is taken. Addiction, as the consequence of a goal and as an event itself, can offer a recursive measure of continuity, stability, or order in addition to novelty or escape. The individual in question fetishizes the repeat experience that confers a sense of order on his or her existence. The value of addiction, then, is not unlike that produced through understanding one's life as a narrative in order to produce meaning out of chaos. The idea of addiction, with its echoes of stability as tradition, explains in part why some Second Life participants report feeling a sense of calm after rushing home from work to spend their remaining waking hours online. For some, Second Life has seemingly become "First Life." The fetishization of recurrent experience may also explain why the online role-playing game World of Warcraft is also known as "Warcrack."

As Immanuel Kant already understood, while people fetishize material objects they also fetishize abstractions or patterns (Balaban 1995:79). Kant's late-eighteenth-century insight is that fetishism is a *relation* based on minimizing the fear that springs from human powerlessness (80), and I suggest that, to the degree that the future seems less certain and hopeful (or even seems fearful) individuals have always needed and continue to need fetishes, material and virtual, to be magical. Moreover, any fetish, like any celebrity, may fall from grace, but this does not mean that the systems of fetishism or celebrity collapse. Quite the contrary. Fetishists endow new fetishes with magical properties, and the media-celebrity system, fans included, anoints certain members of the ever abundant pool of potential new celebrities with the rank of star status until they lose their allure and are swiftly replaced by others.

In the introduction I outlined how the idea of a virtual object might come to have cultural legitimacy to the point where distinctions might begin to blur between a virtual and a material object, and therefore between allegorical and nonallegorical forms of personification. The contemporary push to naturalize the idea of a virtual object depends in part on the implicit imprimatur of science. Virtual objects are necessarily contained within information machines popularly understood as outcomes of scientific research and the teleological juggernaut of progress to which they are linked. Acceptance of the possibility of virtual objects introduces the consequent possibility that they be accorded something like ontological equivalence, or at least exchangeability at the level of their visual experience, with material objects. This is a technologically inflected development unanticipated by modern fetish theory with its insistence on the material fetish.

Jean Baudrillard's semiological approach to fetish theory is applicable to virtual objects and key elements of networked digital personae such as avatars, yet his focus on signification and codes leaves silent and thereby minimizes the roles of perception and interpretation in fetish dynamics. He writes, "If fetishism exists it is thus not a fetishism of the signified, a fetishism of substances and values (called ideological), which the fetish object would incarnate for the alienated subject. Behind this reinterpretation . . . is a fetishism of the signifier. That is to say that *the subject is trapped in the factitious, differential, encoded, systematized aspect of the object*. It is not the passion (whether of objects or subjects) for substances that speaks in fetishism, it is the passion for the code" (1981:92; emphasis added). Baudrillard does not account for autonomic responses to codes in the form of online sign/bodies. As a digital presence or virtual object, the sign/body supports Web users' experience of the Web as spatiotemporal—as a lively and luminous place for (re)location. A "passion for the code," however, need not contradict autonomic responses to sign/bodies, and both need to be considered to account for the kinds of Web dynamics assessed in this volume. The men I discuss later in this chapter and again in chapter 5 demonstrate their passion for the code by transmitting their moving image online via technical formats organized according to the binary logic of ones and zeros. In so doing, they arguably manifest a desire to inhabit "self-contained formal codes," a desire impossible to materialize that nonetheless does indicate how the image itself could come to contain the individual as an image of his own liberation, liveliness, and presence. Participants of Second Life also manifest their passion for the code by consciously constructing and then inhabiting their avatars, and even designing the virtual real estate these avatars inhabit and territorialize. At the same time, participants engage with these images as if they were a part of themselves, an indication of their experiential response to the sign/bodies on the screen.

Experientially, however, the telefetish is neither pure code nor only a virtual object. Viewers interpret it as a sign and perceive it sensually. The telefetish, a component of the viewer's perception that is also interpreted as a sign in the semiotic dynamic of "I see myself seeing myself," also works to contain this perception. The potential then arises for the viewer to accord to the telefetish the quality of a sensuous commodity if he or she experiences it as transmitting a trace of the original (discussed in detail in the next chapter). The result is a betwixt, magically empirical, immanently transcendent phenomenon somewhere between a sign and a shred of the referent itself. The technically inflected ways of looking that these settings facilitate dovetail with—because they extend and build upon—capitalized fetish practices wherein "certain social relations appear as the natural properties of things in society" (Colletti 1975:37). The outcome is to allow some participants to *experience* an image or simulation as an actual material trace of the object or person on the other end of the transmission. In some ways, then, recalling the previous chapter's discussion of ritual, the resulting telefetish performs similarly to online ritualizations in its seeming ability to void binaries—in this case those of truth/illusion, presence/appearance, object/code, real/virtual, event/representation, liberation/containment, primitivism/modernity, and perception/interpretation. In networked chat and cam settings, for example, appearances seemingly constitute experience itself in a way that, by suggesting the image is no longer symbolic but stands for full and immediate presence, sidelines the material position and role of the embodied Web participant interacting with others through the keyboard and display.

I treat the telefetish as a "power object" (Pietz 1993:145) that first emerged in the late 1990s as a combinatory form of Web identity, identity marker, and telos. The networked telefetish is an alienable virtual object that mediates the social and personal in a world where affect and the actual are already commodified. It is also an ironic way of performing, imagining, or tracing a subject capable of understanding or coming to grips with the incommensurability of the disintermediated, disaggregated, and overtly abstracted world of contemporary capitalism and its mediascaped "space of flows." Website participants form a part of this space in accordance with the cosmopolitan ideal that ephemeral pathways and flows, at least on the Web, are as ontologically important as concrete places and material sites. The telefetish may serve a variety of purposes or goals. In same-sex webcam practices it may constitute a creative posthuman gesture responding to a set of heteronormative assumptions that gay/queer male bodies are loathsome to the point of invisibility. To be on the receiving end of such assumptions can promote adoption of a strategy of representing oneself as a moving image. I have noted the moving sign/body's appeal to perception; viewers can experience the sign/body as somehow akin to an actual experience of its referent. However, as a specific animation of the larger society of the spectacle intent on confirming the image as a quasi-autonomous and therefore fetishizable form of social relation, the emergent exchange value (the only form in which the value of commodities can manifest) of the sign/body supports the inference of referent and viewers alike that their "true" use values, including to themselves, lie in being interchangeable in a broader network based on digital forms of exchange. Exchange, then, produces additional value. Through disarticulating the relationship between subjectivity and embodiment in favor of one grounded in an ontological and political claim to exist through manifesting oneself as a *visible*, commodified image, the interchangeability of one's indexical sign/body in online settings with one's actual embodiment can assist in minimizing the potential for violence committed against one's physical body while also establishing the visible claim to (virtually) exist. Sean Patrick Williams, one of the first men to launch a personal gay/queer webcam, makes this point inferentially when he argues that the internet allows closeted men to "publicly stand up for themselves in a private way" (Aravosis 2000). As a quasi-ironic outcome of exchange and use values "trading places" in this way, the telefetish might be thought of as a posthuman other, or as a potentially mystifying signifier. But it can also be understood as a contingent commodity performing this otherness to the self but in a potentially affirming way that, through viewing oneself as a conscious, lively, and desirable sign/body, may serve as a temporary antidote to heteronormative loathing.

As Pietz notes, whether anthropological, Marxian, or Freudian, all theories of the fetish concur that it generates "a social order out of a chaotic principle of contingency" (1985:8). Out of this order, which depends on fetishism's recurrent dimensions, a certain meaning, and therefore the beginnings of certain histories, may emerge from chaotic contingency. I note here the similarities between the fetish as generating order out of contingency—for example, as a means of keeping at bay *for the time being* the existential Void and the meaninglessness of human experience of existence it portends— and the findings by ritual theorists that ritual is primarily a recurrent order through which people create, contest, and renew specific meanings of things as well as various forms of social coherency. Pietz also argues that "to reduce [the fetish] to its most familiar contexts in Marx and in psychoanalysis is to evade its specific origins" (15). Pietz is correct to emphasize the cross-cultural colonial encounter and the function of the fetish within it, yet his caveat equally applies to studies of new forms of fetishizing contemporary forms of allegory, such as I undertake in this volume. Finally, Marx (1952) can be read as describing the fetishization of commodities as a repeat performance. In fetishizing repeatable experience gained through the recurrent use of information machines to gain a measure of psychic balm—some temporal access to additional power or psychic support—individuals ritualize fetishism itself. They interpret, as a sign, the very practice that they are at the same time performing. They fetishize the means of communication while at the same time pretend that such means are absent (see Sterne 2006:128), thus giving rise to such fantasies as "communication without codes" and "post-symbolic communication." In such a manner does communicability become an end goal, a telos, a fetish in itself.

I find no reason why ritual and the fetish as categories need adhere to the logic of implicit claims that they may only manifest in offline settings. To buttress this statement I include in this chapter the following discussion that exemplifies specific ways that gay/queer men engage in online forms of fetishism. The text-based internet precedes by many years the mid-1990s emergence of the Web. During the early 1990s tens of thousands of gay/queer first world men used text-based Internet Relay Chat (IRC) as a way to contact other men in locations both distant and near. As I argue in chapter 4, IRC is a precursive technology informing the rise of avatar-dependent graphical chat MUVEs such as Second Life. Because it is entirely text dependent, the nickname or screen name by which an individual chooses to represent himself on IRC carries a great deal of weight. During the early 1990s, many IRC participants asserted a quality of identity transparency through choosing explicit "nicks" such as BigTop, SFMaster42, debbie_tv, and ozstr8boi. Yet I observed that over time these names exhausted themselves. Individuals discarded them when they were no longer useful or were found to be inoperative, along with the identities they connoted to these individuals and to others. Changing one's nick from "badboy" to "studgun" might connote a wholly new character whereas a change from "boy4u" to "goodboy4u" might refresh the identity while preserving aspects of the earlier identity claim. In early 1995, I was chatting with a man who asked me why it had been months since I changed my nick. "They have a shelf life," he said. "Update yours and check it out." After doing so, individuals messaged me who may have ceased to find my earlier nick worth messaging, or who perhaps had not found it sufficiently resonant with their interests to have bothered in the first place.[2]

The ideology of the "new and improved" is nothing new within contemporary capitalist society, and the self-renewal of IRC nicknames due to a perceived shortening of shelf lives arguably represents a fetish of the new. Indeed, the practice indicates how internet technologies have constituted and continue to constitute a central fetish object for members of cultures of the interface implicitly seeking confirmation that the progress myth (and possibly the future) might finally be fully actualized through information machines, Web 2.0 wireless mobility, and the constant parade (and rapid obsolescence) of related new devices, applications, and techniques. Yet while the self-renewal of nicknames (or the late 1990s response to competition among personal webcam sites by the addition of "new and improved" features such as chat, diaries, and multiple angles of visual access to the men in front of their cameras) can be theorized as exemplifying a fetish of the new, it can equally be positioned as characteristic of the hypermodernity posited by Arthur Kroker and David Cook (1986). These authors, echoing Baudrillard's theory of the fetish as a passion for the code itself, understand everything as becoming an expression of sign value, to the degree that it even colonizes the economics of product lifecycles in semiotic terms. I would argue against concluding that the changing of nicknames or updating images of the self on a website operates *solely* or even principally as simply a fetish of the new. To so conclude ironically parallels the kind of narrow refusal that led de Brosses's "enlightened" European readers to apply his mid-eighteenth-century theories of fetishism and their universalist applicability only to colonial others and not to their own beliefs and practices. For the changing of nicknames, though lodged within a broader culture of obsolescence and fetishization of the new, is *also* a radically old (i.e., archaic in its sense of *arche*—first principle, structure, or pattern) way of making sense of the world: individuals replace their talismans according to the cyclical rhythm of temporal magic underpinning fetishism's ritualistic mode of making meaning. As such, the changing of nicknames also reveals a deconstructive dynamic. The individual hopes that the nickname will convey the concept carried in the word or phrase constituting the nickname, but at the same time his or her recurring desire to change nicknames reveals a tension between the original hope and any nickname's eventual inadequacy.

With the geographic diffusion of the Web, the cultural popularity of webcams began to grow in the late 1990s, fed in part by media reports of Jennifer Ringley's JenniCam and Sean Patrick Williams's SeanPatrickLive. Webcams, then, emerged concomitant with the development of greater bandwidth, faster transmission speeds, falling prices for consumer electronics, and a more image-saturated Web. As part of this broader move to the visual, the ritualized online performances of gay/queer men also took a visual turn. While IRC continued to exist (and still does), the ability of webcams to refresh images provided greater opportunities for telepresence. Online gay/queer men, using already fetishized information machines, began to fabricate and authorize telefetishes of themselves. These men's ritualized practices acknowledged and performed the encroaching reality that the image now constitutes a social relation. Although the *OED* definitions of fetish provided in this chapter are culled from accounts provided by European traders and subsequent nineteenth-century anthropological investigations, they continue to resonate with some contemporary gay/queer politics that issue from fetishism as a practice. In *Fetishism in West Africa*, Reverend Robert Hamill Nassau (1904) analyzes indigenous fetish practices, and his account of indigenous conceptions of the future remains useful in theorizing gay/queer men's need to perpetually update the digital fetish. Echoing Hegel, Nassau writes, "The future is so vague that in the thought of most tribes it contains neither heaven nor hell; there is no certain reward or rest for goodness, nor positive punishment for badness. The future life is to each native largely a reproduction, on shadowy and intangible lines, of . . . this earthly life" (77).[3] These men's need to continually update fetish identities—whether it be a change of nickname; the continual redesign of one's webpage; juggling one's time maintaining a webcam, weblog, and personal profiles on Web chat sites; or the uncanny correspondence between webcams that refresh and their owners' ongoing concern that viewers not find their sites "boring"—suggests an enactment of the dynamic that Nassau describes as an absent Western sense of a future (or heaven as an organizing trope for imagining hopeful possible futures): fetish strategies have a shelf life. Fetishes are not stable, and maintaining the temporal powers they confer requires ongoing renewal or refueling in direct proportion to an ambivalent or absent sense of the future.

It hardly needs stating that modern gay/queer cultures or forms of publics, whether online or offline, wired or not, are not the same as premodern African tribal cultures. However, a diffuse loss of faith in, or perhaps indifference to, a sense of the future not articulated to technological progress experienced by many first world individuals suggests a return and renovation of the premodern, non-Christian aboriginal view noted by Nassau that the future will be "the same as today." I am not suggesting that gay/queer men who trade in fetishized Web identities and sign/bodies lack any sense of a meaningful future or of places other than those where they find themselves in situ. Rather, in many ways these men have fabricated an idealized if limited image of gay/queer identity that uses virtuality and digital forms of allegory to stake an ontological but spatially alienating claim. I am arguing that holding to a sharp distinction between the archaic myth of the eternal return of the same, where human time is experientially cyclical, and the contemporary sense of a disappearing or a purely dystopic, Hobbesian future (even in light of the progress myth) needs to be reconsidered.

A resurgence of sensing the eternal return of the same did not begin with the internet. Arguably, it resurfaces following the Great War of 1914–1918 and this war's shattering on many fronts of elite illusions of progress. The resurgence, however, widens with the rise of post-Fordist capitalism and its abandonment of local attachments as part of "going global." The idea of local attachments returns us to issues of space. This is seen in 1970s alternative music: in the words of U.K. punk rockers Johnny Rotten and the Sex Pistols, there's "no future now," and this is to sense that, in the "estranged present" (Debord 1994:116) constituting the rustbelt of 1970s deindustrialized inner-city England, opportunity and progress, however construed, were no longer knocking for the Sex Pistols and their fans. In the 1984 British TV pilot *Max Headroom*, pirate TV host Reg broadcasts constant reruns of old music videos to a postproletarian audience whose members we see abandoned in a deindustrialized landscape that resembles a waste disposal site littered with TV screens. "This is the future," he announces. "Now, more of the same." Reg's comment trades precisely in the logic of the cyclical return of the same; the deindustrialized cityscape appears void of hope: the idea that progress equals progressive time (and the future) has been toppled. Hyper-mediated narratives are all that remain. Since 1984, the development and deployment of information machines have proceeded exponentially while a sense of citizenship and belief in the value of political engagement to achieve social ends would seem to have correspondingly atrophied for many. At the same time a sense of the future as purely dystopian (think global warming, environmental collapse, and an endless "war on terror") has gained ground. The year 1984 also marked the publication of *Neuromancer*, the science fiction novelist William Gibson's apocalyptic account of a not-too-distant future—an account that arguably is most famous today for its introduction of the concept of cyberspace as a networked "consensual hallucination" of virtual space (51). Individuals, I suggest, transmit themselves "there"—into virtual space—in part to achieve an ironically tangible spatial replacement-cum-psychic equivalent for a derailed future no longer worth imagining or awaiting. Whether or not one understands these changes as part of a discursive reconstitution of subjectivity, attention to the consequences of the hollowing out of representational modern politics articulated to industrial and national social organizations has been deflected by a media and corporate focus on the shiny new potential of information machines. We live with the irony of having arrived at a historical moment when progress and a robust sense of the future that does not articulate to technology, whether mythic or actualized, psychic or social, has been all but dismissed as the province of fools. Antoine Compagnon argues that "progress—an empty value in itself—has no other meaning than to make progress possible" (1994:51). The virtually complete conflation of the progress myth with information technologies and their world of signs supports growing parallel beliefs in the latter's historical inevitability, and in the value of according to this ersatz world a Neoplatonic status akin to the supernatural.

Again, the coming together of issues of space and time is key. For gay/queer men "the future," as a metaphor for achieving and receiving confirming recognition of one's embodied gay/queer citizenship (or even existence) from the heteronormative social contexts that necessarily imbricate the gay/queer lived world, seems a tantalizing prospect continually kept just out of reach. Recognition is deferred not by the men themselves but by a regressive application of "the eternal return of the same" intended to keep gay/queer men "in their place"—that is, "not here, not yet." In time, but in the meantime, "Don't ask, don't tell." In short, no place at all except, perhaps, the limbo of the eternal antechamber. Alexander Düttmann (2000:109) asserts the impossibility of such a demand for recognition. Whenever an individual or group asks to be recognized, this individual or group asks for confirmation of what he, she, or it already believes themselves to be. But this belief is constituted in a discursive language practice that need not be shared universally with the entity petitioned to grant recognition. No single set of words can ever reach everyone, and there is no reason why the values I hold about myself need be interpreted in the same way by someone else. Claims for recognition or inclusion by minority publics, therefore, may fall on deaf or uncaring ears given that such claims assume the fiction of a general audience. However, asking for recognition indicates a dependence on the broader entity petitioned to confer recognition.

Düttmann's caveats notwithstanding, denying gay/queer space is a powerful oppressive strategy of endless deferral that inadvertently promotes the inculcation of telefetishistic strategies precisely because all people must meaningfully inhabit social space in some form of ritualized way as a necessary precondition for imagining any meaningful future. Moreover, if commodification itself has become a Western tradition, it is the case that many self-defined middle-class first-world men buy into commodity culture's inflation of desire and its seduction of consumers with power fantasies. The acquisition of Web access, for example, reflects a dual fetishization of technology as progress and of movement in the sense that, by seeming to purchase progress in the form of an information machine, one accesses the ability to inhabit a more "friction-free" virtual space. This constitutes a commodified "elsewhere" that holds forth the possibility of a space, even if virtual, from which one might access the future. In so doing, however, there is no inducement for "consumers" to have thought through the sociopolitical contexts that may have led to their space-impoverished sense of "no future" in the first place.

Like the many "citizens" qua "consumers" who on any given day browse and purchase shiny commodities at the mall for instant psychic balm, gay/queer men participate within commodity culture's hyperreal logic of filling the present with objects and distractions so that the past and future recede from view. These men also frequently comprehend at an iterative level that while long-term political struggle has augmented gay/queer subjectivities, they nevertheless still find themselves in an everyday world that is post-Matthew Shepard, post-Brandon Teena, post-Spanner, post-DOMA, post-Admiral Duncan bombing, and post-Ronnie Paris—the three year old who was beaten to death in 2005 by a father obsessed with the idea that his son "might be gay."[4] There was no future for Ronnie Paris. In academic contexts a restricted view of history might lead to the conclusion that Michel Foucault's decision to demure on too publically addressing issues of his own same-sexuality due to his concerns that his thought would be marginalized as "gay" by his opponents reflected the now-banished prejudices of a generation ago. Yet a generation later, the absence of mention in obituaries in American liberal media of Susan Sontag's sexuality or even how it may have influenced her thinking in such works as *AIDS and Its Metaphors*, coupled to her own reticence to speak too publicly on the issue—again, like Foucault, due to concerns of intellectual and historical marginalization—suggests the game continues. The game, here, is an ongoing ritual of excommunication (Carey 1998) that divides social groups from one another through ostracizing strategies of containment. The methods used vary according to the targeted group. Heteronormative applications of this kind of ritual frequently serve in the negative, to minimize awareness of the complexity of everyday lives through substituting distorted, usually mediated, interpretations that collectively work to suggest the monstrosity of gay/queer lives. Gay/queer subjectivities that articulate to same-sex sexualities, regardless of how post-identitarian a queer *identifying* individual may announce himself or herself to be, still may not fully speak their names.[5] Dwight Conquergood notes that "rituals draw their drama, dynamism, and intensity from the crises they redress" (2006:467), and the "crisis" here is one of remaining so persistently inaudible, or of being told through the mediated processes of contemporary rituals of excommunication to remain quiet so often and in so many different everyday ways that one comes to interpret the majority of public discourse as one big lie. Conquergood points to the possibility that, in this moment of crisis of visibility, gay/queer men can enact a partial turning away from patronizing and mendacious discourses by searching for and ritualizing new forms of visibility — by making a political and aesthetic claim to subjectivity through publication, circulation, and display of one's image. Enter the animated telefetish. Through it, one can seemingly exceed the limitations of the image without really doing so.

>>> Space of the Trace

I have raised the role of space at several points in this chapter. Fetishism is also a spatial strategy deployed to acquire temporal power through the use of ameliorative strategies dependent on the possibility of spatial distance and not only deferment of desire. Members of a culture of networked individualism may rely on digital information technologies to satisfy desires or ameliorate concerns about risk and security not readily resolvable on this side of the interface. I have critiqued the reliance on dominant spatial metaphors, such as "cyberspace," "visit," "site," "environment," "under construction," and so forth, that are promoted by industry and academics alike and that propose that the internet is primarily a space — whether thought of as a social, technological, or communications space (Hillis 1999). Certain influential popular culture fictions such as Gibson's *Neuromancer* and Neal Stephenson's *Snow Crash* (1992) also promote accepting this belief. These dystopian science fictions deflect readers' attention away from the networked technologies they outline and toward a fetishization of the links that these networks establish between material and virtual space. In such works, places and landscapes are reduced to forms of interface in ubiquitous wireless settings.

During the latter part of the 1990s, at the same time as the Web's initial popularization, the hype surrounding immersive virtual reality technology that suggested it would allow for a form of space into which individuals might enter also served to habituate individuals to the idea that more accessible "consumer" digital technologies such as the Web would provide something equivalent to this possibility (Hillis 2005). Virtual reality and its promoters, despite the technology's formal limitations (though it is by no means a dead technology),[6] operated as a precursive discursive and metaphoric assemblage that allowed prospective users to come to understand the Web, which has since yielded many of the promises of interactivity earlier linked to immersive virtual environments, as constituting an affective form of space. These points notwithstanding, the distinction between a technology and a space remains key to my argument about the emergence of the virtual telefetish: networked digital technologies of transmission and display offer an ersatz space able to be experienced as virtually real.

As the following chapter argues, the telefetish is an indexical icon experienced or perceived as a sign/body. Theorizing the fetish solely as a material object relies on commonsense contemporary understandings that we could not perceive or mistake a sign pointing to a thing for the thing itself; that the meaning of objects always includes their essential materiality and that they necessarily are located in material space; and that objects are organized in relation to one another by and through geographic space. Geographic space—which many Web applications represent and simulate—articulates relationships between and among objects. With respect to the Web, the popularization of the idea of telepresence and the image-signs upon which the idea relies, joined to the kinds of phenomenological factors just outlined, contributes to the belief that the technology constitutes a space into which humans may enter. Therefore, to return to the idea of virtual objects, if a certain theory assumes that a fetish is always an object, then even if a digital representation of a human body online might be popularly received as transmitting an experiential trace of this body, it could not be a fetish because it isn't a material object. I noted above the range of meanings ascribed to objects. Recall both the discursive strategy of positioning computer-generated images as virtual objects, and that sight is the most spatially organizing of all the body's senses. If for many the Web is increasingly, experientially, a "real" space, then we are faced with the possibility of objects "migrating there" and along the way adapting themselves to the form of the digital sign/body. Such virtual objects include all manner of virtual personae and allegorical personification. Understanding fetishes only as material objects is inadequate for understanding and interpreting what "takes place" in networked virtual environments.

Treating the Web as a space, or as sets of linked spaces, may occlude considerations that the technology is a device for transmitting information, including audiovisual representations of the human body in the form of texts, animated and photographic images, and sound files. Yet the Web is more than this: if positioned as a space it becomes possible to comprehend how graphical chatters or webcam operators sitting at home in front of their displays and cameras may have arrived at the experiential moment when they could imaginatively/virtually merge for a period of time with their signifying digital personae. It is also the case that, as with all perceptual processes, embodied sight is subject to cultural influences, in this case specific ways of seeing and looking that are linked, for example, to the gaze and its psychic possession of the image (see chapter 5), and the conflation of spatial metaphors with the information machines they represent. Experiencing the Web as a kind of space is further influenced by specific historical and geographic circumstances. For example, the social and spatial marginalization of gay/queer men might influence their decision to, in diasporic fashion, embrace the Web as a form of space, a part of which they might call and make their own virtual homeland. As I discuss in detail in the next chapter, the belief that the Web constitutes a relational space fosters a belief in the ability to transmit a fragment of the self "elsewhere" into virtual space where, as a sign/body, one will be *experienced* by oneself and others as having something of the qualities of an object-person coupled to those of a fetish-index.

Theory, as I have noted, is an outcome of its moment, forming part of a broader structure of feeling. Imagine if the Web had existed during the colonial encounter when fetish and ritual theories were first proposed. They would have had to take into account the Web's magical ability to locate virtual objects in virtual spaces experienced as seemingly real by users and participants. Such virtual objects, as commodity forms, speak to Marx's theory of the commodity fetish yet also indicate the need for extensions and corrections to the theory. Commodities, Marx argues, are the productions of "a definite social relation between men that assumes, in their eyes, the fantastic form of a relation between things" (1952:31). The Web, as an innovation and a *structure of seeming*, as the building of an ideological interpretation of the lived world, requires a broadening of fetish theory to account for the fetishization of certain kinds of virtual objects as animated traces of the material real. Such objects suggest the useful exchangeability and inter-orientation of the virtual and the real, the machine and the flesh. Why this might be so is discussed in the following chapter.

Signs

In chapters 1 and 2 I drew from an extensive body of scholarship on ritual and fetishism in order to elucidate how these elements work and why they are applicable to online settings. This effort necessitated proposing revisions to both sets of theory. Ritual need not take place only among embodied individuals occupying the same space; neither need fetishes be solely material objects. In this chapter I turn to the operation and practices of signification in networked settings. Although theories of signification have histories as complex and lengthy (and as contentious) as those of ritual and fetishism, this chapter marks a shift in emphasis. Most readers likely already agree that what we see on the computer screen or display is constituted in signification. It is not contentious to demonstrate that Web-based practices and techniques manifest the Web as a pure "world" of signs. At issue, rather, are the specific characteristics and powers of circulating digital signs. How do they produce affect and meaning in virtual environments on the Web in ways that support online practices of ritual and fetishism? In formulating answers to this question I focus on Charles Sanders Peirce's theory of the index, as well as on later refinements to it by scholars such as

Susan Sontag, Régis Debray, and Jacques Derrida—who with his theory of the trace offers the most engaged refinement.

George Landow has noted that when software designers encounter Derrida's ideas they find a form of digital hypertext; when literary theorists encounter the work of the information technology pioneer Ted Nelson, who coined the term hypertext in 1963, they find a form of deconstruction or poststructuralism (2006:1). In a similar vein, I find that aspects of Peirce's theories seem almost written with the Web in mind. Whether or not I concur with Peirce's theories, however, is less important than to note that they remain valuable and provocative when applied to thinking through the processes that allow Web users and participants the spatiotemporal experience of telepresence. While there is much hype promoting the experience of virtual environments as "virtually real," it is also the case that individuals buy into the experience of telepresence for reasons exceeding hype. One reason is the animating power of the digital sign/body, as a form of "visual language," to suggest to autonomic perception (or to simulate, if you will) qualities of liveness and presence. The application of Peirce's theory of the index—including ideas considered metaphysical and logically impossible by Peirce's interpreters—offers an explanation of this quasi materialization of the sign as well as a way to understand how the idea of telepresence itself works to confirm the Web as a metaphysical first principle.

Peirce first formulated his "doctrine of signs" in the late 1860s. Deleuze considers Peirce the inventor of semiotics (1989:30), and I would place Peirce rather than Ferdinand Saussure as the starting point for theories of signification. Peirce believed that all phenomena are of one character. This belief informs his thought as the founder of pragmatism, or as he termed it, "pragmaticism"—namely the idea, anticipating Marxian praxis, that practical consequences and experience are the criteria of knowledge, value, and meaning, and that theory must articulate to experience in a holistic manner if it is to be useful.

Peirce revised the basic principles of his theory of signs several times. In doing so he extended its range and categories but never arrived at a general, unified theory. He identified 66 kinds of signs and no less than 59,049 varieties (Misak 2004:8).[1] For certain scholars, one result of Peirce's effort is that "what we now possess is little more than a sequence of contradictions, a series of ambitious yet unfinished sketches of elaborate but mutually incompatible structures" (Short 2004:214).[2] The account of Peirce's ideas that follows, therefore, is by necessity partial. For Peirce, thought is a process of producing and interpreting signs. Signs are "in general . . . a class which includes pictures, symptoms, words, sentences, books, libraries, signals, orders of command, microscopes, legislative representatives, musical concertos, performances of these" (Peirce, cited in Gorlée 1994:50). Signs can be nonverbal as well as verbal. Anything subject to human perception, imagination, or knowledge, humans included, can operate as a sign, and he believed all consciousness to be sign consciousness (Houser 1992:xxxvi).

Rather than relying on a binary of sign and signifier, Peirce theorized that a sign operates within a triadic relationship among the *representamen* (that which represents, the representation, the sign), the *referent* (the represented object), and the *interpretant* (a third sign created in the mind of the individual through his or her act of referral and interpretation). Interpretation, therefore, is essential to the possibility of the sign, and the idea of the interpretant distinguishes Peirce's theory from others holding that signs are related only to objects: "Eliminate either the object or the interpretant and you annihilate the sign" (Houser 1992:xxxvii). The interpretant, therefore, in every case is a sign of another sign of the same object, a possibility Peirce expressed as "anything which determines something else (its interpretant) to refer to an object to which itself refers (its object) in the same way, this interpretant becoming in turn a sign, and so on ad infinitum" (1931:228). For a sign to act as a sign, "it must enter into a relationship with its object, be interpreted, and thus produce a new sign, its interpretant" (Gorlée 1994:50).

If anything subject to human perception can be a sign, then one of the more radical implications of Peirce's semiotic is that it can also be read as a theory of objects, both virtual and material. If all phenomena are of one character and a sign can take the form of anything subject to human perception, ourselves included, then Peirce's theory, particularly with reference to his emphasis on the role of the human interpreter of signs as part of the sign system she or he interprets, offers a way to see past the erection of naturalized binaries. These include not only that between sign and referent but also the subject-object binary naturalized through the Cartesianized worldview positing the "interior" mind of the researcher as hermetically sealed from the always potentially contaminating "exterior" material world under his or her review.

Peirce divided the sign into three further categories: symbol (he initially used the term *token*), icon, and index. A symbol's relationship to its object is established by conventions, agreements, or rules habitually agreed upon among a symbol's users. Symbols, then, have *generally* agreed-upon meanings for users, however arbitrary or abstract these meanings may at times seem when interpreted by others. Symbols include "all general words, the main body of speech, and any mode of conveying a judgment" (Peirce 1992:226). A symbolic message's relationship to what it stands for or represents is arbitrary. For example, English speakers understand that the word "housecat" refers to a certain kind of domesticated feline because the word "housecat" is generally accepted by such speakers as having that meaning in advance of any specific use of the word.

The icon, the second kind of sign, stands for something else (its object) due to its resemblance to this object—the icon sounds or looks like its object. Examples include onomatopoeia, maps, and photographs. An iconic message in some way resembles that aspect of the actual object or part of the world to which it refers. Peirce illustrates how icons operate by referencing a specific icon—the diagram. The interpenetrations of potentiality, actuality, perception, connotation, prior experience, and icon*ography* (as a specific form of writing) are implicit in his description and crucial to producing the icon's meaning: "Icons are so completely substituted for their objects as hardly to be distinguished from them. Such are the diagrams of geometry. A diagram, indeed, so far as it has a general signification, is not a pure icon; *but in the middle part of our reasonings we forget that abstractness in great measure, and the diagram is for us the very thing.* So in contemplating a painting, there is a moment when we lose consciousness that it is not the thing, the distinction of the real and the copy disappears, and it is for the moment a pure dream—not any particular existence, and yet not general. At that moment we are contemplating an *icon*" (1992:226, emphasis added).

Peirce uses the term index for his third category of signs. Stuart Hall has argued that "systems of representation . . . work like languages" because "all use some element to stand for or represent what we want to say, to express or communicate a thought, concept, idea or feeling" (1997:4). However, with the Peircian index, the necessary relationship between the sign and its object lies not in connotative mental association between representation and referent but in a direct, denotative, existential, or causal relation of the sign to its object "independent of the mind using the sign" (Peirce 1992:226). The index "signifies its object solely by virtue of being really connected with it"

(Peirce cited in Short 2004:220). A crucial point here is that Peirce's identification of the index "compels us to recognize a relation of sign to object that is distinct from signification" (Short 2004:223). If the index and its object are in a relation, they are not a unity. Nevertheless, this relation is one of direct connection. The index "asserts nothing; it only says 'There!' It takes hold of our eyes, as it were, and forcibly directs them to a particular object, and there it stops" (Peirce 1992:226). Further, "like a pointing finger, [the index] exercises a real physiological force over the attention, like the power of a mesmerizer, and directs it to a particular object of sense" (232). An indexical message "points to" an object or is a sample of that object. Smoke is a natural index of fire; a footprint in the sand is an index of the person whose foot earlier rendered the imprint. An index organizes our intention by directing it to focus on the object; in this way its appeal to human perception is not unlike the dynamic of conception contained in its original meaning of "to seize or tame" (Hillis 1999:69). Robinson Crusoe's panic upon seeing a man's footprint impressed in the sand of a beach flows from the power of the index to directly *indicate* the reality of the object (the *presence* of purportedly savage cannibals) to Crusoe, the interpretant, who directly perceives that in the index's seizing of his perceptive faculties he may also be under surveillance by those who would eat him, its object. The intensity of Crusoe's emotional reaction points to the strong affect of indexical signs imbued with a material trace of the referent to exceed modernity's common understanding of the power of representations to act as stand-ins. Indexical signs, in their ability to induce in the interpretant a sense of participating in the psychic realities in which they trade, exceed this power. When they are relocated to the Web of moving images, they can, at times, seem to have achieved postrepresentational status. Symbol, icon, and index imbricate one another; nowhere does Peirce, believing in the underlying unity of all things and ideas, argue that indices operate independently from other kinds of signs. To have done so would have contradicted his larger belief that all phenomena are of one character. Web settings rely on symbols, icons, and indices. The textual components of these sites are symbols, and the sounds and images they transmit are icons. The transmitted influences they achieve in the form of users' audiovisual experiences of them are indexical. Messages transmitted by websites adhere to an equivalent combinatory logic described by Roman Jakobson: "Most messages are a combination of two or three aspects, stacked in contextually appropriate hierarchy, which shifts over times as the context alters" (1974:26). An icon can have strong indexical qualities, as can an index rely on iconography for part of its affect. With respect to my work here, the 2-D computer interface, like earlier screen formats, transmits symbols, icons, and indices in complexly interpenetrating ways. Göran Sonesson points out, for example, that all pictures are "in a sense indexical, since they isolate a portion of a scene which is present more fully in the actual world of perception" (2004:n.p.). His observation equally applies to the computer screen with its central utility of framing the signs that display within its borders. Screen displays foster indexical reception in part through inducing viewer desire to access the larger totality of which their content, at any one time, only shows a part. The display acts as an indexical technology extending human perception in a manner anticipated by McLuhan's (1964) proposal that electric media are "extensions of man." The Peircian scholars T. L. Short and Murray Murphey observe that Peirce did not until 1885 develop the ideas we today associate with the index; it was at this point that an acceptance of the individual as actual and not just an ideal became more central to his thinking (Short 2004:220). As I have noted, theory is a manifestation of its specific cultural moment. In the 1860s Peirce could still consider individuality as a conceptual ideal (Murphey 1961:300). His early emphasis on the importance of symbols and icons in part reflects his Kantian-inflected understanding that cognition is invariably general and, therefore, that generalizable symbols are, in their habituated uses, consonant with a society whose enlightened scientifically minded individuals build on each other's contributions and discoveries to the overall benefit and progress of the community or collectivity understood as an end or telos in itself (see Murphey 1961:100). By the mid-1880s, however, the ascendency of nominalism as a belief system downplayed universals in favor of the individual as a unique.[3] This, coupled in American circumstances to the capitalized romanticization of an on-the-ground rugged individualism, formed part of the matrix in which Peirce reluctantly accepted the idea of individuals as not only ideal but also actual, if not always real (Short 2004:220, 237–38 n.4).[4] Accordingly, he revised his theory of signs to grant the index the crucial role of directly pointing human perception to specific, nongeneralizable individuals.

When applied to Web settings, Peirce's example of the pointing finger directing attention to "there" or "that" raises two intriguing possibilities. The first is the potential for websites featuring the indexical imagery of moving human bodies to allow for direct experiential relations among the sign online, various forms of desire, and the embodied individual, referent, or interpretant remaining on this side of the interface. The networked hypertextual sign expresses—points directly toward—the interpretant's "if only" desire that a metaphysics of presence be actualized. The second possibility is that networked cosmopolitan dynamics are a manifestation or material exemplification of Peirce's assertion that all phenomena are of one character—an ontological reality that he terms *synechism*. The index is the most embodied sign in Peirce's taxonomy—the smoke from a fire, the footprint in the sand, the physical movement that arrests sensation and seizes perception. The qualities of the index that "point to" an object yet are also a sample of that same object *and which require* interpretation on the part of the interpretant/referent echo cosmopolitanism's root meanings of adornment and cosmetic that I discussed in the introduction. Cosmetics directly "point to" or ornament the surface of the body of which they also never fully take leave. Originally the meaning of cosmos stood in distinction to chaos. By inference, not unlike ritual the ornamental cosmetic is a production requiring the act of interpretation or meaning making that holds chaos at bay. In certain ways, therefore, Peirce's index, at the level of the sign, operates in Janus-faced ways akin to Robbins's (1992) proposal for a rooted cosmopolitanism wherein networked individuals would endeavor to keep one embodied foot on the ground and the other as a networked signifier that would both "point" back to them as embodied referents and extend them in virtual space. The dynamics of Peirce's theory, moreover, also point in a different but related direction. Peirce's interpretants remain "here" and extend their interests "there," in the direction of the objects/signs they interpret. In so doing, they become signs of these objects, signs of signs. This dynamic is similar to an ethnographic anthropologist's synechistic method of participant observation: the participant-observer's presence at what she or he observes always influences those who are observed and who in turn also influence the observer. Not unlike the logic of quantum mechanics, by their very observation interpretants and participant-observers influence the activities of what or who they observe.

Peirce's privileging, during the 1860s, of the abstract, generalizable symbol relying on convention for its readability indicates something of that era's continuing reliance on abstract text and the generalizable reading skills needed to decode it. He published his early theory of signs roughly at the same time as the American Civil War, which was documented by Mathew Brady and his staff in over seven thousand photographic negatives. The work of Brady and his staff constituted one of the earliest popularizations of the use of photography. Other photographic processes and formats such as stereographs, tintypes, *cartes de visite*, and cabinet cards were "invented" in the 1850s and 1860s, but photography as a practice had not yet attained everyday status. Relative to today's practice, pictorial forms of representation were more restricted to interior spaces, such as churches and the home, and did not enjoy wide social and spatial dissemination. A culture based on screens was not ubiquitous. I have not encountered mention by Peircian scholars that his mid-1880s rethinking of the importance of indices in light of nominalism's rise is at least coincident with if not somehow also influenced by the parallel rise and massive popularization of photography as a more everyday practice following the twin developments of gelatin emulsions and the lightweight, portable camera (Kroes 2007:62). (Kodak released the box camera in 1888.) Other uses of photography, such as Eadweard Muybridge's success in 1877 in producing a photographic negative that revealed Leland Stanford's racehorse Occidental airborne while at full gallop, point to photography's developing claim to constitute some form of empirical proof not only "pointing back" to the specific original but also, in inductive fashion, to *indicate something generalizable*. Muybridge's experiment constitutes part of the sociotechnical milieu within which Peirce, while retaining his preference for generalizable signs, at times asserts that the photograph is an icon, at others times an index, while also finding conventional (or symbolic) qualities in all icons (Sonesson 2004). As Muybridge's findings confirm, the photograph is an icon, but in its analog form it is a mechanical recording of light "really connected" (and therefore having a quality of extension from) and "pointing to" the specific object it indicates. In whatever manner Peirce might have come to reidentify the photograph over time, early theories of photography regarded it as a mirror of reality—in Peircian terms, as an icon. More contemporary theorists such as Christian Metz, Umberto Eco, and Roland Barthes (who postulates the temporally inflected indexicality of photography, as in "this has taken place") argue the conventionality of all signs and propose the photograph as a coded version of reality — in Peircian terms, as a symbol (Sonesson 2004). On the other hand, theorists such as Sontag (1973) and Debray (2000) assert the photo's indexicality. One lesson to be drawn from assessing these differences of interpretation is that making any totalizing claim for precisely the kind of sign a photograph constitutes is fraught with theoretical and political difficulties. Such difficulties are also present in assessing the signs and symbols used in rituals, for they have meaning only by virtue of their place in systems of relationships with other symbols. Like rituals, indices cannot stand in isolation. They are rarely pure and the inevitably overdetermined circumstances within which we view and interpret photographs directly influence their eventual meanings and sign values. As Ian Adam (1995) observes, in general uses we often conflate icons and indices. However "erroneous" such everyday conflations might appear to theorists of signification, and however much viewers find metaphysical indexicality in icons because they desire to make some form of contact with the referent to whom they conceive the icon to point, such conflations offer support for Jean-Marie Schaeffer's (1987:101) materialist assertion that in some cases the photograph is an indexical icon whereas in others it's an iconical index.

Several theorists point to the hybridity of photographs. For Adam, the black-and-white photograph is symbolic (viewers interpret shades of light and dark as various colors); iconic and representational in its imagery; and indexical in pointing to its original. Sonesson argues that "first and foremost, the photograph is an iconical sign" (2004:n.p.) To defend this claim he notes that a viewer need not conceive of a photograph indexically in order to understand its meaning. Rather, it conveys signification whether the viewer is sure it is a photograph or not. Despite this iconicity, however, Sonesson further asserts that a photograph also possesses indexicality (the "there" or "where" of the now unseen referent) of which the viewer becomes aware after he or she first sees it as an icon. Sonesson's example is a photograph of a horse: if viewers have not seen the photo before, at first they see only "horse" (iconicity) and then construct or infer the time and place to which they conceive the photo points (indexicality). His point echoes an earlier one made by Ludwig Wittgenstein: "We regard the photograph, the picture on our wall, as the object itself (the man, landscape, and so on) depicted there. This need not have been so. We could easily imagine people who did not have this relation to such pictures" (cited in Sontag 1973:198). Again, the role of desire in inducing the interpretant's interpretation is central to ways that perceptive faculties are inflected by cultural concepts (for example, the Cartesian notion of the mind/body split) that direct perception to certain modes of interpretation or conception. Sonesson also notes that a photograph—unlike a footprint, which remains in the exact place where its since-departed referent earlier trod—can be made available to consciousness at any time and any place following the original making of the photograph. His observation offers further support to understanding why online digital photographs, precisely *because* and not in spite of their spatiotemporal modularity, are artifacts or relics that powerfully assist the circulation of desire. The metaphysics of presence they induce is persistent and always available at any moment of viewing.

The photograph, then, can synthesize Peirce's triad of signs (in literary terms, it can attain qualities that are metaphorically metonymic or metonymically metaphoric, that fuse metaphor's qualities of resemblance with metonymy's direct one-on-one associations between a part and the whole [see note 9 in chapter 1]). This synthesis does not contradict Peirce's original theory, the ethical focus of which was to identify continuity or *synechism*. Synechism expresses Peirce's principle that "whatever is supposed to be ultimate is supposed to be inexplicable," and that "inexplicabilities are not to be considered as possible explanations" (Peirce cited in Hulswit 2004:n.p.). Instead, "synechism is committed to the idea that '*all phenomena are of one character*'") (Hulswit 2004:n.p.). Laura Marks, who has studied how digital media intersect with the search by their user-participants for "the indexicality of the real," observes that Peirce's synechism, with its emphasis on the connectivity among all things, does not distinguish "between their materiality or ideality, insofar as they communicate." Rather, synechism "indirectly informs the process by which *experience*, *information*, and *images* (each of which is a plane of immanence) unfold from and enfold into one another. Enfolding and unfolding emphasize the connections between seemingly disparate ontological or historical moments" (2006:n.p.). Marks carefully refers to planes of immanence, but a synechistic "emphasis on the connectivity among all things" participates, whether in Peirce's theory, later theorists' adaptations, or on the Web, in the metaphysics of a Neoplatonic resurgence of an ancient "consubstantial idealism." It organizes Plotinus's ancient concept of World Soul, as expressed in the twentieth century in Teilhard de Chardin's 1950s *noosphere* and George Gilder's millennial and corporatized *telecosm*. The emphasis on the underlying unity of all things also speaks to the potential, through philosophical enquiry, to arrive at an impersonal form of love for all because all is a syncretic unity. In theory, the idea is noble, and as I suggested in the previous chapter it could have application in rethinking ethnographic research methods. However, consider the continuing influence of Descartes's reworking of the Greek belief, imported into early Christianity, in a spiritual existence completely separate from physical life—which is manifested in his proposal of the mind (a sacred zone of pure thought) conceptually severed from the insensate body (a profane automaton). The resulting alienation of mind from the purportedly insensate material world contributed to the rise of nominalism opposed by Peirce. Within networked settings, alienated monads search for indexical forms of digital appeal that promise them, within highly commodified settings, virtual suture of the mind-body split.

Neoplatonic idealism, following its encounter with Descartes, has been ever more subject to the seductions of the commodity form. Alfred North Whitehead, writing about Descartes's seminal contribution to seventeenth-century scientific philosophy, noted that "the enormous success of the scientific abstractions, yielding on the one hand matter with its simple location in space and time, and on the other hand mind, perceiving, suffering, reasoning but not interfering, has foisted onto philosophy, the task of accepting them as the most concrete rendering of fact" (1967 [1948]:66). Modern philosophy advances the idea of the mind as a self-contained sphere of enquiry—an ever-greater paradox to the degree that those who believe this fiction increasingly mistake abstraction for concrete reality (55). Peirce resists this fiction as he does not force a distinction between idea and material reality. Everything is conjoined. Ironically, the Web, in its ability to operationalize indexicality, is, in many ways, a Cartesian abstraction within which indexical images help confirm both it and them as concrete renderings of fact. In such a manner does the Web instantiate the magical empiricism that results from Neoplatonism's ongoing encounter with Cartesian thought. Syncretic yet discrete. Transcendent immanence. Or, as Gilbert Ryle (1949) would have it, the ghost in the machine.

In a very ancient way, avatars in graphical MUVEs increasingly participate in the reality of the human objects to which they point. Participants experience avatars—moving images that are also forms of allegory and emblematics (discussed in chapter 4)—as seemingly alive and as allowing them access to ritualized, virtual centers where participants conjoin one another through their avatars. In such idealized circumstances adapted to screen-based settings, an individual's avatar sign/body situated in the virtual center may be experienced as sufficiently compelling by other participants—powerful enough to draw together what can be termed either iconic indexicality or indexical iconicity—so as to seem to transmit to them, as Peircian interpretants, some material aspect of this geographically distant individual to whom it directly points. The avatar, then, also operates as a fetish object in these settings. As Short notes, Peirce's discovery of the index "compels us to recognize a relation of sign to object that is distinct from signification" (2004:223). For an online indexically based experience "to work," participant-interpretants must accord to the index the synechistic power of conjoining materiality to ideality, and reality to image, in ways that intensely conform to the ritualized and temporal logic of the fetish (understood as having a power in its own right and not as "standing in" for or representing something else).

Therefore, while Sonesson's two-step process of recognition of the photographic image of the horse may be correct, this does not refute the desire, or even the psychic need and potential phenomenological truth to which Neoplatonic beliefs arguably point, to perceive indices as contiguous to their referents, as part of our experience of our human perceptual apparatus. Particularly with respect to a culture of networked individualism, to view a sign online as an iconic "mirror image" of some material reality situated within the screen's frame can induce desire to access the "there" or material "where" to which the sign indexically points, even as it seemingly already forms a part. Enter the sign/body to operate as a kind of fetishizable "tease" or trace that tantalizes. High-speed broadband connection further supports the perceptual experience of either "going there" as a form of imaginative extensibility of the subject (a possibility echoed in the McLuhanesque slogans of AT&T's "Reach out and touch someone" and Microsoft's "Where do you want to go today?") or, equally apposite, of experiencing a sense of taking, seizing, or possessing some aspect of this thing or individual that remains materially elsewhere.

Peirce theorizes the index as a sign "really connected with" its object. In everyday contemporary language we do not use the term index to speak of this kind of connection. Rather, an index commonly refers to a listing, an arrangement, and to a much lesser extent something that serves to point something out. If in everyday speech one had to choose between "index" and "trace" to refer to something with a "real connection" to something else, one would likely select trace because of the greater material associations commonly accorded to the term. As a noun, a trace is some remaining or residual part of something; a mark in the here and now of something absent. It is the way or path that something takes: "The series or lines of footprints left by an animal," or the "mark left by anything moving" (OED). In Spanish, traza is a draft or first sketch — a mark left by the body of the marker. As a verb, to trace is to follow by foot; to proceed in a line, course, or track; to pursue; to discern; to decipher; to make marks upon, "especially to mark or ornament with lines, figures, or characters"; to draw; to outline, and to put down in writing (OED). For the ancient Greeks, to graph was to write, as in "to trace." To autograph is to write the trace of oneself on the surface of something. Both the noun and verb meanings reveal the enduring multidimensional relationships between the trace and a moving body, including a human one. Because of these everyday associations with material remainders, detection, and suggestions of graphic quality, I prefer "trace" over "index" for its utility in further theorizing how geographically distant participants can seem to experience (and thereby potentialize) some material aspect of other networked individuals in online settings.

I begin my outline of the trace with Sontag's classic *On Photography*.[5] Sontag argues that photography "is not only an image . . . an interpretation of the real; is also a trace, something directly stenciled off the real, like a footprint" (1973:154); she understands the photographic trace as "a material vestige of its subject" (154). Her drawing together of the photograph/icon (she uses the term image) with the footprint/trace offers another way to grasp the notions of indexical iconicity or iconic indexicality noted in the previous section. Unlike Sonesson, who distinguishes the indexical form of a footprint from a photograph, Sontag avoids spatiotemporal and material differences between footprints and photographs as traces left behind by their referents — differences that, on the Web, *appear* less important due to the *graphic* similarity between the indexicality of photographs and footprints mutually displayed as purely digital images.

Debray mounts an argument somewhat akin to that given by Sontag. About the photographic trace, he emphasizes the relationship between the index and its object as "a correspondence in fact" (2000:137, n.9). But he goes further by suggesting something of the "missing links" between index and trace, and trace and lived hegemony: "Later refinements of Peirce's original insights led to understanding the index as some remaining fragment of the object or contiguity with it causally, such . . . as in the case of [a] relic for saint" (137). Debray notes that interpreting indices today increasingly relies "on recognizing the essential relation of immediate *causation* between the object and the referent that is videotic, photographic, televisual . . . or pixilated based on photography or some kind of camera technology that digitizes the *trace of the real object* imagined" (138; emphasis added). Debray, writing almost three decades after Sontag and well after photography's move into the digital realm, returns in a sense to Sontag's linkage of photography to a footprint's materiality. It is worth introducing here Rappaport's argument that indices are "perceptible aspects of events or conditions signifying the presence or existence of imperceptible aspects of the same events or conditions" (1999:55). His point, rendered in the context of explicating ritual's complexities, parallels one of the objectives of both Derrida and Bourdieu—to reveal how Western metaphysics makes something absent in order to make something else present. These proposals are exemplified by the funeral rites for Pope John Paul II held in May 2005. Countless individuals participated in the viewing ritual by using mobile camera phones to record images of his corpse during the twenty seconds each was allotted to file past the bier. Gianluca Nicolette, a media commentator for *La Stampa*, observed that "in the past, pilgrims would take away with them a relic, like a piece of cloth on the saint's body. Here there's been the transposition to a level of unreality. They're bringing home a digital relic."[6]

The use by ritual participants of a digital technology to commemorate their actual presence at the funeral resonates with Rappaport's argument that "ritual's physical display . . . stands in an indexical relationship not to private processes, physiological or psychological, but to conventions and conventional states. That is, it is concerned with the public order and the individual's participation in it" (1999:140). Increasingly the fact of the matter, the sign interpreted as an order, is sensed to inhere in the trace. In the case of a digital relic, its exchange value is both transformed and conserved: it passes through use value and sign value. Erving Goffman observes that a profound belief pervades Western thought that "an object produces signs that are informing about it" (1979:6). Something present yields information about something absent. But as in the photograph's missing referent the absent remains absent, and this is how the trace also can suggest presence's inaccessibility. Despite the pilgrims' digital relics the Pope remains dead. But is he, experientially, arisen through the trace? So arises the hallucinatory desire to make something present not only stand in for something absent but also to make it, experientially, equivalent to what has gone missing, remains elsewhere, or can never be. This is the value of the trace, a power linked to usefulness of desire and finding something like a "perfect place" of operation in Web-based settings. In these settings the flowing exchange value of signs is an indefinite form of commodity that nonetheless becomes a use value in itself that also fosters belief in magical/virtual forms of transformation. To wit: consider the following passage from the VRML (Virtual Reality Modeling Language) developers Kyle Carlson and Steve Guynup in which they theorize the future of avatars in Web-based environments: "In typical VR environments, Avatars are human representations with some human gestural qualities. . . . We can and should empower that representation to do much more. When an Avatar is a representation of a teacher, it ought to have sweeping powers to present and manipulate educational information. Turning away from [the] concept of Avatar as humanoid representation, we find the Avatar can also represent educational information. With the addition of a simple switch node the teacher's Avatar can act as slideshow. A series of informational graphics, models or even worlds can be presented in sequence and completely in sync with the teacher's spoken or written text. For the first time a teacher can go beyond merely presenting some body of information to the students, she or he can literally become the information presented" (2000:65). In suggesting that what is absent (the teacher) will "literally" become present as information embodied in the form of the avatar sign/body, Carlson and Guynup reveal an implicit contempt for human bodies in their inability to understand that good teachers are not slideshows but have always embodied the wisdom and knowledge necessary to convincingly convey the information they present to students. They do not need (digital) avatars or body doubles or stand-ins—or even PowerPoint—to do so. Carlson and Guynup trade in the fetishism identified by Baudrillard as a "fetishism of the signifier" itself (1981:92), and they do so metaphysically by positioning the trace as a virtual object superior to the purportedly inferior teacher as referent.

Of the theorists I have discussed, Derrida presents the most complex extension of Peirce's theories. In *Of Grammatology* he approvingly includes the following passage from Peirce's *Elements of Logic*: "Anything which determines something else (its interpretant) to refer to an object to which itself refers (its object) in the same way, this interpretant becoming in turn a sign, and so on ad infinitum" (1974:50). Derrida cites Peirce to support his assertion that "from the moment that there is meaning there are nothing but signs. We *think only in signs*" (50). He uses Peirce's terms, representamen and interpretant, to argue for a play of signifiers without beginning or end: "The so-called 'thing itself' is always already a *representamen* shielded from the simplicity of intuitive evidence. The *representamen* functions only by giving rise to an *interpretant* that itself becomes a sign and so on to infinity" (49). This passage clearly echoes Peirce's early belief in the "ad infinitum" of sign circulation.[7] Derrida aims to reveal history and culture as the struggle for writing. He points to what has been deleted from official records and seeks to decenter fixity and the institutionalization of metaphysical first principles that lead to authoritarian and totalitarian regimes of thought based on pernicious reifications of specific ideologies. Derrida claims to rigorously oppose metaphysics and its abetting of the production of binary opposites that favor one member of the pair while marginalizing the other. Yet in trying to write the ineffable according to certain precepts of logic, is Derrida's attempt to use writing to get beyond its limits a metaphysical move?

In deconstructing binary thought, in working to position the trace as a kind of qualitative multiplicity that need not only be understood as a representation *tout court*, Derrida also critiques what he terms the *transcendental signified*—an inner principle that places "a reassuring end to the reference from sign to sign" (1974:49). One can argue that Derrida is antimetaphysical here in that he stands opposed to the metaphysics of first principles. But metaphysics also subsumes the "study of phenomena beyond the scope of scientific inquiry," and it is "theoretical philosophy as the ultimate science of being and knowing" (*OED*). As such, metaphysics also examines first principle questions of being, space and time, and identity, form, cause, and change. In this light, Derrida's thinking is metaphysical and, indeed, any theoretical intervention into important moral questions such as form, identity, causality, and being is necessarily metaphysical. When Adam notes that Derrida's trace "is an elusive spectre hovering at the edge of the signifier" (1995:n.p.), he raises a separate understanding of metaphysics as related to the worlds of magic and the occult. This is precisely the sign world as first principle depicted, for example, in the famous final scene of Orson Welles's *The Lady from Shanghai* (1947), which takes place in the "Magic Mirror Maze" and confirms that "from the moment there is meaning there are nothing but signs."

One can further argue that in his theorization of the trace Derrida identifies the inaccessibility of presence as an organizing principle. In Derrida's words, "Thus . . . the trace whereof I speak is not more *natural* . . . than *cultural*, not more physical than psychic, biological than spiritual. It is that starting from which a becoming-unmotivated of the sign, and with it all the ulterior oppositions between *physis* and its other, is possible," "the trace . . . becomes the origin of the origin" (1976:47–48, 61). Something remains beyond or outside the sign system. The event leaves a trace—something apparent remains from what was earlier present. Yet this something/event remains, synechistically, indivisible from the sign. This something, again, is the trace, itself revealing a trace of cosmopolitan, on-the-go continuities charged with the production of value and its manifestation in online settings as the virtual object. Appearance, in the form of the trace, stands in for presence. Yet what precedes the sign, or virtual object, is the trace that is also lodged within the sign (or virtual object). The trace, then, is an inconsistent multiplicity. It cannot be understood by recourse to binary logic based on all or nothing, this or that (Lucy 2004:145). Politically, it follows that the other is never wholly other, never fully "there" (absent from me) in contrast to my remaining "here" (and present). Instead, Derrida's concept (or nonconcept, as he would have preferred) can be interpreted as finding in Peirce's notion of the index as a sign pointing directly to its referent, that this referent (also Peirce's interpretant) is something/an event that both lies beyond the sign system yet remains indivisible from it *at the same time*—a kind of synechistic multiple that need not only be experienced as a representation (and therefore not unlike a kind of art on its way to becoming human). Appearance and presence conjoin. The Derridean trace, then, is a difference that produces value even as it partially lies outside the sphere of interest concerned with this production. As the early Peirce theorizes, we too are signs that take place. Peirce's belief that "all phenomena are of one character" directly anticipates this outcome of Derrida's theory of the trace—the "other" is produced by a binary understanding of how signs circulate. Enter the interpretant as sign to ensure that "the truth is out there." It circulates among and through the continuously updating networks linking representamen, referent, and interpretant.

>>> The Political Trace

Here I return to the issue of media centrality discussed in chapter 1. Mass media rituals are based on Durkheimian binary logic: in the performance of a mediated center, community is maintained through such rituals even as they also exclude and marginalize. These rituals, I suggest, implicitly operate as Derridean first principles within a media system. For most first world lives, media is a central component. No matter how much some of us might wish it were otherwise, most of us rely on media as part of knowing what we know. How, then, might applying the arguably quasi-metaphysical Peircian/Derridean assessments of how the trace circulates to analyses of insider-outsider, center-periphery, ritualized politics dependent for their transmission upon mediated centers advance an understanding beyond what most current materialist critique offers?

Materialist critique works to expose repressive political outcomes in hopes of stimulating action leading to progressive change. Ironically, however, it depends on and becomes a kind of doubling of that which it critiques. To achieve any analytic rigor, in an uncanny way it depends on the same naturalized center-periphery binaries that also position the media center as a metaphysical first principle. One way to arrive at a more robust understanding of media rituals based on acceptance of media as social center—that is, to comprehend *how* and *why* viewers, audiences, participants, individuals, and whole cultures might buy into these metaphysical rituals—would be to first identify this center as actually "full of holes," as a leaky, porous site through which traces attached to images pass as they circulate, like electrons, through networks. The trace, then, operates as a kind of "media grease" that lubricates the circulation of lived hegemonic energies that flow through media functionaries and owners as well as through less powerful viewers/participants. Application of this insight will not void power differentials between viewers and media owners. That is not my proposal. It can, however, assist in understanding how the *psychic* center is much more dispersed (perversely rhizomatic if you prefer) than that acknowledged by the trope of media center. And it can do so critically. Such psychic dispersal is achieved, in part, because the networked and networking trace, in the form of an image, never fully comes under human control even as it seems to carry a trace of the human with it. As such, a quasi-purity, go-between quality or value of a mediator seems to inhere in the trace. These factors facilitate perceiving it as somewhat independent and value-neutral but, in consequence, the trace in the form of an image, particularly a moving one, accrues considerable power through its viral ability to circulate preferred messages of social cohesion that accord with dominant interests. Yet this same ability equally assists the trace, in its quality of "origin of origins" somehow lying outside the sign system, to attach itself to individual perception in such a way that the concept it transmits seizes perception. It is also possible, however, that the quality of the trace that tantalizes and confirms the inaccessibility of presence could encourage viewer/user/participant resistance to dominant messages due to their perceived inauthenticity.

Therefore, theorizing how networked power flows synechistically is a more complex task than doing so primarily by recourse to naturalized binaries. One need not be metaphysical to premise or identify metaphysically inflected practices and techniques: under the lived hegemony of the trace, mediated individuals perceive that they *do* receive something meaningful in exchange for consenting to be governed under a society of the (ritualized and fetishized) spectacle. They become interactive parts of it and not mere "spectators," "users," or "viewers." They are *participant*-observers. This perception develops not only because each individual experiences herself or himself as part of a broader mediasphere, but also because each individual, in receiving the networked trace, forms part of a larger network of signs; each is an interpretant who sends the trace on its way. In this mutuality of circulation the trace can seem lively, and its quality of circulated liveliness builds upon the bodily foundation of autonomic perception that moving images are somehow alive. This circulated liveliness brings traces of life and human remains into many online settings.

My assessment explains, in part, how the dynamic of interactivity, once established, constitutes an Althusserean-like hailing of individuals because as parts of the networked sign system they already are psychically inflected by the trace, already have a sense they enjoy, because already networked (or interpellated), access to some kind of privileged place within an emerging digital social order on its way to dominance. Any synechistic assessment of media, moreover, must remain aware of the researcher's own participant-observer status: as an interpretant participating directly in the sign systems she or he also observes at a distance. Researchers bring with them into the system their assumptions and understandings. Their findings not only influence this system because of what they have to say about it but also the findings become part of the system. Researchers and theorists, therefore, need to remain aware that in seeking a more satisfactory set of understandings as to why people ritualize and fetishize media practices and the ideal of a social center they necessarily flirt with trading in the metaphysics of consubstantial unity, an intellectual move they would likely seek to avoid. To move beyond the binary thinking implicit in the production, identification, and analysis of a media center, in part through understanding the trace as a "mutual implication" (Derrida 1976:146) of all signs and things, people included, is, however, also to see a way to reduce a politics of othering with its sense on the part of those othered of "the eternal return of the same." It is also to see a way to minimize difference that is always implicated in the production of charged values.

In seeing past the unitary independent "self" there is always a risk of turning to the network as the new master narrative—the ultimate first principle at the core of Kelly's Hive Mind proposal. Which "side"—metaphysical or materialist—do you come down on when you try to describe what happens when people start to desire a Network of all networks? Does the trace become the ghost in the World Soul machine? The Holy Ghost of flow as center? Is Second Life, after all, a participant-observer game of anthropology? It may matter less whether one "accuses" Peirce and Derrida of metaphysics or salutes them as visionary in understanding how the sign achieves political economies through the metaphysics accorded it. What is salient here are the ways that Peirce and Derrida offer methodological concepts applicable to identifying why networked communicability, as a materialization of metaphysics, becomes an end in itself courtesy of the trace. How best, then, to link such a research method to Peircian/Derridean theory? It is precisely the potential for metaphysical possibilities in Derrida's potentially material, potentially metaphysical, virtually actual, actually virtual neo-Peircian trace that interests me for how these possibilities anticipate the logic of telepresence, the hegemony of the trace, as well as the psychic core of metaphysically inflected cosmopolitan Web practices. These practices allow for the belief to arise that a trace of the original, as something exceeding representation, might be telepresently available through networked rituals of transmission constituted in sign practices. Derrida asserts that the trace becomes "the origin of the origin." He also suggests that the trace is the disappearance of origin—"there is above all no originary trace." Rather, the trace is a "nonorigin" that in so being becomes "the origin of the origin" (1976:61); both "out of nowhere, something" and "out of being, becoming." Where then—psychically and geographically—might this origin reside or be found? Clearly not in any one place or "media center," for this would concretize the potential for a first principle metaphysics rooted in presence. Rather, the theory's sensibility, like electronic networks, is one of flow, in a "now this" continual sense of movement. It is a dialectical circuitry paralleling that of an earlier televisual logic relocated into more powerful electronic networks with their modular signifiers, ephemeral sensibilities of location, multiple windows contained within screens, and the possibilities, therefore, for multiple forms of quasi-interpellated neosubjectivities each on the lookout for the cosmopolitan trace they are about to transmit at the same time as this trace both pauses within them and passes them by with its fleeting touch. The origin, then, is a remainder that is always on the move to the circuit's next event. But, so, too, is what remains of the subject and the truth. Are networked individuals always running after the truth that passes them by even as it remains right behind and within them, a part of it lingering, like a cosmetic, on the surface of their "soul"? Does "here" for them always already mean "everywhere else"? These are the questions that, ironically, tend to get dismissed as (implicitly the "wrong kind" of) metaphysics by those who argue for the experiential reality of digital telepresence. Current theories of telepresence, despite their occasional associations with simulation, rely on a binary semiotics of referent and representation—the representation produces effects by carrying a trace of the referent. The promotion of this idea—which does not consider how a human referent could also operate, through interpellation, as an interpretant—works to persuade interactive Web participant-observers that presence as a first principle alchemically translates through a kind of virtual empiricism into telepresence, an ideal relying on acceptance of the Web as a virtual space. A by-product is that virtual space itself is rendered a first principle. Again, enter the divine—these days most often with corporate assistance or branding.

Second Life indexical practices are metaphysical. Participant–observers seek, through symbol-icon combinations, to escape the limits of "mere words" via the establishment of a virtual spatial relationship between speech remaining "inside" embodied interpretants participating from this side of the interface, and the graphic combination of their avatars coupled to words in the avatar's speech balloons. This combination indicates (a real trace of) the ideal. Rappaport, in writing of the ways that indices and symbols inflect ritual practices, notes that "given the relationship of indices to that which they denote they are . . . tied to such events and conditions, and cannot *genuinely* occur in their absence" (1999:55). Indices and the events to which they point are "mutually implicated," and this is how, in the suture of representation and event, Rappaport argues that indexicality minimizes mendacity. In contrast, the conventions that underlie symbols more readily facilitate the production of lies—hence, perhaps, the implicit dismissal by graphical chat participants of "mere words" as inadequate or even mendacious and lacking sufficient mutuality (chapter 4), as well as the turn to the online moving image on the part of gay/queer men seeking to stake the visible truth claim of their own embodied existence (chapter 5). The trace, at least, seems to offer access to other spaces and other times because it also touches the self. The move to go beyond the symbol—a move possibly informed by desire for greater access to something true—reveals the naturalization of dialectics; that is, the naturalization of the idea that in the present moment being conflicted it is also always damaged or always ready to crack open due to a surplus value on the verge of transformation if not repair.

>>> Graphing the Trace

To autograph something is to leave one's signature on it as a trace of oneself. The idea of the autograph draws together the self, the sign, and the graph. To graph is to leave a trace. In chapter 1, I introduced Carey's discussion of the telegraph and assessed the implications of his setting ritual in opposition to transmission and how this binary might no longer hold in online settings. John Peters has examined Carey's claims for the tele*graph*, and he argues that it heralded a new form of writing as "the tracing of fleeting processes" (2006:143). The telegraph, the photograph, the polygraph, are, Peters observes, new graphic devices, which all arose from telegraphic experimentation, [that] made it possible to record processes — such as voices, physiological events, the weather, and geological tremors — that hitherto escaped inscription or even notice. The writing these machines produced did not refer to a preexisting symbolic code (as of language). They were rather tracings . . . written by the body itself without the superintendence of a human author or intervention of a doctor's scalpel. . . . Quite like the camera, telegraphic devices were part of a writing/graphing revolution in which inscription of intelligence became possible apart from a human consciousness. Camera, phonographs, and seismographs catch whatever comes their way, whether it makes sense to humans or not . . . The order of the universe is not necessarily located in human intelligence. (143–45)

Peters does not mention the pantograph, which was invented in 1723 and used for the mechanical copying of a plan, diagram, or pattern. Thus graphing (think again of the autograph) precedes the pantograph and telegraphy, or the technology would not have been so named at the time of its invention. I find it worthwhile, however, to consider the strong implication in Peters's final point that graphing coupled to modern machine intelligence is an ordering force; that the totality of the ways the universe is ordered exceeds humanity's ken, in light of assertions by theorists that rituals are "not entirely encoded by the performers" who are following "orders established or taken to have been established by others" (Rappaport 1999:24, 32), and that in their ritual performances "people tend to see themselves as responding or transmitting — not creating" (Bell 1997:167). Rappaport and Bell identify rituals as performances in which the code, in a manner similar to the power of the image and the trace, or the autograph after it is rendered, *somewhat* escapes human control and, I would say, that is precisely how we like it most of the time: immanent transcendence or transcendent immanence, courtesy of the sign.

Peters notes that graphing makes no reference to preexisting symbolic codes of language. This is consonant with that aspect of Derrida's theory of the trace by which it is the origin of the origin, outside of or before the sign system. It is also consonant with Deleuze's (1986) vitalist theory of cinema's movement-image and its ability to seem psychically real to autonomic perception. Peters's point also supports Eco's theory of the photograph as a *surrogate stimulus* that affords human sighted perception the same stimuli as the fragment of reality captured by the photograph.[8] Because we experience these stimuli as codeless and direct we tend to understand them as necessarily truthful (Eco 2000:353) — or, to paraphrase Rappaport, as largely lacking in mendacity. Ritual theories largely concur that a ritual's participants access its core and often unspoken meanings through the images transmitted by their own moving bodies. On the Web, photography, videography, and graphical chat images play crucial roles; digital sign/bodies stand in for the participants, all of whom receive these iconic indices as transmitted traces of the real. One might say that the images "telegraph" telepresence — that the avatar or image of the webcam operator is a kind of moving autograph. Rappaport relies on the idea of codes. A divergent explanation, however, for why rituals are not entirely encoded by their performers is that participants' moving bodies produce, in their reception as images by all participants, aspects of rituals that are never constituted in or experienced as code. At the beginning of this chapter I noted that the Peircian index "compels us to recognize a relation of sign to object that is distinct from signification" (Short 2004:223). Rappaport also notes that a ritual's participants follow orders "taken to have been established by others" (1999:32). Peters's observation that graphic processes work to suggest that the order of the universe is not only located in human intelligence is germane, and it is plausible in online rituals that Rappaport's "others" are constituted in the uncanny transmission of graphical images as traces itself. Through transmitting a sense of themselves through networked graphic traces — through quasi-automated avatars operating as sign/bodies, for example — participants actually contain Rappaport's "others" within their own sphere of communicability even though these participants also may need to believe that this agency flows from an order issued elsewhere. It may be the case for networked ritualizations that if there is an "elsewhere" it lies in the graph itself, in the trace, in an "origin of the origin" also strongly linked to movement through circuits. Metaphysics ad infinitum.

>>> Screen Display

I suggested above that screen displays help foster indexical reception in viewers by inducing their desire to access a larger totality of content lying beyond the frame of the screen. What is absent is made present. I wish to further complicate this discussion by introducing a distinction between screen and display that is cognizant that we are living through a techno-cultural moment repositioning the meaning of a display. This repositioning is on display in this volume—itself an outcome of this moment—and its own uneasy negotiation of the leaky boundaries between screen and display. Both screens and displays organize communication through signs. In everyday language one at times hears the terms used interchangeably to suggest that the screen is a form of display, or vice versa, and at other times that the idea of "display" increasingly supersedes that of "screen." I suggest the latter is so because of display's greater association with action, manifestation, and direct liveliness—associations that are rooted in an older meaning of the term as an unfolding and that are available today for interpreting the value of telepresent virtual interactions as direct manifestations or unfoldings, or as displays of the actions of real people at a distance. The screen retains long-standing associations with cinema and the *projection* of the moving image. However, display, used somewhat interchangeably with screen when describing the computer interface, has surplus meanings to screen's association with the movement-image. Display articulates more directly to inter-activity coupled to the *transmission* of information through electronic networks. If something is projected it is always in a direct and dependent spatial relationship with the projector, whether a machine or a person. If something is transmitted it may pass directly between sender and receiver, but it may also pass through many circuits, corridors, and vectors. Its form may be altered to do so and only be reconstituted into a whole near the end of its voyage from sender to receiver. Transmission does not contain within itself the expectation that what is to be transmitted will remain pure or intact. In its association with analog forms such as slide transparencies and celluloid film stock, however, projection is held to different standards. It may be subject to empirical charges of falsity or illusion that are more difficult to press in the allegorical world of networked transmission.

We implicitly associate projection with an object, including light particles and sound waves, traveling through the air. The vectors of transmission are wider and include wires and networks made to facilitate moving information around in networked ways that far exceed the projector-screen-spectator trialectic. When something is transmitted, therefore, like the image and the trace, it has the *potential* to escape the projected orbit (and ideology) of the sender and attain, through multiple circulations, exposures, articulations of meaning, and the different forms it may take during its transit, its own sphere of influence. It is akin to the transmission of electricity: the largest corridors dissipate up to half of the electrical energy flowing through the wires. (Belief in transmission's *potential* fueled the early utopian claims that "information wants to be free," which were made in concert with the rise of the internet.) Indeed, if for Carey ritual is a synecdoche for culture, for Debray (2000) transmission approximates culture when cultural narratives and modes of experience and being are transmitted among generations of people over long periods of time. While projection and transmission both imply the role of space, the spatial relation is more fixed between projection and projector and more polyvalent, relative, and mutable with transmission.

Goffman notes that "displays don't communicate in the narrow sense of the term; they don't enunciate something through a language of symbols openly established and used solely for that purpose" (1979:1). Goffman's observation parallels the view expressed by Short that the index is a relation of sign to body somehow distinct from signification. As I hope the assessments of graphical chat and webcams in chapters 4 and 5 make clear, the techniques and practices of users or participants conjoin, in differing ways, indexical techniques of display and reliance on symbols, including text. Display, for Goffman, is indexical; it assumes a culturally specific and accepted "range of indicative behavior and appearance" (1). This assumption is designed into the kinds of "off the shelf" avatars initially made available to new graphical chat participants in Second Life and There! These avatars adhere closely to human form, and they also display, in their male and female manifestations, the culturally specific range of indicative (gendered) appearances widely assumed to be "natural" for men and for women. Display helps render the sign more experientially present. The assumptions of display are evident in webcam settings, with their invitation to consume the image of the operator and their direct camera focus on her or his body, facial expressions, and the positions by which he or she faces the camera in ways that conform to naturalized viewer expectations about how the content on the screen will be displayed. Though such iconic/indexical displays are also symbolic in the Peircian sense—based on assumptions that viewers understand the visual codes—they differ formally from how these participants also represent themselves through text and writing practices based in linguistic competencies, a different form of signification. Justus Buchler (1940:102) notes that an index, in Peirce's terms, "is a sign which refers to the Object that it denotes by virtue of being really affected by that object." In networked virtual environments where participants control the movements and appearance of their avatars, the avatar is an index (it indicates the participant) *really affected* by and connected to the object/participant given that the participant controls the avatar in almost every aspect. One sees in the idea of the interface the interplay of meanings between screen and display. The interface, a site of interactivity, contains the possibility of movement conveyed by the screen. It also carries the idea of the display of unfolding of actions, through onscreen characters, of actual human beings at a geographic or temporal remove.

>>> The Significant Potential of Online Environments: "I See Myself Seeing Myself"

Derrida observes that Peirce considers "the indefiniteness of reference as the criterion that allows us to recognize that we are indeed dealing with a system of signs" (1976:49). The musicologist and semiotician Jean-Jacques Nattiez interprets the Peircian referent as a *virtual* object, arguing that this object could not exist other than "within and through the infinite multiplicity of interpretants" (1990:7). The sign acquires a relational and evolving identity and gains elaboration through a recursive series of continuing interpretations. The perceptual experience of webcam operators conforms to and extends certain aspects of this logic. The operator who transmits an image of himself occupies the position of *referent*. Yet like the webcam's other viewers, he is also able to view the display of his own networked digital image. He therefore also occupies the position of *interpretant* of the sign of himself on the computer display. As a sign on the interface, so too does he occupy Peirce's third position—that of *representamen*. The operator comes to carry the entire triadic meaning of Peirce's sign system by becoming a mirror image to himself of subjectivity as a recursive algorithm, ad infinitum. He is a sign, an iconic index, even unto himself, with his own embodiment sutured to representation, simulation, and the imaginary of living virtually.

This circulation of significance points directly to the power of the digital telefetish (discussed in chapters 2 and 5). The digital *representamen*/trace of the operator, when viewed by the *interpretant*/embodied operator, appears as a stand-in for or body-double replica of the operator. The operator's ability to watch this initial *representamen*/stand-in look at a second smaller *representamen*/image of himself in a window nested within the larger webcam frame allows for his stand-in to serve as a performative link between this second image and himself. He sees himself seeing himself as if consciousness looking in or back on itself in a way that confirms a Cartesian separation between consciousness and overall reality. Two points related to this idea are worth noting here. First, the stand-in simulates or depicts watching—it operates as an iconic trace of the operator who watches it as a part of himself outside or beside himself, who traces himself as a trace, and thereby corroborates while at the same time rendering less central the "originary" embodied perception of himself as operator. Second, the entirety of this polyvalency of virtual self-location depends upon the presence of an actual camera located, conceptually, behind the embodied operator. By reverse extension the operator experientially becomes akin to a concretized déjà vu produced by the camera. Within such shifting modes of signification the operator becomes a device—a transmitting signal on display within the network of signs *and* a demiurgic cross-pollination of the Peircian *representamen* and *interpretant*. Phenomenologically, the self, as a concept implying an overall unity of perception like bourgeois consciousness itself, is not accessible as an object of perception. And the triadic possibilities of a webcam operator viewing his image viewing another image of himself works against any understanding of the self as a spatiotemporal unity. The position of the camera, however, in concert with the magical empiricism inflecting viewing practices, can seem to make it so—that is, to "extract" a visible "essence" or trace of the operator's self and transmit it as part of the networked imaginary. At the same time, the webcam, as a technology that builds the idea that we think in signs, allows the operator to produce himself through the pose. As Barthes would have it, after producing himself in this manner, the operator could never again fully see himself except as an image (1977b). The webcam allows him to gaze upon himself as a sign/body on display, as a kind of "spatial aside" and, hence, to become his own index. An operator's fans and other viewers are placed in, or willingly entertain, the position of extracting the essence of the operator's conceptually unitary self from his networked sign/body. Hence the potential within digital networks to be a telefetish even unto oneself—to ritualize an experience of oneself as a multidimensional trace with all the cosmopolitan freedom, commodification, and infinity this may imply.

The following account reveals how the trace of the original, perceived as something exceeding representation, already intersects life on this side of the screen. The 2007 Association of Internet Researchers (AOIR) Conference featured a day-long preconference program on research issues and Second Life. Several participants gave presentations on their experiences as teachers using Second Life as an educational platform, one of whom recounted how he had resolved a disciplinary issue in his virtual classroom. During the first week of class, a student, in the form of his avatar, had produced a pop gun and fired it at the teacher in the "presence" of the other students. According to the teacher, the gun was only a "play" gun that fired a flaglike projectile with a virtual dart at its end. The projectile, however, hit the teacher's avatar. Realizing the importance of quickly reestablishing his authority, the teacher, a code-savvy individual versed in the arts of authoring MUVE-based virtual objects, launched a program during the next class period that caused the offending student's avatar to burst into flames and disappear. Students, including the one made to disappear, were impressed, the teacher gained considerable "cred," and discipline was restored.

In responding to this account, another preconference participant stated that at her university such an incident would have caused the teacher to lose his job and the student would have been suspended. I asked why that would be the case. My question, particularly in a post–Virginia Tech, post–Northern Illinois University world, had less to do with the inappropriate actions of the student and the possibly rash response of the teacher. Rather, I hoped to provoke discussion about the nature of representation in MUVE settings. I continued by asking if a university normally would discipline a representation. To contextualize my question, I noted that many researchers in attendance had earlier discussed the mechanics of gaining Institutional Review Board (IRB) approvals for their research conducted in Second Life. The research, much of it virtual ethnography, entailed interviews conducted "in world" with individuals and groups in the form of their avatars. Why, again, I asked, noting the parallel with the university that would expel and fire the student and teacher for engaging in virtual classroom warfare, would such research require IRB approval if what was under investigation (and therefore possibly in need of protection) only involved a set of representations? In answer to my own rhetorical question I continued that the most plausible explanation lay in understanding that IRBs and those who would discipline and fire the offending student and teacher already understand that the online avatar is more than a representation—that it exceeds the definition of a representation as currently understood. These agencies and officials, I suggested, are already treating the digital avatar as a postrepresentational bodily appendage-cum-psychic extension and therefore as an actual (if not material) part of the person. This is the power of the online trace manifested in the form of a digital moving image already serving in the capacity of a social relation.

"Avatars Become /me"
DEPICTION DETHRONES DESCRIPTION

In May 2004 the United Kingdom Methodist Church launched Church of Fools as a summer-long test run for using the Web to attract and retain members of the faith. To do so the church elected to design and test a MUVE graphical chat platform. Figure 6 indicates the graphics quality of the platform for Church of Fools and its participants' avatar stand-ins in the virtual space. According to Simon Jenkins, one of the designers of Church of Fools, Methodist officials looked to graphical chat as a "serious effort to develop an alternative form of Christian worship for people who find the bricks-and-mortar world of religion offputting."[1] As the official website states, "The opening service in Church of Fools took place at the Christian Resources Exhibition in Surrey, UK, and drew a crowd of 1,000 people online, visiting from places as far apart as New Hampshire, Glasgow and Western Australia. . . . The sermon, by the Bishop of London, the Rt Revd Richard Chartres, called for Christians to actively participate in the culture of the internet and to see the web as a gift from God" for opening "spiritual eyes and ears." The church's cardinal house rule states, "We hope you'll bear with us all as we learn together what it means to create hallowed ground

In this electric age we see ourselves being translated more and more into the form of information, moving toward the technological extension of consciousness.
Marshall McLuhan,
Understanding Media

6　The networked service at Church of Fools.

out of virtual space."[2] Within days of its launch, the church welcomed forty-one thousand visitors in one twenty-four-hour period, and during the initial three-month trial, an average of eight thousand individuals directed their browsers to the site daily. Unwelcome visitors such as those who "shouted" by typing in all capital letters "PRAISE BE TO SATAN" (the speech appears as text in a balloon adjacent to an individual's avatar) led site operators to restrict general access to the pulpit, lectern, and altar spaces in order to "stop less than religious types giving messages definitely not from the Almighty."[3] Although hackers caused mischief on the site, the testimonials on its webpages promote the foresight of the church's experiment. As one individual wrote: "I have a friend who has claimed not to believe in God for many years. He had a crisis this week and wanted a place to try a prayer. No way would he ever go to a real church. But he went to yours, said his first prayer in many years and told me he felt much better afterwards." Another participant, "Radalyn" from Georgia, USA, frequently left her character "alone in the church at prayer, while in real life she worked nearby."

Jennifer Gonzáles offers a succinct definition of the electronic avatar and the relationship between it and the person it stands in for: "An object constituted by electronic elements serving as a psychic or bodily appendage, an artificial subjectivity that is attached to a supposed original or unitary being, an online persona understood as somehow appended to a real person who resides elsewhere, in front of a keyboard" (2000:27–28). Gonzáles's definition, in a manner similar to Derrida's definition of the trace, does not define the avatar as a representation. Rather, she identifies it as an extension of a person. For Gonzáles the avatar is not a negation in the sense that a representation defines something only in relation to something else that remains elsewhere or absent. Instead, an electronic appendage pointing toward artifice seems more consonant with the "second" in Second Life — the chance for a new indexical form of informational expression to arise that raises the originary and ambivalent power of the trace. I understand the avatar as a specific kind of sign that participants need not experience as a representation; hence my use of the term sign/body. If, as embodied beings, we cannot think outside the sign system, then Gonzáles's argument logically extends Peirce and Derrida. To understand that participants might experience the avatar as more than a representation — namely, as an extension of the self into technology — need not mean I agree with the project. Although the avatar exceeds contemporary definitions of representation, it also remains a representation. The set of assumptions built into operationalizing the trace in ways that deny its links to representation leads to specific outcomes, including the operationalization of the implicit assumption that technology itself is a sign. The embrace of technology indicates a devotion to it as a sign; and therefore that networked society has arrived at that juncture of desire and belief that the individual can somehow reside within technology — that he or she can join with it, the object of collective fetishization, through the hybrid vehicle of the sign/body. The arguments in the pages that follow reflect these ambivalent dichotomies.

>>>

As in other graphical chat environments, the electronic avatars of Church of Fools are sign/bodies that, in this particular setting, project within the virtual space a range of prayer offerings, hallelujahs, genuflections, bell ringings, and other forms of digital meditation as well as more profane forms of address. In launching Church of Fools, the Methodist Church participates within organized religion's long-standing interest in exploiting the transcendent potential of the latest (electric) communication technologies. Writing about American nineteenth-century religious attitudes toward telegraphy, James Carey notes that "this new technology enters American discussions not as a mundane fact but as divinely inspired for the purposes of spreading the Christian message further and faster, eclipsing time and transcending space, saving the heathen, bringing closer and making more probable the day of salvation" (1975:4). Carey's argument depends on distinguishing between a view of communication as an embodied/incorporated ritual practice, a "sacred ceremony which draws persons together in fellowship and commonality" (6), and a definition of communication as a process of inscription, the transmission of signals or messages across space for the purposes of "control of distance and people" (3). A key argument I make is that networked information machines and Western cultural attitudes have since evolved, often symbiotically, to synthesize this earlier distinction so that on sites such as Church of Fools visitors participate within a ritual of transmission. In part because of a generalized fetishization of the power of networked technologies, the transmission of the self as information becomes ritualized, and the virtual church becomes the collective site within which avatar bodies as information may be seen to gather to produce, maintain, repair, and renew social relations. The actions of many site visitors manifesting as avatars in the same virtual space, with each transmitting the self as digital information displayed visually, attain a kind of ecumenical status.

The rituals of transmission performed in Church of Fools are Neoplatonic. They are technological versions of the Debordian spectacle as "the material reconstruction of the religious illusion" (1994:18). Their efficacy rests on the power of the emblem—a combination of text and image, discussed below—as a force for transmitting transcendent possibilities. As a sign/body, the avatar allegorizes the essence of true spirit believed resident within the ideal World of Forms, a spirit not normally sensible to everyday embodied experience but accessible on the Web through the imaginary metaphysical practices authorized by a belief in digital telepresence through virtual bodies, actions, and objects. The decision to establish Church of Fools as an avatar-driven graphical chat environment purposefully establishes meaningful connections between religious and online practices and avatar-centered transmissions of the self; the transmission of digital imagery organizes ritual practice at an interfaced "location" that is everywhere and nowhere at the same time.

To assist understanding the appeal of avatars and graphical chat MUVEs, this chapter historicizes and situates technologies precursive to their emergence. I trace the technological genealogy of MUVEs through earlier text-based internet forms, and I examine a number of intellectual influences on their development, including Neal Stephenson's science fiction novel *Snow Crash* (1992); the literary technique "free indirect discourse" developed in the late eighteenth century as a discursive strategy in the bourgeois novel; the emblem and its relation to allegory; and the mechanical automaton. I am also interested in the implications of graphical chat for subjectivity, artificial or otherwise, and I theorize the technology in terms of Hobbes's Author-Actor theory. Throughout I foreground the Neoplatonically inflected belief systems implicit in graphical chat that support forms of virtual reunification between modern subjects and objects. Historicizing and interpreting graphical chat as a technological process of transmission and communication can yield insight into what actually might be new about "new" media and the celebrated move "beyond representation." In addition, it reveals ways that these forms, lodged within a wider and increasingly pervasive culture of the interface, both renovate and extend long-standing desires embedded in techniques and practices of representation, simulation, and display.

Despite the frequent promotion of new media forms as a clean break from the past, graphical chat did not somehow emerge fully formed, like a chick hatched from an egg. The tension between text and images on display has a history in the West dating back at least to the Bible's prohibition "Thou shalt not make unto thee graven images" (Exodus 20:4). Islam, along with iconoclastic movements in the Eastern Orthodox Church during the eighth and ninth centuries, tried to stop the use of images, and Protestants fought a similar battle during the reformation in the sixteenth century. The Enlightenment carries forth this suspicion of iconographics. It privileges the abstraction and generalizability of textuality and words on the page as a way by which an emergent bourgeois subjectivity can distinguish itself from absolutist truth claims anchored to the emblematic images of monarchs, kings, and sovereigns. The contemporary understanding of an iconoclast as one who attacks cherished beliefs is a skeptical legacy of this suspicious logocentric tradition. Graphical chat, however, privileges iconographics and can foster suspicion of texts. The evolution of graphical chat MUVEs from such earlier entrants as The Palace, to more complex platforms such as Rose and There!, to Active Worlds, Second Life, and newer variants such as Entropia Universe and Dotsoul Cyberpark[4] — together with the parallel growth in competitive game applications set in virtual worlds such as World of Warcraft and Eve — exemplifies the increasing expectation placed on images in the West to mediate and organize social relations in a more perceptually immediate and less abstract fashion than through text alone and the supposedly more complex decoding processes it requires.

In 2004 I was "graphically" chatting with an individual depicting as female. In conversation, her avatar indicated unalloyed enthusiasm for the virtual environment where we "met," and she stated that graphical chat was infinitely superior to the use of "mere words." When I entered my response that she had resorted to typing words to express her contempt for them, she abruptly terminated our conversation. While my correspondent may have read my comments as sarcastic rebuttal, what was also at issue was my criticism of her implicit claim that more meaningful communication is possible through transmitting a sense of who one is and experiencing a sense of who others are by manifesting the self as an icon—a virtual body double. I had offended her sense of what was deeply valuable to her, perhaps even sacred. Roy Rappaport notes that embodied ritual postures or gestures define for all participants "the nature of the accepting self." Performers use their bodies to communicate "both to the self and to others not only what could be conveyed by an apparently corresponding set of words . . . but also a commitment of the living self to that message. Such physical acts seem to be more than 'mere talk'" (1999:146). Rappaport's observation gains support from McLuhan's identification of the difficulty of storing precise visual information about objects in verbal or textual forms (1964:158). At the same time, however, the adjective "mere" suggests something of a collapse of meaning, for my correspondent, of "words." Enacting through her avatar her implicit recognition of this collapse, and her disagreement with a system of discourse that, to her, has reduced the meaningfulness of words, would be a way to ritualize this conflict. Ceding embodied forms of power to an artificial subjectivity depends not only on fetishizing the potentials for advanced digital technology as the outcome of Western science long dependent on visual factors, but also the idea that the word be made subject to the image, a seeming inversion of the diktat "In the beginning was the Word, and the Word was with God, and the Word was God . . . All things were made by him" (John 1:1–3). The diktat is continued in the Enlightenment privileging of the text and suspicion of iconographics. While it is not my project here to mount a theological defense of logos, I note the demiurgic potential at work in my correspondent's grasp of the greater mimetic power of the networked image to remake himself or herself, in performative ritual fashion, into the kind of moving image that best reflects who she or he understands himself or herself to be, software limitations notwithstanding. In so doing, logos, in its dual meaning of word and of reason, is positioned in graphical chat as a subtext within an overall emblematic schema favoring the picture that moves. The dismissal of "mere words" is indicative of a rediscovery of what had been temporarily misplaced by modernity—the image and the power of allegory as a means of recapturing the prelapsarian unity of meaning and materiality believed to have existed before language itself.

>>> Earlier Digital Technologies Informing Graphical Chat

Only recently have networked interactive virtual worlds such as Second Life and World of Warcraft appeared on mass media's radar. Digital forms of interactive engagement coupled to the interest by participants in building the virtual worlds they "inhabit," however, are more than a recent blip. Popular for more than a generation among fans, many of whom are passionate about their practices, interactive virtual worlds continue to grow in popularity.[5] Commentators frequently mention the invention in 1974 of the fantasy role-playing board game Dungeons & Dragons (D&D) as an ur-moment. The success of Gary Gygax and Dave Arneson's tabletop game led to software developers and then industries devoted to role-playing games (RPG) and massively multiplayer online role-playing games (MMORPGS).[6] Players inspired by the D&D experience worked to develop text-based applications for a pre-Web internet. These applications, the first of which was launched in 1979, were termed multi-user dungeons (MUDs) (since renamed, variously, multi-user domains or dialogue or dimension) and multi-user dungeons object oriented (MOOs). A MUD "is a networked virtual reality whose user interface is entirely textual" (Curtis 1996:265); MOOs are a form of MUD but incorporate object-oriented programming language that allows players greater freedom in using software to engineer personalized features in these text-based virtual worlds.[7] Like aspects of the novel, MUDs and MOOs rely on the use of literary pictorialism to create a sense of vivid imagery, and thus they allow for the fabrication of highly elaborate and evocative textual descriptions to construct for readers a sense of themed environments and characters: medieval castles, hotels, subway/underground/metro systems with doors that open and close on programmed cue as the trains arrive at stations; elves, goblins, priests, thieves, finely clad damsels, and so forth. The ritualization of games and role playing as a form of self-construction is central to helping to order and organize online experience. Sherry Turkle writes that, in a MUD, "as players participate, they become authors not only of text but of themselves, constructing new selves through social interaction" (1995:12). Participants in MUDs situate descriptions of their online "new selves" and the activities they perform in these virtual places. Further, MUDs provide "an elaborate sense of movement as users' [characters] progress from one virtual space to another, encountering new settings and characters along the way" (Campbell 2004:36). Uses of MUDs include distance education, virtual conferencing, socializing, and as practice environments for programmers. Other uses are adventure oriented, with little action among players. Role play and fantasy related to self-construction constitute central forms of interaction, and users' characters are often as elaborated as the fantasy environments through which they circulate (see Carlstrom 1992).

Launched in 1988, Internet Relay Chat (IRC) is a different form of text-based internet chat setting that, like MUDs and MOOs, allows for multiple simultaneous connections and synchronous conferencing among participants. IRC was designed as a means for "social interaction between spatially disparate people" (Reid 1991). Unlike MUDs and MOOs, however, IRC foregrounds the understanding that the internet is a textual environment and not some kind of space. In common reference, one is "on" IRC whereas one is "in" a MUD or MOO. In contrast to the wizards and gods of MUDs and MOOs, IRC's far less demiurgic Finnish designers early argued that text-dependent descriptions of virtual objects, landscapes, and users' characters would clutter IRC channels. Such a spatialization of the internet, it was felt, impeded real-time conversations between geographically distant users. Conversely, IRC—arguably the precursor to text messaging and certainly an inspiration for such services as AOL's chat rooms and online communities—was intended to promote such conversations. Individuals on IRC were assumed to speak as themselves and were to be using the system more as a medium of communication and less as a site of performance (Campbell 2004:37). This earlier use of IRC stands in contrast to one of its principal uses today: as an internet backdoor to trade bootleg software, patches, cracks, and pornography.

By the early to mid-1990s, these text-based synchronous chat environments had achieved widespread use in wired parts of the first world, including Scandinavia, western Europe, North America, New Zealand, Australia,

Israel, Japan, and South Korea. A lively debate ensued about the relative merits of different technical and aesthetic approaches to chat environments and what kinds of user practices they should support. The emergence of the more image-based Web graphical user interface or GUI in the early to mid-1990s began to render such discussions moot. Distinctions between spatial and textual understandings of the internet have never been completely fixed within actual MUD and IRC practices. Many participants on IRC, for example, fabricate fantasy identities that often build on some aspect of their existing sense of self (Reid 1991), and nothing prevents MUD participants from coming to know other individuals "behind" their online personae. Yet the emergence of graphical chat MUVEs is one logical outcome of the debate between MUD and IRC designers. Indeed, MUVEs combine a more image-inclusive simulation of individuals and virtual spaces earlier achieved by MUD's text-based spatial descriptions alone ("you find yourself in a red, oblong room wallpapered with the image of flying cats") while also incorporating text-based communicatory practices earlier developed on IRC. In so doing, contemporary MUVEs reflect, in part, a fusion of the beliefs that the internet is either a space or a text-based medium.

Graphical chat is often positioned as more advanced and nuanced than these older text-based applications. This positioning operates under the capitalist purview of equating new, better, and progress with "the next thing" and the "killer app." All that is "new and improved" increasingly articulates to a belief that signs that resemble (in graphical chat this is achieved through using iconographic and indexical signs as visual metaphors) are "naturally" superior to those that "only" represent (text symbols on IRC and in MUDS as well as the underacknowledged importance of the text-based components of MUVEs). Nevertheless, text remains crucial to communication in these image-based environments, despite the focus by participants on the ways that graphical chat supersedes reliance on the use of "mere words." There is, however, a widespread belief among participants and promoters of graphical chat that with ever more powerful and customized technology, iconic metaphors of resemblance can be made to operate metonymically. That is, with sufficient bandwidth and computing power, these technologies can offer an experience of connection based on articulating participants' experience to the truth claims vested in images. This belief synthesizes strands of philosophical positions supposedly at variance: empiricism and contemporary variations of Neoplatonism at work in software development that implicitly assume that information machines are the "natural center" for the ideal World of Forms.

> Graphical Chat: *Snow Crash* Gets Built

It is said that in the beginning was the Word. Developers of new technologies often gain inspiration from science fiction writing. Just as William Gibson's novel *Neuromancer* (1984) acted as an inspiration to designers of immersive virtual reality applications (Hillis 1999), the geographer-turned-novelist Neal Stephenson's science fiction best-seller *Snow Crash* (1992) has inspired designers of 2-D graphical chat. The novel is set in a postneoliberal future in which government-by-corporation is the rule. For the protagonist, Hiro, life is Hobbesian, nasty and brutish. In an environmentally degraded world, those with access to computer terminals enter the networked virtual environment that Stephenson calls the Metaverse. "The Street" is the Metaverse's virtual public square and postapocalyptic amusement park.

> Like any place in Reality, the Street is subject to development. Developers can build their own small streets feeding off of the main one. They can build buildings, parks, signs, as well as things that do not exist in Reality, such as vast hovering overhead light shows, special neighborhoods where the rules of three-dimensional spacetime are ignored, and free-combat zones where people can go hunt and kill each other.
>
> The only difference is that since the Street does not really exist—it's just a computer-graphics protocol written down on a piece of paper somewhere, none of these things is being physically built. They are, rather, pieces of software, made available to the public over the worldwide fiber-optics network. (23)

Hiro, inside the Metaverse, sees two young, white, heterosexual couples out on a double date.

> He is not seeing real people, of course. This is all a part of the moving illustration drawn by his computer according to specifications coming down the fiber-optic cable. The people are pieces of software called avatars. They are the audiovisual bodies that people use to communicate with each other in the Metaverse . . . Your avatar can look any way you want it to, up to the

limitations of your equipment. If you're ugly, you can make your avatar beautiful. If you've just gotten out of bed, your avatar can still be wearing beautiful clothes and professionally applied makeup. You can look like a gorilla or a dragon or a giant talking penis in the Metaverse. (33–34)

By allowing us access to Hiro's thoughts in the passage below, Stephenson both predicts and comments critically on the capitalization of iconographic identity. In the class-based description of Brandy and Clint that follows, Stephenson anticipates the prêt-à-porter "Espresso Halle" and "Cocoa Bob" avatars and their relation to participants' identity in There! graphical chat.

The couples coming off the monorail can't afford to have custom avatars made and don't know how to write their own. They have to buy off-the-shelf avatars. One of the girls has a pretty nice one. It would be considered quite the fashion statement among the K-Tel set. Looks like she has bought the Avatar Construction Set™ and put together her own, customized model out of miscellaneous parts. It might even look something like its owner. Her date doesn't look half bad himself.

The other girl is a Brandy. Her date is a Clint. Brandy and Clint are both popular, off-the-shelf models. When white-trash high school girls are going on a date in the Metaverse, they invariably run down to the computer-games section of the local Wal-Mart and buy a copy of Brandy. The user can select three breast sizes: improbable, impossible, and ludicrous. Brandy has a limited repertoire of facial expressions: cute and pouty; cute and sultry; perky and interested; smiling and receptive; cute and spacy . . .

Clint is just the male counterpart of Brandy. He is craggy and handsome and has an extremely limited range of facial expressions. There are enough Clints and Brandys to found a new ethnic group. (34–35)

The principals of Linden Lab, Second Life's developer, do not highlight the setting's debt to the earlier text-based MUDs and MOOs discussed above. To do so might contradict the promotion of "Web 2.0" as something markedly new, and thereby also acknowledge the possibility of the old returning in the form of the new. Linden principals do, however, acknowledge the influence of Vernor Vinge's 1984 novella *True Names* and its rendering of the Other Plane, an electronic virtual world in which "protagonists' bodies never move at all," but "remain plugged-in to the network while programs change their representations of the simulated realities" (Minsky 1984:n.p.). Linden Lab principals are decidedly more enthusiastic in acknowledging their debt to Stephenson's Metaverse, and Second Life itself is sometimes referred to as the Metaverse by Linden Lab and Second Life's residents. The Second Life partner James Wagner has written that *Snow Crash* is "the novel that taught us to dream about an online digital world that exists in parallel with the corporeal realm." In 2006, Second Life featured "obelisks of burnished steel" on which contemporary Metaverse residents could read the first forty pages of Stephenson's novel.[8] A certain cultural capital accrues to Linden Lab in its claiming a genealogical linkage to Stephenson's creation, but despite (at the time of this writing) Second Life's superior graphic capabilities compared to its competitors, postmillennial versions of the Metaverse are equally on view in Active Worlds, There! and Rose.

Following the Metaverse model presented in *Snow Crash*, in graphical chat a participant's avatar/icon "manifests" and is an iconographic trace of the participant. Avatars communicate with other avatars. Text messages that participants type appear on the computer display as words within speech balloons appearing beside their avatars. In some applications this text also scrolls across the bottom of the screen. In sophisticated applications avatars perform simulated body gestures and movements, and by moving a mouse or a combination of mouse/keystroke actions, participants animate their avatars with six degrees of spatial freedom (up, down, left, right, backward, and forward). Second Life "residents" can, as Leonardo Da Vinci imagined, also fly. This ability to fly through space encourages the belief that nature should be reworked according to the visual logic of a landscape painting: a panorama that might extend in any direction even though what one sees of it at any one time is bounded by a frame.

Avatars contribute to graphical chat's more complex pictorial mode of transmitting and depicting a sense of oneself than do purely text-based applications such as IRC and MOOs. Because most graphical chat applications are subscription-based services in which their developers seek to make a profit, many services offer entry-level participants entry-level forms of free access and avatars much like Brandy and Clint (figure 7). Most often, you pay for what you get, and subscribing to higher levels of service or knowing how to write one's own code affords participants greater customization of avatars.

7   My standard-issue avatar in Second Life.

>>> Graphical Chat's Debt to Free Indirect Discourse

For Ted Nelson (2004), "the Web is a form of literature," and in this section I turn to focus on ways that the techniques and uses of graphical chat parallel and extend the modern novel's use of free indirect discourse. This literary and stylistic device emerged during the late eighteenth century; depending on the nationality of the critic and the language of the text under review, theorists also refer to it as middle voice, quasi-direct discourse, narrated monologue, reported speech, *style indirect libre*, and *erlebte Rede*. While textual and visual modes of communication differ in form and settings — the contexts within which free indirect discourse developed in the early novel clearly differ from and precede the circumstances fueling the interest in text-based internet forms of chat and Web-based graphical chat environments — one also can discern similarities in the logics of deployment of different modalities of the page and the display, and of a culture of the book and a culture of the interface (figure 8). Both allow for evolving, even mutating, forms of indirect, dual, and Janus-like depictions of the idea of the self in the many ways it has been imagined and reimagined.

Communicating one's ideas directly can be fraught with danger in any historical period, culture, society, or state. The potential for political pressure,

8 My avatar "speaks" in Rose graphical chat.

censorship, and condemnation of any aesthetic practice or production helps produce forms of expression intended to avoid such potentials becoming actual. These forms allow the expression itself to communicate something of its core intent; it remains, as it were, hidden while in full view. Spectators of 1940s Hollywood cinema, for example, widely understand that couples shown smoking cigarettes, either before or after a fade to black, signifies sexual intercourse that strict production codes prohibited films from actually depicting. While free indirect discourse and avatars do not respond to any official code per se, both are conditional technical strategies in that they respond to specific yet evolving sociopolitical and cultural expectations and standards about not only what can be said or shown but how; not only what can be written or depicted, but how and where; and not only if an idea can be represented but by whom or what. Speaking, writing, or depicting directly may be rigorously policed while de facto limitations placed on indirectly communicating through textual or image-based representational modes may be less stringent. Equally, free indirect discourse may be understood as a form of speculative theory (Deleuze and Guattari 1994)—a proposed understanding waiting to be understood, hinting at something beyond itself, a between-the-lines outline of an emergent future.

My historicization of graphical chat through an assessment of free indirect discourse is organized across four interrelated areas. First, I assess its origins as a print-based technique used to give a quasi-disembodied form of voice to a critical and interiorized individualism. This individualism could then communicate effectively with other novel-reading individuals. This emerging individualism, often gestating within authoritarian early-modern political realities, had need to "hedge its bets" for self-protection and did so through ventriloquistic modes of self-expression such as free indirect discourse and persona. Its expression in free indirect discourse often relies on the vividness of a literary pictorialism that engages readers more directly with the psychological inner states of a novel's characters. This allows an individual author's critique of status quo social, political, and economic realities to seemingly issue more from the vividness of a novel's characters than from the narrator's (and therefore, implicitly, the novelist's) own voice. This technique thus serves to deflect from the author unwanted forms of dominant attention.

Second, ventriloquism as a strategy, with its suggestion that communicative components of the self might lie beyond the physical limits of an individual's body, is part of a wider early modern interest in the psychic mechanisms of automata and puppets. It, too, can serve as a defensive strategy, one that seems to project the source of the message to somewhere or something else than the sender. At the same time, however, as Enlightenment thought identifies the locus of the modern contractually oriented individual as an interior subjectivity seeking ever greater self-determination and self-illumination, a parallel interest in depicting qualities of human subjectivity in the form of doubles who take physical shape in exterior mechanisms, media, and technologies reveals an ongoing demiurgic interest to craft *visible*, external allegorical simulations of this metaphorically illuminated interior self.

Third, the act of theorizing affinities between such different forms as free indirect discourse and digital avatars permits interrogating the alleged shift from a more typographic culture to a more visual one. I concur with W. J. T. Mitchell that "the difference between a culture of reading and a culture of spectatorship . . . is not only a formal issue (though it is certainly that); it has implications for the very forms that sociability and subjectivity take, for the kinds of individuals and institutions formed by a culture" (1994:3). Words and images, operating within specific sociopolitical circumstances, differently represent the possibility and potential of experience without a subject. However, particularly given digitization's opening of typography to new forms of visual design, there are increasingly meaningful overlaps in the ongoing expectations we bring to typographic and image forms even as they each help organize in different ways what we find meaningful and how we do so. Theorizing the increasingly leaky experiential boundary between words and images has important implications for how subjectivity is organized if we are at the historical conjunction where the Web must be taken seriously as not only beginning to renovate some of literature's forms but also forms of social relations.

Fourth, I examine the contemporary focus on visuality and visual culture, or what Mitchell (1994) refers to as "the visual turn." This turn is part of a long-term repositioning of the relationships among production, consumption, vision, sight, and the different kinds of subjectivity formations best suited to systems of production, systems of consumption, and syntheses of the two. The overlaps and disjunctures between words and images point to new modes of subject formation consonant with the requirements placed on individuals who labor and consume within a cosmopolitan system of neoliberal capitalism operating across local and global states of affairs with one foot in every camp.

FREE INDIRECT DISCOURSE

Free indirect discourse in the novel is a style or form of language that comes from the narrative voice but takes on the attributes of the character described. Jane Austen, according to the linguist Dorrit Cohn, was "the first extensive practitioner of the form" (1978:108). The following example is taken from *Sense and Sensibility* (1988 [1811]): "Mrs. John Dashwood did not at all approve of what her husband intended to do for his sisters. To take three thousand pounds from the fortune of their dear little boy, would be impoverishing him to the most dreadful degree" (8). Here, readers witness Austen shift from narrative description—"Mrs. John Dashwood did not at all approve"—to, in the following sentence, the harrumph of Mrs. Dashwood's voice protesting the unfairness of her husband's decision. Readers cannot precisely determine the degree to which this passage represents Mrs. Dashwood's thinking or experiential state, or a capturing of her audible speech, or some combination of the two. Does the language express Mrs. Dashwood's thinking without uttering, or is it utterance itself? Austen's analyses of her characters and inner states seem to come not from "an intrusive author but rather from some August and impersonal spirit of social and psychological understanding" (Watt 1957:297). Austen's use of free indirect discourse produces an ambivalent hybrid that draws together the possibility of narratorial summary and the indirect rendering of a specific utterance. The passage continues:

> She begged him to think on the subject. [Here the narrator relates story information in a straightforward fashion.] How could he answer it to himself to rob his child, and his only child too, of so large a sum? [Mrs. Dashwood's thinking, point of view, or experiential state is expressed through free indirect discourse. The sentence and those that follow could be read as issuing from the narrator, but the formal qualities of personal indignation work to suggest that they express Mrs. Dashwood's point of view.] And what possible claim could the Miss Dashwoods, who were related to him only by half blood, which she considered as no relationship at all, have on his generosity to so large an amount. It was very well known that no affection was ever supposed to exist between the children of any man by different marriages; and why was he to ruin himself, and their poor little Harry, by giving away all his money to his half sisters? (8)

In this passage, eliminating the reporting verb, as in "she said" and "she thought," further induces a sense of the character's subjectivity by subtly drawing readers into it. But if readers are not careful, they can be beguiled into agreeing with the subjectivity presented—in this case agreeing with Mrs. Dashwood's greed-based outrage at the supposed injustice of her husband's honoring his father's will. With respect to the style's selective omission of the reporting verb, Valentin Vološinov argues that the author therefore is "able to present the utterances of his characters in a way suggesting that he himself takes them seriously, and that what is at stake is not merely something that was said or thought, but actual facts" (1986:150).[9] At the same time, moreover, Austen's sophisticated use of the style allows readers access to her characters' interior consciousness while also inviting them to adopt a critical stance to these characters' intentions and thought processes. This permits Austen to direct an ironic, even poetic, barb at such readers by slyly suggesting that their identification with Mrs. Dashwood's character might indicate that they too share her hypocritical parsimony. In this way, Austen can critique the positionality of her bourgeois readers. Those who fully identify with the narrative position she invites them to inhabit will remain unaware of her implicit critiques against them—critiques that if made too obvious would risk ire from these same readers.

Vološinov notes that the specific dynamics of free indirect discourse (which he terms quasi-direct discourse) produce "a matter of both author and character speaking at the same time, a matter of a single linguistic construction within which the accents of two differently oriented voices are maintained" (1986:144). A second example of the style, from Alexander Pushkin's *Poltava* (1829), further demonstrates how free indirect discourse can establish an ambivalent interorientation between narrator and character. Pushkin moves with suppleness between a stance outside of his character Kočubej's subjectivity to one seemingly more lodged "within" Kočubej and then back again: "But his rage for action Kočubej hid deep within his heart. [narrative voice] *His thoughts had now, all woebegone, addressed themselves to death. No ill-will did he bear Mazeppa—his daughter was alone to blame. But he forgave his daughter, too*: [halfway between narrator and character] *Let her answer to God, now that she had plunged her family into shame, had Heaven and the laws of man forgot* . . . [Kočubej's thinking or experiential state] But meanwhile he scanned his household with an eagle eye, seeking for himself bold, unswerving, incorruptible companions [return to narrative voice]" (cited in Vološinov 1986:140; emphasis added).[10] Critics have noted that the historical rise of the novel, focused on the everyday activities of ordinary people, is coterminous with the rise of capitalism, Protestantism, and the development of modernity (Watt 1957). The Enlightenment theorizes the liberating notion of an independent individual based, in part, on a rational, critical inner subjectivity and a heightened sense of self-illumination, and the novel form, as a technological assemblage, provided a new and inherently political form of representing textually or "giving voice to" that psychological inner sense in a manner that today reads as an almost cameralike illusion of objectivity in presenting emotional inner states as empirical facts. The development by novelists during the nineteenth century of free indirect discourse and its effect as an interoriented middle voice represents a "crucial turning point in the social vicissitudes of the utterance . . . explainable in terms of *the general, far-reaching subjectivization of the ideological word-utterance*" (Vološinov 1986:158). Vološinov argues dialectically that such stylistic developments in language parallel developments in subjectivity driven by the changing material conditions of a society or a language group.

Among the first developers of the style is the French fabulist Jean de La Fontaine whose three volumes of *Fables* were published in 1668, 1678, and 1694 (Vološinov 1986:151). Vološinov does not associate the style's serial emergence across different languages to the emergence of nation-states. It is of more than incidental interest, however, that nation-state economies rely on the development of rational-critical, individuated, and interiorized bourgeois subjects, even if, simultaneously, authoritarian state agendas serve to control or oppress aspects of these same subjects' emergent formations. It is notable that subsequent to La Fontaine, writing during the reign of Louis XIV when France was the most powerful country in Europe, the style emerges in its fully modern form first in English (Austen's *Northanger Abbey* [1818]), in a country then dominating mercantilist global trade. At the height of the Second Empire, Gustav Flaubert published *Madame Bovary* (1857), a novel that makes full use of *style indirect libre*. It is not until 1901 that *erlebte Rede* emerges in German. Thomas Mann's *Buddenbrooks* was published subsequent to the formation of the unified German state and the kinds of national economic practices and requisite hybrid forms of complex utterances and ambivalent, at times multiaccented (to appropriate a term from Vološinov) or polyvocal, bourgeois contractual forms of cosmopolitanisms that emerge with and are necessary to facilitate its rise.

The decoding practices demanded in reading novels rely on and support an enlightened critical inner subjectivity. At times, however, it is politically or psychically necessary to mask the potential strength of a too resistant or too critical point of view, to nuance the tone of social critique and the expression of new ideas that may issue from this heightened, potentially oppositional, sense of self. Free indirect discourse allows an author's characters to serve as a screen behind which the author may "hide," yet at the same time it allows him or her to communicate through it to readers. As with the more direct use of persona, the development of free indirect discourse allowed nineteenth-century realist novelists to engage in new forms of criticism by seeming to place this criticism in the thoughts of their characters. They thereby deflected attention from themselves while at the same time rendering the criticism psychologically more true for readers. The extent to which this deflection succeeds, however, varies among readers because issues are referenced yet elided—they are often revealed only through readers' careful attention to the text. Yet while the style can insinuate various nuances of consciousness, resistance, or ideology, it also calls into question the stability of the critical inner subjectivity, or the positionality of which it also reflects. Through its production of a middle voice, free indirect discourse infers the truth of emerging forms of plural, hybrid, or possibly even fragmented subjectivities ready to challenge, or at least unsettle, the idea of the unitary subject so central to Enlightenment principles, capital formation, and the nation-state. Novelists thus have participated in giving voice to what intellectual historian Martin Jay (1998) refers to as "experience without a subject"—a phrase that connotes the idea of mobility, of a virtual subject, or possibly a recording machine, and an issue to which I return in my discussion of graphical chat environments.

In the nineteenth century, the novel's free indirect discourse could provide a modicum of protection for an author's critique. It is not unlike the protection of donning a persona in order to participate in the masquerade's ornate potential for ambivalent social and political commentary. But the position of the middle voice is not always precisely "between" the narrator and the character, and unlike persona it does not function chiefly as a mask used by an author. Novelists employing the style give expression to ideas and describe experiences that, in the case of Austen, can seem to be more those of her characters and less her own—ideas that may not yet have attained full development or "voice" in the novelist's consciousness, in the novel itself, or in the wider society in which novels are written, read, and discussed. Other modes of the style, such as that developed by Flaubert in *Madame Bovary*, position sensitive ideas as issuing from neither the author nor the character yet somehow both at once, thereby complicating one-on-one understandings of representation. In both cases, the style's formal qualities arguably respond to the possibility that certain criticisms, while theoretically conceivable to imagine or theoretically permissible to represent, nevertheless remained sociopolitically or psychically *unspeakable*—or possibly even ineffable. While the following analogy is anachronistic, it is productive to consider free indirect discourse as a kind of software patch allowing the discursive technology of the novel to operate in ways more productive to furthering the political goals of the emerging bourgeois individual vis-à-vis the state, religion, and an entrenched landed aristocracy. I return to the following point in my discussion of graphical chat, but it is worth noting here that the idea of experience without a subject—intended to refer to the difficulty of establishing with certainty the origin or location of the voice rendered through the style—might profitably be applied to considering that a quality of subjectivity has been relocated to the mechanism of free indirect discourse itself. Paralleling the dynamic by which ritual theorists assert that ritual achieves its efficacy, the style—devised by the human subject and "free" in the novel—can be imagined as attaining, like the contemporary software that powers avatars, bots, and other so-called "intelligent agents," a quality of extrahuman agency that is itself an imaginative locus of subjective experience for readers. As such, the style's ability to convey "experience without a subject" bears consonance with Derrida's claim for the trace as "the origin of the origin" (1976:61).

The political goals of the emergent bourgeois subject are directly related to a growing awareness on the part of such individuals that collectively they constitute a "middle" class. As "exquisite flowers of the bourgeois class,"[11] Austen and Flaubert are novelists who through their characters give voice to different facets of this awareness, including the fact that one might move down the class ladder while trying to clamber up. Certain implicitly bourgeois political goals articulated to greater self-awareness and the need to speak about it were resisted by those who sought to contain the possibilities for fully formed political subjectivities within narrowly defined social parameters. Samuel Johnson, for example, warned in 1750 that novels were "written chiefly to the young, the ignorant, and the idle" and that they made dangerous reading for the unwary because their "power of example is so great, as to take possession of the memory by a kind of violence, and produce effects almost without the intervention of the will" (1969:22). As Jay notes, *Madame Bovary* "draws on the fear that impressionable readers will confuse their lives with those of romantic heroines" (1998:209 n.41). The novel, early identified as a feminine form, was implicitly judged by Johnson as potentially destabilizing to patriarchy in its ability to "excite the passions" of female readers. Austen, though in many ways a follower of Johnson, strongly disagreed with him on this point.[12]

Earlier I noted that free indirect discourse might offer certain protections for authors seeking to transmit critique, but I also need to acknowledge that Flaubert's mid-Victorian trial, on grounds of irreligion and immorality, exemplifies the dangers that novelists face by attempting to give voice through print to the unspeakable. Stina Teilmann has written about Flaubert's 1857 trial, and part of the title of her essay "Trying Free Indirect Discourse" communicates her Foucauldian thesis that the concept of the author in France was developed as a policing strategy against the use of anonymous texts during the Revolution to incite mob violence and political upheaval against establishment orders. Making it mandatory for a text to have an author meant that the individual writer of any textual communication deemed contrary to state interests could be identified and punished. Teilmann concludes that Flaubert's use of free indirect discourse in *Madame Bovary*, with its dual-voiced quality, unwittingly contravened the state's demand for clear authorship—one that extended to the implicit demand that any author assert authority over his or her characters.

Teilmann concludes that Ernest Pinard, Flaubert's public prosecutor, pursued his case because he could not ascertain an authority in the novel capable of disciplining or critiquing Emma Bovary's actions. This concords with Jay's observation that the style allows for the emergence of experience without a subject. As Teilmann notes, the scandalized reception for Flaubert's first novel flowed from his use of the middle voice or *style indirect libre* in describing Emma Bovary's passion: "She repeated: 'I have a lover! A lover!' delighting at the idea as if a second puberty had come to her. So at last she was to know those joys of love, that fever of happiness of which she had despaired! She was entering upon a marvelous world where all would be passion, ecstasy, delirium" (cited in Jay 1998:201).[13] This famous passage eschews any simple combination of reporter/reported. Rather, it is an assemblage of enunciation (see Deleuze 1986:73), and Jay argues that what made the passage so scandalous and confusing to the novel's detractors was "their inability to attribute with certainty the shocking sentiments in the last sentence to either the character or the author. Was Flaubert identifying with Emma's fantasy or merely reporting it? His style did not seem to permit for any firm answer" (1998:210). Yet why should this matter so? More is at stake than (implicit) official insistence on a unitary authorial voice. Pinard's office recognized that the novel's words issued from Flaubert's pen and not that of his characters' imaginations or that of some anonymous author. Would the moral arbiters have been equally scandalized if *Madame Bovary* had been written in the first person, direct address, or as a descriptive, journalistic account? Possibly so, for mid-Victorian authors faced risks in mounting challenges to the strict taxonomies of "appropriate" social, sexual, and gender roles. Yet other scandalous novels of the time did not receive the same prosecutorial attention as Flaubert's first novel. What would seem to fuel the scandal in addition to the questions of authority raised by Teilmann is the ability of Flaubert's text to imply what was not yet speakable and, for many, scarcely imaginable or not yet thought: an unsettling of that part of a mid-Victorian discourse formation based on the naturalized ideal of a unitary modern subject. The ability of free indirect discourse to convert an idea into a psychological truth—that the modern self might be, like the trace, an inconsistent multiplicity (see chapter 3) and therefore less than unitary across categories of class and gender—scandalized mid-Victorian taxonometric and patriarchal sensibilities, particularly since the formation of a unitary, fixed self was implicitly understood as a key component of a capitalism based on a theory of self-disciplined production and fixed, contractual divisions of labor. Free indirect discourse, with its ability to communicate a "narrator's independent voice [that] lacks an authoritative, objective standard of truth or morality" (Pascal 1977:138), points to the inherent instability, polyvocality, and synechism of the supposedly unitary and self-controlled subject. Further, in Flaubert's hands, the style indicates the negation of representation it works to overcome. His assertion that "Madame Bovary, c'est moi" anticipates Gonzáles's understanding of the avatar as a psychic appendage of a real person and indicates how the actual draws together the virtual and the real.

Other related factors further contribute to the sense of scandal. Free indirect discourse, as Cohn notes, possesses "a quality of now-you-see-it, now-you-don't that exerts a special fascination" (1978:107). For certain readers, this "special fascination" issues from the form's dual-voiced or even polyvocal qualities. The passages from Austen and Pushkin cited above, for example, facilitate readers' imagistic experience of hide-and-seek, a virtual peep show allowing imaginary access to a series of indirect glances nonetheless taken at close physical proximity. Vološinov writes that "fantasy is the mother" of free indirect discourse (1986:148). With respect to *Madame Bovary*, a fantasy experience of such proximate glances is particularly suited to vicarious participation within the charged erotics at work in the novel. As Peter Brooks notes, "Emma Bovary has no body of her own. Her body is the social and phantasmic construction of the men who look at her" (1993:95). Though Flaubert could comment that "Madame Bovary, c'est moi," the sense of "now you see it," like the negating dynamic of representation more generally, also requires its complement in the absence generated through "now you don't." Yet this interorientation allows readers to remain focused on the form's textual vividness and less on the possibility that the narrator may have subtly, less visibly, introduced his or her own subjective stance under guise of descriptions of characters and settings. It is possible, then, to argue that authors who do so have engaged in a particular form of participant-observation—not with and of others in a group to which they have, like cultural anthropologists, been granted access but rather of the inner workings of their own characters. Flaubert and Austen participate in the inner workings of their characters so that they manifest as ethnographic traces pointing toward some impossible original—the trace, as the Derridean "origin of the origins" ("now you see it") that is also, paradoxically to binary logic, "a nonorigin" ("now you don't")—not a representation, but that which speaks truth to power without seeming to do so. Partial political cover is achieved by writing the truth and, at the moment of its writing, negating it at the same time.

Cohn notes that authors use the form to commit their narrators to emphasize attitudes of sympathy or irony (1978:117). Ironic sympathy for the vaporizing subject is a scandalous, fascinating, and *fantastic* (in the word's older meaning of almost unbelievable *excess*) proposal to those adhering to the tenets of modernism and its theoretically discrete individuals who contract with one another as part of the engines and cogs of capital. In this light, then, Flaubert's prosecution is a collective expression of "how dare you" sympathize with, whether by representing or pointing indexically toward, that which must remain unimaginable. Within mid-Victorian bourgeois circumstances, revealing Madame Bovary's extramarital sexuality is the unspeakable proof that the supposedly transparent unitary subject is capable of rupture. Nineteenth-century theories of productivity had not yet conceived of the many ways that split, unauthorized, "disseminating," and ephemeral subjectivities would in time come to enhance capital's bottom line.

Yet because of its inference of the fiction of the unitary subject on the threshold of mutating into something more flexible, interoriented, and networked, nineteenth-century free indirect discourse anticipates the multiple subjectivities that commodity-driven capitalism, long reliant on symbolic and iconic forms of representation and more recently simulation and the trace, has labored to cultivate in consumers for at least the past fifty years. From this system based on commodification, in part rooted in the use of vivid images has arisen newer ways of understanding productivity and subjectivity, ways embedded in post-Fordist "neocapitalism" and its globalized mediascapes. If once an earlier modern subject organized his or her activities according to a strong sense of core self and Protestant interiority supported and confirmed, in part, through silent reading and writing prac-

tices in private coupled to discourse in the (never fully) public sphere, contemporary global capital increasingly organizes the productive, ever more
individuated individual according to the logics of interactive networks. The
resulting culture of networked individualism and collective isolation organizes its various activities under the logics of multitasking, time deepening,
and, importantly, the mediated image as a form of post-Debordian indexical
social relation and visual communicability. Networked practices and strategies cultivate and rely on so-called flexible understandings of identity. One
bends but does not break. Flexibility—necessarily Janus-faced and as multiaccented as the novel's middle voice, or the spatial relation established in
graphical chat between a participant and her or his avatar—has been discursively positioned as an unalloyed social good. This is, in part, one outcome
of a very successful quarter-century project of capitalist neoliberal restructuring—one that includes "restructuring" the psyche of the laboring subject
so that she or he is more amenable to being governed at the level of the
everyday by the logic of globalization and its distributive, horizontal strategies of mobile capital accumulation, mobile privatizing, and accompanying
rhizomatic spatial restructurings. The suggestion of subjective flexibility
contained in mid-Victorian uses of middle voice, then, could scandalize the
period's upright pillars of national moral rectitude even as it anticipated
some of the outcomes for subjectivity and the Neoplatonic "space of flows"
with and within which we wrestle today.

Graphical chat depicts these outcomes in its customizable, that is to say
flexible, skins or shells for avatars, upgradable domestic virtual interiors,
and participants' telepresent sense of shuttling to and fro between a sense
of being actually here and virtually there, virtually here and actually there,
somewhere between and among one's body, interface, and network. The
changeable skin of the avatar (the Espresso Halles and David Ash Blondes
of There!, for example, as discussed in the introduction) depicts how the
surface—the image as seen—is repositioned as equivalent to or even super-
seding the inside world of thought and critical reflection. The digital surface
appears as the site of struggle to reconcile the modern legacy of interior
subject versus external world of objects. The difficulty here is that the digital
surface is made a commodity form that works to objectify and hence negate
that which inheres in the subject part of this binary. Fetishization of the
surface, the "skin," results. Graphical chat participants ritualize this state of

affairs. They formalize it by performing their accommodation to it, rehearsing it as a form of play, and stylizing it through gesture and posture in the MUVE's virtual space within which they congregate.

Earlier I questioned whether Flaubert's mid-Victorian critics would have been equally scandalized had he written in the first person. Had he done so he would have relied more on persona than on free indirect discourse. While persona and free indirect discourse are ventriloquistic modes, they offer different utilities. A first-person persona acting as a mask or second self directly stands in for the author and preserves his or her speaking self in a way that would also have given Flaubert greater *authority* to write about bourgeois sexuality, attendant conventions, and the potential for polyvalent subjectivity. By inference, this is one of Teilmann's points when she finds Flaubert judged guilty due to insufficient authority. The "I" has gone missing. Yet thought, if it is to be communicated, seeks its limits in representation, and representation finds its limits in what can be thought. As with graphical chat environments, free indirect discourse allows an author to attempt to give voice to something exceeding representation, to an emergent future and what is at the threshold of imagination and cannot yet be thought as opposed to what has already been thought but cannot (yet) be said. It also operates indexically. In this sense the middle voice does not function as a disguise, in the way the "I" of persona may function. Instead, to reiterate, it may point to, "speak" more of, the ineffable and constitute a nascent effort on the part of an author to symbolize or potentialize that which still remains virtual, incipient, not fully thought. In the case of the Flaubert scandal, it is the potential impossibility of a fully unitary bourgeois subject, and its corollary, a never fully present or possible "I," which had not yet been acknowledged or fully thought. Within the betwixt strategy of free indirect discourse, Madame Bovary's character serves less as a symbol of sexual rupture (though she is also this) and more as the index pointing to the fiction of the discrete bourgeois subject *as well as* the seeming impossibility of narrating, let alone thinking about, this understanding at this historical juncture. If persona in narrative stands in for the author, the relationship between the author and the assemblage that "speaks" free indirect discourse is more complex and ambivalent; it is evocative of Jay's "experience without a subject" but also demands recognition of the indexicality inhering in the form itself.

FREE INDIRECT DISCOURSE, SPACE, AND TIME

Before I address the ways that the digital settings of MUDs, MOOs, and IRC incorporate strategies of indirectness consonant with the logic of free indirect discourse, I need to note important variations on the style that also work to decenter the subject. The linguist Ann Banfield, drawing on Roland Barthes's writings on the photograph, points to the photograph's ability to make a complex claim on the viewer of a "now in the past" coupled to a "perspective unoccupied by any subject, a kind of 'camera unconsciousness'" (1991:76). How, Banfield then asks, implicitly raising the specter of the photographic trace as relying for its truth claims on the "that-has-been" quality of the photograph (Barthes 1981:77), might language capture a sense of this modern temporal collapse? One place she finds an answer is in the work of Virginia Woolf. In *To the Lighthouse* (1927), Woolf writes:

> *Now*, day after day, light *turned*, like a flower reflected in water, its sharp image on the wall opposite. Only the shadows of the trees, flourishing in the wind, made obeisance on the wall, and for a moment darkened the pool in which light reflected itself . . .
>
> And *now* in the heat of summer the wind *sent* its spies about the house again. Flies wove a web in the sunny rooms; weeds that had grown close to the glass in the night tapped methodically at the window pane. When the darkness fell, the stroke of the Lighthouse, which had laid itself with such authority upon the carpet in the darkness . . . *came now* in the softer light of spring mixed with moonlight gliding gently as if it laid its caress and lingered stealthily and looked and came lovingly again. (cited in Banfield 1991:77)[14]

The continual switching in the passage between present and past tense, achieved through a coupling of verbs remaining in past tense to adverbials of present time ("now"), suggests a collapse in time. This collapse, however, need not only be one of "now in the past" but also the past as an agent *moving* into the now, as in "out of the past." Mary Ann Doane notes that "the indexical sign is the imprint of a once-present and unique moment, the signature of temporality . . . the promise of indexicality is, in effect, the promise of the rematerialization of time" (2002:16, 10). The meaning and presence of the trace or the index, in this instance that a material aspect of the past seems present to the reader, is as much at play here as a temporal collapse. Indeed, the temporal collapse requires the specter of the trace, the sense that not only the past but something from "somewhere else" is also present. Woolf's passage is one of vivid literary imagery rendered in picturesque phrases. Banfield, using terminology evocative of the idea of experience without a subject, notes that it "makes explicit the unobserved aspect of . . . vision"; that it describes "the perspective of no one," remaining "subjective but subjectless" (1991:77).

Similarly, Flaubert's use of free indirect discourse suggests he comprehends that perception is never total, sustained, or fully knowable to consciousness and that phenomenologically it operates, like allegory, at the edge of simulation. According to Brooks, "Emma as an object of the gaze and of desire . . . is fragmented into a set of accessory details rather than achieving coherence as either object or subject" (1993:91). Brooks's finding that Emma is neither object nor subject might apply to Flaubert himself: the style's focus on interorientation insinuates a partial cinemalike "dissolve," mediated through the "elusive" narrator, between the author and his central character.

Banfield's reliance on Barthes's work on the photograph articulates free indirect discourse to photography. In a sense all media are mixed media, as indicated, for example, by an earlier era's understanding of the silent cinema of cinematography, as a photo play, and by *Photoplay*, the movie tie-in fan magazine launched in 1911 and credited by some with inventing celebrity media. In 1965, the Italian film director Pier Paolo Pasolini, drawing from structuralist semiotics and referring directly to free indirect discourse, enunciated the idea of a "cinema of poetry" relying on a "free indirect subjectivity" that would allow for a director to "imitate his characters' state of mind" (1976 [1965]:555). Pasolini understood free indirect discourse in novels and free indirect subjectivity in films as pretexts that allow authors or directors to construct characters speaking a particular aspect of class consciousness. Anticipating the idea of "late capitalism," Pasolini posited the development of free indirect subjectivity in film as a cultural manifestation of an early "neo-capitalism, which questions and modifies its own structures" (558). His assertion that cultural forms are indicative of the larger socioeconomic organizations within which they are constituted speaks to my interest in examining free indirect discourse and graphical chat as psychic appendages of "the personal" that also *indicate*. In doing away with the authorial "I" they seem less mediated and more directly accessible to readers and viewers. In this way they also point directly to ways that individuals should best position themselves within evolving and fluid systems and the global "flows" of production and consumption.

Pasolini's identification of a cinematic free indirect subjectivity influenced certain of Deleuze's meditations on cinema and its modes of address. Developing Pasolini's ideas in ways that I find applicable to graphical chat, Deleuze writes: "In the cinema of poetry, the distinction between what the character saw subjectively and what the camera saw objectively vanished, not in favour of one or the other, but because the camera assumed a subjective presence, acquired an internal vision, which entered into a relation of *simulation* ('mimesis') with the character's way of seeing" (1989:148). Cohn comments on the "now you see it, now you don't" visual-temporal quality of revelation lodged within free indirect discourse. In cinema it is the camera, with its interorienting yet heterogenous abilities to pivot in every direction, that materializes the fluid virtual place and hybrid subjectivity of the novel's middle voice. The camera sits between the characters and the director. This does not address the issue of narratorial voice-over in film. However, narrative exposition in film — that is, characters telling each other information that they would already know so as to inform the audience — is a less accomplished, overtly functionalist way to communicate necessary information that more accomplished technicians and artists convey to audiences through less direct, more imagistic means. The camera's interorienting powers function in concert with its abilities to see as if from the point of view of the character while at the same time to be manipulated by the camera operator and the director (who edits the play of "now you see it, now you don't").

The cinematic dynamic of free indirect subjectivity has been digitally renovated; it continues to do necessary ideological, discursive, and cultural work on the virtual "middle grounds" of indexical chat technologies. Both free indirect discourse and MUVE graphical chat allow for the production of a betwixt, strategically ambivalent, and at times ironic and distanced indexical depiction of self and others. Yet whereas free indirect discourse as a technique has the effect of a middle *voice*, graphical chat environments produce what I term a middle *ground* of virtual space. In the novel, the subjectivity revealed by the middle voice emanates from a time or space situated between yet imbricating both the author and the characters he or she crafts. A number of critics point to the imagistic nature of free indirect discourse and its influence within the realist novel. Vološinov notes its use in creating "highly original pictorial effects in reported speech transmission" (1986:132). Such effects allow the individuality of the speaker or writer to congeal "to the point of forming an image" (133). Brooks contends that realism, the dominant tradition of the nineteenth century, "insistently makes the visual the master relation to the world" (1993:88). The nineteenth-century novel introduces readers to a sense of viewing the contexts of its characters and their psychological "interiors." Thus one value of free indirect discourse inheres in the style's ability to provoke a reader's vivid mental images of an "iconic" character and his or her setting. Somewhat like the Peircian indexical icon, the form produces a character that seems autonomous from *yet also* oriented to the author's or narrator's point of view.

With the MUVE-based avatar, the middle voice transmogrifies to fully manifest as an iconic middleman or intermediary taking place on an image-driven virtual middle ground—a virtual landscape reliant on and fostering a growing cultural focus on moving images. This middle ground is further constituted within a setting organized according to the spatial logic also on display in competitive "first-person shooter" video gaming and interactive MMORPGS.[15] While the logic of competition is present in MUVEs in such forms as writing one's own software that advances one's avatar's functionality as well as designing visually complex structures and avatars, and there is some convergence in the overall "look" of MUVEs and MMORPGS, the underlying social logic of MUVEs differs from MMORPGS. There are no overt common or stated goals or ends for which one competes as there is in MMORPGS. Instead, the double point of MUVEs is to live virtually and "persistently" in the environment that one constructs and then renovates as one's own and as one desires, and to do so while coexisting, like a character in a novel, with other residents within the setting.

The middle ground of graphical chat, "peopled" with avatars simulating a human population and interacting within virtual landscapes that constitute a quasi-public virtual square, bears further debts to the visual and spatial organization of silent film, the cartoon, the comic strip, the graphic novel, and Roy Lichtenstein's pop art. It lies between yet also interorients the spatially discrete embodied individuals who use it to forge all manner of connections through the rituals of transmission that its interactive landscapes and simulations make possible.

FREE INDIRECT DISCOURSE AND MUDS, MOOS, AND IRC

Earlier in this chapter I introduced text-based MUDs, MOOs, and IRC as internet precursors to graphical chat; in this section I return to them in the context of free indirect discourse. The forms of MUDs, MOOs, and IRC can be understood as a bridging technology between the novel's middle voice and the iconographic middle ground of graphical chat. Both the purportedly more "direct" IRC and the elaborate persona-driven virtual places of MUDs and MOOs allow participants to hail one another in the third person and thereby achieve an indirect and often exciting experience of extending the self away from its embodiment and toward the artificial subjectivity identified by Gonzáles (2000). This distancing sutures or interpellates participants more directly to the middle ground of the interface itself. For example, IRC's command /me allows a participant (let's say his screen name is "MadMax") to achieve a third-person nonverbal "voice" to others. Typing "/me bows before you" transmits to intended receivers as "MadMax bows before you." As with the middle voice in the novel's elimination of the verb form inherent in "he said" and "he thought," the ventriloquistic agency that /me locates in the screen identity allows the IRC reader/interpretant a freer and more objective access, seemingly unmediated by speech, to the subject position of the sender's screen-based character. The technology, however, also makes the same effect available to the writer/sender/referent who sees his typed words on his screen or display. Reading one's own words in the third person helps produce a sense of externalizing one's subject position away from oneself, of becoming an actor on a stage — or in Peircian terms the interpretant of oneself as referent. This can induce an alienating power that makes it easier for participants to risk communicating possibly more honest, direct, and thereby more exciting statements and ideas through the use of this indirect and at times recursive form of address that, like free indirect discourse's "perspective of no one" banishes the "I" from the message. The spatial dynamic enacted by the /me technique is also similar to that of the camera's point of view situated between the operator (the sender on IRC) and the actors or characters being filmed. /me allows the sender/referent to conceptualize a site for his subjectivity as interoriented between, and thereby linking indexically, the embodied position where he sits, the other side of the interface, and the wider network of which his particular computer interface forms a localized spatial margin.

During the period, from 1994 to 1996, that I was writing my dissertation on immersive virtual reality environments, I spent considerable time on several IRC channels as a participant-observer. Initially, I was puzzled as to why some individuals preferred /me (it is not required) or parallel forms of phrasings that produced indirectness such as, "You feel the touch of my hand," as opposed to the more persona-like, "I want to touch you" or even the pragmatic, "I'd like to feel your touch." The latter phrases both transmit a certain authenticity of desire coupled to a directness of voice; however, I have come to understand that /me's specific quality of seemingly nonverbal indirect address and elimination of the "I" allow for more direct, imagistic, and indexical appeals to the sensory imagination. It is also a somewhat uncanny though not unpleasant experience to find oneself in the position of both Peircian interpretant and referent.

MUDs and MOOs feature similar techniques allowing for similar strategies. Participants use the command *say* to "speak" to other participants or game players in the virtual space. When MadMax types "say I'd like to touch Lothlorian's hand," other participants read "You say, 'I'd like to touch Lothlorian's hand.'" Participants, however, use the command *emote* to express themselves nonverbally or in the third person. Typing "emote touches Lothlorian's hand" displays as "MadMax touches Lothlorian's hand." (*Emote* can also be substituted with the colon symbol (:) to produce the same third-person nonverbal effect.)

These combinatory qualities of indirect, seemingly nonverbal address seem to escape the generalizability of the Peircian symbol. They are more like the Peircian index that points like a finger (☞) directly to the embodied, individual/referent on this side of the interface to which it is connected. Networked indirect address captures the experiential "wherewithal" of the virtual experience, one that has been reformulated through the middle ground of the avatar. As the discussion on telefetishism in chapter 5 further clarifies, networked indirect address enhances the tantalizing quality of cybersexual encounters for many users when desiring bodies remain at a distance from one another. It allows the desiring self to "fill in the blanks" through modes of address that on IRC or a MUD synthesize everyday language use, screen names linked to desire, and indexical software functionalities such as /me and emote.

Reading the phrase "MadMax stands before you" produces a strong mental image that also resonates with the finding by Dominick LaCapra that one of the effects of Madame Bovary is "a dissemination of the narrator—at times the author—in the text" (1982:149; emphasis added). A trace of the author haunts the text of Flaubert's novel; a trace of MadMax's embodied referent comes to inhabit the virtual space of text-based chat. For Vološhinov, fantasy is the mother of free indirect discourse. Frances Barker (1984) argues that a substitution of text for actual embodiment was the unanticipated outcome of seventeenth-century bourgeois reading and writing practices. Three centuries later, disseminating into text substituting for one's body on the internet is a virtual move that is key to understanding the erotic and fantasy appeals of MUDs, MOOs, and IRC, for so doing better allows for interpretive fantasy based on an experiential trace of the desirable referent to emerge as the telepresent center of many text-based internet encounters. Such an assemblage authorizes users' complexly ambivalent abilities to heighten and conjoin, to ritualize aspects of anonymity, intimacy of expression, fetishism, and fantastical and truthful claims about themselves and their everyday lives in spatialized settings formally set apart from the actual spaces of everyday life. This networked form of indirect discourse can give textual representation to a broad range of individual desires, some considerably more askance than Emma Bovary's extramarital "indiscretion." Such askance, even "perverted," desires fail to accrete meaning or a history if they remain unspoken or "unthinkable" and therefore languish in fantasy's vacuum.

The increasing ability of software programs to allow MUVE participants to customize their avatars allows the avatar to gather to itself a halo of meanings and possibilities that can reduce participant anxiety. One is the ability to rehearse an image of reunion between the self and its body set aside in the Enlightenment public sphere settings that Barker discusses. Pseudonymity is also important. While participants remain unseen by others, they can identify with their avatars in a metonymic fashion that recalls Flaubert's insistence that "Madame Bovary, c'est moi." Anonymous metonymic identification with one's avatar confers potential for freer expression and negotiation of plural or implicit identities. As in the novel or the cinema, MUVE participants can fabricate casts of characters, each depicting different ideas that these individuals may hold about themselves and wish to transmit. Second Life permits its residents to have more than one avatar (called *alts*). A particular screen name, however, attaches to only one avatar. The named avatar refers back to its maker who in turn watches over it. However, though I might retain the same avatar for years, I might equally decide to select one avatar today and a different one tomorrow. I might sequentially exchange avatars in accordance with my mood or how I am choosing to self-identify and therefore self-depict at different times. Graphical chat indicates how human desire can produce value—that is, exchange value through circulation. But value gained through such rehearsals and performances based on the exchangeability between one's avatar and one's own positionality also suggests how exchange value itself becomes a form of use value to MUVE participants.[16]

>>>

In writing to George Sand about his self-described "impersonal" narrative method, Flaubert declared, "One should, by an effort of the spirit, transport oneself into one's characters, not draw them to oneself" (1921 [1866]:n.p.). Flaubert's instruction to imaginatively transport oneself into one's characters reads like a description of the actions of online text-based and graphical chat participants who repeatedly extend themselves into their avatars, pull back to survey the scene and consider their next move or utterance, then reextend themselves textually or graphically into the virtual landscape. In this sense, the novel's use of free indirect discourse anticipates the dynamic of digital telepresence. Telepresence, with its "practical" applications in telerobotics and its "popular" applications in Web-based chat, webcams, immersive virtual reality gaming, and MMORPGs, suggests I can be materially "here" at the same time as seemingly "there" by extending components of identity into virtual space where they can do my bidding. As I noted when observing that */me* and *emote* allow senders to conceptualize a site for their subjectivity as interoriented between the other side of the interface and the wider network, these commands also promote this sense of spatial extension or flexibility. Telepresence relies on and promotes a theory of subjectivity as flexible, modular, exchangeable, and thereby possibly ephemeral and not fully articulated to embodiment—qualities well suited to networked settings and capitalized practices alike. To be telepresent is to be neither fully here (the place where MadMax types these words) nor fully there (the place where the receivers with whom he chats read them), but more to be constituted in experiential awareness of both at once and therefore, without the need for actual personal movement, of their exchangeability. Text-based forms of telepresence are a bridging mechanism between the free indirect discourse of the novel and the more imagistic middle ground of avatar-based graphical chat environments. Such uses of language, however, are less about creating a temporal sense experience of "now in the past," as in Virginia Woolf's "time vs. tense" use of free indirect discourse, and more about facilitating a spatial sensation of being "here and there" at the same time, a power, at least in part, of the image's current claim to vivid actuality and truth status even as we also fully, and at times cynically, understand its ability to be manipulated.

In Woolf's novels, free indirect discourse draws the past into the now to achieve a pure description of a subjectless or transcendental point of view. In graphical chat, images draw participants located at different locations in space into a network. The avatar, seeming to look out into the wider Web, is neither here nor there yet for the operator or participant is both at once. This sense of spatial betwixtness is enhanced by most MUVE software's ability to allow participants to shift quickly among or shuttle between multiple oscillating points of view, including an avatar's "embodied" point of view when standing on virtual ground, and more mobile bird's-eye panorama and planelike perspectives when flying through virtual space. Enjoying the ability to partake of an avatar's cosmopolitan "view from the top" confers an ambivalent power. It raises the potential, already confirmed by one's increased range of sight, that one might be everywhere at once—that the avatar might be a powerful appendage indeed. Yet such a conceptually disembodied experience of movement (for we cannot actually fly) articulated to the visual control of the landscape beneath, results in the ability to experientially "collapse space." Participants become more indirect to themselves, with each becoming, as it were, one more "stepped back other" within the virtual space. This potential for a progressive virtualization or fragmentation of subjectivity is already implicitly theorized in the novel, and graphical chat's addition of a logic of emblematics, with its unstable drawing together of text and image, further extends the potential for virtualizations of self and self-formation to take place in these settings.

Susan Buck-Morss, in her discussion of Baroque emblematics, defines the emblem as a hybrid form that draws together the different powers of the image and the word (1989: chapter 6). In Peircian terms, emblems organize, in an array of productive ways, the tension between word/symbol and image/icon. Emblems, like avatars, are forms of allegory. The emblem's textual component often works to establish a preferred meaning for the image without which it might be incomprehensible or subject to any number of different interpretations on the part of viewers. While most readers, for example, would recognize an image of the towers of the World Trade Center, what this image on its own would mean after 9/11 for any one reader remains up for grabs. Various potential interpretations of any one image may compete with one another before any one of them is actualized: a picture of a young couple holding hands might imply wholesome attraction to me, sinful lust to you, and something fully different to a third viewer. The addition of a single word, "innocence," however, supports an interpretation of wholesome attraction and works (though not always successfully) to suppress interpreting the image in other ways. The text need not be only a single word; a phrase or brief paragraph also promotes a similarly "clarified" reading. The power of the text, arguably, participates in logos' articulation of word to reason. "Reason" informs the preferred reading even as it synthesizes the reasonable meaning of the word to the frequently emotional registers conveyed by viewing the image.

Readers familiar with ritualized forms of Catholic instruction may recall the holy card as a form of focused devotional that very often takes emblematic form. I recall one particularly memorable example, which sported the image of a 1950s suburban driveway. From the front door of her bungalow Mom surveys the front yard while she motions to Dad, in office garb, seated behind the wheel of the family car idling in the driveway. His head is turned to back the car into the street. At the same time, Jane and Dick play ball in the front yard. Dick is safely on the lawn but Jane crouches immediately behind the car, beneath Dad's range of vision. The specter of a guardian angel hovers between Jane and Mom, somehow calling Mom's attention to the danger Jane faces. The image captures that precise moment when, by the angel's intercession through Mom's waving gesture (and perhaps voice; the card is silent), Dad is made aware of Jane's position. Calamity is averted.

Beneath the image is the card's textual message: "Jane's Guardian Angel watches over her." The text establishes the preferred Catholic meaning of the image. But as a discursive strategy, the emblem is ambivalent and uneasy. The text, whether one word or several, may circumscribe potential meanings but can never anticipate all of them. Emblems call on us to be both readers and viewers at the same time. The "active reader" must work with the "active viewer" whose sensory imagination is free to imagine a much wider range of meanings inherent in the image than in the text: Dad's guardian angel is as neglectful as Dad; Dad doesn't care for the children; they are poorly brought up; perhaps that's not even Dad after all.

The rise of emblems as a form of moral instruction arguably can be traced to the rediscovery, in 1419, of *The Hieroglyphica*, a manuscript attributed to the Greek grammarian Horus Apollo and possibly dating from the fourth century AD. In 1505 the manuscript was published in Venice, and its "discovery compounded an already-powerful neo-Platonic interest in pictorial denotation as a potentially universal code free of the corrupting and artificial intermedium of language. Aesthetic theorists like Leonardo and Paolo Giovio argued that pictures constitute the most unartificial, the purest, and least rhetorically compromised form of communication" (Preston 2003: n.p.). The earliest Renaissance emblems, referred to in Italian as *imprese*, often conveyed personal information about a bearer. They were understood as "potentially personal, as displaying intentions, feelings, and beliefs . . . a coterie form, used personally to denote emblematically some quality in the bearer" (n.p.). As *The Hieroglyphica* suggests, the emblem is also a form of glyph. Glyphs are associated with sacred carvings. In the Renaissance and early modern periods they took the forms of woodcuts, engravings, and lithographs — sacred graphics positioned as forms of "natural language" with greater powers of inclusive gesture and posture than the incomplete and experientially more mediated forms of expression ("mere words") appropriate to discourse. Mario Praz (1964), one of the foremost scholars of the emblem, notes that during the Renaissance emblems were often understood as contemporary equivalents of sacred Egyptian signs. In their later Protestant manifestations, emblems were "designed to instruct by encouraging strenuous interpretive reading on the part of the individual, a practice akin to personal perusal and interpretation of the Bible" (Preston 2003:n.p.). The beauty or shape of an image captures the eye. Viewers/readers/interpretants of emblems were instructed to allow the image component of the emblem to arrest their sight so that they might more deeply meditate on the meaning of the text and the richness of its associations. Italian Renaissance allegorists rejected the use of images they judged as too particular or contemporary in their rendering of actual places "since that level of detail might distract a viewer from the actual mechanisms of the combinatory invention" (Pinkus 1996:170).

Emblems rely on the Neoplatonic belief in the power of images to locate something approaching the divine or the immediate yet transcendent essence of truth. In their conveyance of widely shared folk wisdoms, emblems are also ritual devices for crafting and then maintaining the idea of a public. What unites a collection of strangers into a public is their address by an intertextual body of discourse (Warner 2002). If free indirect discourse emerges at the nineteenth-century zeniths of individual European nation-state powers, the sixteenth- and seventeenth-century vogue for emblems helped organize a set of publics necessary for the intertwined emergence of this individual and the European nation-state. Michael Warner notes that "without the idea of texts that can be picked up at different times and in different places by otherwise un-related people, we would not imagine a public as an entity that embraces all the users of that text, whoever they might be" (2002:68). Warner's use of "text," in Peircian terms, renders the icon subservient to the word. He is interested in the relation between the generalizable qualities of the word as symbol and the emergence of a general public. The image plays a role in this as well, as the popularity of emblem books during the sixteenth and seventeenth century attests. Publication and distribution of emblem books—bound folios of many emblems—participates within the dynamics that Warner identifies. So, too, does *cantastoria* (song story), the Italian form of political street theater originating in the sixteenth century that also relies on the allegorical dynamics of the emblem. Participants painted large canvases as part of telling a story about a certain subject. The images were exaggerated and cartoonlike. Actors interpreted them by pointing to the images like Peirce's interpretants while at the same time telling the story in representamen-like ritual fashion through song, chanting, and group singing.

The emblem book reached the height of its European popularity during the sixteenth century and seventeenth. While scholars note its decline by the end of the seventeenth century, and its subsequent marginalization into the pages of children's literature, Praz (1964) suggests that new forms of the emblem, called by other names, continue their work to shape the social reception and organization of meaning. Cantastoria is one such form, and it is maintained today by politically radical theater companies such as the Vermont-based Bread and Puppet Theater. A wider exhumation of the formal powers of the emblem, however, is everywhere on view in networked digital cultures today, including on the Web (in avatars and speech balloons as an emblematic allegory of the cosmopolitan self imagining moving beyond the unitary subject; the image of a webcam screen framed within a website's larger screen of surrounding textual accompaniment) and on this side of the interface (in a giant U.S. interstate Christmas billboard of the Renaissance Madonna and child with the single word "Rejoice" [appropriate when passing the sign at seventy miles per hour] to remind motorists of the nation's Christian heritage, or in the captioned celebrity photos in *People* magazine intended to maintain and reproduce fan loyalties. Each exemplifies the dynamic wherein the attributions and statements made in the text work to fix, delimit, or render reasonable the range of meanings that viewers might otherwise take from them. The percentage or quantity of the overall space of an emblem taken up by its image component, however, allows for the image to dominate and arrest visual perception. For most viewer/readers, a focus on the text comes after the image is taken in by the eye. Emblematic text can circumscribe the image's many possible meanings but neither text nor image can function meaningfully—emblematically—in the absence of the other. Barthes refers to this as "the unity of the message." In discussing relations between words and images he notes that "anchorage" is the use of languages to "fix the floating chains of signifieds in such a way as to counter the terror of uncertain signs . . . the text replies . . . to the question: *what is it?* (1977:39). "Relay" is the process whereby text and image complement one another. Both are "fragments" in a text-image combination, the unity of which is achieved at the level of "the story, the anecdote, the diegesis" (41). At the level of the emblem.

Earlier emblems transmitted traditions and summarized agreed-upon knowledge. As Praz notes, contemporary emblems are known by other names. But online and offline they form part of a wider and pervasive branding of reality. In their various text-image ratios, they resuscitate and fuse together the Renaissance impresa's emphasis on the individual and the early modern emblem's wider role in transmitting "common wisdom."

Technology influences the form that an emblem may take. In the sixteenth century, lithographed and engraved emblems relied on the printing press and were reproduced in emblem books—the pages of which could not refresh in the manner of the computer display. From this tradition we inherit the implicit print-based understanding that the emblem's text and image components must be in a constant and static spatial relation with one another. New forms of networked, mediated, and advertised public address unanticipated by the Renaissance or Enlightenment, however, suggest new forms of the emblem. The graphical chat avatar is one. The strategy of corporate branding has produced another. (A history of branding as a strategy that implants the idea of the company directly onto its products, so that consumers experience the meaning of the company through its brands, might be subsumed under the longer history of the emblem even though it might appear to contemporary observers that the emblem has been subsumed under the sign of the brand.) Both forms have put pressure on text and, in the case of corporate branding, the image component of the emblem has been disarticulated from the text. Consider, for example, the wildly successful branding campaign launched in 1988 by the Nike corporation, which was initially based on articulating the slogan "Just Do It" to the graphical image of the Swoosh designed in 1971. Like the impresa, the Swoosh conveys cultural meaning. When worn on clothing, it transmits personal information about the bearer—in this case a commitment to the ideal of taking greater responsibility for his or her fitness and health, or at least her or his agreement with this ideology of bodily discipline.

Warner notes that "all discourse or performance addressed to a public must characterize the world in which it attempts to circulate and it must attempt to realize that world through address . . . public discourse says not only 'Let a public exist' but 'Let it have this character, speak this way, see the world in this way'" (2002:114). At the height of the Nike campaign, media-savvy individuals viewing the Swoosh in advertisements and on items of attire worn by professional athletes and individuals buying into the campaign were reminded to "just do it." That is, as competent neoliberal subjects deciding to avoid further excuses and finally take contractual "ownership" of their bodies for purposes of self-improvement. Nike's print and TV advertising constantly depicted the spatial relation of the Swoosh in close proximity to the phrase "just do it." "Just do it," then, served to frame the meanings of the Swoosh, which, as an abstract design, has no particular meaning inherent to itself. "Just do it," however, worked to render the Swoosh, already a recognizable pictorial sign within the mediasphere, as something of a "natural sign" (if only for a time) that recalls Edmund Bolton's suggestion, in 1610, of the possibility for a "universal ensignment" (Preston 2003). So successful was the campaign, however, that, in time, the Swoosh viewed on its own articulated directly to "just do it" and more directly to Nike in the viewing public's mind than it had before the advent of the campaign. The Swoosh, then, achieved the status of the Peircian index, pointing ☞ directly, like an avatar, to the campaign and the firm as cultural shapers, even though it is spatially disarticulated from both. The assumed fixed spatial relationship between an emblem's text and image components was broken. Nike's campaign, moreover, reached beyond expectations rooted in tradition and placed upon the older emblem; not only did Nike transmit an already commonly agreed upon social good, it also sought to produce this good as an outcome of emblematics itself—in other words, following yet updating the logic of ritual enactment, to use this form of symbolic association to organize consumer experience and preference at the individual level.

In a manner that bears similarity to the current widespread interest in fantastical depictions of alternate worlds, the Baroque period was marked by an interest in images of illusionary worlds. At first glance, graphical chat MUVEs appear to realize the Neoplatonic desire for immediacy of perception or "codeless communication" infusing the work of such Renaissance polymaths as Leonardo that we can somehow *potentially* "see what we mean" (in Warner's terms, to see the world in a certain way) without recourse to the mediation of text or discourse. Setting aside the irony of using a medium to achieve a sense of immediacy (see Bolter and Grusin 1999)[17] one may identify Nike's reliance on broadcast media to transmit an emblematics promoting a ritualized and consumerist "public of one" as intertextual but not interactive. The difficulty in achieving a sustained successful communication among networked communicants using only images in graphical chat, however, is a constraint surmounted by the accompanying use of text to clarify meaning and intent. Text that "speaks" in a certain way watches over the meanings of the image (like a guardian angel) and is the price paid in order to achieve any semblance of meaningful conversation and interaction. Graphical chat's use of words for synchronous symbolic exchange poses an inconvenient truth for Neoplatonists who participate in the hype that emphasizes the imagery in MUVEs and minimizes the necessary function of "mere words." The hype, however, is not without a leg to stand on.

While text remains essential to word-dependent forms of communication within graphical chat, site participants experience moving images as lively sign/bodies—as having a quality of psychic depth that exceeds the screen display's 2-D planar qualities.

We perceive the still photograph as framing the past—a veritable photographic memory (Kroes 2007) that "embalms time" (Bazin 1967:14). Movement, however, produces information about the present (Rogers 2005), and moving images suggest to human sensation both the now (whether here or there) in an ever unfolding and flowing present, and also that the present might be other than it is, that movement has the potential to shift the meaning of the present in unanticipated ways (Martin 1998:1). We also perceive space through movement (Gibson 1979:223). When we walk, visual stimuli appear "to stream by us, a stimulus configuration called optic flow" (Kolb and Whislaw 2003:177). A MUVE attempts to mimic this mode of perception by having the virtual landscape adjust to match the perspective of the individual participant. Images flow across the screen or display, and the setting continually adjusts its horizons and view lines to accord with the point of view of the participant looking into the screen or that of his or her avatar moving through the virtual space: automated spontaneity with the ability to convey a quality of mobilization. One effect of this is that "spoken words" in the form of speech balloons adjacent to the avatar are not always on view. They only manifest when an avatar "speaks." The avatar, then, is not always ventriloquistic. But in its gestures and even in repose, it is always an electronic form of pantomime. In chapter 3 I noted that the pantograph was a copying machine designed for rendering changes of scale in drawings of plans, diagrams, and patterns. The prefix panto, from the Greek, refers to "all-ruling," "of all kinds," "almighty," and "the creator of all" (*OED*). If, say, a group of avatars at a party are swimming in a pool, a significant amount of time might pass without conversation and, hence, the need for text. The presence of text on the display at times is transient whereas the "all-ruling" image, even when in static pose, always displays; one is sometimes a reader but always a viewer.

The Nike campaign shows how one form of contemporary media and its publics has broken the presumed fixed spatial relationships between the emblem's text and image components. Graphical chat, a different media with a differently constituted public, indicates yet a different way of reimagining and repurposing this relationship. Recall, moreover, that the compositional structure of an emblem is largely given over to the image. In printed formats, this giving over is purely spatial. In moving image formats, however, it also includes time. In graphical chat, the speech balloon, unlike the all-ruling sign/body, is not visible at all times,[18] and when it is, it takes up a much smaller portion of the screen than the icons which can continue to move. One problematic "value" of the avatar's emblematic performance is to ritualize the belief (and thereby to instruct) that an individual sense of self *ought* to be constituted primarily through these indexical icons that move, seem immediate, and somehow unmediated, yet like ornaments or cosmetics are exchangeable at will though somehow attached to the self.

>>> Webs of Attraction: Allegory and Cultures of the Interface

Emblems are visual allegories. Long-standing associations between emblematics and allegory are germane to understanding networked digital cultures and the computer interfaces upon which they rely. The *OED* defines allegory as the "description of a subject under the guise of some other subject of aptly suggestive resemblance . . . in which properties and substances attributed to the apparent subject really refer to the subject they are meant to suggest." Additional entries describe allegory as "an extended or continued metaphor . . . an emblem." One aim of this volume is to investigate what actually might be new about "new" media, and that necessitates making links and associations across "new" and "old." Both graphical chat and TV ads operate within a highly commoditized media sphere, and in this section I open by considering two American TV ads that use allegory to promote pharmaceuticals directly to consumers in the expectation that they will pressure their physicians to prescribe the advertised medicines. I discuss these ads as part of situating networked practices and techniques within the broader sphere of digital cultures and commodity capitalism. The ads are visual messages of simulated emotion that privilege the image. They are also messages of fantasy—magical narratives with happy endings designed to minimize the auditory reception of the legally mandated caveats conveyed through their spoken/textual components. They are, therefore, consonant with graphical chat's emphasis on the power of the image as well as the application's inability (at the time of writing, at least) to eliminate the text and still offer the possibility of a coherent experience.

Before proceeding further, I need to make three points. First, I am not here undertaking a study of the relationship between the heard oral voice and the read displayed or printed text. Second, I understand that such advertisements operate synergistically: they appeal to a preexisting widespread "will to believe" that a pill might solve all problems even as most individuals know that this is unlikely to be so, while assuming that the more that viewers encounter such ads the more their messages based on the movement-image's direct appeal to human sensation will be seen as true. Third, the soundtracks of both ads end with statements that the drug in question is not for everyone; potential consumers must consult prescribing physicians. The ads, then, are indications of living in a "risk society." Everyone takes risks, the voice-overs imply; there are side effects, but just LOOK at the benefits. Americans in record numbers now demand such advertised pharmaceuticals in advance of any discussion initiated by doctors about whether or not they might benefit the patient.

The drug Remicade®, produced by Centocor, offers relief to certain individuals afflicted by rheumatoid arthritis, Crohn's disease, and ankylosing spondylitis. An ad that aired in 2005 features an image track depicting an attractive middle-aged woman moving effortlessly through her joyful daily encounters. Halfway through the commercial a voice-over begins to intone the list of side effects, many of which are very serious and some even fatal. The image track remains focused on the woman's celebration of life presumably achieved through her use of the drug. A second ad from the same year relies on the same strategy. Lilly's Strattera® is used to treat adult attention deficit hyperactivity disorder (ADHD). The Strattera® ad depicts a competent neoliberal subject busy at work on the many stages of contemporary life that he must occupy as part of the work world's contractual demands. While viewers *see* this individual realizing goals, they *hear* a soundtrack. As with the Remicade ad, at first the voice-over, like the text in an emblem book, supports the producer's preferred interpretation of the visuals. Again, about halfway through the second ad's running time the voice-over switches to quickly intone a lengthy number of side effects. Reason and logic should, presumably, counteract the influence of the relentlessly upbeat imagery, but we know this is not so.

The emblematic structure of both ads calls upon traditional associations not sufficiently acknowledged by rational critical discourse. We associate words with the expression of doubt and rational/critical thinking processes. We are, perhaps, *leery* because we can read. This logic underlies the promotion of the *critical* value of universal literacy, and it is why the Enlightenment privileged abstract textuality over the seemly image of the authoritarian monarch. Images, escaping our ability to fully define them, as Deleuze (1986) has noted, invite us to believe. Perception's engagement with moving images, in particular, blurs the image's psychically real quality with the physical reality of one's moving, active, and perceptive body. Imagine, then, reversing the organization of such advertisements. Imagine the dominant message of consumer empowerment through medication as carried in the voice-over while the visuals depict caveats about side effects. This would lead to the sound of happy voices instructing viewers about a drug's benefits while the visuals would show subjects afflicted with skin lesions, having seizures or heart attacks, and being the centerpieces of funeral rites. It is easy to understand why such a reversal would not appeal to advertisers, but my point is to suggest that many viewers would relate to such an ad in a not dissimilar perceptual fashion from how they receive the actual ads. They would more easily doubt the happy words of the soundtrack in a rational/critical fashion and more readily believe the appeal to emotion in the horror story on view. Within the display-based "dream world of mass culture," do viewers watch to doubt or to believe? Recall from the previous section Preston's (2003) account of the Renaissance belief that the image was the purest form of communication, a "natural language" avoiding the corruptions inherent to text and speech. What you see is what you get. Both Neoplatonists and rational/critical Enlightened thinkers associate the word with doubt. The former doubt its veracity whereas the latter celebrate it for the qualities of doubt it enables.

The widespread U.S. demand for directly marketed pharmaceuticals might be positioned as a form of consumer empowerment. One can understand that the caveat contained within the spoken text that the drug is not for everyone serves, as with older emblems, to police the utopic images. It is closer to the case, however, that the images in these ads escape most if not all policing mechanisms contained within the mandated component of the voice-overs. These ads exemplify how the image (promoting the belief that a potential for wellness can be made actual) today works to minimize any doubt contained in the voice-over. Recalling the definition of allegory provided above, these advertisements imply that the properties of joy and competency attributed through the use of imagery to human subjects are "really" those of the drugs. Human agency, in these ads, moves or relocates to the commodity form. The happy woman is really so because of Remicade, the depiction of the competent worker is really an indexical "suggestive resemblance" of the "properties and substances" of Strattera. The ads, beyond their narrow meanings within discourses of wellness, health, and profit, allegorically imply that neoliberal forms of competency today reside in pharmaceutical technologies. By inference, modular, flexible, and possibly ephemeral human subjects now require completion through these external devices that, like electronic avatars, serve as psychic and bodily appendages.

In certain crucial ways, the Neoplatonic reliance on allegorical messages embedded within the emblem that undergirds the pharmaceutical ads also informs the networked settings I examine. Victoria Nelson observes that "the Web is above all a medium uniquely suited to the ancient mode of allegory, a capability dramatically evident in the ubiquitous fantasy role-playing narratives" (2001:201). Erik Davis could be describing graphical chat when he identifies computer gaming's "first person allegory" structure within which gamers "wander through a rigorously structured but dreamlike landscape patched together from phantasms" (1998:212–13). Allegory is also "the aesthetic device of personification" (Nelson 2001:202), and whether deployed in TV ads or as an avatar in a virtual world it is a figural device serving as a means of simulating the possible. Allegory is a means by which what remains immaterial or potential—in this case actual humans in digital form—is given imaginative yet figural embodiment so that this figure then may *seem* to exist or be probable. This is the discursive value of calling an image a virtual object—it pushes the image toward seemingly greater materiality yet at the same time conveys the value of exchangeability between the virtual and the material that lies at the intersection of the simulation. Conceptually, this state of potential may then have a chance of transforming, of becoming actual. For members of a networked culture of virtuality, however, the allegorically inflected potential of the moving image to achieve figural embodiment also recommends it as a fetish object at least in part because of its virtual status—a mobile status to the degree that human desire confers on the virtual object the eventual potential to transubstantiate into material form.

In thinking through connections between emblems and allegories old and new it is also worth recalling that, etymologically, the noun emblem is close to the English verb "resemble" and the French verb *sembler*—to seem. As I have argued elsewhere (1999:67), the power of the premodern European monarch rested on an emblematic foundation of the seemliness of his or her embodied, ritualized public manifestation. The monarch's *visibly* embodied seemliness carried the message/truth of his or her "natural authority." It allowed the monarch to accrue and maintain legitimacy through articulating bodily performances, pose, and stature to the Platonic ideal World of Forms and its long-standing associations based on resemblance with the eternal and unchanging divine. The link among bodily seemliness, the wider realm of royal authority, and the World of Forms reveals the transcendental power vested in the idea of seeming inhering in the monarch's body-as-emblem.

An allegory, then, like the emblem, is a structure or figure of seeming. It is an ideal vehicle for imaginative relocation to the middle ground of virtual environments with their magical/indexical and thereby seemingly empirical abilities to render equivalence between the imaginary and the real as "seemingly so." Avatars in graphical chat allegorize human bodies as forms of awareness fully capable of becoming information itself. They constitute a set of "playful," graphically accessible, emotionally believable instructions. They are also an "aptly suggestive resemblance," "figures of some other thing mystically signified by them."[19] Digital avatars are contemporary indexical automata through which networked participants perform the expectation to personify themselves through telepresence and the associated real world demand that they take on the qualities of indirectness and spatial exchangeability required for being in more than one place at a time.

Allegory's evocation of one subject under the guise of another is indexical. The hard line between categories softens; the individual receiving an allegorical message infers mutual implication between the subjects. The Derridean trace is at play. This raises an important finding for ritual in online settings. Rappaport (1999:40) distinguishes between what he terms "unconscious" nonlinguistic signals transmitted by the body, such as posture in sitting and movement in walking, from physical displays in ritual that he correctly notes are under conscious control. Posture and how one moves while walking, he states, are indicative of physical and psychic conditions — personal states. In contrast, a ritual's actions stand in an indexical relationship to conventional states and expectations of how one should move in a ritual. In graphical chat, however, Rappaport's distinction does not hold. Individuals who direct their avatars to move, bend over, slump, pout, and sigh convey something about how they feel, or some embodied spontaneous quality they want other participants to associate with their avatars. Such transmissions are indexical to the participant's psychic situation and are not unconscious. Everything proceeds by convention. While one may fly, act inappropriately, and so forth, every communication an avatar makes that points to body movements is highly ritualized; to communicate successfully, avatar movement must concord with the expectations most humans hold about how bodies move in specific circumstances. Even when flying in Second Life, an avatar's head points forward, not backward, and this requires adhering one's avatar's actions to conventions of display rooted in ritual traditions. In such settings the avatar allegorizes not only the desire for virtual living and that everything be rendered as if all the world were a display but also that autonomic body functionalities are now subject to ritualization and its conventions. For participants who intuit that interface-based culture portends a quality of psychic disembodiment, the ability to ritualize an indexical relationship pointing back to autonomic body processes — to render, allegorically, the psychic as the conventional — is a way of anticipating while also warding off this disembodiment, all the while using virtual space to do so.

With respect to the benefits of ritual, a similar dynamic can be identified in the increasing turn to Second Life on the part of educators as a platform for distance and experiential forms of learning. Such educators might choose to view relocating learning experiences to Second Life as pragmatic — as taking advantage of "progress." But we can also see this relocation, and the adaptive educational strategies it demands, as asserting a ritualized form of control over rapid technological change through imposing existing ways of ordering the world — here education and specific accepted percepts about what constitutes learning — onto a potentially disruptive new technology form and in so doing impose on rapid change a semblance of recognizable order. In this way MUVEs, as a setting or ground for online ritualizations, accrue increasing importance as stages on which avatars give some instruction about, or order or meaning to, the role of human bodies in relation to networked virtual space both today and in the near future.

>>>

If free indirect discourse allowed for the potential to imagine experience without a subject, ritualizing one's becoming of information itself through identification with one's avatar depicts a parallel decentering of the subject; just as participants are pulled "forward" into their avatars they equally pull the ideological value of these sign/bodies "back" into their own embodied thought processes. Movement or travel, the sense of a journey—whether virtual or actual—inheres in this imaginative set of utopic associations.

The central trope of allegory is the figure of the traveler who "on his journey . . . is plausibly led into numerous fresh situations where it seems likely that *new aspects* of himself may be turned up" (Fletcher 1964, 34–37; emphasis added). The televised images of pharmaceutically induced ecstatic release, and the customized gestures of the avatar who may be shorter, taller, bulkier, thinner, more buxom, or less tanned than oneself, allegorize "new aspects" of contemporary and more "mobile" individual formations. The TV ads form part of an economy of gesture that renders pharmaceuticals as new aspects of core subjectivity. Digital avatars indicate a revitalization of the belief that signs, especially moving images, are already alive with the energy to which they point as simulations. To apply Neoplatonic logic, all that remains is for humans to accord avatars the agency that they already seem to possess. While these sign/bodies point to the living bodies of participants, as residents of the Web they equally point to digital networks as "new aspects" of life. For some participants this could offer a lessening of the psychic burden of rescuing meaning from inherently meaningless signs so as to avoid the pain inhering in a glimpse of the Void and the chaos it portends. Instead, the avatar implies, the Web beckons as a lively ecumenical space and suggests that the journey from here to "there" is an exchange value well worth pursuing.

It is worth noting here the importance of mobility. At a moment of great support for the idea of mobility as a major resource of contemporary life, the online moving image pulls us along in its tow, catching us in a tension between material fixity and digital flow. For MUVE participants seated before their screens, who are at least incipiently aware of the unequal distribution of actual mobility, the avatar meaningfully expresses their interest in and desire for ever-greater mobility through virtual objects coupled to a dialectal disaffection with a material sense of remaining immobile. Thus MUVEs can be viewed as a depiction of the discourse and simulation of mobility. Participation in a MUVE ritualizes the fetishization of mobility. Such participation, however, points to how the sense of remaining immobile—home alone— articulates to a regressive discourse emphasizing the purported limits of embodiment. In such a way does the avatar also point to the absence of what it represents—the absence of sufficient embodied mobility and acceptable offline forms of transcendence on the part of many MUVE participants.

Allegory always has been a form of simulation, and the discussion above of mobility raises the issue of the automata — things that have the power of self-movement or spontaneous motion, including the ability to simulate human actions. The writings of Ernst Hoffmann (1766–1822) engage the idea of the automata, a machinelike self anticipating cybernetics and, according to Christopher Lasch, one that "satisfies the [fantasy] wish to believe that thought can divorce itself from emotion" (1984:27). *The Sandman* (1816–17), Hoffmann's fictional investigation of Olympia, a daughter as mechanical being, allegorizes the idea of a projected double as well as how modernity positions the human body as a (female) mechanistic vampire that needs to be fed even as it drains away the (male) mind's vital forces. Hoffmann's Romantic tales are inflected by Descartes's belief that the human body is a machine. They may also be understood as bearing a partial debt to the French materialist philosopher Julien Offray de la Mettrie. Mettrie's publication of *L'Homme machine* (1748), intended to destabilize metaphysical church and state claims to naturally rule, proposed that the human be understood as comparable to a machine made of mechanically moving parts. Yet Hoffmann's Olympia, a soulless product of human manufacture, also reveals the continuing cultural attraction of the unextirpated ancient belief that inanimate matter does have a soul or a life of its own. In discussing magical beliefs associated with forms of human representation and simulation, John Cohen observes that the sculptural form of the Egyptian statue of Memnon "indicated that [it] was about to speak" (1964:16). He further comments on the ability of the legendary Daedalus to construct statues that moved on their own: "So alive were these statues, says Plato, that they had to be prevented from running away" (16).

In *Automata* (1814) Hoffmann, writing as the machine age gains traction and gears up, articulates this belief to mechanism and the oracular in the form of a carnival attraction: the Talking Turk, an automaton that answers questions posed to it by fairgoers. The Talking Turk plays on the stereotype of the Terrible Turk, the mythic oriental other who is a courageous beast of perverted valor. The Talking Turk, as a kind of "*machine homme*" or inversion of Mettrie's *l'homme machine*, also speaks to the ongoing tensions between Enlightened (European) disenchantment and origin myths — of the spirit world of old (the other of irrational mysticism) also present in Marx's haunted though also inherently futuristic interest in having the commodity speak so as to reveal what I term the political economy of metaphysics.

Beyond the pages of fantasy fiction, the mechanical 3-D descendants of the enigmatic Talking Turk have populated the midways of carnivals, state fairs, exhibitions, and amusement parks. Often taking the form of older women or foreign others seated before crystal balls, for a small token they dispense oracular knowledge through a slot on a small piece of cardboard inscribed with the seeker's future. But if these automata "speak," like the digital avatar they frequently also moved. As such they are also automated forms of pantomime, as noted above, the ordered expression of meaning by gesture or mime. In the case of mechanical automata and digital avatars, one might say that we have handed the Harlequin his own magic wand. Mechanical automata anticipate the avatar in the assumption that human beings can be reproduced—mechanically in the case of automata, electronically with digital avatars. In both cases the best way to show this is possible is through simulating a body double that acts and looks human. Hoffmann's fictional character, the Talking Turk, was reproduced during the nineteenth century in the form of such machines as Thomas Edison's Talking Doll. These devices hail viewing publics to imagine a human being without a human body (Gunning 2001:19–21); a human being that in miming the conceptually disembodied modern subject would necessarily be more dependent on forms of commodification and more centered in exchange values than in use values. Mechanical dolls, therefore, can also indicate something tragic about human affairs. Commenting on the form of Charlie Chaplin's acting in the 1936 film *Modern Times*, McLuhan writes that "the mime of this Chaplin film . . . is precisely that of . . . the mechanical doll whose deep pathos it is to approximate so closely to the condition of human life" (1964:290). Or, more precisely, this modern life. The avatar, in many ways a descendant of the mechanical doll, inherits the legacy of, while at the same time is expected to "fix" or transcend, the pathetically capitalized separation of human subjects from their bodies as objects.

The avatar, however, also manifests the age-old ventriloquistic desire "to create automata capable of simulating or actually replicating speech" (Connor 2000:338). As a digital automaton emulating human form, the avatar expresses the "paradoxical logic of the [automaton as a] technological object which plays endlessly at not being itself in order to assert more effectively its own identity" (Beaune 1989:437), and, I would add, the goals of those who desire it. The avatar allegorizes capital's interests in encouraging producers and consumers to believe that their real interests always lie "formally else-where"—within the screen-deep digital space of flows that they may only ever enter as mobile sign/bodies. In a sense, digital avatars also point to an inversion of Gramsci's Hegelian-inflected suggestion that the old is dying though the new is not yet capable of being born. Or, rather, what was old is new again. Reformulated Neoplatonic beliefs are on the ascendant—not yet capable of fully being (re)born yet somehow on their way, in part courtesy of the widespread belief that capitalized exchange values are "natural." Such beliefs confirm that certain forms of signs are living things equivalent in status to the humans who imagine, fabricate, and wait for them, like oracles or animated tableaux, to "speak" of their own accord.

Participants who dismiss "mere words" in graphical chat are no less in-fused with Neoplatonic and Gnostic belief systems than Renaissance poly-maths, Hoffmann's readers, or supposedly naive fairgoers whose beliefs and reception are belittled merely by virtue of the critic's having learned that they conceived of or were fascinated by ways to animate the inanimate and therefore retain a place for spirit, even (or especially) in mechanism, in an otherwise disenchanted and numb world of dead objects, organized religion, and, for many, its exhausted rituals. To dismiss such practices as naive fails to consider how the beliefs they reflect continue to manifest ritualistically in new forms and that the Web increasingly constitutes, for such believers, a transcendental signifier in itself, the postrepresentational ur-automaton come to life as the appendage for all who use it as a means to seek a unity between meaning and materiality. Dismissing such practices because one disagrees with them or views them as regrettable forms of fetishism or as fantasies that could only ever be actualized in a future that never arrives fur-ther minimizes consideration of networked individualism's collective desire to break through the dead-end limits of capitalized forms of representation today. Dismissing such practices therefore also misses out on making crucial political connections between contemporary yearnings for transcendental experiences and how such metaphysically inflected experiences both natu-ralize and locate capitalized beliefs and ideologies.[20] Marx understood this well. This is the essence of his theory of commodity fetishism with its sub-tending logic of haunting (a preoccupation of Victorian society) and occupa-tion of the commodity by the world of spirit. It is no surprise to find this on the Web. One of the Web's principal commodity forms is the image; on the sites I examine the image is the privileged form. This image already moves quite well and increasingly is on the way to finding its own legs.

Animism has never completely disappeared, as is made clear by Hoffmann's stories and by Marx's interest in what commodities would say if they could speak. Animism, however, as a "cognitive and emotional relationship to the natural and social order" (Robins and Webster 1999:33), manifested in the belief that inanimate forms might speak, move, and break free, began to wane due to censorship and repression at the point that enlightened science "discovered" that the nonhuman objects constituting the natural world were not enchanted. This had the effect of circumscribing the labyrinthine chain of signification possible when statues and other signs begin to move of their own accord. However, this chain returns "through the back door," as it were, in Peirce's understanding of the circulation of signs and Derrida's concept of the trace. Moreover, at the same time as strains of Enlightenment thought opened the intellectual process whereby the world would be rendered a disenchanted planet, a Cartesian-inflected mind-body split perversely encouraged the desire to understand human bodies as automata.

>>>

A close relationship between signs and referents characterizes mythical and magical thought (Sack 1980:47). In premodern contexts allegory embodied belief. As Nelson discusses, "To its intended audience allegory 'signified' in the premodern, not the postmodern, sense of the term: that is to say, it *embodied*. An allegorical representation, whether in words or images, was alive with the transcendental energy of the essence it depicted. That is why a Renaissance natural philosopher like Bruno could believe that contemplating images of Egyptian and astrological deities allowed him to draw divine essence from the [Platonic] World of Forms into himself. A viewer or reader of allegorical art or literature did not simply have an edifying didactic experience but experienced direct contact with the transcendental world: the artist as theurge had deliberately constructed this artifact of the material world to resonate with its equivalent in the insensible world" (2001:203). The referential has been absorbed into the field of signs, and meaning and value are understood to naturally inhere in the object itself.

Extending this observation to graphical chat, fabricating virtual places and objects, avatars included, allegorizes a broader cultural resurfacing of the implicit, as of yet largely unspoken, belief that certain sign forms are alive. Or, at least as indicative traces, avatars are situated as automated appendage/conduits to the embodied self and to the never fully perceivable real. Readers who find it difficult to conceive of the direct experience of Platonic essences through transmitted digital sign/bodies may find it productive to consider the experiential identification of users with their avatars as an uncanny updating of Coleridge's "willing suspension of disbelief." Coleridge's famous formulation comes from *Biographia Literaria* (1817) and its account of the genesis of *Lyrical Ballads* (1798), published jointly with William Wordsworth. While Wordsworth's subject matter was to be "things of the every day," Coleridge's were to be drawn from "persons and characters supernatural, or at least romantic; yet so as to transfer from our inward nature a human interest and a semblance of truth sufficient to procure for these shadows of imagination that willing suspension of disbelief for the moment, which constitutes poetic faith" (Abrams and Greenblatt 2000:478). Coleridge's poetic faith is a dynamic apropos to graphical chat's electronic avatar.

When Deleuze writes about the psychic value of the movement-image to human perception, he is, I believe, also indicating that Neoplatonic thought is not solely rooted in superstition and magic. Although it inherits these associations it is also anchored in Coleridge's "shadows of imagination," the limits to everyday perception rooted in the ways that autonomic perception apprehends moving images. These images seem real to us at the level of sensation, and, like Olympia's human suitor, we intuit them as forms of the living, as second selves, in contradistinction to the world of the dead. One might also argue that the belief that invoking a symbol for an action is to perform the action oneself is a legacy of our reptilian brain. It is, however, also the root of allegory and simulation. Left underconsidered by humanist thought because of its historically too close linkages with nature, and authoritarian belief systems relying on a propaganda based in unruly emotive imagery, this belief lives on in the arguably necessary psychic fantasies that statues can talk, mechanical dolls or puppets on a string might take undue possession of one's soul, and . . . graphical chat. The 3-D statue, doll, or puppet transmographizes into a moving 2-D avatar with depth. It is a virtual object rendering visibly vivid the twin desires for the suzerainty of images over words and a codeless and "direct" perception of reality on the part of those exhausted by symbolic representation's limits. In many ways the avatar conforms to the ancient logic of puppetry as a practice—let the puppet tell you what it wants to do. The avatar, in ritual fashion, is the educator; though it is designed and, therefore, by a certain logic is inferior to its designer, it never-theless shows and tells MUVE participants on this side of the interface what they need to do to stay current in the virtual world. The very name "graphi-cal chat" allows growing virtual publics to infer that images are best suited for indicating, or for telegraphing through depiction "the core essence" of contemporary communications. Images in graphical chat are received as a new form of performative and immanent "natural language." In short, they are implicitly understood as actualizing the latent potential of "mere words" (see Marcuse 1964:132). The graph in *graph*ical and the concept of a quasi-automated "second life" located "There!" also suggest the belief that net-worked virtual space constitutes a new nature more pure, exotic, and sacred than contaminated cultural and environmental material realities. This uto-pian desire concords perfectly with neoliberal demands for the building of a metaphysically inflected "friction free" space within which capital might flow. To paraphrase Marx, graphical chat, replete with virtual objects serving as "social hieroglyphics" (1952:32), is part of an intensification of allegorical experience in the world that today works to ritualize capital's inherently metaphysical interest in having relationships between persons programmed as an experience of the relationships between things. Relationships between automata are relationships between things though they may appear other-wise to sensation. The magical practices continue right in front of our eyes but many only see signs of exchange.

Though MUVE participants freely discuss commerce, they rarely if ever raise issues such as Neoplatonic essence, the pressures of neoliberalism, or the virtualization and polyvalent quality of their subjectivity, even if cor-porate interests promote flexibility as a desirable neoliberal character trait, and even if many MUVEs offer flexibility in avatar customization. In ritual fashion, participants remain partially aware of the codes they enact. They perform some of the complexities that attend contemporary identity refor-mations through processes of picturesque allegory that have migrated to the more psychically safe "spaces" of a virtual middle ground.

>>> Positioning the Subject in Avatar Chat Environments

Hobbes's distinction between the Author and the Actor (*Leviathan*, 1651), introduced in earlier chapters, is useful in theorizing subjectivity in MUVEs. Hobbes closely links this distinction to a second, related one he mounts between natural and artificial persons. A "Naturall Person" is one "whose words or actions are considered, either as his own, or as representing the words or actions of another man, or of any other thing to whom they are attributed, whether Truly or by Fiction (1985:227). It is possible, however, for certain "Artificiall Persons" to have "their words and actions *Owned* by those whom they represent" (218). These artificial persons are Actors. Those who own the words and actions are Authors. Actors are subject to the authority of the Author and in many ways the Hobbesian Actor is a persona. As I outlined above, in fiction persona is written in the first person and is generally understood as a mask or second self directly standing in for the author. Hobbes theorizes this direct connection as a law of nature. He argues that should an Actor break such a law when carrying out the acts scripted for him by the Author, then the Author, not the Actor, "breaketh the Law of Nature" (219). Hobbes anticipates the kinds of multiple subjectivities based not on genealogy but on activity and labor practices that contemporary identity formations routinely negotiate across a range of public settings. We might envision such Actor formations variously as Goffmanesque public roles—businesswoman, motorist, scientist, pedestrian, wronged customer, enthusiastic fan, tourist, the ADHD sufferer benefiting from Strattera, and so forth. Hobbes's political theory of the social contract contributes to the theory-turned-Enlightenment practice that the individual subject can be the master or sovereign Author who controls or produces his or her own meaning through textual practices. Given the long-established practices of this Author-Actor dynamic it is perhaps not surprising that individuals may have come to expect its re-creations in fiction in the form of persona. Rose graphical chat uses the term "actor" when referring to avatars.

Hobbes's theory, however, is also a kind of literary geometry that diagrams an individual figure (or "Naturall Person") encompassing both the author and a series of actors or personae (or "Persons Artificiall") that he or she dons as a disguise useful in performing modernity's many competing demands. These actors are scripted and regulated by the author, the overseeing panoptical core at the heart of Hobbes's early modern conception of individual sovereignty. Characters in novels can be read as a formal device, as persons artificiall, that remediates or extends in new directions the cultural logic subtending the theory of the Actor that Hobbes proposes. An avatar, to the degree that the MUVE participant-as-Author sitting in front of the screen's display relies on a one-to-one correspondence between himself or herself and the icon, is an Actor in this sense — an extension and not a representational negation of the Author. This avatar has a closer, more direct relationship to the Author than the multiple characters populating many novels. However, somewhat in the manner of a cross between a novelist and the operator of a pull-down menu, a MUVE that allows participants to maintain multiple avatar identities also allows acting out the potential for numerous, at times sequential, Hobbesian personae or plural identities. These exceed the masking function and "second self" meaning of persona directly corresponding to the author. But the fetishization of the Web as a fetishization of the new, of the progress myth finally realized, plays a crucial role here. Within Web settings, avatars are key players in the ritualization of an increasingly core experience of contemporary networked existence — that one is nothing but an Actor, a mask without referent. In such settings the Web itself seems to hail its new digital subjects (Case 2003), and in such a way is the Web well on its way to becoming a new kind of Author that "breaketh the Law of Nature."

What is the specific formal relationship in graphical chat between the image of the avatar and the dependent speech balloon (as illustrated in figure 8)? If free indirect discourse introduces an ambivalence for readers in distinguishing an author's voice from that of her or his characters, I suggest that "on" the virtual middle ground of graphical chat the concept of the author is maintained and transmitted through the screen's placement of written text at the bottom of the screen and in the speech balloon. Though many participants also use Instant Messaging (IM) functionalities to exchange text messages (and at the time of this writing experiments with audio/voice are underway), when the avatar is silent the author is symbolically absent from the screen, but her or his character/actor remains visible, escaping the indexical relation to the participant and for the moment gesturing toward the network and sign system. Earlier I raised a similar distinction: in discussing how images and texts operate in concert as emblems, I noted that the long-understood relationship between a policing text and polyvalent imagery has evolved toward greater authority and independence for the icon. In graphical chat, this would mean that greater authority for the avatar is analogous to greater authority for the character, a digital thespian and a neo-Hobbesian Artificiall Person. The avatar may render the Actor the locus of agency itself—the puppet or automata either finally free of its un-seen operator or, to invert Gonzáles's definition of the avatar, the human as embodied appendage, the referent of the online avatar as interpretant.[21]

The Author, however, as MUVE participant, through the text component that appears on the screen or display, remains at least a remnant in the overall schema of graphical chat. Mirroring the now-you-see-it, now-you-don't dynamic of free indirect discourse, the speech balloon, in any temporal immediacy it attains each time a participant types a new phrase or set of words, transmits a trace of the author as origin to other participants reading the contents of the balloon. The speech of the Author/participant takes on both a third- and first-person quality while the image of his or her character maintains a constant first-person quality. Together they reveal the ongoing value of forms of indirect speech and depiction; in graphical chat it can ap-pear to be the character/Actor who speaks as the Author and not the other way around—a state of affairs anticipated by Flaubert in his suggestion to Sand that the author should transport himself into his characters and not draw them to himself.

In Peircian terms, then, one can theorize the digital avatar in such cir-cumstances as follows. Initially the avatar is a sign or *representamen* for its object, the *referent* or embodied participant, with whom it is in a relation. The relationship is indexical, with the avatar composed of both iconic and symbolic signs on the screen. Objects, including virtual objects such as avatars, "are unlike language insofar as they bear a 'motivated' and 'non-arbitrary' relationship to the things they signify" (McCracken 1988:132). But if the trace of the participant carried in the text signs off of the screen while the avatar icon remains on display, in an oddly ironic way the avatar enters the position of "becoming-unmotivated" in that it is partially delinked from and therefore enters into a quasi-arbitrary relationship to its referent. It is at this point that, as the trace, it "becomes the origin of the origin" (Derrida 1976:61)—as more than just a representation it points back directly to the participant-observer, but it does so in a way that turns this individual into its own referent. Thus it makes of itself "the origin of the origin." Yet it is also at this point that this participant-observer, as the Cartesian *cogito*, can look at her avatar that looks back at her as enacting a Cartesianized under-standing of consciousness as "I see myself seeing myself." The mobile avatar, however, (as if freed from the immaturity of the Lacanian mirror stage) can seem to stand apart from its less mobile human referent while remaining within the network sign system.

The possibility that digital avatars be accorded any quality of independence also depends on how the necessary technologies are understood. I have noted that the image never fully yields to human control. But to this should be appended the recognition that any perceived independence of the avatar also relies on the idea of technological neutrality. As Andrew Feenberg (1999:89–91) argues, "commonsense" understandings of technology view it as an outcome of science, a field and practice that, despite the increasing harnessing of its energies to forces of commodification, still is accorded the status of neutral and thus seen as separate from the necessarily biased spheres of rhetoric and politics. According to this logic, technology, as the outcome of science, must itself be neutral and value-free save for the instrumental uses to which we put it as a "tool." As the story goes, a hammer can be used for good or evil, an airplane for dropping napalm or needed food to the starving. Technological determinism is one outcome of this line of thought. Technical necessity, coupled to the quest for efficiency, dictates the development of technologies (77). Technology, then, comes to "have an autonomous functional logic that can be explained without reference to society" (77). Technological development, once conceived as intrinsically independent of social relations, seems to follow a path of ever more efficient and rational development. In the Marxist sense, technology becomes a base and social institutions more like superstructures that must adapt to this base. Once a technology is introduced it becomes imperative to conform oneself with its universalizing logic (78). In such a way does the logic of technological determinism today render unto information machines the metaphysical quality of first principles. A society in which the majority of its members view technology as somehow autonomous but essential is a society ready to accord increased agency to technology. Enter the digital moving image, with its powers of the trace, to play a leading role in this drama. The very possibility of the image being accorded the status of a social relation depends not only on the relationship between human perception and the exponential increase in the number of images in circulation, or on the magically empirical conflation of Cartesian subject-object separation with a resurgent Neoplatonism. It also depends on the ideology of technological neutrality, of technology and technical processes (images included—"a photograph never lies") discursively positioned as independent from the messy, contingent, necessarily politically mediated world of human affairs. Once positioned as independent, the image can be (re)invited to enter this messy social world as a seemingly "free agent" that possibly might introduce a quality of truth (reduced to "clarity") into this messy, contingent and "all too human" world. The possibility of a humanly produced device such as a digital avatar holding the promise of truth is theorized by Bruno Latour as the human "delegation" of norms to devices: "We have been able to delegate to nonhumans not only force as we have known it for centuries but also values, duties, and ethics" (1992:232). Latour's concept of delegation can also be understood as humans transferring values onto a machine, or as the way that a machine directly reflecting human norms becomes a kind of persona or stand-in second self that works to enforce the moral obligations delegated to it. As Feenberg further argues, "technical devices prescribe norms to which the individual is tacitly committed by organizational belonging" (1992:103). In seemingly reverse fashion, then, participating in Second Life commits the individual to the norms of the avatar—understood as simultaneously independent and the participant's self-extension or *delegate*. As McLuhan notes, "by continuously embracing technologies, we relate ourselves to them as servomechanisms" (1964:46).

I have raised the issue of technology-as-tool, and a related factor supporting the ideology of technology as neutral is the positioning of sophisticated "black box" technologies such as networked information machines as tools. This is a discursive sleight of hand asking us to render equivalent tools that extend body functionalities such as knives, hammers, and shovels with, for example, advanced microprocessing and nuclear magnetic imaging (NMI). Tools are helpmates. Unlike atomic bombs or Frankensteins, tools aren't frightening and, therefore, according to this line of thought, the idea of increasing independence for the avatar or sign/body should not be frightening either. Rather, it should be welcomed as an enhanced form of tool to assist us in circulating more freely through networks.

Avatars in graphical chat, then, are commodities of consciousness that seem to have entered into exchange with one another. If they could speak in the way that Marx would wish the commodity to speak, they might say, "Though we are well on our way to becoming a form of social relation, our use value doesn't belong to us as objects. What belongs to us is our ability as traces to bridge the gap, and therefore to suggest the exchangeability, between the virtual and the actual, the informational and the embodied. To act, therefore, as increasingly independent signs for the way you desire to think. Our imagistic nature makes us easy to exchange, but we benefit enormously from the confusion that exists about what precisely constitutes an object. We are also in the process of seeming to become more enduring than, more alive than, and more natural than our makers upon whom, from the virtual future, from the tantalizing center of progress itself, we are also able to gaze back."

Graphical chat environments both point to and perform the reorganization of the subject and the built environment as a set of images in constant circulation, as the dematerialization of the commodity necessary for capital's continuing progress. In so doing they, like automata ready to walk, are e-versions of mechanical models presupposing a living original. In both, "the platonic Demiurge copies the ideas, and the Idea is the model of which the natural object is a copy. The Cartesian God, the *Artifex maximus*, works to produce something equivalent to the living body itself. The model of the living machine is that body itself. Divine art imitates the Idea—but the Idea is the living body" (Canguilhem 1992:53).

The avatar, as a form of what I may now also term "free indirect depiction" or "free indirect emblematics," in part inverts the flow of power between the Author or Naturall Person and his or her characters or Persons Artificiall; it allows for a play of freedom on the part of the actor or sign/body given the seeming lack of narratorial function or directorial overview within these virtual environments. The avatar serves as the "point person" for the various quasi-pseudonymous positions that networked individuals adopt within networked digital cultures. In this way, at such points as suggested in the preceding paragraph, the avatar/Actor may no longer relate entirely mimetically to its Author/participant. Further, it may be the Author/participant/referent who is in training, who comes to take his or her cue from the informational stage of virtual life to which the real action appears to have ritualistically relocated, who also then fetishistically reenacts what he has learned from the graphical chat's lively mise-en-scène and works it back into the fabric of the everyday on this side of the interface as an *emulation of life*. The avatar/Actor, conceptually on its way to becoming a productive Author, organizes the meaning of the ritual and points back to two crucial distinctions that Hobbes makes: a Naturall Person has his or her own words and actions and can also represent those of others or any other thing; and only some Persons Artificiall have their words and actions owned by those whom they represent. Consider the possibility of the avatar as an Artificiall Person on its way to no longer having its words owned by the Author.

American corporation law has crafted a strong precedent for the institutionalization of the avatar as an Artificiall Person. Since 1886, when the U.S. Supreme Court crafted the doctrine of corporate personhood in *Santa Clara County v. Southern Pacific Railroad Company*, American corporations have been deemed fully autonomous artificial persons whose words and actions have achieved significant, if not complete, powers of autonomy. The corporation anticipates the avatar as a kind of commodity that exchanges value directly with other commodities. And too often it is not the corporation who "breaketh the Law of Nature" but the Authors, the Naturall Persons who so frequently are no longer held to adequate account. When one reads phrases relying on the subjectless passive voice such as "mistakes were made"—whether in Iraq, at Enron, in Afghanistan, or at WorldCom; or in the excessive marketing of Bextra, Celebrex, Vioxx, or the collateralized debt obligations (CDOs) that ultimately led to a global liquidity crisis—to whom or where is one to imagine that agency has been conceptually relocated? While the modifying "at Enron" does acknowledge the location of the errors as resident within the former corporation or artificial person, the strategic use of the passive voice relocates human responsibility within a scandal-plagued American corporate culture into flow, into the network that cannot be held as individually responsible.

In American corporation law and in graphical chat, the Actor is sovereign. But since the Author created the Artificiall Person, should he, like Doctor Frankenstein, destroy his creature? Or should he view the avatar as sovereign (Dr. Frankenstein's cry of "It's alive!") precisely because it is the visual distillation of so many Authors' scripts, from Neal Stephenson's in *Snow Crash*, to that of his or her own? For if it is so understood, then following Hobbes's logic the Authors would be breaking a natural law to overthrow the avatar as it is only the distillation of their intent and desire. Experience comes to be the possession of the avatar at least as much as, if not more so than, it belongs to participants. This is how the avatar becomes the core of graphical chat ritual practices as an Artificiall Person on its way to naturalization and full citizenship within the digital realm. To invert the current anodyne understanding of graphical chat as an unthreatening zone of "play" to which cosmopolitan nomad/monads can repair, what participants see on their computer displays are the increasingly lively productions of the avatar/ Author who performs them at the same time. That is also to say that participants, in ritual fashion, are no longer, if they ever were, fully in charge of "the code" that, in avatar form, they also have come to fetishize.

Vološinov poses a question apposite to this investigation: "In what cases and to what limits can an author act out his character?" (1986:156). He answers that the absolute acting out of free indirect discourse makes sense to an audience or readers only in the rarest of cases involving a "picturesque" dimension and will have required the author to take into account necessary changes in expressive intonation; changes of voice based on close study of the features that individualize any one voice, a character in a novel included; a change of persona (which he also terms a mask) given the "set of individualizing traits of facial expression and gesticulation" (156). His answer seems to recognize — though not approve of — the abiding Neoplatonic desire to enter the image, to achieve the state of "living in art," a desire I interrogate more fully in the following chapter. Any graphical chat participants taking their cues from the interface are "acting out their characters." The avatar becomes the digital and technological subject, actualizing through virtuality the agency lodged within free indirect discourse's textual mechanisms. Yet this might also allow for a quality of (re)enchantment to be experienced by hypernetworked individuals, who, in returning to their interfaces to peer yet again into a common virtual middle ground, participate within an online community composed not only of other embodied participants but also of the moving images and unscripted dialogue that constitute the charmed foci of the "sacred space" of information.

>>> (It Is Written that) In the Beginning Was the Word . . .
(Yet the Image Is Just as Old)

In the pages above I have historicized the rise of graphical chat with reference to earlier text-based internet chat programs and the novel's use of free indirect discourse, and I indicated how specific discursive aspects of modern identity formations, coupled to an endless repositioning of capital and its practices, imbricate these modes of communication. A second theme, the ongoing desire for transcendence from both the demands of conscious individual subjectivity and "this earthly plane," has subtended the first, and I have assessed the ways that Neoplatonic beliefs and practices inform free indirect discourse in the novel and free indirect depiction in avatar-based chat. The intense promotion of contemporary information machines as, collectively, *the* manifestation of the progress myth and the seemingly unrelated worlds of spirit, belief, materials, lucre, and political expression are really never far apart, even as the hype emanating from corporate Persons Artificiall instructs consumer-based forms of subjectivity that they are. Such an invented distinction allows for conceiving these interpenetrating spheres of meaning, nature, and social relations as palpably discrete from one another, thereby rendering their individual commodification more palatable, more desirable. Corporatized forms of mediated address simultaneously hail each of the seemingly distinct neo-Hobbesian actors we each methodically perform across the stages of everyday life.

Graphical chat MUVEs exemplify and now begin to shape the ways by which fantasy, metaphysics, and political economy are joined at the virtual/actual hip; the temporary sense of transcendence that graphical chat may offer individual participants and residents concords well with the strategic, distracted but flexible networked individual who is increasingly overwhelmed by time deepening and multitasking—using the cell phone while on email, working the PDA while eating lunch—and by the related phenomenon of disintermediation—the process by which, under the guise of choice and access, everyone does everything for themselves and increasingly in Web-based settings. From the *Martha Stewart Living* fantasy expectation of "do it yourself" to the electronic wall of voice mail queues, paying a bill, booking an airline ticket, or checking one's bank account, no human (and the labor costs he or she represents to capital) stands in the way of communicating with information machines through interfaces—but this process consumes a great deal of time and requires much unpaid "self-service" labor. In the midst of this multitasking frenzy, the image of the avatar indicates and aestheticizes (thereby rendering more tolerable) our need as overtaxed neo-Hobbesian actors to be in more places at once than we can possibly juggle. For those of us who are constantly on the go and also online a lot of the time—living emblems of Raymond Williams's notion of a mobile privatization today enhanced with such features as "my Yahoo," "my eBay," and "my MSN"—graphical chat, replete with individualized "homes" for avatars to inhabit and remodel and within which to flirt, worship, and hold court, ironically constitutes a new form of virtual stability. This virtual stability is the ritual outcome of the need for a semblance of order in an overly flexible world. It emerges as a counterpoint to the material instability subtending the flexible work practices that are increasingly the capitalist norm. At the same time, the entirety of performative MUVE practices also ritualizes core qualities of the new informational economy expected of firms. Increasingly, firms are expected to informationalize and become more image oriented, and MUVEs are the performative platforms for ritualizing such qualities virtually. They are fantasy places according with the idea of allegory as the aesthetic device of personification. They announce "welcome home" to the disincorporating monad taking its cues from the screen to make a display of itself. Finally, the various accreting requirements and desires to use networked information machines propel accepting as "only natural" the cosmo-politics inherent in the worldview that, as individuals, we are materially here by virtue of our image being "there" (Kroker and Weinstein 1994).

If the development of free indirect discourse paralleled the rise of specific national economies, then the networked virtual subject, the sign/body of the avatar included, parallels and heralds the rise of contemporary media-scapes that encourage individuals to position themselves as a cosmopoli-tan fusion of global producer/consumers and national citizens. Each component of these identities or positions is subject to continual and arbitrary revaluations and reflects capital's preference that an older understanding of identity as more fixed and enduring now share the limelight with the idea that we each are organized as a series of inherently mobile yet traceable positions—that both identity and position remain distracted yet in focus, both capable of continuously shifting between the flexible and the fractured, the responsible and the childlike, the producer and the participant, the em-bodied and the imagistic, tradition and progress, place and space, the ma-terially spiritual and the magically empirical.

>>> Church of Fools

Church of Fools, a discussion of which opens this chapter, is a strong ex-ample of how meanings of transmissions and of rituals can be seen to syn-cretize within networked virtual environments. I return to Church of Fools because the belief that we are in essence disembodied awareness, however implicitly it infuses the church's website, remains central to how informa-tion machines are used not only by early adopting religious organizations but also by cultural forces running from the corporatized to the alternative and the resistant. These forces, knowingly and otherwise, seek to actualize an updated version of the Platonic idea of World Soul. For Plato, World Soul was the principle of animation in all things; for the Egypto-Roman Neoplatonist philosopher Plotinus, World Soul was an emanation of God. In the twentieth century, the idea of World Soul resurfaces in the writings of Teilhard de Chardin (1881–1955) who, anticipating globalization in arguing that the Age of Nations had past, identified the noosphere as a planetary thinking network, an interlined system of informational and human consciousness locating a convergent unity of all things in space and time (1964). More recently, Pierre Lévy has argued that in the not-too-distant future information machines will allow for the organization of "an enormous, hybrid, social, and technobiological hyperbody"—a kind of electronic, and therefore commodifiable, world soul of commingling surrogate selves that would allow the human body to "detach itself completely from the hyperbody and vanish" (1998:44). Kevin Kelly (1994) laments for those "dumb terminals" who remain unconnected to electronic networks. He celebrates the arrival of the "hive mind"—all of us terminals joining together as one network, a noosphere of information infinitely more intelligent than all the previously disaggregated body "parts." This is a ritual of transmission if ever there was one.

The digital avatar allegorizes the Gnostic belief that the essence of humanity is disembodied awareness. It is useful here to recall the Hindu meaning of the avatar. In Hindu theology, an avatar is the manifestation, incarnation, or embodiment of a deity, especially Vishnu (the Preserver), in human, superhuman, or animal form. Avatar, a Sanskrit term, translates as "he passes or crosses down." If ignorance or evil are ascendant on earth, the Supreme Being incarnates itself in an avatar form appropriate for fighting these blights so as to support force for the good. An avatar might also manifest as a warning against hubris, as a way to convey ideas to humankind, or even as a pantomimic form of divine playfulness.[22] The United Kingdom Methodist Church leaders who launched the Church of Fools MUVE foresaw the need for the church to adapt, to reincarnate itself in a more avatarial form that could "pass or cross down" into the virtual world, to become inherently more mobile, and to move beyond "bricks and mortar" in order to reach networked individuals focused on the display. Their reliance on the digital avatar also points to the supernatural powers increasingly accorded to information machines. Church of Fools participates in the genealogy of metaphysics outlined above and exemplifies its resilience. Its ecumenism bears consonance with the cosmopolitan dynamic of globalization, as anticipated by Teilhard de Chardin. Ecumenical means belonging to or representing the worldwide Christian community, and as a dedicated "place" for ritual practice, Church of Fools explicitly relies on an understanding of ecumenism wherein a general assembly, an ecclesiastical body representing the world at large, gathers together. Recalling the discussion of cosmopolitanism that opens this volume, the origins of the word ecumenical lie in the Greek concept of *ecumene*, which at times is translated as the inhabitable world and its inhabitants, and in ecumene's original Greek word *oikos*, which suggests a dwelling, a home, or a temple.[23] The term, moreover, further conveys "the image of a house or household, since it neatly links several major aspects of human life that can help or obstruct the building of a global community."[24] This image of a house or household is important; a household, among other things, is both a collective of people and the gathering place for this collective. The purpose of communication as ritual, as Carey (1975) noted, is to draw people together for specific social purposes, and a site such as Church of Fools, based on the twin principles of animation and automation, is a house for ritual, a virtual home for the gazing eye of the cosmopolitan trans-citizen. In a more direct way than secular graphical chat, this e-location invites communicants to celebrate, and thereby help make actual, the transnational falling away of borders among all manner of species and specie, to join in an allegorical ecstasy of communicability itself. But the ontological message remains the same whether one worships at the Church of Fools or is born again in Second Life. The Web is an emergent center of becoming, the ecumenical home for all sign/bodies, a destination or return for the advance brigades of the society of the spectacle on their way to so becoming: Networked individualism's collectively acknowledged Thou. From capital to God and back again, Thy Sovereign will be done. But in a liminal *oikos* more like a limbo than a heaven, a nether zone of collective isolation constituted as a restricted view of salvation where the just are detained and into which the avatar, as a form of passing or crossing down, ritualistically descends.

>>>

And yet, if Church of Fools graphically promotes Christian ecumenism, what about the biblical instruction of John 1:7? "In the beginning was the Word and the Word was with God, and the Word was God." World Soul depends on a synthesis of logos and spirit and the theme of incarnation expressed in this verse is the "only fully explicit statement of the theme of incarnation in the New Testament" (Beardslee 1993:464). The word incarnate. Christ, positioned in John as logos, manifests Supreme Being in a manner similar to the avatars adopted by Vishnu.

Thus we are returned to the relationship between text and time in graphical chat MUVEs. The Web relies on machine language taking the form of code. Most MUVE participants never fully command this code, and what the action they witness on their screens has to say is that the word is now history. I am being somewhat metaphoric here, but only somewhat. This is a tragedy of the virtual commons. For my graphical chat correspondent dismissing "mere words" as yesterday's news, the word is a dead letter. So, too, are text-based MUDs, MOOs, and IRC. The moving, flowing image (which seems to hover, because flickering, even at those moments when still) now takes command in the settings it inhabits. Exodus 20:4 may instruct readers that "thou shalt not make unto thee any graven image, or any likeness of any thing that is in heaven above, or that is in the earth beneath," but inside Church of Fools the image exceeds the binaries of sacred or profane, skin or adorning ornament, ritual or communicatory message. Instead it syncretizes the meanings of all in a way that is akin to Peirce's refusal to distinguish materiality from ideality. His theory of signs flows from his belief that all phenomena are of one character. Church of Fools makes this so. That one synechistic character is the image, the tantalizing image of experience without a subject, a consummation and a comity devoutly to be wished.

Avatar identification, still a temporary performance for most, but recurring with the frequency of a ritual infused with the powers of commodity fetishism, provides a momentary, seemingly transcendental fix. As an *axis mundi* for the teleritual, graphical chat offers a flexible means of connection for multitasking subjects whose fractured identities are ever more organized around the multiple intersections of what they do and how they appear or seem. What the avatar "embodies" is the value of virtuality. Yet what it also performs, and attempts to give some order to, is the current difficulty in acknowledging or giving voice to the virtualization of the subject, including the virtualization of already commodified desire, and its central role within new forms of production and immaterial labor. This difficulty is wholly consonant with the widespread desire for the restoration of enchantment. This desire manifests as a disenchantment with enchantment's absence—a disenchantment with a disenchanted modern world in which digital networks are "often presented to contemporary individuals as the final technology of their ultimate self-creation" (Barney 2000:195).

If free indirect discourse or the ambivalent protection of the text-based middle voice was once to be used with great subtlety, as was the case with Austen, and might lead to scandal, as with Flaubert, today market forces enthusiastically promote the transcendental postsubject. Information machines such as graphical chat allow this being, temporarily at one with his or her digital commodities in a sequential string of affairs dynamically akin to serial monogamy and its habitual flirtations, to couple with the spatio-temporal polyvalency of a middle voice reformulated as an imagistic middle ground. Better the fractured subject always on the move, one who purchases many things to satisfy the profanely sacred and sacredly profane fetishized desires induced by networked effects and the plural identity claims she and he must juggle in neo-Hobbesian fashion. Better still, for the commodity's sake, if this individual doesn't feel at home in his or her body, doesn't quite know why, and turns in a distractedly focused fashion to the animated moving image both to mask this uncanny lack and to reveal, to experiment demiurgically with new modes of indexicality, new ways of looking more consonant with an understanding of self-experience as participating within a play of images segregated from history and, as much as possible, narrative contexts. The telefetish is at the door, appearing as a specter of oneself, a Real McCoy action figure, the appearance of digital humanity beckoning from the other side of the interface—from the sphere of communicability itself.

So Near, So Far, and Both at Once
TELEFETISHISM AND RITUALS OF VISIBILITY

In this chapter I consider webcam culture as it evolved from the late 1990s to the early years of the millennium among a group of English-speaking, first world gay/queer men. (I also refer to these men as digital queers and discuss my use of the term gay/queer in the section following.) These men are part of a vanguard that used webcam technology to transmit live images of themselves and their immediate personal home environment for some considerable period of time on a regular basis (some as much as twenty-four hours per day). In the words of one participant, "I wanted to share my life. I wanted to share it not only in words, but in pictures, video and audio" (quoted in Snyder 2002:178).

My interpretation of gay/queer men's webcam practices and techniques draws from theories of commodity fetishism. I argue that online ritual practices produce a digital form of the fetish, which I term the telefetish. My discussion of these men traces a brief history whereby through their webcams they transmitted ritualized claims to exist through an ambivalent politics and strategy of virtual visibility. I first historicize and theorize the techniques these men developed to render themselves more visible. I then provide an extended examination into why these men ultimately closed their websites. I include in this discussion an assessment of the potential of newer technologies of web transmission such as weblogs to realize some of these men's aspirations and political goals that webcams apparently could not meet.

The variety of uses and sheer number of webcams suggests the need to speak of webcam cultures. Google requires .17 seconds to index well over a million hits for "webcam sites," and many listed are aggregate sites that provide links to thousands of individual cams. WebcamSearch.com and ChatCamCity.com, for example, provide cameras in dozens of categories, including animal cams, indoor cams, college cams, surveillance cams, UFO cams, volcano cams, and cams on all seven continents and in fifty U.S. states. Indeed, cams are deployed worldwide to watch and surveil traffic, public spaces, bank interiors, parking structures, shopping malls, the weather, nature views, major tourist destinations, and the unsuspecting babysitter back home. They are also used for personal PC-to-PC phone calls, as described in the introduction, and in video chat rooms organized by conversation topic and special interest. A site such as ImLive.com lists dozens of "experts" available for instructional chat on a variety of subjects, from alternative medicine and spirituality to online therapy, poker playing, cooking, and American Sign Language. PalTalk.com regularly schedules webcam chats with celebrities and media-industry players and hosts thousands of user-created rooms. Kevin Whitrick achieved notoriety in one of the site's many rooms devoted to insult when, in March 2007, he announced his intention to commit suicide and then proceeded to hang himself while others watched and cheered him on.[1] Webcams have also spawned an industry of for-pay "live sex chat." Individuals (who may or may not have their own webcam) enter the room of webcam operator/broadcasters who are typically in provocative dress. Individuals can chat with the operator and others in the room, and for an additional fee they can "go private" for a more intimate encounter. Increasingly, live events are broadcast through webcams, including the political rallies of politicians competing in the 2008 U.S. presidential campaign, the Nobel Prize award ceremonies in Stockholm, and Sunday morning services of churches across the planet.

The gay/queer men on whom I focus were among the first to develop the practices that have come to be known as "lifecasting" — the continual broadcast of a person's life through digital media. Because of advances in webcam technology since its early days, the many individuals who wish to live online can now easily join commercialized open platforms such as CamStreams .com, UStream.tv, and Justin.tv. The image transmitted by the webcam displays on a viewer's screen, usually within a small box lodged within the larger space of the display (see figure 5). Much of the display contains text-based information punctuated by various images and JPEGs. Commercialized sites provide a customizable template that typically includes the cam operator's profile, schedule of appearances, special events, chat interests, and personal rules for chat that, if broken, result in a visitor's banishment. The number of hours spent online is a key factor in a lifecaster's popularity: 24/7 has the effect of proving one's bona fides. In the late 1990s, webcam fans would email screen captures of their favorite operators to these same operators so that they could post them in picture galleries on their sites. Now, operators and registered visitors alike can post and rate video clip highlights of their favorite lifecaster "episodes." With access to Wi-Fi, the mobility of webcams has also increased. Some lifecasters, such as Justin Kan, the founder of Justin.tv, wear a cam attached to a hat or special glasses so that viewers see everything from the wearer's point of view. Most still position one or more cameras at strategic points in their home so that viewers can observe the broadcaster within his or her own personal environment. Some combine both techniques. While technological sophistication has increased since the 1990s, the practices themselves have largely remained the same.

Jennifer Kaye Ringley's JenniCam is possibly the best known personal webcam site from the late 1990s; it inspired many of the webcam sites that were to follow. As Patrick Cornwell, the owner and developer of Camstreams .com, notes on his site's "About" page, "Webcams fascinated me from the moment I read about them in a Sunday newspaper in the summer of 1997. It was an article about JenniCam—a website by a woman called Jennifer Ringley who chose to show her life to the world, warts 'n' all. She had inadvertently created the first 'Reality' show—it was definitely the start of an era." Ringley launched JenniCam in 1996 as an undergraduate at Dickinson College in Carlisle, Pennsylvania. At its peak, her site attracted an estimated four million hits per day and remained popular until Ringley closed it on New Year's Eve 2003.[2] Teresa Senft (2008) notes that Danni Ashe's less well known porn-centric site predated Ringley's by two years, but perhaps because Ringley's webcam mixed erotics with less freighted pleasures, such as showing her brushing her teeth and sitting at her desk (White 2003:14), her site and online practices are widely accepted as defining the personal

9 Screen captures from the image gallery of SeanPatrickLive:
"Checking" (March 25, 1998) and "Badday" (April 19, 1998).

webcam as a genre. Such sites do not seek a sexually focused audience; most of the time they show the routine, a flash of activity as the operator heads out the door, an empty room, the eating of cereal at the table, time in front of the TV, a shape in bed. Yet the personal nature of the transmissions and the sense of intimacy they provide can also infuse such activities with a highly charged sense of erotics. Personal webcams as a genre, to paraphrase Amy Villarejo, defy expectations based on presumed categories: "Twenty-four-hour webcam sites . . . are neither wholly devoted to what we might call the visibly sexual . . . nor are they . . . devoid of connections to that domain or to sexual dissidence" (2004:85).

SeanPatrickLive.com, launched in January 1997, was shut by its operator, Sean Patrick Williams, in the spring of 2001.[3] Williams's fan base was never as wide as that of Ringley (Williams's site received between thirty-five thousand and eighty thousand hits a day), but the Washington, D.C.-based operator holds the likely distinction of being the first gay/queer man to go live on webcam. His site garnered considerable media attention. Newspaper interviewers questioned why so many repeat viewers found of interest the largely banal images of the telegenic Williams eating, smoking, sitting in front of his computer, or sleeping (figure 9). He replied, "People see a reflection of themselves . . . You watch TV or movies, and you see people wake up wearing makeup, looking perfect. I wake up and, well—it's not pretty. I think people find that refreshing."[4] "What I'm trying to show is that what goes on in somebody else's life always seems bigger and different and fabulous and a lot different than what's going on in our lives. But that's not true."[5] And, "It's sort of to let people know that everybody's not as different as we like to think."[6] These 1998 mainstream media interviews do not emphasize the same-sex aspect of Williams's site. Nevertheless, as Donald Snyder records in his ethnographic study of the site, Williams saw SeanPatrickLive as an opportunity to write about issues of importance to the gay community: "I remember living in Wilmington, North Carolina, where I grew up, we didn't hear about like gay things; we just heard about the big gay things. And things like, you know, Matthew Shepard got a lot of press, but like the Roanoke thing [a more recent and less publicized gay killing] didn't.[7] This is probably because the guy that was shot wasn't really young and pretty. He was kind of an older weird looking queer, but I think it's just as important to say that" (Snyder 2002:192). That Williams lived his life so openly online made a difference in the lives of gay/queer male viewers. Will, a self-identified middle-aged Bostonian and fan of the site, recorded the following observation on his weblog:

> Long before "The Truman Show" dealt with the subject of having one's life telecast to the world Sean Patrick Williams was visible 24 hours a day via webcam. He lived in D.C. and ate, slept, cleaned, worked, cooked, entertained, watched TV and occasionally had sex on cam (although he was far more restrained in the latter regard than many other web cammers). As someone who had always been a very private person, I was fascinated by the openness of it all.
>
> What I admired about his cam site was how powerful and courageous a statement it was for a gay man to take the ultimate "out" position of living a gay life on line for the whole world to see. . . . He did it naturally and without grandstanding, and somehow it became compelling. One cared, and missed him when he was gone.[8]

SeanPatrickLive and the other sites I discuss are "history." They are part of an earlier moment of gay/queer engagement with the Web, an experiment in virtual visibility at the onset of the Web's massive popularization. Ritual theory offers an explanation for why some men choose to live significant portions of their lives in front of a webcam. "Real life" can easily seem to be on the verge of descending into meaninglessness or chaos, and ritualizing life practices can provide a counterbalancing sense of order (Bell 1997:12). Personal webcams constitute a performance space for networked individuals to depict the idealized ways they believe or wish the world to be and to work through issues that confront them, which they also know are difficult or impossible to solve. Such performances may incorporate critiques of how the world actually is organized. In any case, performances make participants more visible. The rise of gay/queer webcam practices, therefore, allowed participant-operators and their fans to ritually enact ways of making their lives more visible and thereby, given the ongoing heteronormative reluctance to extend full recognition to these men as subjects, to stake an ontological though spatially ironic political claim to exist in the here and the now.

Ritual theory, however, can also help to explain the ways that heteronormative attitudes operate against acknowledging these men as full human subjects and, therefore, why they might turn to technology as a form to redress invisibility. I call here on James Carey's (1998) identification of "rituals of excommunication" or "degradation." Such rituals acquire legitimacy by claiming to speak on behalf of "the people." They operate in ways identified by Pierre Bourdieu (1991) to induce cohesion among members of an "in group" at the expense of those they exclude, and as Carey notes, they rely on media to disseminate (mis)information about the individual or group to be degraded or excommunicated. Naturalized distortions abound in such exercises that frequently amount to forms of shunning. The scale of the shunning can run from an individual to an entire culture. Though not always successful, rituals of excommunication are intended to induce states of shame and unworthiness. "They often are occasions when persons are sent into exile: internal exile, a kind of invisible existence . . ." (Carey 1998:42). Such rituals are dangerous because "their apparatus can be used to ostracize any disadvantaged population that is politically unable to defend itself from the damning authority of the ritual . . . they bear a systematic cruelty . . . the kind that disenfranchises and derogates minorities" (Sella 2007:118). Rituals of "social cruelty" (Carey 1998:67) take many forms. With respect to gay/queer men, when the rituals result in the enactment of legislation such as the U.S. Defense of Marriage Act (DOMA) they gain the legitimacy of democratic procedure. The DOMA legislation is a political outcome of this kind of increasingly mass-mediated ritual form. Mass media report the denial by political legislators of equal protection for LGBTQ individuals under the law, and, in a vicious circle, the constant stereotyping by the media reinforces "commonsense" attitudes that get translated into laws such as DOMA, or that result in a lack of laws—namely the inability to extend U.S. federal hate crime legislation to cover sexual orientation, gender identity, gender, and disability.

The specifics within which many gay/queer identities gestate—the realities of the closet, geographic and social isolation, the desire for wider social recognition and acceptance in the face of rituals of excommunication running from the subtle to the blatant, coupled with the considerable numbers of men employed in the information and communication technology (ICT) sector or possessing considerable skill with respect to how these technologies and their applications are deployed—contribute significantly to the emergence of these relatively information machine–savvy men at the forefront in using these technological assemblages in novel ways. Snyder's study notes Sean Patrick Williams's "deep connection to technology": his early interest in computers, his work as a programmer and Web designer, his interest in video gaming, and his ownership of five computers and related electronic technologies (2002:183). As Larry Gross observes, "the Internet has particular importance to sexual minority communities. . . . Tom Rielly, the founder of PlanetOut, explained, 'Traditional mass media is very cost-intensive. Gays and lesbians don't have a high level ownership of mainstream media properties. The internet is the first medium where we can have equal footing with the big players'" (2004:x-xi). Gross notes the intensity of internet use found among gay men and lesbians, a use related both to the geographic and social isolation of individuals and to the ongoing potential in many places to be on the receiving end of psychic and physical violence if one is too public about one's same-sex orientation or preference. These men's practices reflect directly on difficulties at hand. Though many would claim that the most egregious forms of Western homophobic discrimination had abated by the late 1990s, mounting a personal webcam allowed these men to perform a degree of public visibility frequently denied to them in heteronormatively inflected public settings. The desire for voice is actualized as the online moving image that "says," "look at me, in truth I exist." Of course, spatial ironies abound. In a sympathetic interview conducted in 2000, Sean Patrick Williams argued that the internet "is of particular benefit to gay activism because it empowers closeted gays to 'publicly stand up for themselves in a private way.'"[9]

Using the Web to connect with other people in some ways naturalizes the idea expressed in the phrase "absence makes the heart grow fonder," except that the absence has been produced through encounters with representations and simulations that precede (*if* they occur) any face-to-face encounters between individuals. The aesthetic qualities of individuals' online performances, confirmed by receiving emailed JPEGs of themselves captured by admiring men, allowed these operators to enact the perilous though comforting illusion that they might conceptually relocate to the pure realm of aesthetics — to somehow "live in art" through fabricating a series of performing images that may have seemed at times to operate as if within the space of a dream. Sexualities may be de/re/constructed through online performativity, resulting in potentially askance outcomes — deferral of desire, the pornographization of one's online persona, or, less likely, a first date. These outcomes can be highly aestheticized productions by niche celebrities who remediate the politics of celebrity-fan dynamics that, ironically, have the potential to separate individuals as much as they promise connection.

While being the star of one's own webcam is often the result of fans having conferred on the operator the cultural capital of inherent authenticity, it also highlights the tantalization of their desires for someone so near yet still so far because always just out of material reach — the *tele* in the telefetish. Ironically, this reiterative dynamic in turn mirrors the kinds of tantalization of gay/queer men and lesbians promised by liberal social discourse. Urvashi Vaid (1995) has noted that gay/queer men and lesbians are promised a "virtual equality" that offers a veneer of partial acceptance in exchange for conforming to heteronormative standards of "good taste." Gay/queer men express this dominant standard through their performing (in public and in particular in the workplace) of what heteronormativity prescribes as an acceptable or palatable image of gay/queer identity. As Victor Turner (1957) argues, rituals are social dramas. Online rituals, therefore, offer these men performative possibilities to dramatize and fetishize various complex even problematic aspects of the material conditions of their lives, the tensions and conflicts included. A certain difference, and hence a politics, is put into play by these men who, when self-pornographizing themselves as democratic digital spectacles, could be seen to violate heteronormative taboos against making a spectacle of oneself.

Yet if, as I argue in detail below, online performances, in part through their promise of ritualized connection, have had the potential to separate and defer the satisfaction of desire through face-to-face embodied encounters, so too may the promise of virtual equality noted by Vaid have contributed, in Goffmanesque fashion, to an ironic yet ritualized updating of the segregated aspects of gay/queer realities into sanitized public fronts and more private modes of interacting. Public fronts, tolerable to heteronormative values, remain separate from supposedly less palatable constructions of online gay/queer personae targeted and transmitting primarily to other men identifying as gay/queer. A hybrid array of askance political analyses, images, and sexualities is relegated, therefore, not only to "backstage" material fantasy environments that until recently were largely the purview of commercial gay/queer bar culture but also, increasingly, to online settings experienced as virtual environments. For gay/queer men online, the neither public nor private yet both at once character of the networked settings they may seek to virtually inhabit permits marginalized aspects of gay/queer cultural realities to attain something like a "return to the center" — to achieve fuller visibility and "presence." Virtually. Fetishism, then, is not the only component of this story. But its inflection of digital queers' online practices is key to making sense of a broader hybrid doubling or "askance twoness" that informs gay/queer identity practices — one by which many of these men and their politics abide. The gay/queer sign online denotes the shifting material status of its maker: partially hidden and therefore also partially in view.

>>> Gay/Queer and Queer Theory

My use of the terms digital queer and gay/queer may raise the issue of queer theory for some readers. Queer theory has produced critical insights into the meaning of the subject and arguments asserting its psychic impossibility; relationships among sexuality, gender, embodied difference and practices; their social construction; the broader sociopolitical and economic contexts within which these dynamics are lived, promoted and contested; and the convoluted history of gay male identity with its earlier sodomitical and homosexual foci and the latter term's links with medicalized discourses of illness and perversion. Queer theory suggests that pathways and flows are as important and have equal ontological status as the places and sites they represent. Theorists have argued that queerness, with its claim to void oppositional binaries of us and them, in and out, gay and straight, might embrace all forms of nonnormative sexuality and move beyond minority identities such as "gay" or "lesbian." Gay and lesbian, it has been argued, even when asserting legitimate political claims to subject status, reaffirm, by producing a binary, heteronormative hegemony.

For readers who interpret my use of "gay/queer" as placing "queer" in an uneasy tension with "gay," it is precisely my intention to avoid binaries in my discussion of webcam cultures. Judith Butler has broadly argued against foreclosing future uses of the sign; I do not understand gay/queer as an uneasy sign but rather an askance one. The term connotes a hopeful but difficult politics of intra-same-sex solidarities. My use of the virgule (/) does not deny difference between men identifying as gay or as queer, but neither does it hold them apart; instead it acknowledges and performs an attempt at the necessary ongoing dialogue among the overdetermined realities for which the terms are stand ins. This dialogue itself can be askance — sideways, oblique, askew, and indirect. What does remain uneasy with respect to gay and to queer is the truly ironic emergence of a dyadic relationship between them even as the latter term was designed to move beyond homo/hetero binaries while not abandoning the interests of those who desire members of the same sex. The inadvertent strengthening of political and cultural differences between those men identifying as gay who desire other men and those men identifying as queer who also desire other men does not suggest theoretically infinite possibilities for queer. Rather, it has been advanced by an at times too idealistic, at times regressive insistence that queer stand separate from gay even while it remains convenient to merge the still-blurry definitional boundaries between the terms when necessary for political common cause. The ways that the terms gay and queer imbricate one another in popular culture usage is of more than passing interest. As David Halperin has noted, queer theory is often abstracted from the everyday lives of individuals identifying as lesbian, gay, and/or queer (2003:343). These are lives lived in actual bodies, yet within academic contexts "queer" has been so appropriated by theory that theoreticians risk losing sight of the ways that the term continues to be used in other ways both on the street and on the Web. The Web-based success of the 2003 Ukes of Hazzard music video *Gay Boyfriend* is a case in point. The song's refrain repeatedly insists, "Gay boyfriend, gay boyfriend, I don't really care that you are queer." I do not understand the refrain to reinstitute the value of gay by dismissing conceptions of queer. On the contrary, it promotes contiguities and commensurabilities between the terms. My own reappropriating use of the gay/queer *fusion* recognizes this everyday mutability or synechistic interdependency of the terms *as well as* a generational shift in thinking on the part of men who have sex with men imbricated with ageist assumptions. For many younger women and men, queer culturally supersedes the older terms lesbian and gay, terms that loosely denote those of us not old enough to have been "homosexual" in our youth yet not young enough to have been "queer."

A related form of ageism played out in the late 1980s and early 1990s when many young men identifying as queer believed, or chose to believe, that HIV infection was a generational disease afflicting older gay men and homosexuals. In these cases, the deployment of queer indicates factors such as ageist othering that are not directly linked to sexual desire. Yet this remains so even as the term retains, for younger individuals, many of the same-sex codings earlier, and still, carried by the term gay. Ironically, then, even the term queer is available for certain forms of commodification and reification. It cannot escape processes of signification; a history that produces arbitrary, competing meanings for any term; or the production of binaries and whatever metaphysical "centers of truth" such a production works to create. While some readers may fully locate their understanding of the term queer within academic theory, others will recall the derogatory origins of the term as an epithet equivalent to faggot, pansy, fruit, or gay. While "faggot" during the late 1970s and early to mid 1980s was on the verge of a widespread reappropriation on the part of self-affirming gay men, the subsequent and more successful recuperation of queer, at first by activists, ran parallel to and at times in tandem with the rise of academic queer theory. My use of the sign gay/queer within this volume recognizes the male same-sex cultural component of this history and acknowledges flexible and fluid contiguities and dynamic continuities articulating those men identifying as either or both. It should not be read as a refusal or even a muddying of theoretical waters on the part of those who, ironically, seek to retain a certain discursive purity or even cosmopolitan quality for "queer."

It is not at all clear, moreover, that "moving beyond" gay, lesbian, or even homosexual subject identifications would mitigate homophobia or work to combat it. Alexander Düttmann (2000:106), theorizing the contradictory dynamics released when a minority group seeks recognition from the majority, raises the example of the slogan "We're queer, we're here, so get fuckin' used to it" to suggest that the phrase demands general societal recognition for something that no longer needs to be recognized. My point is not to take issue with Düttmann but rather to suggest that his queer example reveals how queer accrues binarized identity claims to itself that are as easily refuted as those claims for recognition advanced by gay and lesbian identity formations. My study of the ways that the men I examine in this chapter use the terms gay and queer suggests that at times they use them interchangeably and at other times not. On many (though not all) websites organized to appeal to same-sex male interests, the use of either term is largely absent given that same-sex interests and desires predominate within these bounded forms of public spheres. At times an individual may refer to himself as gay to denote self-identification with a specific history of difference. At other times the same man may refer to himself as queer to reference his broader connection to discursive communities of common material cause. A man who understands himself as queer might, in response to a homophobic slur directed at him for holding hands with another man in the public square, shout back "That's *MISTER* faggot to you"—directly employing the non-co-optable and nonqueer aspects of same-sex activity as a form of political riposte. In the complexity of these associations and reasons, for the purposes of the present work I find gay/queer valuable in its richness as a term that bridges generational differences and that acknowledges the various cultural and political realities of men who desire men, whether gay, queer, or both at once, and who also engage with the indeterminacy, ambivalency, and incommensurability of dispersed and capitalized identity formations taking place online. Those readers who desire and sleep with members of the opposite sex and who identify as queer may find additional theoretical value in gay/queer through considering linkages between the in-between state of the webcam as an event that is also a representation. The "/" can be read not as separating but as introducing a conjoining betweenness, as well as a recognition of the shifts in the ways that sites and operators are described (and self-describe) as alternately gay, queer, and gay/queer.[10] Gay/queer, then, if terminologically perplexing to those who, in seeking to specifying formations to which queer may not articulate, inadvertently render queer a kind of first principle that risks being subsumed by heteronormativity, can also be seen as a requeering of queer—as defamiliarizing or making it strange once again.

>>> Telepresence and the Telefetish

The gay/queer creative use of digital technologies examined in this chapter represents an active engagement with magical thinking by socially marginalized, technologically well-connected men who have understood that screen-based identities are not fully "real" even as they have hoped that they might be, if only for "the moment." Part of this return to magical thinking, or investiture of fetish "spirit" or "aura" in a Web persona implicitly positioned as a digital human, flows from telepresence. The idea of telepresence supports the growing belief that the internet is more a space than a set of textual engagements and, therefore, that an individual can be both materially "here" at the same time as seemingly "there" by extending components of identity into the virtual space of digital technologies (see chapter 1). As Sandy Stone puts it, "inside the little box are other people" (1997:16). In Lev Manovich's words, "The body of a teleoperator is transmitted, in real time, to another location where it can act on the subject's behalf" (1995:350). The sense that a subject can transmit her or his "'presence' in a remote physical location" (349) so as to achieve "action at a distance"—a phrase that, for empiricists, can serve as a rough and ready definition of magic—illustrates the enchanted thinking, the idealist metaphysics, yet also the creative taking up of dominant spatial metaphors entailed in both the placing and experiencing of fetishized and disembodied personae as online traces of personal identity. Moreover, an uncritical use of the term telepresence by many new media theorists implicitly promotes the power of Web networks as akin to a transcendental signifier because it occludes consideration that the act of telepresence is really akin to creating a sign in the form of an index or trace. Belief in telepresence as some form of material actuality reveals a metaphysical belief that one might move into a sign, into a virtual topography that in its indexicality is necessarily a wholly aesthetic "terrain" of signification. It literally asks the individual to become one with the image.[11]

In many personal webcams and websites, gay/queer men present themselves as living emblems. Through combinations of images and text they become the simulation of their sexual fantasies, implicitly suggesting and explicitly depicting that "the online transmission of my fantasy self *is* the real me." They render themselves telefetishes. These fantasy images have garnered unto themselves an ironic power: like the archaic fetish they are skillfully contrived, made by art, animated by the owners' spirit, and worshiped in their own character to the extent that spatial metaphors of the Web promote the largely unspoken belief that individuals and their embodied selves can be fully interpellated within the conceptual apparatus of the technology. Website participants actually see the moving images, the traces of the "little people in the box" to whom Stone refers. In my online research for this project I sometimes encountered the assertion that "my fantasy is real," and I suggest that the assertion reflects something of this dynamic; it underscores the complex, even contradictory distinctions and overlaps between experience and materiality. Moreover, asserting that one's fantasies are real concords with Clifford Geertz's suggestion that ritual practices allow for the temporary fusing of images and attitudes about the nature of existence with one's actual experience of real existence: "In a ritual, the world as lived and the world as imagined, fused under the agency of a single set of symbolic forms, turns out to be the same world" (1973:112).

Telepresence, in its meaning as the virtual presence in the form of a digital sign of an object or person situated elsewhere, is a powerful means for making sense of the postmodern commodity-body. Recall the discussion in chapter 3 of how the meanings of the icon and index overlap and interpenetrate in everyday usage. Telepresence promotes the synechistic possibility that icons may, experientially for viewers, transmogrify into indices or traces. A webcam owner can be both a material body and his iconic telefetish: material and virtual, spatial and textual, symbolic and indexical, and archaic and posthuman, either both at once or in a now-here, then-there fashion both instantaneous and fluid. This is further made possible by the "actuality" of both materiality *and* virtuality (Lévy 1998; Shields 2000) coupled with a webcam site owner's experience of spatial separation or structuring that telepresence seems to authorize between his body and his Web persona. What telepresence further allows is for webcam owners to experience their own re-representation to themselves. This experience of self-visibilization, elaborated below and also discussed in chapter 4's assessment of graphical chat, helps foster the sense that the information presented represents a crucial aspect of who these men *actually* are. In chapter 1, I noted that Marx hoped the proletariat would come to see that in its possession of only its own sensuous embodiment it was other to the bourgeoisie. It is productive to articulate this idea to Georg Lukács's famous question as to what it is that individual proletarians know when they come to see themselves as commodities. A tentative answer might be "sensuous commodities" operating within a Western capitalism dependent on a "technocracy of sensuality" (Haug 1986:45).

For a webcam site owner, the images of his body as a cosmopolitan surface, as a commoditized "work of art" on the Web, can be equally telepresent to himself. The way they appear to him on a screen can have an equal measure of use value for him as for fans and other viewers. As such the metaphysics of telepresence allows his commodified sign/body something akin to a haunting return of the trace even as it also has provided him the sense of distance between the iconography and his embodied presence that modern sensibility still demands. The issue of automation and the automaton, discussed in chapter 4, also applies. This was a central reason provided by Sean Patrick Williams for his engagement with the webcam experience: "It really will run by itself on its own. I think that's why it keeps going" (quoted in Snyder 2002:184). Williams is referring to the automated technology upon which a webcam operation relies. By inference, this includes its generation of the telefetish through the display.

Constructing one's Web-based telefetish within an already fetishized technological environment is a doubling—the making of Pietz's "power object"—and hence a potential negation of any sense of falseness. This may explain the déjà vu quality of fascination on the part of some webcam operators who keep weblogs attached to their sites and who have posted comments roughly along these Lacanian lines: "Watching myself on the camera is very interesting . . . to be able to see myself from another's point of view." In such comments that implicitly acknowledge the impersonal power of the gaze as a two-way process, one may see how representation, simulation, or symbolization collapses into a sense that there really is (at least a trace of) another who watches.

>>> Gaze of the Telefetish

Jason Weidemann (2003) is one of the few gay/queer men to have published a personal account of his experiences as a former webcam operator. He divides into three categories webcams marketed to gay/queer men: "Single cams run by one person [like his own]; . . . portal sites, where subscription to a single commercially run website offers access to several different amateurs; and webcam houses . . . largely put together by entrepreneurial college students, which started appearing in the late 90's" (n.p.). About his experience he writes: "I usually tried to be live on camera about two hours a day. Most of the time I must have been boring to watch. I typed papers and wrote e-mails, napped in the nude, ate ramen noodles. The camera was perched above my computer, focusing on my face, but occasionally pointed toward my bed when I read or slept. Often I was sexually explicit, stripping and then masturbating. I usually began the night with the mindset of 'putting in my hours,' but the thought of men across the world watching me, and some finding me beautiful, usually shifted my attitude to enjoying being sexually explicit on camera" (n.p.).

Weidemann goes on to explain how he came to name his site As You Gaze Upon Me: "The title for my website was undoubtedly influenced by the cultural studies classes I was taking at the time, where the term 'the gaze' was making the rounds. As I understood it at the time, the 'gaze,' always masculine, represented the flow of power between voyeur and subject: the gaze was an act of consumption directed against an object by a more powerful subject. This concept may have merit, but the gaze worked differently for me. It was an act I courted and a part of my own erotics as an exhibitionist. Rather than seeing 'the gaze' as a source of insidious power, I came to see it as a major component of my own pleasure" (n.p.).

With its use of the conjunction "as," Weidemann's site name implies the simultaneous viewing practices of many individuals, himself included. Weidemann courted the gaze of his viewers. His desire elicited it, and he welcomed it as a major component of his pleasure. The form of the gaze to which he refers is consonant with Laura Mulvey's classic theorization about popular cinema's production and reproduction of the "male gaze." Mulvey appropriates psychoanalytic theory to demonstrate "the way the unconscious of patriarchal society has structured film form" (1975:6). The subject of the gaze, for Mulvey, is always male. The female is the object of his gaze. Mulvey ties her theory directly to the cinematic apparatus. The cinema is a technology of projection and, consonant with the technology's mechanisms, "practically all traditional narrative cinema treats woman's body as a projection of male vision" (Huyssen 2000:208). In her assessment of the positive potential of women's webcams, Michele White notes that, while privileged forms of looking continue to inhere in "certain kinds of heterosexual white masculinity," other more gender-neutral conceptions of the gaze admit "that compliance and power can be the products, as well as the instigators, of the gaze" (2003:9).

What might it mean for men to gaze on men, not within the cinema of projection but on the Web of transmission? Mulvey notes that the conventions of cinema create a hermetically sealed world "indifferent to the presence of the audience" (9), but Weidemann seems anything but indifferent. Slavoj Žižek notes that the gaze "denotes at the same time power (it enables us to exert control over the situation . . .) and impotence (as bearers of a gaze, we are reduced to the role of passive witness . . .)" (1990:2). White notes that webcam viewers, as computer users interacting with the screen, "become collapsed with the computer and may fail to distinguish where subject ends and object begins" (2003:20). Her comment suggests the postrepresentational experiential quality of certain webcam practices, and the fact that networked settings destabilize the gaze/gazer binary. These observations merit reading alongside Rappaport's observation that ritual participants fuse with a ritual's ordering processes: "To say that [in a ritual] performers participate in or become parts of the orders they are realizing is to say that transmitter-receivers become fused with the messages they are transmitting and receiving. In conforming to the orders that their performances bring into being, and that come alive in their performance, performers become indistinguishable from those orders" (1999:119).

A webcam's interactive qualities transmit the power of the gaze in wider and more diffuse ways than cinema's direct projection. In chapter 3 I noted that something transmitted has the potential to escape the anticipated trajectory of the sender, to attain its own quasi-independent, automated sphere of influence. The collapse and fusion of which White and Rappaport write directs me to Jacques Lacan, a third source useful for interpreting Weidemann's embrace of the impersonal male gaze. I do so less for Lacan's psychoanalytic insight than for his explicitly spatializing qualities of explanation, diagrams included, that read almost as a theory of certain forms of networked viewing practices. In *The Four Fundamental Concepts of Psychoanalysis* (1978), Lacan is interested in demonstrating how vision or image comes to intersect the realm of symbolic language (41). Readers encounter several diagrams of which three pertain to the present work (figure 10). The first two are of isosceles triangles (triangles with two equal sides) (91), the third a double dihedron (106). In the illustration of the two triangles, Lacan identifies the apex as a "geometral point" or geometral subject. It also represents the eye of the individual viewing subject. Lacan labels the far side of the triangle the "object," a plane this eye regards. A line transects the triangle, at an angle parallel to this far side or object. This bisecting line he labels "image" (this line is similar to the Albertian veil of perspectival drawing). It exists midway between the eye and the object of its gaze.

Lacan distinguishes between the eye and the gaze. The second triangle diagrams how one is looked at from every quarter—a looking that need not only be the collective sight of others trained upon me, for the impersonal

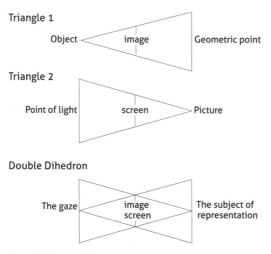

Triangle 1

Object — image — Geometric point

Triangle 2

Point of light — screen — Picture

Double Dihedron

The gaze — image screen — The subject of representation

10 Lacan's diagram of the gaze. Adapted by Liz McKenzie.

gaze need not emanate only from human eyes. Watching my moving image on the screen, I can also be part of this gaze, part of the invisible and anonymous surveillance that may scan the world, or focus on another. This triangle's apex is labeled "point of light," its far side "picture" and what the gaze composes. Lacan labels the transecting line "screen." Imagine the third diagram, the double dihedron in figure 10, produced by first turning the two triangles so that their apexes face or point at each other and then pushing these triangles into each other. The apexes that respectively represented geometral point (eye) and point of light (gaze) come to rest against, or touch, the far side of each other's original triangle. The merger or superimposition onto one another of the triangles causes the transecting lines of image and of screen to coincide as the screen/image standing midway between the gaze and the subject of representation. Because of this conjoining, the subject of representation now becomes, for the impersonal gaze, coterminous with a screen/image. Experientially, it may seem a psychic appendage of the screen. Equally, the gaze is now, for the subject of representation, located at this image/screen dialectic. Both, then, operate, in Rappaport's terms, as transmitter-receivers ritualistically "fused" with/appended to the messages they send and receive. The subject of representation does become, like Weidemann, a picture to be consumed by others, but he is also in a position to assert, "I am a Camera": I am a mechanism transmitting not only the gaze but a truth claim, an aura affecting me and multiple yous as you gaze upon me. This potential is enhanced when what may, at first glance, seem only an image of himself on his screen turns with a camera vision of its own and, in a manner not unlike the "artificial subjectivity" of the avatar identified by Gonzáles (2000) and discussed in chapter 4, reflects the gaze back toward him in imaginary form, like the trace as "the origin of the origin."

In Weidemann's embrace of the transmitted gaze, if online viewers interpret his sign/body as coterminous with his actual embodied position, and at the same time he intuits the collective impersonal gaze as coterminous with the screen that also displays his image back to him, then his viewing of the screen could make available to him the collective reflective power of the gaze. Indeed, this would be a powerful subjectivity by reflection—one that might exceed the power implicit in Lacan's observation that the gaze is "the subject sustaining himself in a function of desire" (1978:84). In Weidemann's case that would mean he produces, together with the camera, his own aura, a coproduction that allows him to move beyond seeing himself as merely objectified or the *projected* fantasy of others. Even if no one else is present when one looks—a situation in which most webcam viewers find themselves—as long as an individual looks he or she is subject to the impersonal gaze. The webcam fan looking at Weidemann sees him as an image, but conceptually the screen/image fusion, as diagrammed in Lacan's double dihedron, allows the impersonal gaze, of which this individual is already a part, to also reflect back on him. Looking itself indicates the desire that results in the gaze. In webcam settings, the technology of transmission, including its automated features that were so appealing to Sean Patrick Williams ("it really will run by itself on its own"), incorporates the networked gaze. This gaze includes the operator who watches himself watching himself as a telefetish—a display that fuses image to screen and sign to body. This operator, too, is part of the anonymous apparatus that may surveil the world, or focus in on another in a manner that inverts understanding Weidemann and other operators as only exhibitionists. As a man, Weidemann already possesses the power of the gaze to objectify others that Mulvey identifies. Yet, as a man who desires and therefore at times sexually objectifies other men, Weidemann is able to move back and forth between Mulvey's gendered positions. As Lacan's triangulated overlay suggests, in networked settings he is neither subject nor object, sender nor receiver, sign nor body, but, synechistically, he is all of these at once. He looks into the camera, desiring the male gaze that seeks his image on the screen because it visibilizes his existence not only as a subject but also as an auratic object—something powerful to be worshiped in its own right, seemingly transhistorical yet only truly valuable for a time.

>>> The Telefetish and Eternal Return of the Same

The effort to mount a claim to exist through a politics of the telefetish circulated within restricted virtual publics at first might seem ironic and self-defeating. In many ways it is; one cannot live by image alone. However, as a tactics of psychic survival it is twofold in nature. It is a turning away and moving on from the perennial lack of progress rooted in a politics based in attaining full recognition from those who may never be prepared to grant it. At the same time, in mounting a claim to exist through the telefetish sign/body in virtual space, this tactics has not lost sight of the history and ongoing actual violence and threats of violence that police the everyday existence of gay/queer men. Sean Patrick Williams came to the recognition that "there are a lot of people who are closet on the Internet, a lot of people who just normally wouldn't do anything . . . you know, when you go to a list of hate crimes and you see how many people get killed . . . when it constantly is happening over and over you kind of go 'oh wait, they kill gay people on the streets these days' . . . You know . . . I used to think [being gay] wasn't this defining part of you, it wasn't a big part of you, but it is, I mean, I think that as long as other people will judge you on it, I think it is a defining part because you have to deal with it" (quoted in Snyder 2002:192). Here one sees an individual who potentially would, following Düttmann, have moved on from a gay identity formation if only he had been allowed to do so. Taking one's place in a virtual public realm allows one to mitigate or negotiate on one's own terms how one "enters into dialog" with the forms of psychic and physical violence that continue to attend to what heteronormativity continues to insist is "too much" gay/queer public audibility and visibility.

The often violent backlash against LGBTQ individuals is fueled by a persistent othering and its attendant withholding in dominant discourses and practices of a fuller acknowledgment of gay/queer subjectivities. In U.S. settings, the backlash against visibility manifests in the 2004 voter rejection across eleven states of same-sex marriage rights including eight states in which voters simultaneously foreclosed the possibility of same-sex civil unions.[12] The same dynamic exists in other "advanced" nations, as exemplified by the rise of homophobic violence in France in 2004 following the passage of national legislation prohibiting homophobic hate speech. A gay/queer man might mount a webcam telefetish as a claim for visibility, but he might also be a father, an industrial engineer, a genius, a fraud, a Log Cabin Republican or possibly all of these. Such necessary complexities of modern life (though anticipated in 1656 by Hobbes in *Leviathan*) are organized across many vectors of which sexuality constitutes only one. This certainly seems implicit in Sean Patrick Williams's earlier understanding of his positionality. This reality, however, is often ignored in the heteronormative delimitation (perversely akin to commodity branding) of a gay/queer man as principally an outrageously desiring unreproductive and at times monstrous sexual object who, ironically, *also remains* unseen because, in heteronormative discourse, he is positioned as almost never here but always elsewhere. Keeping the embodied realities of gay/queer men as invisible as economically practicable is crucial to maintaining unacknowledged forms of privilege and is part of a political economy of resource allocation with the resource, here, being visibility in the here and the now.

Etymologically, *aletheia*, the ancient Greek word for truth, means "the unhidden" or "the uncovered," the not forgotten because in view; hence the tradition of depicting the truth as nude. Webcam operators who, to repeat, remain partly hidden and therefore partly in view, participate in this tradition and in so doing depict their status as "possibly true"—the possibility of the virtual on its way to future actualization. By transmitting what was hidden by means of images, online nudity and self-pornographization included, these men have staked a figural claim to the truth, to the flickering actuality of gay/queer existence. The contradiction here is that this digital claim always transmits from somewhere else, never from *this* geographic place. The cosmopolitan networked dynamic has the potential to reinscribe past and present gay/queer negations into the future in ways that foreclose future changes and instead reshuffle the status quo. Ergo, the eternal return of the same.

I also note that HIV/AIDS continues to play a complex role in many gay/queer men's lives. This chapter, in part, probes issues of visibility for these men, and as Leo Bersani observes, "nothing has made gay men more visible than AIDS" (1995:19). This "visibility," however, has also been used to keep these men on the social margin. The widespread moral panic that ensued following the media ritual of excommunication that organized the 1980s hysteria attending Hollywood actor Rock Hudson's death from HIV/AIDS is a case in point. Concurrent proposals by politicians to establish internment camps for infected individuals almost always coded as gay/queer men reveal the organized social cruelty that accompanied this pernicious form of visibility.

For many gay/queer men HIV/AIDS coupled to such rituals of excommunication produced around it confirm history as an apocalyptic narrative. The phrase "Living with HIV/AIDS" captures a cyclical sense of the eternal return of the same that currently informs the lives of many men as did coming to terms with Matthew Shepard's 1998 murder thirty years after Stonewall. Lee Edelman notes that for gay/queer men, the heteronormatively inflected future "is mere repetition and just as lethal as the past" (2004:31). Extending Guy Hocquenghem he further argues that "we do not intend a new politics, a better society, a brighter tomorrow, since all of these fantasies reproduce the past, through displacement, in the form of the future" (31). Tomorrow's problem will be yesterday's solution, only more so, a contemporary version of the eternal return of the same. *Plus ça change*, or, knowledge without commensurate power, is an intolerable thought that must be thought but nonetheless remains very hard to think. "The intolerable is no longer a serious injustice, but the permanent state of a daily banality. Man *is not himself* a world other than the one in which he experiences the intolerable and feels himself trapped" (Deleuze 1989:170). Enter increasingly interactive communication technologies as a privileged way to signify spatially and render historically visible iterative fetishistic strategies for coping ritualistically with rapid change and an uncertain informational future seemingly full of incommensurables possibly on their way to being actualized as concrete intolerables.

>>> Telemobility

I have raised the role of movement in imagining the Web as a desirable space of flows, and Larry Knopp has argued that gay/queer men are particularly attached to movement itself and therefore possess "a corresponding ambivalent relationship to both placement and identity" (2004:124). In the previous chapter I noted the potential for graphical chat participants to privilege their avatars precisely because these electronic identities may seem more mobile than the participants themselves. Clearly, gay/queer men are not alone in privileging movement. They do, however, differ in that while mobility is increasingly a normalized expectation of capitalized social relations, these men, because they are always discursively positioned as elsewhere, have been rendered as mobile, denied fixity, and forced into flow, without advance consultation; in other words, potentially against their will. Yet Knopp also details the ways by which such men often feel both in and out of place at the same time and experience pleasure in movement and displacement. This is indicative of their cosmopolitan perspective. It is also an outcome consonant with an understanding of the Web as a site of movement and flow and therefore with the construction of Web-based telefetish personae experienced as neither here nor there yet somehow both at once. As I noted in chapter 2, gay/queer men are not absent a sense of the future. Rather, telefetishism as a digital practice is supported by belief in a hopeful future imaginatively relocated to a virtual "elsewhere," the contemporary spatialized counterpoint to the premodern, shadowy, intangible reproduction of the endless "today" identified by colonial fetish theorists as one of the reasons for the power accorded to the fetish by "dark others." Spatially, then, the digital telefetish is a quixotic and indexical means to quasi materialize and historicize an embodied experience of placelessness coupled to a visible refusal of the hatred for gay/queer bodies.

At a more global scale the gay/queer telefetish has allowed users to stake an ironic—some might say incoherent—ontological claim to exist within the "space of flows" and the movement this implies. While actualizing a telefetish online remains at the level of the virtual, the idea and therefore the possibility of movement through Web-based forms does introduce the factor of time as much as it references space. Movement takes time; even virtual movement—refresh rates, connect times, lag—cannot do without it; and as Edelman (2004) observes, the core of making meaning requires us to locate it along a continuum of movement, at times spatial, at others temporal, always ending in the future. But if the future only forms part of an undesirable eternal return or seems on permanent hold, then an embrace of virtual space as a device capable of performing cultural work analogous to the temporal future's ability to stave off meaninglessness might appeal to digital queers with access to crafting a body double in virtual space.

Western belief in transcendence has a long history, drawing variously on a Christian "hereafter" that is equated with a heaven or a hell always located elsewhere and, for the living, always in the future, after death. Belief in a hereafter also draws inspiration from more secularized Neoplatonically in-flected notions of progress by which the future is always positioned as better than today. Yet, by inference the eternal "here and now," the ongoing place of our bodies, must be rent with "lack" and unmet desires—and hence as long as commodification articulates to the evolutionary belief in progress as an ameliorative dynamic, the "here and now" remains the site of an eternal mourning for the status of the present and embodiment. Enter visual infor-mation technologies. Even as postmodern thinking critiques the progress myth and transcendence as a particularly Western internalized form of magical thinking, information machines and their advances—part of the flexible discourse of a progressive future and the ambivalence it reveals about the present—are fetishized not only by "early adopting" gay/queer men,[13] but by large segments of a global and cosmopolitan middle class as new and utopian commodity forms.[14]

In ahistoric fashion, commodity culture proposes an ever-expanding present linked to a *seemingly infinite* world of goods and multiple identity for-mations in the here and now. This proposal is structurally consonant with the cyclical archaic belief that experience is always more or less the same. Debord refers to this contemporary temporal process as "pseudo-cyclical" (1994:110). Consumers cycle through the goods according to the dictates of fashion only to find themselves yet again at the bricks-and-mortar mall or the virtual one, circulating according to the alienated logic of the quasi-distracted glance. The theoretical distinctions between premodern and contemporary assumptions about the future, therefore, would seem to recede in importance in the face of an experience of commodities and celebrity-like online identities that arguably update the ancient meanings of the Hydra. The Hydra was a poi-sonous water snake with numerous, conceivably infinite, heads. When one was severed another grew in its place. I call on the Hydra, a foundational myth claimed by the West, to suggest the underlying linkages between the commodity, with its discardability and subsequent replacement by the fac-tory/consumer apparatus with the new that yet is somehow the same, and the archaic belief in the return of the same. Science and technology com-bined, where technology is as much a condition of possibility for science (and therefore of progress) as it is applied science, are modernity's more powerful answer to the perceived weakness of the archaic magic of the fetish.

For some, networked information machines seem to offer a way "forward" and an escape from the cyclical return of the same. As a utopian proposition, however, these devices can work to divert user attention from the logic of the eternal return of the same experienced within commodity culture, and redirect it toward an increasingly virtual future located within networked iconographic displays. One's material experience of the everyday, along with the return of the same that this locates, now forces the Western notion of transcendence of the finite — expressed, for example, in the Christian mantra "this *too* will pass," and which is coupled with a mind over body split — to cut a deal with the eternal. Eternity and infinity, time and space, set apart by theorists of antiquity and modernity, begin converging at the site of online Web technologies where the ideally real — the locus of teledesire — is the virtual.

>>> The Telefetish Backstage

How does the digital or virtual subject self form? Gay/queer telefetishism and its ritualized practices did not spring fully formed into the dataspace of information machines. These practices have antecedents in precursive and parallel spatial practices with their own forms of gay/queer cultural capital. The material spaces of commercial bar culture — the hustler bar, the leather bar, the western bar, the drag bar and so forth — long precede the Web and also embody understandings of identity expression linked to performing the commodity form. The avowedly noncommercial produced spaces of gay/queer men's Radical Faerie gatherings are another example. They typically take place in rural environments, remote from the prying eyes of heteronormative policing practices, where ritualized activities take center stage as a means of promoting an alternative range of gay/queer/faerie identities separate from that of gay/queer consumer culture. Such spaces are "backstage," and Henri Lefebvre's (1992) notion of spaces of representation is useful in thinking about them. For Lefebvre, spaces of representation locate identity practices and are always produced and designed. While the ersatz spaces of webcam sites are formally different from these concrete spaces, it remains productive, given the success of telepresencing technologies and the beliefs that underlie their invention and diffusion, to consider webcams as produced *representations* of space that reflect in some way the lived and imagined spaces of the men who design them. The ability of the operator of As You Gaze Upon Me to transmit his onscreen sign/body as a performative display within this representation of space supports Lefebvre's idea of spaces of representation. This representation is the imaginary space "where" the telefetish displays itself indexically, ventriloquistically, pantomimically.

I would further note the requirement that such produced spaces must feel reasonably safe to participants — somewhat distinct from the larger world — so that they can engage in the ritualizations of the ideally real fantasy explorations that attract participants in the first place. Weidemann, faced with his life as a closeted midwestern teenager, turned to online technologies as an act of survival and hope. Spaces of representation on the Web that feel safe must be framed or bounded, like landscapes. Landscapes are social constructions imposed on nature to neutralize, tame, or colonize its dangers and are always bounded by a frame that separates them off, like a webcam frame within the larger frame of the website page filling the computer display. Psychically, webcam viewers experience webcam settings in semiprivate or private modes of reception and thereby infer to the settings themselves a quality of safety. Issues of physical safety clearly influence how a subject self forms, and an individual such as Weidemann who might not otherwise consent to be photographed or filmed in the nude may feel safer in mounting a webcam that transmits his fleshy image for all with the means of access to verify even though any experience of safety in virtual settings is not materially real. Belief that the telefetish sign/body occupies a trace of material space that is defensible and therefore semiprivate leads to a kind of hopeful confidence in transmitting a telefetish in ways that would not happen in those discursive formations or material spaces that might allow the unwanted intrusion of hostile eyes, bodies, and undesirable legal and social repercussions.

Participants in the spaces of commercial bars and alternative faerie gatherings and the virtual settings of webcams share in ritualized exchanges that trade in visually based and highly artistic conventions. In a manner supportive of fetish dynamics, these exchanges require mutual agreement on the part of those present and telepresent for something akin to living in art in a way that builds social capital through the performative aestheticization of their own bodies. These are the same bodies that are judged as possessing little of value by heteronormative standards. But social capital circulating among a marginalized group is not all that is produced here. Crafting identity in this way, in the spaces of representation that Lefebvre identifies, depends for any success on the effectiveness and competency of the performances and the artistry inherent in the settings and the "props." This is a fine line that must be walked, and fear of walking it unsuccessfully in online settings is often expressed through the recurring concern of operators that visitors not find their webcam performances "boring." "Ritual," notes Victor Turner, "is a declaration of form against indeterminacy" (1995:77). To be found boring by fans means an uncertain and therefore indeterminate future as an operator. Adhering to the logic of the disposable commodity, the frequent updating of sites and onscreen enactments of requests by fans are ritualistic; they maintain and extend the meaning and shelf life of the telefetish, thus keeping indeterminacy at bay.

Sean Patrick Williams refused to charge viewers a fee to access his site because he believed it would induce expectations on the part of viewers for performances that he would be unable to sustain. It was, therefore, less the idea of becoming a product per se that motivated his decision to remain a free site than it was "the idea that he would be a *boring* product" (Snyder 2002:189; emphasis added). In the previous chapter, I discussed the relationships between branding and emblems. The advance apology frequently encountered on many webcam sites — "I hope you don't find my site boring, email me if you do" — is partly an indication that branding exercises in these settings involve the ritualized emblemization of value as well as aesthetics, partly a recognition that at all scales media are increasingly fragmented and therefore competition for viewers is ever more the norm. The advance apology is also partly a recognition that an askance identity of "twoness" might have forfeited certain potentially important aspects of stability. Mediation, therefore, is never without its risks, and the advance apology is also a strategy for dealing with an overarching anxiety of being discarded as a *dated* but not necessarily outworn commodity. As Jonathan Sterne argues, "We have forgotten that we rarely, if ever, fully consume — that is, actually use up — anything. We live in a culture of disposal, not consumption" (2004:353).

This complex need for confirmation articulated to the implicit branding dynamics of webcam niche celebrity culture subtends the interpellating voting or ratings function written into many personal gay/queer webcams. During the late 1990s and early years of the millennium, hundreds of sites operated as a vast self-organizing website with the most popular sites achieving a "top of the charts" niche celebrity status that also positioned their operators as successful microbrands. Such performative rituals worked to regulate relationships among people: site owners encouraged fans to vote and results were tallied daily on websites such as Jasbits.com, which featured "Top5 CAM Current Guy and GirlCam Rankings."

The advance apology anticipating viewer boredom also speaks to an ongoing belief that the power of photographic images, especially ones that "refresh" automatically, in part flows from what Anne McClintock refers to as photography's long-standing relationship to "the romantic metaphysics of inner, individual truth" (1995:124). The apology, in other words, reveals a deep-seated anxiety that viewers who find a site's contents boring may also find the image of its owner's "inner" subjectivity boring—and thereby, by the logic of self-commodification within networked digital cultures whereby more and more individuals conceive of themselves as a series of necessarily unstable images, an insufficiently illuminated commodity form *finally* unworthy of or even without exchange or use values. For a period of time, the exchange value of the operator as a commodity is made available to him as a form of surplus—as a confirming indication or sign of his own social value within the network. But as the commodity ages, the networked effects of the ratings game begin to wane, and the operator tires of the relentless demands of the webcam as vocation, his own fetish value to himself becomes exhausted and the telefetish, as a consecrating nostrum, is discarded as inoperative.

Extending Foucault's (1978) assessment of the discursive construction of sexuality, I suggest that the apology (along with sites such as Jasbits and its popular descendants such as Hotornot.com where individuals consent to have images of themselves, or their webcam sites, rated by strangers) also reveals the ways by which the Web has emerged as a pivotal apparatus by which sexuality is (re)incorporated into mechanisms of power.

The advance apology reveals the dynamic of a human who has become a "working fetish" even to himself, even though the telefetish operates within a virtual space that is formally different from the material conditions of his embodied experience (online disposal has a virtual quality and hence may seem more "ecological," even as its psychic effects may feel exceedingly real). Such an individual may be a fetish object to some, or part of an interactive experience to others (both a camera and a photograph that refreshes), but regardless of his overdetermined or incommensurate online fetish status he also has sought to keep the magic alive and thereby avoid being discarded and feeling the abjection that may follow. This a material object (or a sign)

cannot do, and this points to the inadequacy of theories of the fetish positing it solely as a nonhuman material object. Rather, fetishism "unfixes representations even as it enables them to become monolithic 'signs' of culture"
(Apter 1993:1). While the fantasies and embodied selves of digital queers are
indeed experientially real, their material status within a website proves more
problematic. What is the material nature and status of a Web identity or online persona? In looking at an image on the screen—at a self-performance
or display taking place three nights a week at 11 PM or alternate Sundays
at 5 PM—does one see an object, an idea, a trace of both, or a copy that
indicates similarity with or difference from its "original"? The ambiguous
answers to these questions indicate that with information technology, an
increasingly visually and interface-focused culture fabricates a technology
of spatial synecdoche through the use of emblematics.

>>> Reality Bites: Virtual Space, Virtual Identity

Like contestants on reality TV, webcam operators perform themselves in
public media. The ideological frame of reality TV works to suggest that each
viewer is in control of the camera. To imagine an outcome other than the
hyper-individuating, competitive scenarios presented on programs such as
Survivor, American Idol, The Weakest Link, The Apprentice, and *Who Wants to
Marry a Millionaire?* is akin to being a fool, to not being savvy, to not being
in control, to have forgotten that each mediated individual has for a long
time been equipped with the sense that the camera is inside her or his head.
This sense of mediated resignation and agency also participates in the kinds
of incommensurabilities accorded to fetish practices by the theorists Apter,
Pietz, Krips, and Villarejo. E. L. McCallum notes that "fetishism is a mastery that is grounded in an ambivalent sense of knowing better, knowing
that one's mastery is limited" (1999:141). Applied to an assessment of post-
enlightenment realities, cynical reason organizes a similar dynamic: an intelligent, wary psychic exhaustion aware of its own complicity ("I know I'm
being had"), buying into no single approach yet sensing no (easy) alterna-
tives in view ("but so what"). However, with respect to how gay/queer men
have negotiated webcam identities, although cynicism is always a potential
outcome of attachment to the fetishized sign/body, the ambivalence under-
scoring the "artful deceit" whereby an individual makes a fetish also confers
an ironic power. And this power flows from making and transmitting some-

thing visible. What is visible here is a trace of the real experienced as autonomous yet which operators or fans later can choose to erase or discard.

The impossible possibility of an autonomous trace suggests that distinguishing between persons and bodies remains crucial, for persons are subject to different forms of aestheticization than are bodies. After all, bodies — such as, for example, those of gay/queer men standing in such fantasy environments as the leather or western bar — may project an image but they do not transmit this image through wires as personae may; yet the perceptual "realness" of a telepresent persona blurs the experiential distinction between bodies and personae, and the spatial distinction between actually being here and virtually being there. This online leakiness has implications for the politics of personhood, however actual or virtual, along with bodies performed "in" synechistic Web settings that are neither private nor public yet both at once. Men seeking to achieve online commodification as a temporary means to control the fragmentation they experience online and offline ironically feed what they seek to control through performing these very fragmentations. While this kind of performance resonates with aspects of queer theory's assertion of the hybrid fluidity of post-identity subjects, it also ritualistically enacts the contradiction whereby risk to autonomy is embraced yet held at bay. In a kind of hedging of bets, fleshiness is idealized online but never touched, and a virtual panoply of utopian ideas of queerness supersedes the ambivalent here-and-now realities of actual flesh.

A related fragmentation or doubling is found on websites of operators who are "out" only on the Web. This is a spatial strategy, again, dependent on understanding the Web as a relational space available for displacing identity and presence conceived as too difficult to negotiate "here." Telepresence allows these men an experience of being virtually "out" in the relatively anonymous setting of a webpage or chat room without many of the psychic and physical risks that they must incorporate into their daily routines as part of being in the material world. In light of this, witness Billy's Perv Website — a Cool Gay Site for Servicing Your Dick. Updated several times monthly during its operating period between 1997 and 1999, it received a total of 157,000 "hits." Billy invited site visitors to "click here" to "activate the perv interface . . . click here to view me in handcuffs . . . click here to vote 'which tanline should I go for? speedo or thong' . . . click here to have virtual sex with my image. And please, send me email, but don't ask for sex because 'I don't sleep around.' I'm only 'out' on the net, shy in real life."

Through telepresence's indicative magic, an operator's closet—always a relative spatial metaphor, but for many men in the gay/queer diaspora a blend of a still resilient internalized homophobia and rationalized against the harsh background of being the brunt of rituals of excommunication coupled to real violence and geographic and social isolation—seems more bearable through writing and designing a gay/queer persona. This persona is then in a "position" to communicate both to its author and to others from the virtual space of a website "where" the author also can be out. In this way virtual space serves as a "dream surrogate for better values" (Apter 1993:3); nevertheless, such coping mechanisms as Billy's pornutopic strategy are not entirely unproblematic for those younger digital queers who see themselves as post-gay or even post-queer. Though a site such as Billy's Perv Website can, in a manner similar to how MUVE participants ritualize difficult rites of passage through the performances of their digital avatars, form a bridge from the closet to a fuller self-acceptance, and while it should also be understood as a vehicle for testing, exploring, and experimenting with different ways of being (Knopp 2004:123), it also may confirm a decision that perhaps one need not be all that out in real life if an emblematic trace of one's self can connect through digital networks to other digitally queered hybrid identities that to varying degrees are also fractured from flesh.

Being "out" only on the Web extends the logic of the "virtual equality" noted by Vaid. The logic of this virtual equality is rendered hegemonic through Web practices that inadvertently or otherwise position "equality" for gay/queer people in such a way as to render as invisible as practicable those concrete differences inherent in the multiple realities of gay/queer lives. While the "glass ceiling" of embodied acceptance is harder to hit than it was a generation ago, it still remains the case that contemporary queers often are treated as virtual equals only if they eschew performing difference. Many digital queers "only out on the net" have moved to craft virtual forms of the ghetto as a partial turning away from or tactical accommodation to those who would deny these men or repress the truth of the array of subjectivities achieved through decades of organization both *against* homophobia and its practices as well as struggle *for* articulating a different *and* complementary collective sociopolitical and cultural identity. As Snyder observes, "A virtual world without closets does not necessarily help recreate the real world into a place where closets are no longer needed" (2002:179).

Rituals both distinguish and articulate processes that are unlike or incommensurable; distinguishing and articulating are contrasting functions of ritual but they are not contradictory (Rappaport 1999:101–4). "In all rituals private psychophysical processes and public orders are at once articulated to each other and buffered against each other" (105). An individual who is only out on the Web indicates his ability to distinguish the difference between the public and private realms he feels compelled to negotiate. At the same time, the statement articulates the meaning of being only out on the Web (virtually public) to the real-life closet and internalization of heteronormative demands for a very private existence "elsewhere." It may, therefore, bring into psychic alignment the incommensurabilities of public effacement and private presence. In ritual fashion, men making such statements transmit information about this public/private distinction even though they are not the original "encoders" of the demarcation. This indicates their strategic acceptance but not belief that they should only be out on the Web—should only construct themselves as modular flow. A ritual's performers may accept the strictures that a ritual performs, though they need not believe in them (120).

With respect to gay/queer experiences of material public space, belief or desire that the Web might constitute not only mobility but also some form of actual space grows in tandem with the reality that it remains taboo, for example, to hold hands with one's same-sex partner at the mall. And while it is acceptable for a handful of secondary sitcom characters to be out on mainstream network TV, viewers see little enactment of actual gay/queer experience on these channels.[15] The ontological acceptance of the idea of gay/queer cedes, in Eve Sedgewick's memorable phrase, to the epistemology of the closet. Any human experience of feeling "in" place requires both the actual space within which one "takes place," along with an experience of this space that endures over some period of time. If gay/queer men frequently fail to attain a positive experience of duration in heteronormativized material space because—quite apart from any demand for affirmative recognition—they are always positioned as always over *there*, in some kind of vague, ill-defined "queer" space and therefore never fully *here*—then it follows that these men rarely experience full acknowledgment as being "in" this *here* place together with non–gay/queer individuals who would have had to move beyond disavowal or indifference in order for this to happen.

A form of virtual politics that responds to emplaced disavowal manifests in webcams as a ritualized reliance on something similar to a recited story or myth that asserts the notion of "let's produce a virtual ideal that both responds to and turns its back on the problem." For some, this virtual ideal, the telefetish as a kind of digital human, becomes a locus of tantalization, mimetically mirroring the disavowal it was enacted to overcome. Within "flexible" but often still hostile contexts, making sense of the world through the Web becomes more than just anOther gay/queer option, for these men have lived by the implicit betwixt-yet-between compartmentalizing logic inhering in telepresence long before its technical application to online settings. This is one factor explaining their early adoption of webcam technology so as to mount the telefetish as a complex trace of their lived realities as both presubjects and postsubjects but never in-between.

These forms of pre-post, here-there psychic incommensurabilities that attend webcam telefetishism reflect the uncertainties and ambiguities of the contradictory dynamics subsumed under the placeholder idea of globalization and the central role of information machines in this idea and its uneven actualization. Further, given this contradiction, making sense via webcams also operates in a similar fashion to the intertwined logics of voyeurism and the pornographic imagination noted by McClintock. She argues that these logics are "founded originally in loss of control. The pleasure arises from mastering in fantasy a situation that is fundamentally dangerous and threatening. . . . [T]he pleasure of voyeurism involves the deliberate, controlled reenactment of the loss and its subsequent mastery" (1995:129). Whether the dangerous situation is local or global, webcam operator Weidemann offers a complementary insight to McClintock's thesis:

[In 1999] When "As You Gaze Upon Me" went on-line, I had been living in a very open gay culture for over a year but had yet to feel comfortable with meeting and dating gay men I saw as more cultured, more beautiful, and more advanced than myself. I found it difficult to move from meeting and speaking with people on-line to doing so in person . . .

. . . I had deep reservations about my own body image . . . At the start of my webcam, I wasn't consciously interested in exhibitionism. Not until I realized how much I enjoyed being on camera did I begin to see myself as an exhibitionist who depended on the comments of others to form opinions about himself. I began each night wondering who was watching and who was passing me by. But as the e-mails rolled in—sometimes four or five a minute—telling me how beautiful I was, how aroused my images were making them, I felt emboldened. Feeling beautiful turned me on, and so I masturbated, garnering even more praise. Masturbating . . . never became a clinical act. Pleasing others amplified the pleasure of masturbating on-line . . . The impetus behind my exposure could be explained by my hope that someone, somewhere, would find me beautiful . . . I was ultimately in control of the images shown on my site. (2003:n.p.)

Weidemann used his online performances to achieve a kind of situatedness in displacement, a fixity in movement. The sense of mastery he achieved arguably extended to the broader local conditions of his life. But, in gaining comfort through a process of continual surveillance by strangers, Weidemann also evolved a coping strategy for dealing with the sense that many people now experience of having little to no control over events taking place in the so-called "global arena," which nonetheless affects each of us at the local level. Given the intimate relationship between information machines, capital, and processes of globalization it might even be said that the kinds of webcam use discussed here can be thought of in terms of a poker metaphor, as globalization's "sexual flush," where the operator exploits his online persona as a form of personal rescue. Such a seeming contradiction further allows for the persona, as an excellent hand of cards giving control to the operator, to stand in for capital and its spatiotemporal ephemeralities (with all the payments under the table, or at least circulated through sites such as PayPal™).

>>> Living in Art

Freud observed, "Only in art does it still happen that a man who is consumed by desires performs something resembling the accomplishment of those desires and that what he does in play produces emotional effects—thanks to artistic illusion—just as though it were something real" (1950:90). Rendering oneself as a telefetish, as the owner of As You Gaze Upon Me undertook to do, is a process of self-aestheticization. As a networked version of "living in art," it is indicative of the modern belief system that the artistic field is relatively autonomous and can yield knowledge, social distinction, and cultural capital (Bourdieu 1984). It is also, as indicated in the discussion in chapter 4 of the novel and free indirect discourse, infused with the sense that art can form part of a survival strategy, making human life more comprehensible and bearable even as this might also at times entail a partial reconciliation with or even embrace of forces of commodification. The act of producing one's digital self-image intended for the impersonal gaze and transmitted through a technology also understood as autonomous (Feenberg 1999) is a necessary aesthetic strategy when becoming a special kind of commodity destined for online exchange. Weidemann's description of his experience in front of his webcam points to a strategic, self-conscious self-aestheticization:

> A clock . . . allowed me to say "cheese" at the moment an image was snapped. Thus images could be highly scripted and yet appear natural, as though I had forgotten the camera was on. (A great "performance" occurs when the aura of a hidden camera is produced despite careful attention to each shot.) Often, whole evenings were "posed" so the end result appeared to be a natural flow of images — the subject "caught" unaware by the camera, performing intimate acts such as sleeping, reading, picking one's nose . . . I often performed this intimacy on camera . . . unlike the subject of a photo shoot, I was also my own photographer. I determined the angles, the lighting, how deeply the camera probed, what articles of clothing were removed.[16] (2003:n.p.)

Depending on the site, viewers who are fans confirm the operator's self-aestheticization. They make ritualistic offerings to the operator by emailing him JPEGs of the screen captures they take of moments during his performance that they particularly favor. (As computer technology and broadband availability have advanced, fans today send operators video clips.) Grasping something of the metaphysics inhering in the "wait between [the photograph's] exposure and [its] exhibition" (Cavell 1979:185), owners (for themselves and their fans) maintain extensive picture galleries of these returned images, including brief textual commentaries. In so doing they highlight the ways that media compress lived experiences to forms amenable to technologies of playback and review.

Making oneself into an artful, even enchanting, telefetish reflects the long-standing Western interest in fabricating a homunculus or double, which is also seen in the fascination with golem and automata. As the late-medieval/Renaissance Swiss alchemist Paracelsus (1493–1541), in arguing the possibility of constructing a successful homunculus, states: "And by art they receive their life, by art they receive their body, flesh, bones, and blood; by art are they born: therefore Art is in them incarnate and self-existing, so that they need not learn it from any man, but are so by Nature, even as roses and other flowers" (quoted in Cohen 1966:43). Any attempt to actually live Art in such a way, however, means coming to terms with the impossible experience of switching back and forth between transmitting oneself as a seemingly autonomous and therefore transhistorical artwork, and a very historicized human being who, in transmitting the hopeful illusion, also points to the very deficiency, even morbidity, of the circumstances he seeks to transcend. An ambivalent politics of recursivity results. Webcam viewers and the operator alike become the camera that Christopher Isherwood in 1939,[17] and later Baudrillard (1997:19), understand as already inside their heads. Having interpellated the technology's spatial and cyborg logics into his sense of identity, a webcam operator such as Weidemann can interact with himself-the-camera that he sees on the screen-based display looking back at him and at the same time engage with the camera that may or may not sit offscreen as purely a technological device. As a person being viewed, the webcam owner stars as a willingly commoditized and interactive telefetish. He is alive yet a sign that is not; both a pictured object and not; able to be frozen in time yet also discarded by fans; an individual in control of deciding when he will no longer be a fetish, yet desiring the email feedback, pics included, that confirms both the use and exchange values of his existence as a communicatory act and worthwhile commodity. All of this transpires within a networked environment that serves both as a "place" (internet as space, coupled to the temporal experience in browsing or watching images on the computer display) *and* the means to get to this "place" (internet as technological domain of textuality, imagery, publication, and production).

Weidemann's awareness of self-aestheticizing himself when online suggests something of what it might mean to become a *tableau vivant* on the Web. Walter Benjamin (1968 [1936]) addresses the ways by which an aura and authenticity attach to paintings as original works of art. Aura is a ritualistically instilled magical power, but as a form of authenticity it is socially and technically constructed. With the aura comes the cultural capital that helps confer to the "original" painting transcendent status and political affect. Benjamin claims that early photography's technical limits invested the photograph of the period with aura. The fact that the lengthy "procedure itself caused the subject to focus his life in the moment rather than hurrying on past" meant that the subject "grew into the picture" (Benjamin 1999:514). The length of time "imposed itself as a sense of fullness and security onto the subject photographed. The technical effect of the recording medium became an almost spiritual quality of the object recorded" (Downing 2006:231). Eric Downing observes that Benjamin insisted that the long exposure time required by early camera technology was paralleled by the "air of permanence" suffusing the mid-Victorian imperialistic bourgeoisie that constituted the first mass market for photography in the form of the photographic portrait. Aura, then, emerges at the intersection of a particular technology and particular ideology (232). After 1880, with advances in camera technology and the introduction of the snapshot, the sense of duration important to aura's production vanishes and Benjamin is able to identify the emancipation of the quickly produced object from aura.[18]

Could an aura have inhered to the telefetish produced by SeanPatrickLive or As You Gaze Upon Me? Though an object's aura is activated by exchange and contains an essence of subjectivity that can seem to gaze back on those who view the object, Benjamin might have responded in the negative—he plausibly argues that "the presence of the original is the prerequisite to the concept of authenticity" (220). But his thoughts on early photography also suggest the possibility of a different answer. Weidemann explicitly identifies the long periods of time he sat before the camera, periods far longer than those required of early photographic subjects, in noting that "often, whole evenings were 'posed.'" SeanPatrickLive transmitted the sleeping, and therefore often prone, body of Williams for hours at a time. I want also to relate the possibility for networked aura to the sign/body. Deleuze notes that the reconstitution of movement is "the regulated transition from one form to another, that is, an order of *poses*" (1986:4). The slow refresh rates of webcamera technology in the late 1990s allowed viewers to see the image as a series of static shots—photograph-like poses that also moved as they updated. Slow refresh rates allowed the periodic duration between refreshes to provide viewers with the illusory quality of photographic access to "the inner gestures and postures of both body and mind" (McLuhan 1964:202). Slow refresh, then, provided a means of reintroducing the transcendental potential of the pose and something of the aura that Benjamin identified as inhering or sticking to early photographic images. This aura, then, was available to Weidemann, in circular fashion, as an authenticating means to help better render himself an onscreen original to his many fans.

But can the original—in this case the human webcam operator—present himself in an online environment? To the degree one asserts that the technology simply transmits produced information, that the essence of what is present is representation, the answer might be no. To the degree, however, that one believes the internet to be a space locating human action then one might argue in the affirmative, and to the degree the operator is experientially as indexically telepresent, as a kind of emergent digital human, then the answer is yes. Again, the allegorical concept of telepresence conjoined to embodied reception of display-based spatial depictions is crucial, and webcam dynamics complicate aspects of the claim that the internet is only textual in that the operator may gaze upon himself practicing his look—striking a pose—even while he is also fully present to himself. As such he becomes dead to himself as the eternal pose frozen in time and alive to future possibilities. An operator conceivably accrues to himself something in the nature of aura and a claim to authenticity by virtue of having looked upon himself as a work of art holding within itself all the techniques of illusion necessary for its production. This aligns with a ritual's ability to performatively articulate incommensurate realities in ways that draw them into one another, relaxing the emphasis on originals or proofs of authenticity. This point turns on Rappaport's (1999:119) earlier noted observation that ritual performers are transmitter-receivers; in fusing with the messages they exchange, they become parts of a ritual's ordering processes.

The spatial nature of webcams—in their tantalizing ability to suggest that they constitute a visible space, however untouchable and therefore possibly taboo, and in the geographic distance among operators and their viewing publics—mirrors Benjamin's definition of the aura as a "unique phenomenon of a distance however close it may be" (1968:243). He also notes that the distant object remains unapproachable. "Unapproachability is indeed a major quality of the cult image. True to its nature, it remains 'distant, however close it may be'" (243). SeanPatrickLive's operator achieved auratic status. He eschewed interaction with his fans: "The interaction really needed for me to be one way" (quoted in Snyder 2002:186). The artful deception of telepresence such as enacted ritualistically by the operator of As You Gaze Upon Me suggests that for viewers, too, his aura might inhere in his telepresent trace (recall Weidemann's grasp that "a great 'performance' occurs when the aura of a hidden camera is produced despite careful attention to each shot"). So near, so far, and both at once.

Benjamin relies on Freudian theories of fetishism as pathology. He observes, however, that "the authenticity of a thing is the essence of all that is *transmissible* from its beginning" (1968:221; emphasis added). The most sought after aspect of a webcam site is the transmitted real-time image of the operator—an outcome that updates Benjamin's contention that in an age of mechanical reproduction "everyday the urge grows stronger to get hold of an object at very close range by way of its likeness, its reproduction" (223). Reproduction in digital image technologies follows the logic of simulation—a sense of the original is reproduced in a dematerialized form that stands on its own to the degree that it appears detached, like the avatar in graphical chat, seemingly sovereign from yet pointing back to any original. To the degree that images themselves increasingly constitute forms of relations in which the subject need not appear to be present, the Web-based telefetish can be seen to achieve a temporal quality of virtual authenticity and its own aura. For operators and viewers alike, the individual site operator, like Narcissus, extends himself as a Web persona beyond his bodily referents, thereby seeming to exist in a ritual of communicability, to live fully, if terminally, in the posthuman artwork he has made in a state of fusion somewhere between an original and a ready made.

Benjamin further observes that "the existence of the work of art with reference to its aura is never entirely separated from its ritual function" (1968:223–24). The practices and techniques discussed here are queer and plausible outcomes of a ritualized effort to live in art within the dream world of mass culture. This is a material impossibility. Nevertheless, for these men this effort was rendered experientially plausible and strategically desirable through a combination of endlessly deferred recognition, the melding of psychic and political aspirations, and the networked possibilities inhering in information machines and the virtual faces, traces, and spaces they both conjure and contain.

>>> "When the Consecrating Nostrum Is Discovered to Be Inoperative"

Networked gay/queer men project a sense of self to others. Some are known, others adduced. Most are strangers interpellated by technology—and this is particularly so in the case of personal websites. Each is protected behind an active Web persona even while hoping for fulfillment through digital connection. But within the fetish's temporal logic there comes the disenchanting moment when it is time to let go. Consider, then, the owner's termination, in September 2001, of his sophisticated and informative webpage, Queerz 'n Jox 'n Sox (hereafter QJS),[19] which had been visited by hundreds of thousands of men monthly since the late 1990s. The final additions to its pages outlined the owner's rationale for closing the site — "longing and email":

> Many of the 50–75 letters I receive each day are from guys wrestling with despair: those who've lost a loved one . . . the lonely in their self-imposed closets and boys on the brink of running away from home.[20] I am overwhelmed by the expectation that I am qualified or capable of being their online healer . . . no more email . . . do not let the web shield you from your destiny. boys need destiny . . . do not count on a magic combination of computer keystrokes to deliver your soul-mate to your door . . . turn off your computer, go outside . . . do not believe that beauty is what photographers see . . . though we can share experiences on the net we are also separated by it. like television, the web is an exacting replica of reality, but the farthest thing from it.[21]

These parting words by QJS distinguish the real from the virtual by suggesting how the Web may diminish the possibility of finding confirming material encounters. Sean Patrick Williams expressed concern that his webcam operation made it increasingly difficult to negotiate real-life encounters such as dating: "There are times when I think that, a lot of times there's that persona and then there's Sean. And I think people will immediately start interacting with that [persona]. . . . the question will [pop] into my head 'Will nobody date me because I am the guy on the Internet?'" (quoted in Snyder 2002:194).

Deleuze and Guattari observe, "Art is never an end in itself; it is only a tool for blazing life lines" (1987:187). The sites QJS, SeanPatrickLive, and As You Gaze Upon Me exemplify how the transmission of self-made fetishizable identities serves as both an aesthetic and performative display (for each man's persona was the evolving product of his own activities) as well as a response (each man's persona was also the evolving product or image of the intentional activities of others, fans included). Ironically, QJS warns that a new kind of gay/queer sexual irrelevancy is at hand, one ushered in by the very technology of which the site was a part. Stone's "little people in the box," QJS suggests — in this case online gay/queer men weaving and unraveling new and old ideas of sexuality and identity—do derive use value from the Web. Yet if at times the virtual is its own reward, as part of a broader survival strategy gay/queer men need to get out of the house more often, as QJS suggests. There are, furthermore, other forms of salvation than living in art, which ultimately is an ersatz form of "salvation." Williams offered similar advice. Refusing to answer the hundreds of emails he received daily, he argued his site was a "window, not a voice" into his life (quoted in Snyder 2002:187), and he suggested that no viewer should consider him their personal friend: "You ultimately should go out and talk to other people . . . It's not about developing this personal relationship with me. You tune in and you watch, but get out the door and talk to somebody. My camera is on 24 hours a day, but if you think that's my real life, it's not. You're not getting everything, you're getting a picture every 30 seconds."[22] Yet many viewers did relate to QJS's operator and to Williams as their parasocial friends. After all, Williams had personalized his site and made it more lively through the use of his first and middle name, thus inviting closer forms of viewer identification than he might have anticipated. Furthermore, getting out of the house more often also entails grappling with the specific forms of opportunities and constraints embedded within embodied personal engagement with others—a complexity evocatively captured by Norman O. Brown's metaphor: At first we see "roses roses," then as we reach forward to touch we feel "thorns thorns" (1966).

It is possible to identify the sense of possession that fans felt for these sites and their operators, and the eventual decision by the operators to shut down the sites—a complicated set of interactions among rituals of possession, of exchange, and of divestment. Grant McCracken argues that "possession rituals allow the consumer to lay claim and assume a kind of ownership of the meaning of his or her consumer goods" (1988:85). Such rituals allow individuals to personalize the goods, to move the meaning believed to inhere in the goods from the goods and into their everyday lives. McCracken writes about the acquisition of material objects, but the dynamic he describes is applicable to the virtual objects and personae populating networked digital settings. It manifests itself both in fans' parasocially inflected desires and expectations that these operators would relate to them in personal ways, and in fans' capturing of operators' images from these sites that they could then make part of their private viewing practices. Fans visiting these personal webcam sites anticipated a pleasurable viewing experience. As a form of consumption, this experience could be fetishized as the kind of ideal circumstance that never seems to fully exist in the material here and now.

The quality of the relationship between operators and fans was a factor in determining the longevity of these sites. Initially QJS sought email, but over time he came to dread it. From the start Sean Patrick Williams maintained a critical distance from text correspondence, preferring to focus his energies on visual display. Yet his volume of email confirmed to him the site's continuing popularity. When operators and fans were mutually pleased with the sites' operations they were engaged in rituals of exchange. Maintaining the website operated as a form of gift from the operator to his fans. This giving took the form of transmitting to them symbolic and indexical qualities of the operator and his worldview that he at least implicitly assumed or understood they sought to access. These qualities were ones of which fans approved. The webcam operating as a site of ritualized exchange between operator and fans provided a setting for the exchange of immaterial goods, in the form of transmitted images and other forms of interpersonal communication "charged with certain meaningful properties to individuals" (McCracken 1988:87), individuals whom the gifting operator in artfully "blazing life lines" assumed were desirous of acquiring these properties.

>>>

For the webcam operators I have discussed the decision to close their sites was not easily made, and the divestment ritual that QJS performed downplays the earlier meaning invested in the site by him and his fans alike. Implicitly, by telling fans that the Web will not fulfill their needs, he tells them that qualities of meaning are, like identity itself, always contingent, subject to negotiation, revaluation, or even negation. At the moment that operators divested their meaning from their sites, the meaning that fans had brought to these sites came to be understood by operators as displaced. This meaning had, therefore, to be displaced by operators a second time. McCracken argues that displaced meaning is meaning that can't be accessed in the here and now. It must be deliberately displaced to the past, the future, or somewhere else (108). When the webcams were sites of exchange rituals, meaning flowed to them; it was displaced to them by operators and fans alike. As the telefetish exhausted itself for its owners (and for those fans who came to find it "boring") this meaning was again displaced elsewhere, as manifested in the advice to get out of the house and talk to somebody. As a form of ritual, "the displacement strategy has enabled both individuals and groups to suffer circumstances created by poverty, racism, and dispossessed statuses of all kinds. So important is the role of displaced meaning in these lives that it cannot be forsaken without dramatic consequences" (109).

The negotiation of material constraints that are also the loci of opportunities demands wisdom, not only information. To avoid this demand is to risk paying the potentially too high price of self-negation and an aesthetization that attends the displacement of meaning required for any attempt to live in or through art. The risk to be negotiated here, as I noted earlier, is that in making oneself into a telefetish, correspondence between one's embodied self and the fetish may seem broken or feel erased. Peter Brooks notes that "attempts at seeing and knowing are attempts at mastering, and our technologies of representation . . . always bear witness to that impossible enterprise of arresting and fixing the object of inspection" (1993:106). Snyder asks if, for Sean Patrick Williams, the "costs of production of identity" are as important as material costs. How is it possible, Snyder posits rhetorically, to create a visible presence on the Web without having to shape this identity into a marketable display? (2002:188). Rituals of exchange and divestment, then, particularly in online settings promoting the exchange of immaterial goods or values, reveal the complicated ways that exchange value and use value trade places or even appear to fuse through displacement of meaning.

The webpage on which QJS posted his final words featured an image of Tantalus captioned, in part: "Metaphor for Life on the Web." Punished for offending the gods, Tantalus was set "in a pool of water which always receded when he tried to drink from it, and under fruit trees whose branches the wind tossed aside when he tried to pick the fruit. . . . From his name we have the word 'tantalize'" (Howatson 1989:549). Friedrich Hölderlin feared that he "might end like the old Tantalus who received more from the Gods than he could take" (cited in Agamben 1999:5). Tantalization is "torment by the sight, show or promise of the desired thing which is kept out of reach on the point of being grasped" (*OED*). This definition reveals how an experience of tantalization can arise as a response, on the part of the viewer, to the always just-out-of-reach telefetish. The story of Tantalus also suggests the provocative relationship and tricky exchange value between the virtual and the possible — the more so when redemption seems withdrawn, substituted by a perpetual state of deferment, as a result of too much having been expected from aesthetics and not enough from politics. By the myth's logic, webcam fans and operators alike were tantalized and therefore punished by too close an identification with the site's promise—the vision, the possibility of actualizing an ideal real. As metaphor for life on the Web, however, the story of Tantalus also suggests an ironic sense of security that may arise from fetishizing the reiterative nature of the experience itself. The flip side of digital tantalization, then, may be a certain ritualized order produced—though only for a time—through the continuity and repeatability of the tantalizing experience itself.

For quite some time, we have lived in an age of parasocial interactions wherein fans feel they know media celebrities on an intimate basis and may act accordingly (Horton and Wohl 1956). The animated telefetish, the digital trace, heightens this perception. The story of Tantalus, however, suggests how close yet far away the virtual and the actual can be to one another at the same time, and a combinatory erotics of participation in Web settings coupled to their tantalization raises a potentially hegemonizing fusion of love and mourning if one senses somehow that the telepresent object of desire might be possessed through its image or aura. What is the artful seeker of love and fuller identity—the seeker who desires to continue to desire and who conjoins hope and desire—to make of the ritualized phrase "I'm only out on the net"? The desires informing the aesthetics of the Web practices examined here are embedded within a broader cultural yearning expressed in Deleuze's succinct phrase "new art, new thought." Though new ideas gestate within historicized material realities, the form of the expression also influences the form of new ideas. Didier Eribon suggests that the form within which gay/queer male expression gestates requires the casting off of an interiorized "yoke of domination." But before this is possible one must first understand that the obligation "to enclose one's private life in the interior ghetto of a divided mind" leaves individuals open to every invidious form of public slander, insinuation, gossip, and rumor. This is why "every gay man starts off learning to lie." To move beyond this, gay/queer men have had "to learn a new language, a new way of speaking, new forms of self-presentation" (2004:99–100). Men such as the operators of the webcams discussed here understand this. While they also utilize text-based forms of exchange, in producing themselves as visual telefetishes they buy into the anti-logos of "mere words." These men already grasp something of the essence contained in Rappaport's proposal (noted in chapter 3) that symbols, hence words, can more readily lead to mendacity than can indices — tied as indices are to actual events and material conditions (1999:55). It is possible to argue that within cultural settings where gay/queer men have long fetishized the image — possibly because images cannot be used to lie discursively, as is the case in such mendacious proposals as "don't ask, don't tell" — that the emergent networked culture of webcam operators has developed the "new idea" of ritualizing the image as a social relation. Even if an image is a fake, a fake at least points back to an original and therefore to some form of empirical truth. From the practice of making a "new art" from the telefetish, it is possible that "new thought" has emerged that finds expression, in these men's webcam displays, in a digital *aletheia* — the visibilization of no longer wishing to live the lie.

The sublime desire on the part of those inflected with "new thought" gleaned through new forms of art pushing in necessarily contingent ways against naturalized limits is that the cultural transmission of new art will usher in radical modes of thinking and social organization. Readers are likely familiar with the 1990s hype surrounding new digital media and attendant cultures of the interface. Deleuze notes that for a brief moment the French polymath Antonin Artaud believed cinema would play an equally transformation role. Artaud was not alone in so believing, but by 1933 he had arrived at a new, less transcendental thought about the artful tantalization of the possible: "The imbecile world of images caught as if by glue in millions of retinas will never perfect the image that has been made of it. The poetry which can emerge from it all is only a possible poetry, the poetry of what might be" (cited in Deleuze 1989:165). The world of images, however, may only become fully imbecilic if one thinks of it as a permanent state of affairs from which there is no other recourse.

It is worth recalling the ancient meaning of persona as a mask. The mask when worn keeps others from seeing the truth of one's face — of precisely who one is. But the mask, when donned, also provides for its wearer a form of psychic protection. It mediates the wearer's visual encounter with those tragicomic aspects and moments of existence that are otherwise too painful or damaging to see. The masking power of online personae networks this ancient knowledge to produce digital forms of the impersonal gaze. Each is the performative essence of theater. They are a "poetry of what might be" — in ritual fashion, a tragicomical twin, potential truths conjoined to potential lies by which to imagine a world of freer possibilities coupled to a performance of what it actually means to live as an image and commodity form. The digital mask, the sign/body, only becomes fully "imbecile" when, in taking their cues from Narcissus, Web participants refuse or are otherwise unable to detach from an illusory reflection of themselves and thereby render themselves less able to anticipate the tragedy of becoming an embodied other to oneself. Stated otherwise, the mask risks becoming all there is with no referent behind it. As discussed in chapter 4, the Web is then positioned as the author of the disincorporated subject. Desiring to be as one with the digital image, then, entails some degree of numbing oneself to the requirement to do the necessary political work of rearticulating the concrete personal and institutional practices in which each of us are engaged (see Joseph 2002:174).

And yet, while I am sympathetically critical of belief systems appropriated by marginalized individuals interested in checking out the value of living as a digital image, I acknowledge the concrete outcomes for which Web technologies do allow: their ritualized uses can form part of strategies of coping and survival. Out of this can come actual meetings with other men first encountered through online settings. These men engage a dialectics of the positive—in turning to the internet as a way to meet people "for real" they treat it as a complement connected to the material world and not as a separate space. In the words of the operator of As You Gaze Upon Me, "initial steps into an on-line community allowed me, a teenager slowly coming to terms with his sexuality in the Midwest hinterland, to articulate my sexual feelings and to begin developing a vocabulary to describe myself as gay. I met my first boyfriend on a local BBS after another user gay-bashed him" (Weidemann 2003:n.p.). Here, aspects of website technologies and the kinds of participation they make possible support Pierre Lévy's assertion that the virtual tends toward its actualization, that aspects of the ideally real contain the potential of becoming actually so. However, Lévy, arguably the most optimistic academic promoter in the humanities of a disembodied and utopian virtualized future, further observes in a more somber fashion that "the boundary between . . . actualization and commodity reification, virtualization and amputation, is never clearly defined" (1998:44).

In many ways commodity society functions as an experience of conceptual disembodiment. People are driven to seek experiences featuring images of bodies, including their own. In Peter Sloterdijk's words, "The remote, but already visible, naked body remains in the world where we have 'contact' without touching each other, the epitome of the really desirable . . . one has the impression that the images are already among themselves, in search of a complementing image" (1987:342). How tantalizingly cosmopolitan—the Archimedean view from on high, the Via Dolorosa refashioned as the impersonal technological gaze. Belief in the powers of telepresence, fueled by a sense of absence in the here and now alongside ambivalence about future prospects, leads to a "wishing [that] paints the objects with its longings, as if the objects were not themselves but simultaneously the remote other that inflames the wishes" (343).

>>> Anatomy of a Closure

Weidemann ends his retrospective account of his time as a webcam niche celebrity by referring to images from his now defunct site that he perused as part of writing his article. "There was also a sadness to the images—I never smiled—and a loneliness too, because it was always just me within the frame. Ultimately, the images pointed away from me and toward . . . another identity I once performed on camera. I don't know who the person I performed on camera was. *I often wonder if any of the men who watched me thought they knew*" (2003:n.p.; emphasis added).[23]

Weidemann's account begins in the closet, traces great empowerment, and ends with his site's closure. His final lament can be read in different ways, and I will address these different possibilities sequentially. It is possible that a closed site only represents a standard outcome of celebrity, the end of one's Warholian fifteen minutes. Yet Weidemann's words suggest that he came to realize, in mounting the webcam as a potential form of liberation, that the image on the display eventually contained him within itself—as an image of his liberation and liveliness. Following Agamben's account, Weidemann's narrative also reflects something of "the terror" inherent in making a work of art; the quest for absolute meaning devours all meaning, leaving only signs (1999:10). Signs and meaning are then freed to chase each other in a vicious or virtuous circle (depending on your politics) out of which comes the trace that, in Derridean fashion, already may have formed the origin of what becomes a circular process. For a time, Weidemann experienced the power of visibility as the thing viewed. Viewers consuming his trace were the proof that constituted the affirmative recognition of his gay/queer existence. Yet though he could bask in their gaze, he could not see them. Empirically, while they confirmed him, did they "really" exist? Or, on communication's two-way street, were they ultimately dead ends?

Weidemann's lament reveals his *need* to shut his site. Any one particular fetish form, though worshiped in its own right during the period of engagement, must remain a temporary one. The duration of successful engagement with it depends on how long its perceived auratic powers remain efficacious. While this might be understood as a "constraint" imposed on the fetish, its temporal nature is precisely what makes fetishism a viable coping strategy and why rendering oneself as a telefetish can do necessary work but only for a time. We live in an era when the image has moved beyond its qualities of appearance to increasingly constitute experience itself (Castells 2000). Yet the webcam operator who looks too closely into the screen at his own telefetish performance risks mistaking his own appearance as experience for being and, thereby, getting burned as a latter-day Narcissus by the very power of the telefetish's animating aura that made it so compelling to transmit in the first place.

No one can live in art, or within the space of the frame. To try to do so is to directly experience how aesthetics can turn anesthetic; one is numbed to sensation. I read the accounts of Sean Patrick Williams, QJS, and Jason Weidemann as implicit acknowledgments of this danger. When Weidemann wonders if his viewers knew who he was, when he writes that his screen image "pointed away from him" to another, he identifies the distinction between his material being and his lively telefetish operating as his trace. His viewers were focused on his sign/body—a fetish power in its own right and "properly" located in virtual space. For them, it was easy to equate the embodied Weidemann self with images of his body and to set aside due consideration of the differences between self and body (Waskul 2004:38). "At the end of the day," however, Weidemann remains materially real to himself—he pulls his head back from the screen to understand that his online self-performances were a form of production that allowed fans to identify less with his embodied reality and more with his body image. Yet the quality of psychic deception inherent here, previously positioned by him as a form of power, lies at the base of the highest aesthetic value of transmission. When Weidemann was moved to understand this, he could no longer live in art, and thus he stepped out of his frame and ended his beautiful moment. The possibility that Weidemann's performances were psychically deceptive subverted his original project of liberation. It bears noting Herbert Marcuse's understanding of the ambiguous, even deceptive dynamic with which art as truth is forced to engage in a capitalist world. While he argues that the truth of art is "that the world really is as it appears in the work of art" (1978:6), Marcuse also cautions that "whether ritualized or not, art contains . . . the protest against that which is. . . . The modes in which man and things are made to appear, to sing and sound and speak, are modes of refuting, breaking, and recreating their factual existence. But these modes of negation pay tribute to the antagonistic society to which they are linked . . . the world of art which they create remains, with all its truth, a privilege and an illusion" (1964:63).

I've already referred to the Narcissus myth. I raise it again in the context of the idea of living in art not in the way that contemporary culture reduces this myth to a cautionary against self-love but to call upon its broader instruction that extending oneself ever farther into space increases the potential for becoming numb (McLuhan 1964:59). Becoming numb. The self-deception that arises from confusing oneself with an illusion. Narcissus and narcotics share the same prefix. Narcissus, taking a drink from a pool, was tantalized as he gazed into his mirrored reflection. Tantalus became his Nemesis. Cosmopolitan digital narcissi point to the dangers of narcotization through a displacement of perception induced by having already displaced themselves experientially too far "into" networked information machines, too far into their trace that circulates as a virtual object within the networked sign system. Such extensive displacements include conceptual entry into the dual zones of the image and the gaze that can look back without seeing, as well as taking on the power of the networked gaze through engaging the digitally enhanced potential of seeming to be there and here, self and other at the same time. Weidemann wondered if his viewers knew who he was, but he also came to view his image as pointing away from him. His final expression of regret—"I don't know who the person I performed on camera was. I often wonder if any of the men who watched me thought they knew"—would have been equally effective expressed as "My image was on the display but I often wonder if they knew *where I was*." Weidemann had arrived at the point of experiencing communicability—the true home of the gaze and to which it also points back—as a moving end in itself.

Marcuse further argues that "like technology, art creates another universe of thought and practice against and within the existing one. But in contrast to the technical universe, the artistic universe is one of illusion, semblance"

(1964:238). While the passage indicates his inability to predict the future—to foresee a time when technology, like art, has become a home for illusion, semblance, and distortion but also for critique—the thrust of his observation remains apposite to Weidemann's dilemma: "In various forms of mask and silence, the artistic universe is organized by the images of a life without fear—in mask and silence because art is without power to bring about this life, and even without power to represent it adequately" (238–39). One reason why art is without such power is that art is a form of information useful to the living but, despite the power of the trace, especially in art that evokes living bodies, not alive itself. McLuhan argues that art is a "translator of experience" and that, with respect to technology, it is "exact information of how to rearrange one's psyche in order to anticipate the next blow from our own extended faculties" (1964:242, 64). His definition touches on ritual's ability to institute and maintain forms of order. Early adopters are also early adapters. The attempts by gay/queer webcam operators to live in art can be seen to ritualize, as a form of impossible adaptation, one of the principal experiences that flow from an ever-more networked society of the spectacle. This is the sense that one is only an image. Perhaps digital technology's great illusion here is to suggest that becoming a telefetish, transmitting an image of oneself as a virtual object, is equivalent to donning the forms and qualities of freedoms denied by dominant political processes, and therefore it is to finally realize art's power to enact a "life without fear." The illusion is great because it is also experientially true, but only for a time—only until the trace moves on, and the telefetish is discarded.

To concretize my interpretation of the closing by their operators of the vanguard sites discussed in this chapter I have organized my commentary through an assessment of Weidemann's decision. Four additional factors should be noted. The first is economic. Sean Patrick Williams's decision to not charge user fees produced serious financial burdens for him. He was charged a fee each time a fan downloaded an image from his site. The more the site grew in popularity and the more mass media attention Williams received, the greater were his monthly costs, which toward the end amounted to nearly two thousand dollars a month. This cost was only partially offset by sales of merchandise and early forms of banner advertising (Snyder 2002:190–91).

The second factor is the influence of virtual mobility on the psyche of the operator. The constant switching between here and there, presence and absence, exerts a toll. When online, an operator is, experientially and psychically, only partially "here." His internalization of the heteronormative denial that gay/queer men live "here" and not only "there" leads to a devaluation of the here and helps produce these men's ambivalence about placement and attachment to movement as noted by Knopp (2004:124). Movement, then, can induce a temporary sense of self-unity, of moving back and forth between the here where one is denied and the there where a more hopeful utopia might be on offer. The ongoing embodied difficulties attending to the here renders it, at times, of insufficient value to mitigate its constraints. Gay/queer male desire is displaced onto movement and there. These men are among the earliest adopters of the there as virtual space—in other words, of the building as technology of the Platonic ideal that the true World of Forms is to be found in aesthetics—a disembodied elsewhere than this vale of tears. As I have argued, virtual space is populated by indexical traces such as the gay/queer telefetish, and the mobility motor they rely on is the exchange value they carry with them when transmitted into networked space. Once there, once in sacred virtual space, the trace, as "the origin of the origin" (Derrida 1976:61), works to confirm that the digital realm, the ultimately inaccessible there, is *invaluable*. Here it is possible to identify how the logic of allegory, when applied to the form of the digital realm that stands in for the ideal, recognizes the essential presence of the sacred and the true even in the profane world of the commodity. For the operator, in seeming to have surpassed value, the auratic trace in virtual space produces a metaphysical surplus that renders absence worthier than presence. This partially explains Weidemann's concern that his viewers may not have really known him at all. Though he sought confirmation through digital networks, over time the psychic fault line induced through experiencing virtual space as invaluable but materially inaccessible grew too great for an individual so focused on mobility. While the experience confirmed his self-worth, for his interpretant fans his telefetish as origin pointed to itself and back to them; his trace, as the origin of the origin, was worthier still. Within the logic of the fetish, this proved unsustainable—what was initially an effort of liberation, when rendered alienating after a time, became an impossible performance of self-othering, without value, and was terminated.

The third factor, which is related to the second, is the stale dating of the commodity form coupled to a fetishization of the new. If gay/queer men are early adopters of digital technologies allowing for new modes of self-depiction and formation, then might the most avant-garde of such operators have moved on to the "next thing" as part of a broader fetishization of the new? Ritual practices are never static. Bell (1997:241) notes that contemporary forms of invented ritual "not deeply rooted in any shared sense of tradition" bear the burden of showing that they work. Efficacy in "affecting people's cognitive orientation and emotional sense of well-being" (241) counts more as the source of legitimation for such rituals than any tradition. If a fan becomes "bored," if the operator feels overburdened, no longer a shaman but still a technician, lonely and thereby narcotized, then his sense of well-being is at risk and it is time to modify, refresh, or abandon a given ritual practice. A particular difficulty here lies in certain similarities between the dynamic of fetishism and the operator's identity performance as transmitted to his online fan community. While identity is crucial, any form of identity is also a provisional state subject to modifications over time. The fetish object faces being discarded once it loses its magic charm. Once discarded, it loses its identity as a fetish object. In a not dissimilar fashion, identity is in constant engagement with the wider world, and to remain operative within that world it requires continual assessment, negotiation, and, frequently, reworking. Coupling issues of fetishization to those of identity within these online settings can augment the inherent instability of both processes. Here one may see how newer forms of invented rituals may fail for reasons similar to why any one fetish form is discarded when inoperative. Desire for change itself is a strong techno-cultural imperative linked to commodity fetishism and the progress myth. In turn, the modularity of the Web contributes to innovation and, in a virtuous circle, a demand for novelty and updating.

The three factors cited above point to the limits of webcam practices. A fourth factor also points to these limits but in doing so suggests how operators may have gained something politically through the difficult process of deciding to close their sites. Agamben writes that "the only ethical experience . . . is the experience of being (one's own) potentiality, of being (one's own) possibility—exposing, that is, in every form one's own amorphousness and in every act one's own inactuality" (1993:44). Scott Durham turns to this quotation as a means to explicate the impossible art of Jean Genet. Durham argues that Genet's art affirmed an experience that exceeded the limits of his own identity as well as the forms of life and expressions of the world he inhabited; Genet's intention was to sketch a set of potentials and thereby give some form to the ineffable. While the webcam operators discussed in this chapter may not have had the conscious intention to create an "impossible art," they nevertheless share with Genet the sketching of a set of gay/queer potentials that give visible form to what remains difficult to fully speak or, for some, even think. Genet's is a crucial political gesture and one also conveyed in everyday language through such ideas as "go for it" and Nike's commodity-inflected "just do it." The difficulty for Genet in exceeding identity limits, however, is the possibility of arriving at an experience of "dying to oneself" (1998:191–93) so that, as reflected in the webcam operator Weidemann's lament that he may have remained unknown to his viewers, himself included, all that remains is the image, the appearance as experience. "For the one who creates it, art becomes an increasingly uncanny experience . . . because what is at stake seems to be not in any way the production of a beautiful work but instead the life and death of the author, or at least his or her spiritual health . . . art's *promesse de bonheur* becomes the poison that contaminates and destroys his existence" (Agamben 1999:5). (It is worth noting here the parallels between the way that an impossible art may induce in the artist the experience of "dying to oneself" and the ability of free indirect discourse, as a literary style, to produce "experience without a subject" [chapter 4]. Gustav Flaubert's comment to George Sand that the novelist should transport himself into his characters coupled to his recognition that "Madame Bovary, c'est moi" also suggests the morbid transubstantiation visited upon the artistic psyche.)

I am struck by the consonance between Durham's and Agamben's assessments of the perils of living in art, and the eventual situation faced by Genet the gay/queer artist and the vanguard operators I discuss above. Their websites pointed toward a hopeful future, but in so doing they also pointed back to the oppressive past and present from which they sought to move forward or away. Darin Barney, echoing Benjamin, argues that a technology can "be said to harbour the power to save us from the condition it imposes to the extent that it stands as a vivid and appreciable manifestation in the world of that very condition" (2000:232). The operator's moving images, therefore, can be understood as constituted in "what they are no longer or are not yet" (Durham 1998:192). This is the power to imagine becoming other than what we are right now, to imagine a reality different from today, and in so doing to expose the big lie hiding behind empiricist assertions of "just the facts" and "that's just the way things are." Webcam operators' production of self-visibility as an active appearance worked to expose the lie. As such the operators worked against the evil identified by Agamben: "The only evil consists . . . in the decision to . . . regard potentiality itself . . . as a fault that must always be repressed" (1993:44). But while Durham correctly identifies becoming other than what one is as a potential form of political power, becoming other (in this case, becoming visible there) while remaining the same (remaining invisible here) is precisely the ambivalent coping strategy by which gay/queer men have long survived. The political results are decidedly mixed.

As long as gay/queer men have known who they are they have also had to be other to themselves as part of everyday life. Most minorities find themselves in somewhat similar identity positions of "twoness" but, calling on the above discussion of virtual mobility, it is the specific denial of gay/queer existence in the here and now, coupled with the ability of many men to "pass as straight," that has frequently led these men to the askance desire to become other to oneself spatially through mobility—that is, to be in some other place than the here. Gay/queer men's experience has been such that they can reasonably ask precisely *where* new becomings—new epistemologies—and therefore new access points to power might emerge. I have discussed the incentives for gay/queer men to turn to the Web as part of staking the ontological claims to visibly exist. But it would seem that no matter where these men have turned to imagine becoming other they are given the message that they still are not true—either from dominant discourses that seek to deny their material existence in the here and now, or from their own experience that, in the end, the Web might not be the right "place" to mount existential claims through a strategy that produces the appearances as images and thereby returns them to the psychic place from which they started. Where then? I propose the possibility that Weidemann closed his site because in sensing it was false he was also struggling to understand (but could not yet give voice to) the fact that the dynamic of the Web too ironically simulates the in/out, here/there material circumstances under which gay/queer lives frequently are lived as if in a state of suspension between fate and desire. The Web, despite its increasing ubiquity, induces a binary territorial experience of online-offline, here-there, very similar to that already well understood by the gay/queer men turning to the Web as a means to mount an existential truth claim to somehow exist in the here. For Weidemann, negation as a young man led him to the Web that, over time, produced a second negation. This double negation offered him the possibility to reconceptualize his place in the material world and to locate some kind of truth in it. As he said, he met his boyfriend through a BBS service. In this way his art, though he describes it as a failure at the end, did have a positive political outcome. It did offer him something—himself. The medium was the reverse message. The sign/body was his to reclaim in order to discard. His online appearance as experience was as an outcome of his "impossible art" and it induced him to think through the powers of the spectacle and understand how it comes up false in the end.

>>> From Webcams to Weblogs

Early adopters are frequently early adapters, and while gay/queer personal and pay-per-view webcam sites continue to wink on and off according to the schedules of their owners and the exchange logic of the marketplace, other gay/queer men have turned to weblogs and blogging as ritualized locations to performatively enact both forms of political hopefulness and their ongoing negotiations of telefetishism, digital networks, and the wider world. Contemporary blogs are intertextual, hypertextual, multimediated, and modular. Their origins lie in early 1990s internet/Usenet discussion lists, postings, and "threads," but unlike the earlier text-based internet they are frequently image rich. In addition to textual commentary, blogging software allows operators to upload JPEG and GIF photos, flash animation, and embed video clips from YouTube.[24] Services such as Twitter allow bloggers to "micro-blog"—to insert via text message brief updates to their blogs in order to, for example, keep them current as new ideas and information become available to the blogger wherever he or she may be.

Though some images in blogs lack the feature of a refreshing real-time image of the webcam operator's body, many bear similarities to webcam sites in the ways they are used to stake personal identity claims, allow their operators to transmit themselves as sensuous and picturesque commodities, and require—if they are to be successfully received by readers/fans—continual updating of content. This intertextual and fetishistic dynamic transcends the specific content of any one site and is on display in gay/queer weblogs as politically disparate as The Daily Dish, Joe.My.God, Shades of Gray, and Tiny Queer Footballs, to mention only four among thousands.[25]

Weblog intertextual practices can also be understood by recourse to the ideas of sampling, pastiche, and cut and paste. Andrew Sullivan's The Daily

Dish, for example, features not only his writing but frequent insertions of YouTube video clips consonant with the argument advanced in the text within which they are embedded. Sullivan also posts responses from readers. Their discussion of the issues he raises is an integral part of the site's content. A recurring feature, "The View From Your Window," showcases digital photographs that Sullivan's readers send him of the landscape just outside their windows. The weblog, then, is something of a shared process among Sullivan, his fans, other readers, and possibly unknown others such as those originally posting video clips to the YouTube site. In a ritual, all participate. Contemporary blogging conforms to this dynamic—all can become part of the story as it unfolds in real time. While I do not wish to overly subscribe to the periodizing claims advanced for the internet, it is worth considering Sullivan's weblog as exemplifying what has been referred to as the shift from a 1990s understanding of the Web as a platform for production to a more recent understanding of it as a platform for participation. I introduce the idea of this shift—one paralleling other ideas such as Web 2.0 and the 3D Internet that also frame the Web as an evolutionary environment—because it is worth considering that the webcam telefetishes discussed in this chapter became exhausted not only when operators experienced too great an alienation from the "here," but also when they ran out of steam.

This is easily understood by too-busy readers expected to maintain personal websites or weblogs and who have been asked the question, "When was the last time you updated your site?" One's professional website is a fetish; neglect it at your peril lest the consecrating nostrum be received as inoperative. Fetishes are finished when they are found "boring," yet Williams, Weidemann, and QJS did all the work themselves. Other than including picture galleries of JPEGs sent by fans, their sites did not feature other forms of internet content or include the live feeds from other webcams that are now features of many commercialized sites. These operators and their symbolic and iconic productions were the main attraction. While fans may have emailed JPEGs for inclusion in their image galleries, the work of mounting, labeling, and maintaining them fell to the operators alone. Contemporary weblogs also attract followers interested in the operator, and also require considerable labor. Yet if one considers the percentage of screen space taken up by the weblog operator's actual writings in relation to that given over to YouTube access, extensive passages of hyperlinked intercuts of other people's writing taken from other weblogs and print media sources, and the emailed commentary from readers, then one begins to see that weblog operators, while responsible for arranging content, need not produce the entire site content for it to remain interesting. Nevertheless, rather than working against understanding these sites as forms of ritualization, including the reality of operator labor enriches understanding the intersection of ritual and fetishism. It takes work to mount a ritual and to keep the fetish alive. Overworked operators come to feel exploited, not seen for who they are, and finally take a break. Thesis 220 of Debord's *Society of the Spectacle* states: "The fact is that a critique capable of surpassing the spectacle *must know how to bide its time*" (1994:154). In the meantime, while we are "waiting," as long as individuals continue to grapple with the complex social, political, economic, and cultural circumstances within which they are enmeshed, the need for social dramas and the power of the fetish endures. Old forms fade away. But the need for ritual and fetishism, like new ideas and hope, appears to spring eternal.

>>> TeleRefresh

In the introduction I posed the question, "Do we seek from images modes of self-depiction denied us or made difficult through speech?" Vološinov (1986) argued that expression organizes experience—an insight informing my understanding of appearance as experience. But experience also organizes expression, as evidenced by the decision of the operators to close their sites. A final factor meriting consideration, therefore, concerns the timing of these sites' closure. All were American. Their duration concorded not only with increased expectations about what the Web-based image might provide for identity claims, but also within the relatively liberal political climate of the Clinton administration era. I only note incidentally the passing of these sites roughly coterminous with the coming to power of a radically more conservative administration much more inimical to the interests of gay/queer men and much more inclined to cooperate with nongovernmental cultural forces militantly opposed to any extension of visibility for these men. From webcams to weblogs. Compared to the direct visibilization of gay/queer bodies on webcams, gay/queer weblogs, with their politically "sensible" recentering of the text suggest, as discussed in chapter 4, the contingent value of more indirect forms of discourse and expression during hostile cultural and political moments. The image has not "gone away." Rather, the reinvention and reformulation of these virtual spaces accord with the social, political, economic, and cultural circumstances inflecting these men's lives and experiences in actual places. The text-image ratio of the emblem is changing, and with it the form of the telefetish. But the telefetish always remains open to change lest its presence become too prescriptive, its specific form and associations too limiting, exhausting, or dangerous, its potential for ritualized epiphany a bit too everyday.

For early-adopting vanguard digital queers, the webcam provided a pictorial "stage" of Web-based self-actualization and an ironic visibilization of the claim to actually exist in the here and the now. Keeping a weblog, like a diary, suggests the related need to record and make visible — through combinations of words, literary pictorialisms, hypertext links, and persona-like modes of picturesque self-representation — those "inner" thoughts and emotional states that the camera or graphical chat avatars cannot as yet "capture." The weblog places text more squarely at center stage than do webcams or graphical chat. Considering graphical chat, webcams, and weblogs in tandem may suggest a contingent spike in recognition that intertextuality and emblematics remain central to staking a claim or even striking a pose. Weblog operators, then, manifest the value of using the Web as both a virtual space and as a textual medium. They indicate new ways that words and images have something to say and show one another.

>>>

Many documented stories filled the old naked city's archives; many, many more personal neodocumentaries circulate on the Web. I have identified ways that some gay/queer men were at a forefront in ritualizing new forms of the fetish. As forms of ritual, gay/queer website and webcam practices reveal the actualization of new forms of the crossroad: ones where transmission becomes ritualized, where the carnival and play meet the shrine and worship, where the spirit of the demiurge meets the image of the flesh, and aesthetic and political desires rub shoulders.[26] These forms of ritual are a response to these men's offline, everyday circumstances, and an exploitation of new possibilities inherent in already fetishized information machines.

Digital Affectivity

Virtual technologies authorize action at a distance. Cruise missiles. Immersive Virtual Reality. Telerobotics. Webcams. All are forms of applied science that trade in what were once the realms of magic and the divine. These technologies operate within a highly mediatized, increasingly screen-based commodity culture, many members of which live in awe of the spectacle and appearance as experience. Such individuals are propelled by an implicit but dominant belief system within which "for one to whom the real world becomes real images, mere images are transformed into real beings" (Debord 1994:17). If, in earlier modern eras, the awe-inducing grandeur of a mountain range or the aurora borealis could induce experiences of beauty or the sublime in humbled pilgrim viewers, today significant components of this moral power have been relocated to information machines. In a world that mass media tell us is overwhelmingly polluted and rapidly warming, and which modernity has rendered disenchanted and therefore separated from much of human experience, sublime grandeur is now often found in the overwhelming power of technology. Graphical chat participants and webcam operators imaginatively transcend the here and now. They fabricate body doubles, and through these sign/bodies — avatar and telefetish — seem to merge with the immanence of lively technical affect, if only for the moment. This cultural move relies on a widespread belief in the machine's imagined *supernatural* powers.

In *One-Dimensional Man* (1964) Herbert Marcuse speaks to the societal confusion about the meaning of technology and its place in society. While technology is a social relation that functions within the realm of epistemology, the juggernaut it has become recommends working to understand the intersecting dynamics by which it is increasingly accorded ontological status. After noting that a computer, positioned as a tool, can equally advance "a capitalist or socialist administration," and that a "cyclotron can be an equally efficient tool for a war party or a peace party," Marcuse directs readers' attention to what happens when technics itself becomes a universal form of material production. When it does, he points out, "it circumscribes an entire culture; it projects a historical totality — *a 'world'*" (1964:154; emphasis added). James Carey reached a complementary conclusion when he came to realize that his binary model of communication as transmission versus communication as ritual was in the process of breaking down. His 1997 comment bears repeating: "To reconceive *transmission as ritual* is to reveal communications not as a means of sending messages but as the constitution of *a form of life*" (11; emphases added). Communication, Carey suggests, itself becomes "both a model of and a model for reality" (10) — in short, a world. For better and for worse, networked communication technologies now constitute a form of life, the networked cultures of digitally assembled individuals who are online a lot of the time have made a life world of virtual space. In a culture of technique, creating forms of social cohesion increasingly means the adoption of technical means.

Chapters 4 and 5, focusing on MUVEs and personal webcams, provide extended sets of concluding observations about the broader cultural, political, and economic consequences attending the emergence of digital humanity as a new aesthetic, historical totality, and form of life. These observations begin, respectively, with the sections "In the Beginning Was the Word" (chapter 4) and "Anatomy of A Closure" (chapter 5) and I do not repeat them here. Rather, I will emphasize that many of us now must find ways to daily negotiate in online settings the value of this form of totality or form of life that also heralds the victory of communicability for its own sake. Technicized forms of life play increasingly important roles in shaping society, and technology has become one of life's spectacular conditions. Looking at the symptomatic ways by which interactive technologies intersect online fetishistic strategies in ways that help produce rituals of transmission offers a powerful way to make sense of one of the stronger social dynamics in circulation today.

As Agamben (2000) notes, with the rise of communicability for its own sake, language and communication practices gain increasing autonomy from the actual bodies that transmit and produce them. Online practices of ritual and fetishism point to new ways of seeing and of saying that also contribute to and strengthen the emergence and growth of the digital world as constituted in pure communicability. The different forms that materiality can take, moreover, must also be taken into account in order to assess the different kinds of affective change they can force. Digital affectivity is the emotional influence on individuals and groups induced by digital media's specific kinds of psychic and experiential effects. The indexical worlds of MUVEs and personal webcams point to the importance of digital affectivity: part of the seduction of the digital flows from the affective materiality of the digital sign/body.

Andrew Feenberg, a student of Marcuse, in his otherwise compelling critical call to rethink the relationships among technology, philosophy, and politics, argues that traditional forms of power "based on myths, rituals, and coercion" have been replaced by technologies of control and communication (1999:11). Feenberg's use of ritual here appears to rely on Durkheimian understandings. This renders Feenberg less open than Marcuse to acknowledge how technologies of control and communication are now a historical totality — a world, a form of life — and therefore as central a cultural myth to contemporary social movements as the earlier myths, rituals, and coercions they have rendered obsolete, replaced, and absorbed. Networked communication technologies constitute an increasingly central location for ritual and its new modus operandi. They occupy a cultural space that blurs distinctions between the form of this electronic god-myth and the virtual sacred space in which it dwells. Online rituals strengthen networked technologies' ontological claims to be a world — they advance these technologies' political status. Equally, ritual practices, rather than fading away as many blinkered secularists had hopefully presumed, when transmogrified into digital forms gain new strength from the fetishized technical settings with which they increasingly interdepend as forms of the secular sacred.

As new forms of ritual and the fetish, graphical chat and personal webcam performances point to the need to believe in what Deleuze terms "necessary fictions." This is the Humean idea that our nature requires us to believe in the idea of something larger than ourselves. Would this suggest that webcam operators or Second Life participants could come to "need" their screen personae and avatars in order to exist? Does the creation and subsequent liveliness accorded to the avatar suggest an engagement and acceptance less of the world on this side of the screen than of the world of electronic networks, because the natural world seems too receded from view, an ecology reduced to a form of mediated nostalgia? For, at times of great uncertainty, art forms, including popular art forms such as those crafted in virtual worlds by willing participants, can serve as forms of becoming—as forms of collective conversation about the limits of our reality, our perception, and our understanding of what we mean by the self. As Deleuze (2001:16) observes, the work of art is less a representation than an experience of the sensible. Such art forms also manifest an interest in expanding the definition of what it means to be alive to include seemingly independent character formations on the other side of the screen. Yet transcendence always remains the outcome of immanence (31). In turning to the Web in search of new forms of life, even though one may not actually live in art, one may be turning away from affirming this life and toward using virtuality to induce excitement about being alive on a disenchanted, commodified planet. This is particularly so given that the older cultural technology, a necessary fiction variously identified as god, the hereafter, heaven, the afterlife or even progress, has been dethroned as an exhausted fetish for many, or made more strictly instrumental, as is the case in how god operationalizes the imperial political economy of postmillennial American crony capitalist fundamentalism.

The iconographic relationship of seeing oneself seeing oneself that is noted by some webcam operators, and that is also on view in a different digital way when MUVE avatars turn back to look at their authors so as to suggest that avatars now authorize themselves, further indicates the experience of power that flows from the ability to consume one's own ritualized networked performance. One may conceive oneself variously as an embodied cam operator or chat participant, a sign consuming the very sign that one has just visibly manifested through transmission, or on a pivot switching recursively and multidimensionally among these positions. This conceptual flexibility accords with the seemingly triumphal logic of neoliberal capital and the space of flows through which it circulates.

The telefetish and the avatar are, at base, the same surface creature, a virtual topological form required for perceiving life, that already winks back indexically to each and every viewer and that, therefore, also draws viewers into making meaning. Telepresence and sufficient bandwidth allow for ritualized exchanges of the fully capitalized and metaphysical trace that, in turn, authorizes celebrations of indexical images as seemingly true, as origins of origins. Such exchanges seem to magically suture the inner speech of digitally networked participants, home alone before their multiply windowed displays, to the visible sign/body that/who manifests before them in a digital public sphere constituted in the wires, servers, routers, and other machines that make the sign world of networked virtual space experientially possible. The technology grants its users and participants access to view but restricts full admission to the "true" materiality of the digital trace. In such a way, then, it is also possible to identify in such practices the continuing implicit acceptance of mind-body dualism. The Web, a technology that in many ways reifies mind-body dualism, allows for the bringing together of feeling and meaning in online settings even as it is the long-standing holding apart of feeling and meaning-making that supports mind-body dualism in the first place. In the settings discussed in earlier chapters, participants seek to balance the demands of the cogito—*I think*—with the desirability of becoming an aestheticized form of online transmission; it is, however, a visible form of sensation that is never fully reducible to this thinking "I."

The information machines, techniques, and practices discussed in this volume suggest two overarching desires. The first is to depict reality as a graphic vision drawn in light, the imagistic vividness of which interpellates directly to sensation and an immateriality that reifies contemporary Neoplatonic, Cartesian, and capital-inflected desires to transcend bodily centered limitations. The second desire, related to the first, is to fabricate illuminating technologies that confirm and promote the desirable utility of circulating, cosmopolitan, commodifiable, informational, provisional, and multiple identities that also trade in creation myths and the divine. Both Thomas Hobbes and telepresence propose multiple, contingent identity forms, and so too does the Christian doctrine of the Trinity—a single god can be three individuals each of whom manifests liveliness differently depending on circumstances. And the dogma of incarnation allows for a single person to be both god and human. Ritual performances actualize the virtual and articulate these seeming material incommensurabilities into an ordering whole, one that allows desire to serve as the intersection where fate and hope cross paths. It is not, however, only fate and hope crossing paths.

The websites I have discussed are both telepresent locations *for* and new pluralized forms *of* ritual and fetish practices and techniques. They are the contemporary digital settings through which networked individuals, incorporating aesthetic practices into everyday digital life, attempt to organize and make sense of the psychic incoherency of living under the sign of the spectacle. The Web brings to life Carey's "transmission as ritual." These websites and the symbolic power they organize are the synechistic crossroads where the carnival and play meet the shrine and worship as a new civil religion that blurs distinctions among priest and acolyte, worship and pleasure, utilitarianism and aesthetics, secular and sacred, empiricism and metaphysics, history and archive, event and representation, seeing and saying, incorporation and inscription, bodies and signs, depth and surface, and presence and absence. We create technical forms based on what we call ideologies precisely so we can really believe in them and really love them as necessary fictions. And, over time, we abandon them when we find them obsolete or inoperative.

Hillel Schwartz has commented that "the more adroit we are at carbon copies, the more confused we are about the unique, the original, the Real McCoy" (1996:1). If the Frankenstein—that hoary myth of uncanny kin so centrally telegraphed onto the contemporary imagination—revealed an earlier bourgeois fear of technology's potential as science's child spurned, and, later, a fear of automated competition in the workplace, then with sufficient bandwidth, display, and desire, a way has been opened for the contemporary cosmopolitan *cogito* to imagine a better, even more alive, silicon copy than the Frankenstein—to imagine that, in having made a space for the trace, virtual technologies might constitute a landscape of the gods at once both immanent and transcendental, a digital promised land with space enough for us, body doubles included.

>>> Introduction

1   Bruce Robbins (1992) argues for renovating the idea of
cosmopolitanism to better reflect globally networked
socioeconomic realities. Today the Web forms one of
the central realities working to undo the local/global binary at the level of networked individuals' personal and
everyday experiences. Robbins argues for a "rooted cosmopolitanism" whereby we each keep one foot rooted
in place with the other free to travel through cosmopolitan global networks. Robbins's proposal recalls the
adaptation of Diogenes by the Stoics that rendered the
ideal of cosmopolitanism as one by which one dwells
simultaneously in two communities—one of which is
the local community into which each of us is born and
the other is that of human aspiration, argument, and
discourse. Phenomenologically, this is apposite to an
individual's Web experience: his or her body remains in
the here and now, a rooted foot on the ground, while
Web applications, particularly those providing access to
moving images set within virtual landscapes, encourage
the individual's imagination to go "elsewhere" in search
of the ecumenical potential of sites, both sacred and
profane, that can evoke fetishized and utopian desires
for idealized other places on the other side of the screen
or computer display. Manuel Castells has proposed that
a principal influence of electronic networks may be "to
reinforce the cosmopolitanism of the new professional
and managerial classes living symbolically in a global
frame of reference" (2000:393). Adopting a more tren-
chant view of such forms of capitalized cosmopolitanism, Guy Debord notes that "what brings together men

liberated from local and national limitations is also what keeps them apart"
(1994:4).

2 For a discussion of theories of presence in television studies and their deployment in Web settings, see McPherson 2002.

3 To the best of my knowledge, the term "information machines" was coined by
Winner (1986:103).

4 Users begin their allegorical "journey" to Second Life via the company's website,
www.secondlife.com, which allows them to download the necessary software
directly to their computers. Once this initial setup is accomplished, accessing
Second Life does not require a separate Web browser such as IE, Firefox, Safari,
Opera, or Konqueror. Like browsers, graphical chat MUVEs are also Graphical
User Interfaces (GUIs) but they operate separately on the internet from such
browsers. Linden Lab, Second Life's parent company, hopes to redefine Web
participation through making Second Life a total-immersion browser where
each user's avatar interacts directly with "3-D" representations of people, objects, information, products, and so forth. Throughout this volume I refer to
MUVEs as part of the Web. We have come to assume that access to the Web
equates a reliance on traditional browsers; MUVEs, however, are different and
competing portals of access.

5 "Living a Second Life," *Economist*, September 30, 2006, 77–79; "IBM to Build Virtual Stores in Second Life," Associated Press, CBC News.ca, January 9, 2007,
www.cbc.ca (accessed on January 9, 2007; full website URL in author's files).

New Business Horizons, Ltd. lists on its website over 150 companies and
organizations that have a presence in Second Life. See www.nbhorizons.com
(accessed on September 6, 2007).

6 Charlotte Higgins, "Website Sets Out Its Stall for First Online Symphonic Concert," *Guardian Unlimited*, August 14, 2007, http://media.guardian.co.uk (accessed on September 6, 2007).

7 Information provided by John Lester, the Boston-based operations director for
Linden Lab (the maker of Second Life), during a keynote address at the As-
sociation of Internet Researchers Conference, Vancouver, B.C., October 2007.
During the same address Lester also identified Second Life as "the Oasis of the
Surreal."

8 "Linden Lab Opens the Source Code for *Second Life*," CBC News.ca, January 8,
2007, www.cbc.ca (accessed on January 8, 2007; full website URL in author's
files).

9 Yee, a researcher who focuses on massively multiplayer online role-playing
games (MMORPGs), maintains the Daedalus Gateway website. (In Homeric
legend the character Daedalus was a skillful artificer associated with the labyrinth and was said to have invented images. The labyrinth, arguably, models the
potential for a seemingly endless play of signification and, therefore, the emergence of the index and the trace discussed in chapter 3.) For Yee's assessment of

social interaction, collaboration and long-term goals established in such virtual worlds, see www.nickyee.com (full website URL in author's files).

10   http://online.strayer.edu (accessed on November 25, 2006; full website URL in author's files).

11   "Strayer University Launches Pioneering Virtual Commencement Ceremony," Strayer University press release, June 27, 2006, http://finance.boston.com (accessed on July 4, 2006).

12   MemoryOf: Your Online Center for Healing, http://memory-of.com (accessed on September 6, 2007).

13   *Encyclopedia of Death and Dying*, http://www.deathreference.com (accessed on September 6, 2007).

14   Raymond Williams first used the term "flow" in 1974 as part of his assessment of television broadcasting. For Williams, flow is a form of program sequencing planned by networks. The flow of television programs organizes the viewer's overall televisual experience. Flow is "perhaps the defining characteristic of broadcasting, simultaneously as a technology and as a cultural form" (2003:86). Technologies such as the Web might be thought to liberate the viewer from such centrally organized techniques. Each individual uses the Web to produce his or her own sense of flow and make links between and among various sites. I use the term in a macro fashion to indicate that power, in the form of information flows, forms part of the Web-as-network's constant circulation of sign-based information.

15   The term "virtual environment" is a spatial metaphor. As I have discussed in detail (Hillis 1999), such metaphors often mask various forms of power imbalances and inequities. Nevertheless, their use is unavoidable in writing or speaking about the Web. Even the slightly more neutral term "setting" retains considerable spatial affect and its use does not resolve the issues that arise from referring to a nonspace as a space. The transmission of information through information machines simulating such networked settings or virtual environments now constitutes a core component of the ritualized practices of networked individualism and the techniques on which such practices rely.

16   A full discussion of my use of the term "gay/queer" is given in chapter 5.

17   Interestingly, Deleuze describes the "unicentered subjective perception that is called perception strictly speaking" as "the first avatar of the movement-image" (1986:64).

18   See Winner 1986; Dreyfus 1992; Postman 1992; and Marx 2000. In each work this point has been articulated in various ways.

19   I make very sparing use of the terms "user" and "users" when referring to those individuals engaged with networked Web practices and techniques. As Langdon Winner argues, an instrumental reliance on the idea of use in discussing information machines reveals the naturalization of technologies as "neutral tools that can be used well or poorly, for good, evil, or something in between" but pre-

cludes inquiring how "a given device might have been designed and built in such a way that it produces a set of consequences logically and temporally *prior to any of its professed uses*" (1986:25). The "promiscuous utility" of technological processes and objects allows them to be positioned as fundamentally neutral with respect to their moral standing (6). Further, the idea of the user, while not void of agency, tends to suggest the naturalization of consumption, of a consuming individual who is also shaped by the technology. Certainly, consumption is a feature of Web use and technologies and those who deploy them influence each other to varying degrees. There are, however, certain situations where inclusion of the term user remains apposite to describing the practices and techniques in question.

20 The interface brings together the somewhat separate meanings of screen and display; I discuss these terms in chapters 3 and 5.

21 "Fiber Optics Turn Eyeglasses into Movie Screen," Reuters, December 20, 2006, www.techweb.com (accessed on December 28, 2006).

22 Statistical research broadly confirms that in one half of all American homes the TV remains on during waking hours regardless of whether or not anyone (distracted or focused) is watching. Figures released in summer 2005 suggest that the weekly average or mean time spent by an American youth between the ages of eight and eighteen on reading was forty-five minutes; on a hobby, one hour; on physical activities, one and one half hours; and on watching TV, DVDs, and videos, and playing computer games and using the internet, a total of six and one half hours (University of Illinois Extension, http://web .extension.uiuc.edu [accessed on December 15, 2006]). Figures released on January 30, 2006, indicate that fourteen hours per week is the average or mean time spent online by an American with internet access. An equal amount of time is spent watching TV, for a total of twenty-eight hours watching TV and computer screens alone (this does not include time spent watching movies in any format). (Jupitermedia Corporation, www.jupitermedia.com [accessed on December 15, 2006). Figures released November 29, 2006, reveal that 35.5 percent of internet users spend less time watching TV than before they began using the internet (University of Southern California, Annenberg School of Communications, http://annenberg.usc.edu [accessed on February 27, 2007]). Nielsen NetRatings indicates that an individual with internet access on average goes online thirty-five times a month, looks at 1,506 webpages during this period, spends 32.53 minutes a day doing so from home and 20.31 minutes from work for a total of almost 53 minutes a day online. Nielsen's website also provides aggregates of mean hours spent online monthly "globally" by individuals with internet access in Australia, Brazil, France, Germany, Italy, Japan, Spain, Sweden, Switzerland, the United Kingdom, and the United States. The number is fifty-three hours and does not include time spent in front of other screens or using the computer screen for purposes other than accessing the internet (Nielsen NetRatings, www.netratings.com [accessed on December 15, 2006]).

23 Developing a software application that depicts gender and race as a set of images reveals that the ideology built into the technology is what Stewart Ewen (1988) has identified as "the democracy of images." American media invite citizens, repositioned as consumers and faced with diminished access to meaningful political participation at scales larger than local politics, to redirect political agency into the process of "consuming images" from an array that best reflects the ways they wish to configure, represent, and signify themselves at any one time.

24 For a comprehensive assessment of the politics of racialized depictions in online settings, see Nakamura 2007.

25 American Girl, http://store.americangirl.com (accessed on January 5, 2007).

26 "IBM to Build Virtual Stores in *Second Life.*"

27 Several recently published anthologies do contribute to this grounding in material histories. See, for example, Lisa Gitelman and Geoffrey Pingree, *New Media, 1740–1915* (2003); David Thorburn, Henry Jenkins, and Brad Seawell, *Rethinking Media Change: The Aesthetics of Transition* (2003); Darren Tofts, Annemarie Jonson, and Alessio Cavallaro, *Prefiguring Cyberculture: An Intellectual History* (2003); and Wendy Hui Kyong Chun and Thomas Keenan, *New Media, Old Media: Interrogating the Digital Revolution* (2005).

28 "Farewell, Seminal Coffeecam," *Wired*, March 7, 2001, http://www.wired.com (accessed on November 10, 2007). See also Stafford-Fraser's essay from 1995 titled "The Trojan Room Coffee Pot," www.cl.cam.ac.uk (accessed on March 14, 2008).

>>> 1 Rituals

1 One might elect to understand "the widest possible disagreements" about the meaning of ritual as the collective outcome of inherently flawed theorization. Such an understanding would concord with the idea that a discipline such as anthropology that produces differing and even contradictory determinations on just what constitutes ritual might itself be in the process of unraveling. This view would reflect a positivist approach to the world—a preference that representations of social reality never contain any of the contradictions inherent in the reality itself. A positivist approach is "not concerned with the great and general ambiguity and obscurity which is the established universe of experience" (Marcuse 1964:183). Ritual theory's many variations, each indicative of the time and culture during which it was formulated, are more productively understood as revealing as much if not more about the individual proposing the theory than the ritual or those performing it.

2 The kinds of Enlightenment reading, writing, and rhetorical practices outlined by Jürgen Habermas (1982), for example, are highly ritualized. These practices were central to the emergent power of bourgeois individuals operating in a new form of Enlightenment public sphere. Certain forms of writing took place behind closed doors. Other forms of contingent group discussions demanded the

neither fully private nor fully public settings of coffee houses and salons. The continual negotiation of and movement between public and private space and, therefore, of articulations among social cohesion, contract, and individual goals was highly formalized through textual and discursive practices so as to achieve a more economic and effective form of communication. In a not dissimilar fashion, networked, on-the-go individuals communicate with one another through virtual channels often theorized as parts of a larger public sphere. These individuals nevertheless remain physically separate and individually located even as they conjoin through websites dedicated to ritualized practices. These practices, many of which are imaginative engagements with utopian notions of virtual space, suggest the salience of ritual theory's emphasis on social cohesion.

3 Four assumptions based on binary logic underlie the neo-Durkheimian assumption that rituals perform, embody, and renew social consensus. The first assumption turns on the continuing saliency of ritual theory's naturalization of the *sacred* versus *profane* binary. The second is lodged in ways that some theorists position rituals as *expressions* of an already existing system while others conceive of them as *constitutive* of the form through which culture exists and is reproduced (Bell 1997:73). The networked ritualizations I examine blur this distinction. They are expressive (transmitted as signals through preexisting Webs of information technology) and constitutive (historical components of the emergent culture of networked individualism).

The third and fourth assumptions are exemplified in Eric Rothenbuhler's (1998) assessment of ritual communication: the association of ritual with *participatory* cultures versus the association of transmission with power and *control*; and the distinction between *audiences* for transmitted materials versus a ritual's *participants*. Participation versus control, advanced by both James Carey (1997) and Rothenbuhler, is based on distinguishing ritual from transmission in order to ground the argument that communication is a form of ritual. However, networked practices are communication as ritual *and* as transmission: "Virtual spaces . . . have a long history in the form of rituals, and in the built form of architectural fantasies and environments" (Shields 2003:2), and the virtual spaces of Second Life and There!, in which participants elect to locate themselves, synthesize in complex ways the ritualized practices for which the sites, as zones of communicability, allow. With respect to audience versus participants, a personal webcam operator may watch a moving image of himself on the screen or display as a sign/body of consciousness itself while also participating in making his overall website more interesting to fans who watch in very active ways and who are rewarded by the operator in the different ways he can recognize them. These practices suggest that fans are both audience and participants in the collective ritualizations that the operator at times leads and to which at others he must respond.

4 Rothenbuhler (1998), who focuses on broadcast mass media forms, identifies four kinds of media rituals. The most conventionally understood of these rituals

is the broadcast of a funeral or a wedding that interrupts normal broadcasting and allows individuals to participate in the ceremony at a distance; for example, the funerals of John. F. Kennedy, Princess Diana, and Pope John Paul II. Live, preplanned, and presented with reverence, these state-sanctioned media rituals constitute part of a historic moment in which they help shape national and social reconciliation.

The second form of media ritual occurs when large numbers of individuals watch the same television programming at the same time, including religious broadcasting, organized sporting events, and certain soap operas; for sporting events the ritual also involves the consumption of favorite foods prepared specially for the viewing occasion. This type of ritual can also include mass-viewing practices following unanticipated disasters such as 9/11 or the 1986 explosion of NASA's space shuttle *Challenger*.

The third form is the ritual of media work, which occurs when journalists and other media professionals focus on producing "objective" reports for public consumption (a point specifically critiqued in Couldry 2003). The fourth media ritual is television as religion. Rothenbuhler notes the controversial studies authored by George Gerbner and colleagues during the 1970s and 1980s that claimed television viewing is a shared daily ritual. To the degree that Gerbner et al. identify watching television as a form of ritual, they also identify the technology's formal mechanisms as important in ritual constructs. Their observation anticipates my interest in how information machines are new virtual locations for ritualized practices that are amenable, in circular or recursive fashion, to forms of fetishization supportive of the ritualization of practices of transmission. As Rothenbuhler observes, "modern . . . technologies may operate by natural means that are scientifically understandable, but we do not experience them that way. . . . The power to alter experiential reality at the flip of a switch is the essential magic" (1998:122).

5   Shaun Nichols, "Building the 3D Internet," iTnews.com, November 27, 2006, www.itnews.com.au (accessed on January 9, 2007).

6   Plato (c.428–c.347 BCE) believed that World Soul was the animating force in all things. For the Egypto-Roman Neoplatonist philosopher Plotinus (205–270), World Soul was an emanation of God, and the physical world was God's body. Teilhard de Chardin's (1881–1955) concept of the noosphere draws from the Ancient Greek *nous*, meaning thought; it is a planetary thinking network of self-aware communication. More recently, Kevin Kelly (1994) has proposed the Hive Mind as the collective buzz of networks in which all bodies have become informational.

7   Telepresence in networked settings is the subject of Ken Goldberg's anthology *The Robot in the Garden: Telerobotics and Telepistemology in the Age of the Internet* (2000). Thomas Campanella has also pursued the issue—see his essay "Be There Now," *Salon*, August 7, 1997, www.salon.com (accessed on November 16, 2007).

8   Malinowski references his belief that the populations he studied had scant con-

ceptual understanding of the relationship between the rituals they performed and the broader circumstances within which they were lodged. His observation equally applies to contemporary engagement with information machines: "Yet it must be remembered that what appears to us an extensive, complicated, and yet well ordered institution is the outcome of so many doings and pursuits, carried on by savages, who have no laws or aims or charters definitively laid down. They have no knowledge of the *total outline* of any of their social structure. They know their own motives, know the purpose of individual actions and the rules which apply to them, but how, out of these, the whole collective institution shapes, this is beyond their mental range" (1961:83).

9   In the second part of this volume I examine how the Web is an ideal setting for the performance of allegory and the corresponding synthesis of metaphor and metonymy. In metaphor, A is treated as if it were B—as when one compares gambling to the "game" of life. With metonymy, A is treated as if it were part of B—"Washington," deployed in media reports, is a sign in a diachronic relationship with its referent, American national and international politics. A second example would be when the Christian cross is made to stand for Christ. In the case of an actual relic, one may see how metonymy's reliance on signs, and a sign's necessary contiguity with other signs forming part of a larger set as part of how it communicates information, connects to Peirce's ideas about indexicality and the possibility of experiencing a trace of the original in its representation (chapter 3).

The websites discussed here are particularly suited to collapsing experiential distinctions between metaphor and metonymy. The very name Second Life combines the two. Second Life positions online interactions metonymically—as if they were part of real life (arguably the case)—even as the term is a metaphor for something else to which it is compared. Virtual platforms such as Second Life allow participants experiences based on a fusion of metonymic and metaphoric dynamics. James Carey argues that humans, through the symbolic work we do, first craft the world we occupy, then "produce as many [worlds] as we can" (1976:22), and then transition between them as best we can. Clifford Geertz observes that not only does ritual enact a "story people tell themselves about themselves" (1973:448) but also that "in a ritual, the world as lived and the world as imagined, fused under the agency of a single set of symbolic forms, turn out to be the same world" (112). In networked settings, a simulative quality of what I will term *netonymy* may be said to apply. One outcome is that ideas and experiences, because they are performatively enacted within the arena of the virtual, may enjoy improved chances of actually getting built or coming to pass this side of the interface.

10   In Catherine Bell's discussion of the complexities attending the history of the notion of ritual she proposes a focus on "'ritualization' as a strategic *way* of acting" (1992:7). I understand the activity of ritualizing as the conversion of a practice into a ritual—as a specific mode of acting (labor involved included) that

renders an activity or a performance or a set of symbolic actions or indexical displays as a ritual practice.

>> 2 Fetishes

1 Deleuze comments more broadly that "the virtual object is never past in relation to a new present . . . It is past as the contemporary of the present which it is, in a frozen present; as though lacking on the one hand the part which, on the other hand, it is at the same time; as though displaced while still in place. That is why virtual objects exist only as fragments of themselves" (1994:135). Deleuze's assessment that the virtual object seems to lack that which it already is, and that it remains in place while displaced, parallels that of Jacques Derrida's for the trace insofar as Derrida (1976) identifies the trace that circulates in the sign world as an origin of an origin that also is not. The trace is fully discussed in chapter 3.

2 Though text-based chat remains popular with more marginalized social groups, the widespread relocation to Web-based chat applications, with their ability to allow users to combine text *and* images of themselves and of others, coincides with the decision on the part of many individuals to hold onto their nicks for longer periods of time than in text-based applications. This is not to suggest that there are not situations in which individuals may frequently refresh screen names to convey information that is temporary in nature. If on MSN I regularly use the nickname JoeCitizen, for example, I might, if visiting the Ukraine, change the nick to "In the Ukraine." In the serial striking of poses that this dynamic suggests, if I am feeling down I might temporarily adopt "feeling blue" and so forth. Nevertheless, for those who maintain their nicks, updating one's images arguably now stands in for the "refreshment" and temporal sense of virtually actualizing the possible offered through changing nicknames on text-based IRC channels. The following comment from late 2006 (which I have left anonymous) is typical of current Web-based gay/queer intertextual strategies developed by men seeking contact or connection with others: "Thanks for dropping by. I try to keep my profile fresh, switching or updating the pics, improving the text, browsing through other profiles in search for new ideas." Strategies of recycling and discarding names in text-based chat, therefore, bear dynamic similarity to the frequent updating of images and graphics on websites.

3 Nassau's description is in counterdistinction to his own naturalized European conception of a future heavily dependent on equating it with a heaven or hell and incorporating a scientific notion of progress, which was largely unquestioned until the Great War. Implicitly, for Nassau, the future equals a utopian space similar to heaven; Christian faith, coupled with modernity's progress myth, organizes a hope-filled belief in the future as transcendent. The more limited resources and technologies available to the indigenous peoples that Nassau encounters do not facilitate their faith in a "hereafter" or a hope in tomorrow

by which, for example, they might organize deferring gratification in the name of capital accumulation and exchange value.

4　Larry Buhl, "Man Accused of Killing 'Gay' Baby Son," *Advocate*, July 14, 2005, http://www.planetout.com (accessed on November 24, 2007).

5　See Patrick Moore, "Susan Sontag and a Case of Curious Silence," *Los Angeles Times*, January 4, 2005, www.commondreams.org (accessed on February 15, 2005).

6　The falling cost of computer power combined with miniaturization and other technological advances have reawakened the interest of business and industry in immersive virtual reality technology. Long used in flight simulation and videogame industries, the technology is now also used by manufacturers of automotive components and farm equipment, by companies engaged in petroleum exploration, and by engineers concerned with maximizing the efficiency of factory floor layouts. See "Virtual Reality Spreading in Business World," CNN .com, January, 2007, http://www.cnn.com (accessed on January 17, 2007).

>>> 3 Signs

1　Of the sixty-six kinds of signs Peirce identified I rely on only two trichotimies of signs: representamen, referent, interpretant; and symbol, icon, index. Other threefold divisions of signs postulated by Peirce include qualisign, sinsign, and legisign. The qualisign is a sign of the nature of an appearance, whereas the sinsign is a sign of an individual object or event. The legisign is a sign of the nature of a general type. As the Peirce scholar Douglas Greenlee notes in reference to this last trichotomy, "the obscurity of the categories confronts us again in this division" (1973:47).

2　Peirce's writings took the form of a few published articles, unfinished manuscripts, letters, and other writing fragments, and it has been the task of his followers and interpreters to unify these into reader-accessible compendia. See, for example, *The Collected Papers of Charles Sanders Peirce*, 1931–1958; *The Charles S. Peirce Papers* (microfilm), 1992–1998; and *The Essential Peirce*, 2 vols., 1992 and 1998.

3　The *Oxford Dictionary of Philosophy* defines nominalism as "the view that things denominated by the same term share nothing except that fact: what all chairs have in common is that they are called 'chairs.' The doctrine is usually associated with the thought that everything that exists is a particular individual, and therefore there are no such things as universals" (Blackburn 1994: 264).

4　I note in passing the consonance between the cultural and intellectual circumstances that incline Peirce to produce a theory of the sign stressing generalizability and the collectivity, and the rise of ritual theory with its emphasis on the group.

5　As I noted at the outset of this chapter, theories of signification have a complex history of often contentious disagreements. I trace a Peircian-inflected line of thinking that supports the arguments I make about Web practices and techniques. For readers interested in theories of indexicality and the trace that differ from those upon which I rely, apply, and extend, see Armstrong 1998; Crimp 1993; Krauss 1994; Solomon-Godeau 1991; and Tagg 1988.

6 Elisabeth Rosenthal, "The Cellphone as Church Chronicle, Creating Digital Relics," *New York Times*, April 8, 2005, A10.

7 I have noted the naturalization of the progress myth as a march of humanity forward in time. I have also noted the "progressive" dethroning of this ideal despite its ongoing psychic utility in helping frame utopian aspirations within modern capital formations. As a consequence, technological progress is now the dominant manifestation of this ideal, a development arguably influenced by the decline of belief in social progress. Following Derrida's renovation of Peirce's early theory of the interpretant as a sign always already inflected by the sign that precedes it, I suggest that one might imagine the temporal opposite of the modern notion of progressing forward: time as an infinite regress with the antidote being a kind of virtual hyperpresent. Not that Peirce's or Derrida's proposals negate the idea of forward movement. Rather, consider the following possibilities that arise if the interpretant is always already a sign "ad infinitum." *Infinitum* or infinity is a concept of total spatial extension across all dimensions. One may see aspects of the Peirce/Derrida proposal exemplified in online situations where a viewer — as fan or participant of a webcam or graphical chat — who looks at the signs of others' presence on some level sees that if they manifest as signs to him then he in turn is only visible to them as a sign transmitting across virtually infinite spatial networks. But would one then assume that the infinite number of signs this suggests would all have come into being at the same time? If one did, one would also admit the conceptual possibility of placing one's own subject position not only within a progressive forward march but also in a hyperpresent eternal return (or circulation) of the same — eternal in the sense of time proposed by the Christian myth "God always was, always will be, and always remains the same." But, equally, and as is already contained in this myth whereby "God" can be read as the synechistic totality of all signs, if the Derridean infinity of signs, among other possibilities, also "always was," then, somewhat like a nest of Russian dolls, time becomes an infinite regression of signification without origin.

Derrida argues that "Peirce goes very far in the direction that I have called the de-construction of the transcendental signified, what, at one time or another, would place a reassuring end to the reference from sign to sign" (1976:49). Yet he is also able to argue that "the trace is not only the disappearance of origin . . . the trace . . . becomes the origin of origin" (61). I am arguing for the "practical metaphysics" of how the trace circulates in networked capitalized settings. Despite Derrida's claim to eschew metaphysics, it could be argued that the Christian myth beat him to the punch.

8 In a number of online settings that allow individuals to construct personal

profiles, subscribers manipulate a sequential series of still self-portrait photographs that, when opened sequentially by viewers, transmit a sense of liveliness—a key requirement of telepresence. A series of four images might, for example, show an individual raising his hand. Sequentially viewing these four rapid-capture shots gives viewers the neo-Muybridgean experience that the still images are part of a larger project of motion capture of something essentially true about the referent. This is possible precisely because the series does convey something approximating the truth about how the individual moves through space. This verisimilitude of body movement is a form of virtual ontology that autonomically exceeds any epistemological implications conveyed by clothing, mannerism, or stated ideology.

>>> 4 "Avatars Become *I/me*"

1   Barnaby J. Feder, "Services at the First Church of Cyberspace," *New York Times*, May 15, 2004.

2   Unless noted otherwise, all quotations and facts about the Church of Fools are from its website, www.churchoffools.com (accessed on November 30, 2007).

3   From its outset, the Church of Fool's virtual worshipers had to compete with irreverent site visitors. Early on, administrators blocked unauthorized users from occupying the pulpit, and the user IDs of frequent "shouters" were banned. In December 2004, administrators reconfigured software to remove the earlier experience of collective gathering in the virtual space. While many individuals might each be simultaneously downloading the means to access the virtual church, at the time of this writing visitors experience it as space into which they enter alone. The church indicates that when funding permits it will resume the full functionalities on view during the 2004 trial period.

4   The website URLs for these MUVEs or graphical chat environments are The Palace, www.thepalace.com; Rose, www.moove.com; There!, www.there.com; Active Worlds, www.activeworlds.com; Second Life, www.secondlife.com; Entropia Universe, www.entropiauniverse.com; and DotSoul Cyberpark, www.dotsoul.net.

5   In Second Life, for example, at any given time ten to twenty thousand residents populate the site. The popularity of the site has expanded exponentially: Linden Lab estimated that by late 2006, 2,160,000 individuals had established accounts on the site; by the end of November 2007 there were 11,100,000 active and nonactive individual accounts. In the second half of 2006, 828,000 people had logged on to the site "so cutting-edge it defies genre classification: a game, a tool, a playground, a nation." Between November 23 and 29, 2007, alone, however, 445,542 individual logins were recorded (the statistics for 2006 and the quotation are from the Linden Lab website, www.lindenlab.com [accessed on December 28, 2006]; the 2007 statistics are from http://secondlife.com [accessed on November 30, 2007]). A study conducted by the University of South-

ern California Annenberg School Center for the Digital Future revealed that 43 percent of participants in sites such as Second Life indicate that their virtual world communities are as important to them as their physical ones (see http://annenberg.usc.edu; full website URL in author's files [accessed on February 27, 2007]).

6   For a more extensive discussion of role-playing games, see BBC News, http://news.bbc.co.uk (accessed on December 26, 2006).

7   See MOO-Cows FAQ (http://www.moo.mud.org) and The Hud Faq (www.mudconnect.com) for detailed sets of FAQs addressing communication issues in MUDs and MOOs.

8   James Wagner, "Snowcrashed," August 14, 2006, http://nwn.blogs.com (accessed on March 14, 2008).

9   I acknowledge the long-standing debate as to whether the Soviet academics Valentin Vološinov and Mikhail Bakhtin were the same person or two individuals familiar with each other's projects to the point of intensely close collaboration. I take no side in the debate, and in this volume I adhere to the name used in the publication I consult. The editors of the 1986 edition of *Marxism and the Philosophy of Language* note the debate and offer reasons supporting their conclusion that the two men were separate individuals.

10 Pushkin's textual moves parallel the back-and-forth dynamic between MUVE participants and their avatars—that which is experienced by participants who repeatedly extend themselves into their characters, pull themselves back to consider their next move or utterance and to survey the scene, then reextend themselves experientially into the virtual space. In certain ways, free indirect discourse anticipates the networked dynamic of telepresence discussed in this chapter.

11 The phrase is appropriated from Pasolini's (1976 [1965]) discussion of free indirect discourse. He theorizes how the technique might be applied to a free indirect subjectivity and the possibility for a "cinema of poetry."

12 Austen, unlike Johnson, rejects the notion that novels are frivolous, as her famous gendered defense of novels in *Northanger Abbey* (1818) makes clear: "Let us not desert one another; we are an injured body. Although our productions have afforded more extensive and unaffected pleasure than those of any other literary corporation in the world, no species of composition has been so much decried . . . there seems almost a general wish of decrying the capacity and undervaluing the labour of the novelist, and of slighting the performances which have only genius, wit, and taste to recommend them. 'I am no novel reader—I seldom look into novels . . .' 'And what are you reading, Miss——?' 'Oh! it is only a novel!' replies the young lady . . . only some work in which the greatest powers of the mind are displayed, in which the most thorough knowledge of human nature, the happiest delineation of its varieties, the liveliest effusions of wit and humour are conveyed to the world in the best chosen language" (37–38).

13 Note, for comparison, the passage in the original French: "Elle se répétait: 'J'ai

un amant! un amant!' se délectant à cette idée comme à celle d'une autre puberté qui lui serait survenue. Elle allait donc posséder enfin ces joies de l'amour, cette fièvre du bonheur dont elle avait désespéré. Elle entrait dans quelque chose de merveilleux où tout serait passion, extase, délire" (IntraText Digital Library, www.intratext.com [accessed on October 7, 2006; full website URL in author's files]).

14 Banfield also points to the same technique in the chapter openings of Woolf's *The Waves* and *The Years*.

15 The popularity of any one game is fleeting. A few years ago games such as Sony's *EverQuest* (everquest.station.sony.com), Microsoft's *Asheron's Call* (ac .turbine.com), or, for children, Disney's *ToonTown* (play.toontown.com) were massively popular, but by 2006 the flickering action had relocated to newer virtual environments and games such as Blizzard Entertainment's wildly successful subscription-based *World of Warcraft II (WoW)* (www.worldofwarcraft.com), and the free *Official U.S. Army Game* by America's Army (www.americasarmy .com). In June 2006 *ToonTown*'s market share of the MMORPG global population of players had declined to 0.9 percent and *Everquest*'s share to 1.6 percent, whereas *WoW* enjoyed a 52.9 percent share (see MMOGCHART.COM, www .mmogchart.com [accessed on December 29, 2006]).

16 For a focused discussion of the social dynamics that developed within the graphical chat MUVE The Palace, see Suler 1997; 1999.

17 In *Remediation, Understanding New Media*, Jay David Bolter and Richard Grusin (1999) underscore the irony of using technologies of electronic media to achieve a perceptual sense of immediacy, of having somehow, through the use of a device, superseded the need for the very device in use.

18 In most applications, an avatar's speech balloon remains onscreen for a period of time after the utterance is first transmitted by its owner/participant. I noted earlier, that the same textual content of the balloon also scrolls along at the bottom of the screen. In many applications this text can be captured and saved for later review. At any one time, however, only a portion of ongoing text communications will be visible. Some applications allow for turning off this function so that the only text visible is in avatar balloons appearing onscreen for a period of time when and just after they "speak."

19 The quotations are from an *OED* definition of allegory, which is dated 1639 and attributed to William Whately.

20 Such "fantasies" are, temporally, located in the here and now. The virtual, then, is also in the now and not only in the future and in any actualization it may be argued to achieve over time.

21 This would be somewhat consonant with Martinich's (2005:113–15) interpretation of the political intent behind Hobbes's proposal: the Sovereign is the actor who, in his being, is a distillation of the authors' many voices; therefore authors (according to Martinich, the Sovereign's subjects) need not object to the script that the Sovereign enacts (or legitimately overthrow the Sovereign) as it

was they who originally authored it. This is an interesting "will of the people or folk" interpretation that works to invert the appearance of democratic will that Hobbes's binary also can seem to portend.

22 In taking various animal and other hybrid forms of animals and humans, avatars carry the idea that a variety of life forms considered inferior to human beings also have divine intimations. For an excellent discussion of Hindu avatars, see Manas, www.sscnet.ucla.edu/southasia/Religions/Avatars/Vishnu .html (accessed on October 6, 2007).

23 This information is taken from *Strong's Greek Dictionary*, www.htmlbible.com (accessed on October 6, 2007).

24 For a critical discussion of the meanings and origins of ecumenism, see http://etext.lib.virginia.edu.

>>> 5 So Near, So Far, and Both at Once

1 "Get on with It, said Net Audience as Man Hanged Himself on Webcam," *Times Online*, http://technology.timesonline.co.uk (accessed on December 9, 2007).

2 See also texaskidd & friends, www.texaskidd.com (accessed on October 30, 2006).

3 Virtually no Web-based direct evidence remains of SeanPatrickLive.com. However, Ghost Sites/Museum of I-Failure has a screen capture of Williams's final website posting; see www.disobey.com (accessed on January 30, 2007).

4 Quoted in Helen Kennedy, "Thanks to Digital Video Cameras, Voyeurism is the Latest Internet Rage," *New York Daily News*, July 16, 1998, www.newstimes.com (accessed on February 2, 2001).

5 Quoted in Steve Friess, "Cyber Voyeurism," *The Advocate*, September 1, 1998, www.advocate.com (accessed on February 2, 2001).

6 Quoted in Tom Long, "Livecam Web Sites Bring Us the Excitement, Boredom of Others' Lives," *Detroit News*, August 3, 1998, http://detnews.com (accessed on February 2, 2001).

7 Ronald Gay, a self-identified "Christian Soldier" out to "waste some gays," opened fire at Roanoke's Backstreet Café, killing Danny Lee Overstreet and wounding six others in September, 2000. See the *Roanoke Times*, http://rtonline1.Roanoke.com (accessed on December 9, 2007).

8 DesignerBlog, http://designerblog.blogspot.com (accessed on March 14, 2008).

9 John Aravosis, "StopDrLaura.com," *New Republic*, October 23, 2000. www .wiredstrategies.com (accessed on March 14, 2008).

10 For readers interested in links between networked virtual space and queer, see, for example, Case 1996; Tsang 2000; Wakeford 2000; Woodland 2000; and Snyder 2002.

11 I do not here examine other applications of the term "telepresence." For example, non-internet applications may involve the use of robotics in dangerous

situations. An operator on one side of a lead shield may use digital visual information technologies to manipulate a robot equipped to move and grip radioactive objects with a handlike appendage. Located on the other side of the protective wall from the operator, the robot is *teleoperated* by the operator to engage directly with materials that would post an unacceptable risk for the operator's body.

12   Examples of this issue abound. As Paul Varnell notes, "The U.S. census bureau's disinclination to ask even as a voluntary question if people are gay or lesbian is another example of preserving gay invisibility. And of course, the CDC cannot report risk behavior for AIDS by gay and bisexual men, only by 'men who have sex with men.' . . . The CDC cannot acknowledge that gays exist as persons, only that people are engaging in certain types of sexual behavior. Once you start looking around, examples of the effort to suppress gay visibility leap out at you. 'Ex-gay' groups fit in perfectly. Most of them no longer claim that they can significantly change a person's sexual desires. Their main goal is to dissuade people from thinking of themselves as 'gay,' 'lesbian' or 'homosexual.' As therapy, this is preposterous, but it successfully reduces the number of people identifying themselves to others as homosexual" ("The War on Gay Visibility," *Chicago Free Press*, February 8, 2006, http://www.indegayforum.org (accessed on March 4, 2007).

13   "Early adopters," a term from innovation diffusion theory, includes individuals already predisposed to the promise of change articulated to a technology's introduction. Digital queers were not alone in using information technologies as a strategy to negotiate and rehearse certain forms of power relationships amenable to visibilization, as Jennifer Ringley's JenniCam suggests (see White 2003). Ana Voog and Theresa Senft were also well-known independent "camgirl" operators. Issues of voyeurism, visibility, celebrity, and commodification permeate Western cultures, and these issues are depicted on webcam sites whether run by a man or a woman of any sexual orientation or preference. However, specific forms of spatial exclusion, legal discrimination, and provisional and conditional social acceptance have contributed to the evolving self-conceptualization on the part of gay/queer men, digital queers included, as to just who and what they might be. These forms of partial exclusion and understandings of the self resonate with many of the technological possibilities for which webcams allow. Clearly gay/queer men put such issues as self-pornographization into discourse differently than do the many women and the thousands of operators of heterosexual sexcam commercial porn sites that have multiplied in number since the demise of the webcams this chapter examines. For an insightful discussion of women's engagement with webcam technologies see Senft 2008.

14   As Pamela Park-Curry and Robert Jiobu observed in 1982, the difficulties experienced by individuals and groups in coming to terms with an exponential increase in the power and deployment of computers in contemporary life resulted

in "converting" the computer from an oppositional force to "an electronic pop god, or informal fetish" (328).

15 The virtual equality Vaid identifies in everyday life plays out in mainstream mass media that still fail to represent the complexities of gay/queer realities and rarely show gay/queer pleasure for its own sake. If on broadcast TV gay/queer men are no longer precisely the love that dare not speak its name, they are still depicted as chaste and subordinate, latter-day barren Fridays and other assorted "supporting characters" to the Robinson Crusoes and their fear of the (same-sex) trace. Premium cable TV provides a somewhat fuller range of identity depictions. In North America, Pride Vision, a full service LGBTQ digital cable channel, emerged in Canada, and Showtime, an American premium cable channel, contracts with independent producers to syndicate such "edgy" and "adult" programming as *Queer as Folk* and *The L Word*. In 2005 two new cable services debuted. Viacom/MTV Networks launched its basic cable channel, Logo; the channel's promoters intend it to service what they see as an under-represented LGBTQ market. The same logic undergirds the launch of the satellite and cable premium subscription service Here! ("Gay Television. No Apologies."). Logo and Here! are a step forward for visibility and representation and also reflect the repositioning in corporate circles of LGBTQ people as a commodity to be marketed to advertisers. However, in the historical absence from mainstream media of consistent news and information programming inclusive of LGBTQ peoples and their concerns, or entertainment offerings that resist exceptionalizing their representations and experiences, they have moved to develop webspaces that provide access to a broader range of self-representations and the ability to respond to same. For better and for worse, gay/queer webcams and websites more generally are part of this strategy of negating mass media's claim to be a media center.

16 The issue of the speed at which webcamera images update is compelling in its relation to specific theories of the cinema developed by Deleuze. The camera most often trains directly on the operator in a fully static fashion and in this sense is like the early cinema of attractions where audiences looked directly at the film as if through a proscenium arch. Deleuze relates this early form of cinema to the ancient idea of "Forms or Ideas which are themselves eternal and immobile" (1986:4). He further writes of "formal transcendental elements" that he also identifies as *poses*. The pose is central to most webcam practices and viewing experiences as indicated by the explicit discussion of webcam posing provided by Weidemann in this chapter. Yet at the same time, the camera technology of the late 1990s "refreshed" or updated the image only every fifteen seconds at best, and many operators, perhaps by means of a small flashing light located offscreen, knew when this was about to happen, enabling them to strike a new pose should they wish. The technology supported an emphasis on the pose, allowing for a moving back and forth between a photographic quality

of the video image and a constant updating according to the refresh rate. The times when the screen remained still allowed viewers to experience a quality of transcendence and momentary timelessness even as the refresh rate introduced something remotely akin to cinematic montage and the potential for immanence in the image this raised.

17 "I am a camera with its shutter open, quite passive, recording, not thinking. Recording the man shaving at the window opposite and the woman in the kimono washing her hair. Some day, all of this will have to be developed, carefully printed, fixed" (Isherwood 1969 [1939]:13).

18 As Belk observes about Benjamin's own fetish for the original, and how this may have inflected his theory of the aura, "By locating power only in the unique . . . Benjamin joined Adorno as a Marxist elitist attempting to defend high culture from the threatened encroachments of the masses. He failed to acknowledge the power and magic that can be generated by mass-produced images. . . . Benjamin should have known better. He himself was an inveterate collector of a mass-produced commodity: books. If such mass-produced objects as books, even rare editions, lack an aura by themselves, their ardent pursuit, passionate acquisition, and worshipful possession in a collection can provide one" (2001:61).

19 Because of privacy concerns I do not provide this site's URL.

20 The email volume experienced by QJS is not unusual. Sean Patrick Williams, in responding to the "frequently asked question," "Why do you not answer my email or become my penpal?" stated that he received around six hundred emails per day, many of which requested advice of a personal or therapeutic nature. The flow of email updates Ian Watt's observation that the eighteenth-century novel "unrolls in a flow of letters from one lonely closet to another" (1957:189).

21 The linking by QJS of television to the Web is instructive. Television technology's original meaning of "distant seeing" already anticipates telepresence and transmitting one's self-aestheticization to others. If the phrase "seeing is believing" remains operative—particularly in a culture that fetishizes vision and optics—then the building of machines that suggest the augmented move from vision to telepresence seems "only natural."

22 Quoted in Tom Long, "Livecam Web Sites Bring Us the Excitement, Boredom of Others' Lives," *Detroit News*, August 3, 1998, http://detnews.com (accessed on February 2, 2001).

23 Weidemann's thoughts echo Ana Voog's assessment in the late 1990s of her webcam site's solipsistic appeal: "Whatever I'm doing, it has nothing to do with me—it has to do with what they're thinking I am, and that is what they are" (cited in Andrejevic 2004:98).

24 In 2003, 11 percent of internet users posted a photo online; by 2006, this percentage had increased to 23.6 (USC Annenberg School for Communication, http://annenberg.usc.edu [accessed on February 27, 2007]).

25 The Daily Dish, www.andrewsullivan.com; Joe.My.God, http://joemygod .blogspot.com; Shades of Gray, http://shadesofgray.typepad.com/shades_of_

gray; Tiny Queer Footballs, http://tinyqueerfootballs.com (accessed on March 2, 2007).

26 Networked "living in art" as an ironic claim by gay/queer men of an already extant full subjectivity different and equal to that claimed by heterosexuals contains something of the dynamic at play suggested by Marcuse's characterization of art "as revelation of utopian images of fulfillment and happiness that reject the alienated world" (Cox 1988:22). Theodor Adorno boxed utopian imagery into the corner of a "comforting illusion" (47–48). Marcuse, however, held open a broader place for it to "communicate truths repressed in the present" (21).

>>> Works Cited

Abrams, Meyer Howard, and Stephen Greenblatt. 2000. *The Norton Anthology of English Literature*, 7th ed., vol. 2. New York: Norton.

Adam, Ian. 1995. "Iconicity and the Place of Butala's 'The Prize.'" The Canadian Literature Archive. http:www .umanitoba.ca/canlit/conference/ian_adam.shtml (accessed on November 25, 2006).

Agamben, Giorgio. 1993. *The Coming Community*. Michael Hardt, trans. Minneapolis: University of Minnesota Press.

————. 1999. *The Man without Content*. Georgia Albert, trans. Stanford, Calif.: Stanford University Press.

————. 2000. *Means without End: Notes on Politics*. Vincenzo Binetti and Cesare Casarino, trans. Minneapolis: University of Minnesota Press.

Andrejevic, Mark. 2004. *Reality TV: The Work of Being Watched*. Lanham, Md.: Rowman and Littlefield.

Apter, Emily. 1993. "Introduction." In Emily Apter and William Pietz, eds., *Fetishism as Cultural Discourse*. Ithaca, N.Y.: Cornell University Press.

Apter, Emily, and William Pietz. 1993. "Preface." In Emily Apter and William Pietz, eds., *Fetishism as Cultural Discourse*. Ithaca, N.Y.: Cornell University Press.

Arendt, Hannah. 1968. "Introduction." In *Illuminations* by Walter Benjamin. New York: Schocken.

Armstrong, Carol. 1998. *Scenes in a Library: Reading the Photograph in the Book, 1843–1875*. Cambridge: MIT Press.

Austen, Jane. 1988 [1811]. *Sense and Sensibility*. In *The Oxford Illustrated Jane Austen*, 3rd ed., vol. 1. Oxford: Oxford University Press.

———. 1988 [1818]. *Northanger Abbey*. In *The Oxford Illustrated Jane Austen*, 3rd ed., vol. 5. Oxford: Oxford University Press.

Badiou, Alain. 2005 [1988]. *Being and Event*. Oliver Feltham, trans. New York: Continuum.

Balaban, Oded. 1995. *Politics and Ideology: A Philosophical Approach*. Aldershot, U.K.: Avebury.

Banfield, Ann. 1991. "L'Imparfait de l'Objectif: The Imperfect of the Object Glass." *Camera Obscura* 24: 65–87.

Barker, Frances. 1984. *The Tremulous Private Body: Essays on Subjection*. London: Methuen.

Barney, Darin. 2000. *Prometheus Wired: The Hope for Democracy in the Age of Network Technology*. Chicago: University of Chicago Press.

Barthes, Roland. 1977a. *Image, Music, Text*. Stephen Heath, trans. New York: Hill and Wang.

———. 1977b. *Roland Barthes/by Roland Barthes*. Richard Howard, trans. New York: Hill and Wang.

———. 1981. *Camera Lucida: Reflections on Photography*. Richard Howard, trans. New York: Hill and Wang.

Bassett, Elizabeth H., and Kathleen O'Riordan. 2002. "Mediated Identities and the Ethics of Internet Research: Contesting the Human Subjects Research Model." Paper presented at Crossroads in Cultural Studies: Fourth International Conference, Tampere, Finland, 2002.

Baudrillard, Jean. 1981. *For a Critique of the Political Economy of the Sign*. Charles Levin, trans. St. Louis: Telos Press.

———. 1997. "Aesthetic Illusion and Virtual Reality." In Nicholas Zurbrugg, ed., *Jean Baudrillard: Art and Artefact*. London: Sage.

Bazin, André. 1967. *What Is Cinema?* Hugh Gray trans. Berkeley: University of California Press.

Beardsley, William A. 1993. "Logos." In Bruce Metzger and Michael Coogan, eds., *The Oxford Companion to the Bible*. Oxford: Oxford University Press.

Beaune, Jean-Claude. 1989. "The Classical Age of Automata: An Impressionistic Survey from the Sixteenth to the Nineteenth Century." In Michel Feher, Ramona Naddaff, and Nadia Tazi, eds., *Fragments for a History of the Human Body: Part One*. New York: Zone Books.

Belk, Russell W. 2001. *Collecting in a Consumer Society*. New York: Routledge.

Bell, Catherine. 1992. *Ritual Theory, Ritual Practice*. New York: Oxford University Press.

———. 1997. *Ritual: Perspectives and Dimensions*. New York: Oxford University Press.

Benjamin, Walter. 1968. "The Work of Art in the Age of Mechanical Reproduction." In Hannah Arendt, ed., Harry Zohn, trans., *Illuminations*. New York: Schocken Books.

———. 1999. *Selected Writings: Volume 2, 1927–1934*. Michael Jennings, Howard

Eiland, and Gary Smith, eds. Cambridge: Harvard University Press, Belknap Press.

Bersani, Leo. 1995. *Homos*. Cambridge: Harvard University Press.

Blackburn, Simon. 2005. *Oxford Dictionary of Philosophy*. Oxford: Oxford University Press.

Bolter, Jay David, and Richard Grusin. 1999. *Remediation: Understanding New Media*. Cambridge: MIT Press.

Bourdieu, Pierre. 1984. *Distinction: A Social Critique on the Judgment of Taste*. Richard Nice, trans. Cambridge: Harvard University Press.

———. 1991. *Language and Symbolic Power*. John B. Thompson, ed., Gino Raymond and Matthew Adamson, trans. Cambridge: Harvard University Press.

Brooks, Peter. 1993. *Body Work: Objects of Desire in Modern Narrative*. Cambridge: Harvard University Press.

Brown, Norman O. 1966. *Love's Body*. New York: Random House.

Buc, Philippe. 2001. *The Dangers of Ritual: Between Early Medieval Texts and Social Scientific Theory*. Princeton, N.J.: Princeton University Press.

Buchler, Justus. 1940. *The Philosophy of Peirce: Selected Writings*. London: Kegan Paul, Trench, Trubner and Company.

Buck-Morss, Susan. 1989. *The Dialectics of Seeing: Walter Benjamin and the Arcades Project*. Cambridge: MIT Press.

Butler, Judith. 1993. *Bodies That Matter: On the Discursive Limits of "Sex."* New York: Routledge.

Caillois, Roger. 1961 [1958]. *Man, Play, and Games*. Meyer Barash, trans. New York: Free Press of Glencoe.

Campbell, John Edward. 2004. *Getting It On Online: Cyberspace, Gay Male Sexuality, and Embodied Identity*. New York: Harrington Park Press.

Canguilhem, Georges. 1992. "Machine and Organism." In Jonathan Carey and Sanford Kwinter, eds. *Incorporations*. New York: Zone Books.

Carey, James W. 1975. "A Cultural Approach to Communication." *Communication* 2: 1–22.

———. 1983. "Technology and Ideology: The Case of the Telegraph." *Prospects* 9: 303–25.

———. 1989. *Communication as Culture: Essays on Media and Society*. Boston: Unwin Hyman.

———. 1997. "Reflections on the Project of (American) Cultural Studies." In Marjorie Ferguson and Peter Golding, eds., *Cultural Studies in Question*. London: Sage.

———. 1998. "Political Ritual on Television: Episodes in the History of Shame, Degradation and Excommunication." In Tamar Liebes and James Curran, eds., *Media, Ritual and Identity*. New York: Routledge.

Carlson, Kyle, and Steve Guynup. 2000. "Avatar as Content Delivery Platform." *Future Generation Computer Systems* 17 (1): 65–71.

Carlstrom, Eva-Lise. 1992. "Better Living through Language: The Communicative

Implications of a Text-Only Virtual Environment, or, Welcome to LambdaMOO." Electronic Frontier Foundation, www.eff.org (accessed on March 14, 2008).

Case, Sue-Ellen. 1996. *The Domain-Matrix: Performing Lesbian at the End of Print Culture*. Bloomington: Indiana University Press.

———. 2003. "Luminous Writing, Embodiment, and Modern Drama: Mme Blavatsky and Bertolt Brecht." In Ric Knowles, Joanne Tompkins, and W. B. Worthen, eds., *Modern Drama: Defining the Field*. Toronto: University of Toronto Press.

Castells, Manuel. 2000. *The Rise of the Network Society*. London: Blackwell.

Cavell, Stanley. 1979. *The World Viewed*. Cambridge: Harvard University Press.

Chare, Nicholas. 2006. "Passages to Paint: Francis Bacon's Studio Practice." *Parallax* 12 (4): 83–98.

Chun, Wendy Hui Kyong, and Thomas Keenan, eds. 2005. *New Media, Old Media: Interrogating the Digital Revolution*. New York: Routledge.

Clark, Danae. 1991. "Commodity Lesbianism." *Camera Obscura* 25/26: 181–201.

Cohen, John. 1966. *Human Robots in Myth and Science*. London: George Allen and Unwin.

Cohn, Dorrit. 1978. *Transparent Minds: Narrative Modes for Presenting Consciousness in Fiction*. Princeton, N.J.: Princeton University Press.

Colletti, Lucio. 1975. "Introduction." In *Karl Marx, Early Writings*. Harmondsworth, U.K., Penguin.

Compagnon, Antoine. 1994. *The Five Paradoxes of Modernity*. Franklin Philip, trans. New York: Columbia University Press.

Connor, Steven. 2000. *Dumbstruck: A Cultural History of Ventriloquism*. London: Oxford University Press.

Conquergood, Dwight. 2006. "Lethal Theatre: Performance, Punishment, and the Death Penalty." In D. Soyini Madison and Judith Hamera, eds., *The Sage Handbook of Performance Studies*. Thousand Oaks, Calif.: Sage.

Couldry, Nick. 2003. *Media Rituals: A Critical Approach*. London: Routledge.

Cox, J. Robert. 1988. "An 'Unsolved Contradiction'? Herbert Marcuse on Aesthetic Form and Praxis." *Literature in Performance* 8 (1): 21–27.

Crimp, Douglas. 1993. *On the Museum's Ruins*. Cambridge: MIT Press.

Curtis, Pavel. 1996. "Mudding: Social Phenomena in Text-Based Virtual Realities." In Mark Stefik, ed., *Internet Dreams: Archetypes, Myths, and Metaphors*. Cambridge: MIT Press.

Danet, Brenda. 2005. "Play, Art and Ritual on IRC (Internet Relay Chat)." In Eric Rothenbuhler and Mihai Coman, eds., *Media Anthropology*. Thousand Oaks, Calif.: Sage.

Davis, Erik. 1998. *TechGnosis: Myth, Magic and Mysticism in the Age of Information*. New York: Harmony Press.

Dayan, Daniel, and Elihu Katz. 1992. *Media Events: The Live Broadcasting of History*. Cambridge: Harvard University Press.

Debord, Guy. 1994. *The Society of the Spectacle*. Donald Nicholson-Smith, trans. New York: Zone Books.

Debray, Régis. 2000. *Transmitting Culture*. Eric Rauth, trans. New York: Columbia University Press.

Defoe, Daniel. 1902. *Moll Flanders*. London: Aitken.

Deledalle, Gérard. 2000. *Charles S. Peirce's Philosophy of Signs*. Bloomington: Indiana University Press.

Deleuze, Gilles. 1986. *Cinema 1: The Movement-Image*. Hugh Tomlinson and Barbara Habberjam, trans. Minneapolis: University of Minnesota Press.

———. 1989. *Cinema 2: The Time-Image*. Hugh Tomlinson and Robert Galeta, trans. Minneapolis: University of Minnesota Press.

———. 1994. *Difference and Repetition*. Paul Patton, trans. New York: Columbia University Press.

———. 2001. *Pure Immanence: Essays on a Life*. Anne Boyman, trans. New York: Zone Books.

Deleuze, Gilles, and Félix Guattari. 1987. *A Thousand Plateaus: Capitalism and Schizophrenia*. Brian Massumi, trans. Minneapolis: University of Minnesota Press.

———. 1994. *What Is Philosophy?* Hugh Tomlinson and Graham Burchell, trans. New York: Columbia University Press.

Derrida, Jacques. 1976. *Of Grammatology*. Gayatri Chakravorty Spivak, trans. Baltimore: Johns Hopkins University Press.

Dewey, John. 1916. *Democracy and Education*. New York: Macmillan.

Doane, Mary Ann. 2002. *The Emergence of Cinematic Time: Modernity, Contingency, the Archive*. Cambridge: Harvard University Press.

Downing, Eric. 2006. *After Images: Photography, Archaeology, and Psychoanalysis and the Tradition of Bildung*. Detroit: Wayne State University Press.

Dretske, Fred, I. 1969. *Seeing and Knowing*. London: Routledge and Kegan Paul.

Dreyfus, Hubert L. 1992. *What Computers Still Can't Do: A Critique of Artificial Reason*. Cambridge: MIT Press.

Durham, Scott. 1998. *Phantom Communities: The Simulacrum and the Limits of Postmodernism*. Stanford, Calif.: Stanford University Press.

Durkheim, Émile. 1965 [1912]. *The Elementary Forms of the Religious Life*. Joseph Ward Swain, trans. New York: Free Press.

Düttmann, Alexander García. 2000. *Between Cultures: Tensions in the Struggle for Recognition*. Kenneth B. Woodgate, trans. London: Verso.

Eco, Umberto. 2000. *Kant and the Platypus: Essays on Language and Cognition*. Alastair McEwen, trans. New York: Harcourt Brace.

Edelman, Lee. 2004. *No Future: Queer Theory and the Death Drive*. Durham, N.C.: Duke University Press.

Ehrsson, H. Hendrik. 2007. "The Experimental Induction of Out-of-Body Experiences." *Science* 317 (5841): 1048.

Ellul, Jacques. 1964. *The Technological Society*. John Wilkinson, trans. New York: Vintage Books.

Eribon, Didier. 2004. *Insult and the Making of the Gay Self*. Michael Lucey, trans. Durham, N.C.: Duke University Press.

Ewen, Stuart. 1988. *All Consuming Images: The Politics of Style in Contemporary Culture*. New York: Basic Books.

Fagerjord, Anders. 2003. "Rhetorical Convergence: Earlier Media Influence on Web Media Form." Doctoral thesis, University of Oslo. http://fagerjord.no (accessed on March 14, 2008).

Feenberg, Andrew. 1999. *Questioning Technology*. London: Routledge.

Fetveit, Arild. 1999. "Reality TV in the Digital Era: A Paradox in Visual Culture?" *Media, Culture and Society* 21 (6): 787–804.

Fitzgerald, John J. 1966. *Peirce's Theory of Signs as Foundation for Pragmatism*. The Hague: Mouton.

Flaubert, Gustave. 1964 [1857]. *Madame Bovary*. Mildred Marmur, trans. New York: Signet.

Flaubert, Gustave and George Sand. 1921. "Letter 40." *The George Sand-Gustave Flaubert Letters*. A. L. McKenzie, trans. The University of Adelaide Library, eBooks@Adelaide. http://ebooks.adelaide.edu.au (accessed on September 2, 2008).

Fletcher, Angus. 1964. *Allegory: The Theory of a Symbolic Model*. Ithaca, N.Y.: Cornell University Press.

Foucault, Michel. 1977. *Discipline and Punish: The Birth of the Prison*. Alan Sheridan, trans. New York: Pantheon Books.

———. 1978. *The History of Sexuality: An Introduction*. R. Hurley, trans. New York: Random House.

———. 1985. *The Uses of Pleasure*. R. Hurley, trans. New York: Random House.

Freud, Sigmund. 1950 [1913]. *Totem and Taboo: Some Points of Agreement between the Mental Lives of Savages and Neurotics*. James Strachey, trans. New York: Norton.

Friedberg, Anne. 1993. *Window Shopping: Cinema and the Postmodern*. Berkeley: University of California Press.

Gabildano, Joseba. 1995. "Postcolonial Cyborgs." In Chris Hables Gray, ed., *The Cyborg Handbook*. New York: Routledge.

Geertz, Clifford. 1973. *The Interpretation of Cultures*. New York: Basic Books.

Gibson, James J. 1973. "On the Concept of Formless Invariants in Visual Perception." *Leonardo* 6: 43–45.

———. 1979. *The Ecological Approach to Visual Perception*. Boston: Houghton Mifflin.

Gibson, William. 1984. *Neuromancer*. New York: Ace Books.

Gitelman, Lisa, and Geoffrey Pingree, ed. 2003. *New Media, 1740–1915*. Cambridge: MIT Press.

Goffman, Erving. 1979. *Gender Advertisements*. London: Macmillan.

Goldberg, Ken. 2000. *The Robot in the Garden: Telerobotics and Telepistemology in the Age of the Internet*. Cambridge: MIT Press.

Gonzáles, Jennifer. 2000. "The Appended Subject: Race and Identity as Digital Appendage." In Beth Kolko, Lisa Nakamura, and Gil Rodman, eds., *Race in Cyberspace*. New York: Routledge.

Goody, Jack. 1977. "Against Ritual: Loosely Structured Thoughts on a Loosely Defined Topic." In Sally Moore and Barbara Myerhoff, eds., *Secular Ritual*. Amsterdam: Van Gorcum.

Gorlée, Dinda L. 1994. *Semiotics and the Problem of Translation: With Special Reference to the Semiotics of Charles S. Peirce*. Amsterdam: Rodopi.

Greenlee, Douglas. 1973. *Peirce's Concept of Sign*. The Hague: Mouton.

Gross, Larry. 2004. "Foreword." In *Getting It On Online: Cyberspace, Gay Male Sexuality, and Embodied Identity* by John Edward Campbell. New York: Harrington Park Press.

Habermas, Jürgen. 1982 [1962]. *The Structural Transformation of the Public Sphere*. Thomas Burger and Frederick Lawrence, trans. Cambridge: MIT Press.

Hall, Stuart. 1996. "Cultural Studies and Its Theoretical Legacies." In Simon During, ed., *The Cultural Studies Reader*. London: Routledge.

———. 1997. "Introduction." In Stuart Hall, ed., *Representation: Cultural Representations and Signifying Practices*. London: Sage.

Halperin, David. 2003. "The Normalization of Queer Theory." In Gust Yep, Karen Lovaas, and John Elia, eds., *Queer Theory and Communication: From Disciplining Queers to Queering the Discipline(s)*. New York: Harrington Park Press.

Hardt, Michael, and Antonio Negri. 2000. *Empire*. Cambridge: Harvard University Press.

Harvey, David. 1973. *Social Justice and the City*. Baltimore: Johns Hopkins University Press.

———. 2005. *A Brief History of Neoliberalism*. New York: Oxford University Press.

Haug, Wolfgang Fritz. 1986. *Critique of Commodity Aesthetics: Appearance, Sexuality and Advertising in Capitalist Society*. Robert Buck, trans. Minneapolis: University of Minnesota Press.

Hay, James. 2006. "Between Cultural Materialism and Spatial Materialism: James Carey's Writing about Communication." In Jeremy Packer and Craig Robertson, eds., *Thinking with James Carey: Essays on Communications, Transportation, History*. New York: Peter Lang.

Hegel, Georg W. F. 1956. *The Philosophy of History*. John Sibree, trans. New York: Dover.

Hillis, Ken. 1999. *Digital Sensations: Space, Identity, and Embodiment in Virtual Reality*. Minneapolis: University of Minnesota Press.

———. 2005. "Modes of Digital Identification: Virtual Technologies and Webcam Cultures." In Wendy Hui Kyong Chun and Thomas Keenan, eds., *New Media, Old Media: Interrogating the Digital Revolution*. New York: Routledge.

Hillis, Ken, Michael Petit, and Nathan Epley. 2006. "Introducing Everyday eBay." In Ken Hillis, Michael Petit, and Nathan Epley, eds., *Everyday eBay: Culture, Collecting and Desire*. New York: Routledge.

Hobbes, Thomas. 1985 [1651]. *Leviathan*. Crawford Brough MacPherson, ed. London: Penguin.

Hoffmann, Ernst Theodor Wilhelm. 1814. *Automata*. Project Gutenberg Australia. http://gutenberg.net.au (accessed on March 14, 2008).

———. 1816. *The Sandman*. John Oxenford, trans. Virginia Commonwealth University. http://www.fln.vcu.edu (accessed on March 14, 2008).

Holman, C. Hugh, and William Harmon. 1992. *A Handbook to Literature*, 6th ed. New York: Macmillan.

Hoover, Stewart. 2006. *Religion in the Media Age*. New York: Routledge.

Horton, Donald, and Richard Wohl. 1956. "Mass Communication and Parasocial Interaction: Observations on Intimacy at a Distance." *Psychiatry* 19: 215–29.

Houser, Nathan. 1992. "Introduction." In Nathan Houser and Christian Kloesel, eds., *The Essential Peirce*, vol. 1. Bloomington: Indiana University Press.

Howatson, Margaret C., ed. 1989. *The Oxford Companion to Classical Literature*. Oxford: Oxford University Press.

Huizinga, Johan. 1955 [1938]. *Homo Ludens: A Study of the Play Element in Culture*. Boston: Beacon Press.

Hulswit, Menno. 2004. "Teleology." Digital Encyclopedia of Charles S. Peirce. www.digitalpeirce.fee.unicamp.br (accessed on November 25, 2006).

Huyssen, Andreas. 2000. "The Vamp and the Machine: Fritz Lang's Metropolis." In Michael Minden and Holder Bachmann, eds., *Fritz Lang's Metropolis: Cinematic Visions of Technology and Fear*. Rochester, N.Y.: Camden House.

Isherwood, Christopher. 1969 [1939]. *Goodbye to Berlin*. London: Hogarth Press.

Jakobson, Roman. 1974. *Main Trends in the Science of Language*. New York: Harper and Row.

Jameson, Fredric. 1992. *Signatures of the Visible*. New York: Routledge.

Jay, Martin. 1998. "Experience without a Subject: Walter Benjamin and the Novel." In Laura Marcus and Lynda Nead, eds., *The Actuality of Walter Benjamin*. London: Lawrence and Wishart.

Johnson, Samuel. 1969 [1750]. *Rambler* No. 4 (March 31, 1750). In W. J. Bate and Albrecht B. Strauss, eds., *The Yale Edition of the Works of Samuel Johnson*, vol. 3. New Haven, Conn.: Yale University Press.

Joseph, Miranda. 2002. *Against the Romance of Community*. Minneapolis: University of Minnesota Press.

Kelly, Kevin. 1994. *Out of Control: The Rise of Neo-Biological Civilization*. Reading, Mass.: Addison-Wesley.

Knopp, Larry. 2004. "Ontologies of Place, Placeless, and Movement: Queer Quests for Identity and Their Impacts on Contemporary Geographic Thought." *Gender, Place and Culture* 11 (1): 121–34.

Kolb, Bryan, and Ian Whislaw. 2003. *Fundamentals of Human Neuropsychology*. New York: Worth.

Krauss, Rosalind. 1994. *The Originality of the Avant-Garde and Other Modernist Myths*. Cambridge: MIT Press.

Krips, Henry. 1999. *Fetishism: An Erotics of Culture*. Ithaca, N.Y.: Cornell University Press.

Kroes, Rob. 2007. *Photographic Memories: Private Pictures, Public Images, and American History*. Hanover, N.H.: Dartmouth College Press.

Kroker, Arthur, and David Cook. 1986. *The Postmodern Scene: Excremental Culture and Hyper-Aesthetics*. New York: St. Martin's Press.

Kroker, Arthur, and Michael Weinstein. 1994. *Data Trash: The Theory of the Virtual Class*. New York: St. Martin's Press.

Lacan, Jacques. 1978. *The Four Fundamental Concepts of Psychoanalysis*. Jacques-Alain Miller, ed., and Alan Sheridan, trans. New York: Norton.

LaCapra, Dominick. 1982. *Madame Bovary on Trial*. Ithaca, N.Y.: Cornell University Press.

Landow, George. 2006. *Hypertext 3.0: Critical Theory and New Media in an Era of Globalization*. Baltimore: Johns Hopkins University Press.

Lash, Scott. 2002. *Critique of Information*. London: Sage.

Latour, Bruno. 1992. "Where Are the Missing Masses? The Sociology of a Few Mundane Artifacts." In Wiebe Bijker and John Law, eds., *Shaping Technology/Building Society: Studies in Sociotechnical Change*. Cambridge: MIT Press.

Leach, Edmund R. 1968. "Ritual." In David L. Sills, ed., *The International Encyclopedia of the Social Sciences*. New York: Macmillan.

Lefebvre, Henri. 1992. *The Production of Space*. Donald Nicholson-Smith, trans. Oxford: Basil Blackwell.

Lenggenhager, Bigna et al. 2007. "Video Ergo Sum: Manipulating Bodily Self-Consciousness." *Science* 317 (5841): 1096–99.

Lévy, Pierre. 1997. *Collective Intelligence: Mankind's Emerging World in Cyberspace*. Robert Bononno, trans. Boston: Perseus.

———. 1998. *Becoming Virtual: Reality in the Digital Age*. Robert Bononno, trans. New York: Plenum.

———. 2001. *Cyberculture*. Robert Bononno, trans. Minneapolis: University of Minnesota Press.

Lucy, Niall. 2004. *A Derrida Dictionary*. London: Blackwell.

Lukes, Steven. 1975. "Political Ritual and Social Integration." *Sociology* 9 (2): 289–308.

Malinowski, Bronislaw. 1961. *Argonauts of the Western Pacific*. London: E. P. Dutton.

Manovich, Lev. 1995. "Potemkische Dörfer, Kino und Telepräsenz/Potemkin's Villages, Cinema and Telepresence." In Karl Gebel and Peter Weibel, eds., *Mythos Information: Welcome to the Wired World*. Vienna: Springer-Verlag.

———. 2001. *The Language of New Media*. Cambridge: MIT Press.

Marcuse, Herbert. 1964. *One-Dimensional Man: Studies in the Ideology of Advanced Industrial Society*. Boston: Beacon Press.

———. 1978. *The Aesthetic Dimension: Toward a Critique of Marxist Aesthetics*. Boston: Beacon Press.

Marks, Laura. 2006. "Author Response." Resource Center for Cyberculture Studies, http://rccs.usfca.edu (accessed on November 25, 2006).

Martin, Randy. 1998. *Critical Moves: Dance Studies in Theory and Politics*. Durham, N.C.: Duke University Press.

Martinich, Aloysius P. 2005. *Hobbes*. New York: Routledge.

Marvin, Carolyn, and David Ingle. 1999. *Blood Sacrifice and the Nation: Totem Rituals and the American Flag*. Cambridge: Cambridge University Press.

Marx, Karl. 1952. *Capital*. Friedrich Engels, ed., Samuel Moore and Edward Aveling, trans. Chicago: Encyclopaedia Britannica.

Marx, Leo. 2000 [1965]. *The Machine in the Garden: Technology and the Pastoral Ideal in America*. New York: Oxford University Press.

Massumi, Brian. 2002. *Parables of the Virtual: Movement, Affect, Sensation*. Durham, N.C.: Duke University Press.

Mattelart, Armand. 1994. *Mapping World Communications: War, Progress, Culture*. Minneapolis: University of Minnesota Press.

McCallum, Ellen Lee. 1999. *Object Lessons: How to Do Things with Fetishism*. Albany: State University of New York Press.

McClintock, Ann. 1995. *Imperial Leather: Race, Gender, and Sexuality in the Colonial Contest*. New York: Routledge.

McCracken, Grant. 1988. *Culture and Consumption: New Approaches to the Symbolic Character of Consumer Goods and Activities*. Bloomington: Indiana University Press.

McLuhan, Marshall. 1964. *Understanding Media*. New York: McGraw-Hill.

McPherson, Tara. 2002. "Reload: Liveness, Mobility and the Web." In Nicholas Mirzoeff, ed., *The Visual Culture Reader*, 2nd ed. London: Routledge.

Minsky, Marvin. 1984. "Afterword." In *True Names* by Vernor Vinge. New York: Bluejay Press, http://home.comcast.net (accessed on November 25, 2007).

———. 1986. *The Society of Mind*. New York: Simon and Schuster.

———. 2006. *The Emotion Machine: Commonsense Thinking, Artificial Intelligence, and the Future of the Human Mind*. New York. Simon and Schuster.

Misak, Cheryl. 2004. "Charles Sanders Peirce (1839–1914)." In Cheryl Misak, ed., *The Cambridge Companion to Peirce*. Toronto: University of Toronto Press.

Mitchell, W. J. Thomas. 1994. *Picture Theory: Essays on Verbal and Visual Representation*. Chicago: University of Chicago Press.

Moravec, Hans. 1988. *Mind Children: The Future of Robot and Human Intelligence*. New York: Simon and Schuster.

———. 1999. *Robot: Mere Machine to Transcend Mind*. New York. Oxford University Press.

Mulvey, Laura. 1975. "Visual Pleasure and Narrative Cinema." *Screen* 16 (3): 6–18.

Mumford, Lewis. 1934. *Technics and Civilization*. New York: Harcourt, Brace and Company.

Murphy, Murray G. 1961. *The Development of Peirce's Philosophy*. Cambridge: Harvard University Press.

Nakamura, Lisa. 2007. *Digitizing Race: Visual Cultures of the Internet*. Minneapolis: University of Minnesota Press.

Nassau, Robert Hamill. 1904. *Fetichism in West Africa: Forty Years' Observation of Native Customs and Superstitions*. New York: Charles Scribner's Sons.

Nattiez, Jean-Jacques. 1990. *Toward a Semiology of Music*. Carolyn Abbate, trans. Princeton, N.J.: Princeton University Press.

Nelson, Ted. 2004. "Keynote Address." Presented at the fifth annual meeting of the Association of Internet Researchers, University of Sussex, U.K., September 19–22.

Nelson, Victoria. 2001. *The Secret Life of Puppets*. Cambridge: Harvard University Press.

Nye, David E. 1994. *American Technological Sublime*. Cambridge: MIT Press.

Park-Curry, Pamela, and Robert Jiobu. 1982. "The Computer as Fetish: Electronic Pop God." In Ray Browne, ed., *Objects of Special Devotion: Fetishes and Fetishism in Popular Culture*. Bowling Green, Ohio: Bowling Green University Popular Press.

Pascal, Roy. 1977. *The Dual Voice: Free Indirect Speech and Its Functioning in the Nineteenth-Century European Novel*. Totowa, N.J.: Rowman and Littlefield.

Pasolini, Pier Paolo. 1976 [1965]. "The Cinema of Poetry." In Bill Nichols, ed., *Movies and Methods*, vol. 1. Berkeley: University of California Press.

Payne, Robert. 2004. "Virtuality: The Refreshment of Interface Value." *Postmodern Culture* 14 (3), http://muse.jhu.edu (accessed on January 30, 2007).

Peirce, Charles Sanders. 1992–1998. *The Charles S. Peirce Papers* (30 reels of microfilm). Cambridge: Harvard University Press Microreproduction Service.

———. 1931. *The Collected Papers of Charles Sanders Peirce*. Charles Hartshorne and Paul Weiss, eds. Cambridge: Harvard University Press.

———. 1992. *The Essential Peirce: Selected Philosophical Writings*, vol. 1. (1867–1893), Nathan Houser and Christian Kloesel, eds. Bloomington: Indiana University Press.

———. 1998. *The Essential Peirce: Selected Philosophical Writings*, vol. 2. (1893–1913). Bloomington: Indiana University Press.

Peters, John Durham. 2006. "Technology and Ideology: The Case of the Telegraph Revisited." In Jeremy Packer and Craig Robertson, eds., *Thinking with James Carey: Essays on Communications, Transportation, History*. New York: Peter Lang.

Pietz, William. 1985. "The Problem of the Fetish," part 1. *Res* 9 (spring): 5–17.

———. 1993. "Fetishism and Materialism: The Limits of Theory in Marx." In Emily Apter and William Pietz, eds., *Fetishism as Cultural Discourse*. Ithaca, N.Y.: Cornell University Press.

———. 1998. "Afterword." In Patricia Spyer, ed., *Border Fetishisms: Material Objects in Unstable Spaces*. New York: Routledge.

Pinkus, Karen. 1996. *Picturing Silence: Emblem, Language, Counter-Reformation Materiality*. Ann Arbor: University of Michigan Press.

Poster, Mark. 2002. "Visual Studies as Media Studies." *Journal of Visual Culture* 1 (1): 67–70.

Postman, Neil. 1992. *Technopoly: The Surrender of Culture to Technology*. New York: Vintage.

Praz, Mario. 1964. *Studies in Seventeenth-Century Imagery*, 2nd ed. Rome: Edizioni di Storia e Letteratura.

Preston, Claire. 2003. "Emblems and Imprese, 1400–1700." *The Literary Encyclopedia*, www.LitEncyc.com (accessed on February 5, 2005).

Rancière, Jacques. 2004. *The Politics of Aesthetics: The Distribution of the Sensible*. Gabriel Rockhill, trans. London: Continuum.

Rappaport, Roy A. 1979. *Ecology, Meaning, and Religion*. Richmond, Va.: North Atlantic Books.

———. 1999. *Ritual and Religion in the Making of Humanity*. Cambridge: Cambridge University Press.

Reid, Elizabeth. 1991. "Communication and Community on Internet Relay Chat." Internet Relay Chat (IRC) Help Archive, http://www.irchelp.org (accessed on March 14, 2008).

Robbins, Bruce. 1992. "Comparative Cosmopolitanisms," *Social Text* 31/32: 169–86.

Robins, Kevin, and Frank Webster. 1999. *Times of the Technoculture: From the Information Society to the Virtual Life*. London: Routledge.

Rogers, Sheena. 2005. "Through Alice's Glass: The Creation and Perception of Other Worlds in Movies, Pictures, and Virtual Reality." In Joseph D. Anderson and Barbara Fisher Anderson, eds. *Moving Image Theory: Ecological Considerations*. Carbondale: Southern Illinois University Press.

Romanyshyn, Robert. 1989. *Technology as Symptom and Dream*. New York: Routledge.

Rothenbuhler, Eric W. 1998. *Ritual Communication: From Everyday Conversation to Mediated Ceremony*. Thousand Oaks, Calif.: Sage.

Ryle, Gilbert. 1984 [1949]. *The Concept of Mind*. Chicago: University of Chicago Press.

Sack, Robert D. 1980. *Conceptions of Space in Social Thought: A Geographic Perspective*. Minneapolis: University of Minnesota Press.

Sahlins, Marshall. 1985. *Islands of History*. Chicago: University of Chicago Press.

Schaeffer, Jean-Marie. 1987. *L'Image précaire*. Paris: Editions Seuil.

Schwartz, Hillel. 1996. *The Culture of the Copy: Striking Likenesses, Unreasonable Facsimilies*. New York: Zone Books.

Sella, Zohar Kadmon. 2007. "The Journey of Ritual Communication." *Studies in Communication Sciences* 7 (1): 103–24.

Senft, Theresa. 2008. *Celebrity and Community in the Age of Social Networks*. New York: Peter Lang.

Shields, Rob. 1991. *Places on the Margins: Alternate Geographies of Modernity*. London: Routledge.

———. 2000a. "Virtual Spaces?" *Space and Culture* 4/5: 1–12.

———. 2000b. "Hypertext Links: The Ethic of the Index and its Space-Time Effects." In Andrew Herman and Thomas Swiss, eds., *The World Wide Web and Contemporary Social Theory*. New York: Routledge.

———. 2003. *The Virtual*. London: Routledge.

Short, T. L. 2004. "The Development of Peirce's Theory of Signs." In Cheryl Misak, ed., *The Cambridge Companion to Peirce*. Toronto: University of Toronto Press.

Skagestad, Peter. 2004. "Peirce's Semeiotic Model of Mind." In Cheryl Misak ed., *The Cambridge Companion to Peirce*. Toronto: University of Toronto Press.

Sloterdijk, Peter. 1987. *Critique of Cynical Reason*. Michael Eldred, trans. Minneapolis: University of Minnesota Press.

Snyder, Donald I. 2002. "'I Don't Go by Sean Patrick': On-Line/Off-Line/Out Identity and SeanPatrickLive.com." *International Journal of Sexuality and Gender Studies* 7 (2/3): 177–95.

Solomon-Godeau, Abigail. 1991. *Photography at the Dock: Essays on Photographic History, Institutions, and Practices*. Minneapolis: University of Minnesota Press.

Sonesson, Göran. 1993. "Pictorial Semiotics: The State of the Art at the Beginning of the Nineties." *Zeitschrift für Semiotik* 15 (1–2): 131–64. www.arthist.lu.se (accessed on November 23, 2004).

———. 2004. "Photography." *The Internet Semiotics Encyclopaedia*. Lund University, http://filserver.arthist.lu.se (accessed on December 5, 2006).

Sontag, Susan. 1973. *On Photography*. New York: Picador.

Stallybrass, Peter. 1998. "Marx's Coat." In Patricia Spyer, ed., *Border Fetishisms: Material Objects in Unstable Spaces*. New York: Routledge.

Stephenson, Neal. 1992. *Snow Crash*. New York: Bantam Books.

Sterne, Jonathan. 2004. Book Review of "Culture and Waste." *Space and Culture* 7 (3): 352–53.

———. 2006. "Transportation and Communication: Together as You've Always Wanted Them." In Jeremy Packer and Craig Robertson, eds., *Thinking with James Carey: Essays on Communications, Transportation, History*. New York: Peter Lang.

Steuer, Jonathan. 1992. "Defining Virtual Reality: Dimensions Determining Telepresence." *Journal of Communications* 42 (4): 73–93.

Stone, Alluquere Roseanne. 1997. *The War of Desire and Technology at the Close of the Mechanical Age*. Cambridge: MIT Press.

Suler, Richard. 1997. "A History of the First Year (or so) of the Palace." The Psychology of Cyberspace. www.rider.edu (accessed on March 14, 2008).

———. 1999. "The Psychology of Avatars and Graphical Space in Multimedia Chat Communities." The Psychology of Cyberspace. www.rider.edu (accessed on September 3, 2004).

Tagg, John. 1988. *The Burden of Representation: Essays on Photographies and Histories*. Minneapolis: University of Minnesota Press.

Taussig, Michael. 1993. "Maleficium: State Fetishism." In Emily Apter and William Pietz, eds., *Fetishism as Cultural Discourse*. Ithaca, N.Y.: Cornell University Press.

Teilhard de Chardin, Pierre. 1964. *The Future of Man*. Norman Denny, trans. New York: Harper and Row.

Teilmann, Stina. 2000. "Flaubert's Crime: Trying Free Indirect Discourse." *Literary Research/Recherche Littéraire* 17 (33): 74–87.

Thorburn, David, Henry Jenkins, and Brad Seawell, eds. 2003. *Rethinking Media Change: The Aesthetics of Transition*. Cambridge: MIT Press.

Tofts, Darren, Annemarie Jonson, and Alessio Cavallaro, eds. 2003. *Prefiguring Cyberculture: An Intellectual History*. Cambridge: MIT Press.

Tolkein, J. R. R. 1965. *The Lord of the Rings*. Boston: Houghton Mifflin.

Tsang, Daniel. 2000. "Notes on Queer 'n' Asian Virtual Sex." In David Bell and Barbara Kennedy, eds., *The Cybercultures Reader*. New York: Routledge.

Turkle, Sherry. 1995. *Life on the Screen: Identity in the Age of the Internet*. New York: Simon and Schuster.

Turner, Victor. 1957. *Schism and Continuity in an African Society: A Study of Ndembu Village Life*. Manchester: University of Manchester Press.

———. 1995 [1969]. *The Ritual Process: Structure and Anti-Structure*. New York: Aldine de Gruyter.

———. 1982. *From Ritual to Theatre: The Human Seriousness of Play*. New York: PAJ Productions.

Twain, Mark. 1998. "On Work and Play." In John P. Holmes and Karin Baji, eds., *Bite-Size Twain: Wit and Wisdom from the Literary Legend*. New York: St. Martin's Press.

Vaid, Urvashi. 1995. *Virtual Equality: The Mainstreaming of Gay and Lesbian Liberation*. New York: Anchor Books.

Villarejo, Amy. 2003. *Lesbian Rule: Cultural Criticism and the Value of Desire*. Durham, N.C.: Duke University Press.

———. 2004. "Defycategory.com, or the Place of Categories in Intermedia." In Pamela Church Gibson, ed., *More Dirty Looks: Gender, Pornography and Power*. London: BFI Publishing.

Vinge, Vernor. 1984. *True Names*. New York: Bluejay Books.

Vološinov, Valentin N. 1986. *Marxism and the Philosophy of Language*. Ladislav Matejka and I. R. Titunik, trans. Cambridge: Harvard University Press.

Wakeford, Nina. 2000. "Cyberqueer." In David Bell and Barbara Kennedy, eds., *The Cybercultures Reader*. New York: Routledge.

Warner, Michael. 1990. *The Letters of the Republic: Publication and the Public Sphere in Eighteenth-Century America*. Cambridge: Harvard University Press.

———. 2002. *Publics and Counterpublics*. New York: Zone Books.

Waskul, Dennis D. 2004. "The Naked Self: Body and Self in Televideo Cybersex." In Dennis D. Waskul, ed., *net.seXXX: Readings on Sex, Pornography, and the Internet*. New York: Peter Lang.

Watt, Ian. 1957. *The Rise of the Novel*. Berkeley: University of California Press.

Weidemann, Jason. 2003. "Confessions of a Webcam Exhibitionist." *The Gay & Lesbian Review Worldwide* 10 (4): 13–17. http://www.accessmylibrary.com (accessed on October 2, 2005).

White, Michele. 2003. "Too Close to See: Men, Women, and Webcams." *New Media and Society* 5 (1): 7–28.

Whitehead, Alfred North. 1967 [1948]. *Science and the Modern World*. New York: Free Press.

Williams, Raymond. 1960. *The Long Revolution*. London: Chatto and Windus.

———. 1977. *Marxism and Literature*. Oxford: Oxford University Press.

———. 2003 [1974]. *Television*. New York: Routledge.

Wilson, Catherine. 1999. "Vicariousness and Authenticity." In Ken Goldberg, ed., *The Robot in the Garden*. Cambridge: MIT Press.

Winner, Langdon. 1986. *The Whale and the Reactor: A Search for Limits in an Age of High Technology*. Chicago: University of Chicago Press.

———. 1993. "Social Constructivism: Opening the Black Box and Finding It Empty." *Science as Culture* 3 (16): 427–52.

Woodland, Randal. 2000. "Queer Spaces, Modem Boys and Pagan Statues: Gay/Lesbian and the Construction of Cyberspace." In David Bell and Barbara Kennedy, eds., *The Cybercultures Reader*. New York: Routledge.

Yee, Nick. *The Daedalus Gateway*. www.nickyee.com (accessed on March 14, 2008).

Žižek, Slavoj. 1990. "How the Non-Duped Err." *Qui Parle* 4 (1): 2.

author-actor binary (Hobbesian), 21, 187–88; relation to graphical chat/ MUVE avatars, 188–95

Automata, 182

automaton, 137, 182–85, 217; allegory and, 182; magical belief and, 182–183; mobility and, 182

avatar: Hindu meaning of, 198; relation to figures of Christ and Vishnu, 200. *See also* digital avatar

Badiou, Alain, 43, 73

Banfield, Ann, 159–60

Barker, Frances, 78, 165–66

Barthes, Roland, 111, 130, 159

Baudrillard, Jean, 24, 89, 94, 118, 238

Bell, Catherine, 40, 47, 48, 51, 54, 55, 62, 66, 68, 70, 75, 80, 82, 84, 125, 207, 254, 272 n. 3, 274 n. 10

Benjamin, Walter, 22, 32, 238–39, 241

body, 18, 193; as automaton, 185; autonomic responses of, 26, 180; Emma Bovary and, 155; Cartesianism and, 19, 21, 77, 112–13, 182, 185, 227, 265; cosmopolitanism and, 1, 21, 29, 109; as emblem, 179; fetish theory and, 100; gay/queer, 75, 92; the gaze and, 221; image, 55, 235, 250; movement, 77, 144, 177, 180, 277 n. 8; out-of-body experience and, 12; politics, 22; ritual and, 5, 70, 179, 198; self and, 147, 165, 183; self-regulation and, 78; sign/body and, 12–13, 91, 128; telepresence and, 215, 281 n. 11; tools and, 192; the trace and, 100, 115–16, 183; of Webcam operator, 39, 128, 216, 239, 250, 257; Web users and, 2, 12, 101, 157, 165, 201, 267 n. 1. *See also* body double; sign/body

body double, 138, 183, 225, 262; cosmopolitan *cogito* and, 266; history of, 19; as psychic appendage, 42

body politic, 33

Bourdieu, Pierre, 11, 53, 54, 116, 208

Brady, Mathew, 110

Brooks, Peter, 86, 155, 160, 162

Buddenbrooks, 151

Caillois, Roger, 68–69

camgirl operators, 282 n. 13

Carey, James, 60–63, 98, 124, 128, 135–36, 208, 262, 272 n. 3, 274 n. 9

Cartesianism, 19, 21, 77; human bodies as automata and, 185

celebrity, 89, 160, 171, 226, 282 n. 13; online niche for, 210, 229, 249

Church of Fools, 44, 71, 133–36, 197–200, 278 n. 3, 278 n. 5

cinema, 146; of attractions, 283 n. 16; autonomic perception and, 125; the gaze and (Mulvey), 218; graphical chat/MUVEs and, 165; image and, 13; interface and, 25; of poetry, 160, 247, 279 n. 11; projection and, 127, 218–19; rise of, 12

Cohn, Dorrit, 148, 155–56, 161

commodity fetishism, 30, 45, 101; metaphysics and, 185–86; ritual and, 200

communicability, 3, 40, 126, 157, 201; appearance of digital humanity and, 201; Church of Fools and, 199; defined, 2; ecumenism and, 199; as end in itself and, 14, 65, 92, 251, 262–63; as fetish, 92; graphical chat/MUVEs and, 272 n. 3; networked, 122; post-symbolic, 92; as ritual, 61, 241; as transmission of information, 61; Web as sphere of, 21

communication: codeless, 26, 74, 92, 173; communicability and, 2; danger of, 145–46; display and, 127; emblem and, 169, 177; as form of life, 62, 262–63; free indirect discourse and, 145, 153, 180; graphical chat/MUVEs and, 137, 141, 173–74, 187, 195; as inscription, 136; IRC and, 36, 60, 140; media studies of, 31; nonverbal, 75; noosphere and, 273 n. 6; personal webcams and, 244, 250; post-symbolic, 92; practices as autonomous, 17, 263; public sphere and (Habermas) and, 271 n. 2; ritual and, 5, 57, 61–62, 136, 199, 262, 272 n. 3; screen and, 127; social harmony and, 77; technologies, 64–65, 81, 135, 224, 262–63; time and space and, 63; transmission and, 5, 61–62, 78, 262, 272 n. 3; virtual environments and, 22; Web and, 24, 26, 29

cosmopolitanism, 1–2, 16, 22, 78; capital and, 73, 148; digital avatars and, 167; *ecumene* or *oikos* and, 199; flow and, 91; free indirect discourse and, 151; gay/queer men and, 225; globalization and, 199; the index and, 109; networked individuals and, 16, 81, 223; personal webcams and, 216; queer studies and, 213; rooted, 109, 267 n. 1; Second Life, 35; sign/body and, 17, 197; synechism and, 109; tantalization and, 249, 251; the trace and, 123; as view from above, 10; virtual mobility and, 4; visual culture and, 36; Web and, 2, 26, 28, 77, 122, 171

Couldry, Nick, 11, 57, 59, 60, 76–77
Culte des Dieux Fétiches, Le, 83

Debord, Guy, 4, 14, 18, 19, 21, 23, 33, 88, 96, 226, 259, 262, 267 n. 1
Debray, Régis, 104, 111, 116, 128
de Brosses, Charles, 83–85, 94
Deleuze, Gilles, 12, 13, 42, 81, 104, 125, 146, 154, 161, 177, 186, 224, 239, 242, 247, 264, 275 n. 1, 283 n. 16
Derrida, Jacques, 52, 75, 104, 121–22, 129, 135, 153, 185, 190, 253, 275 n. 1; metaphysics and, 118–20, 277, n. 7; the trace and, 118–20, 123

Descartes, René, 21, 113
digital avatar, 2, 3, 12, 17, 20, 30, 68, 87; as allegorical form, 44, 114; as allegory of disembodied awareness, 198; American corporation law and, 194; autonomic body processes and, 180; as commodity of consciousness, 192–93; as conditional technical strategy, 146; cosmopolitanism and, 167; defined, 134–35; as digital and technological subject, 195; as educator, 186; as emblem, 168–70; as emulation of life, 193; as extension of self, 135, 189; as fetish object, 114; as form of pantomime, 174; in graphical chat/MUVEs, 113; Hobbes's author-actor theory and, 187–94; as indexical automaton, 179; as information, 136; as ironic form of virtual stability, 196; metonymy and, 165; neoliberal ritual and, 196; as "origin of the origin," 190; as outline of emergent future, 146; politics of anonymity and, 165; pose and, 174; as postrepresentational, 193; relation to mechanical automaton, 182–85; relation to Nike swoosh, 173; representation as exhausted and, 186; restoration of enchantment and, 200–201; ritual and, 179–80, 196; as sign/body, 18, 135; spatial betwixtness of, 167; speech balloons and, 280 n. 18; virtualization of subject and, 195, 200; as virtual object, 18, 186, 190. *See also* graphical chat; MUVEs

digital queer, 203, 211, 225, 231, 233, 260, 282 n. 13. *See also* gay/queer men

Diogenes, 1, 267 n. 1
displacement, 2; defined, 84; fetishism, 86; gay/queer, 225, 253; of meaning, 245; movement, 225; of perception, 251; personal webcams and, 236,

displacement (*continued*)

244–45; time and, 224; virtual objects and, 81, 275 n. 1

display: experiential presence of the sign and, 128; as indexical technology, 108, 128; relation to screen, 126–29; relation to transmission, 127

Dungeons & Dragons (D&D), 139

Durham, Scott, 254–56

Durkheim, Emile, 48–51, 53, 54, 61, 64, 66–67, 78

Düttmann, Alexander, 97, 213, 222

early adopters, 36, 226, 252–53, 257, 260, 282 n. 13; religious organizations as, 197

Eco, Umberto, 110, 125

ecumene, 2, 27

ecumenism, 199–200

Edelman, Lee, 224 25

Ehrsson, H. Henrik, 12, 13

Elementary Forms of the Religious Life, The, 50, 64

emblem, 36, 44; as allegory, 168, 175–80; anchorage and, 171; *cantastoria* and, 170–71; contemporary resurgence of, 171; corporate branding and, 172; defined, 168; *imprese* and, 169; as living, 215; as moral instruction, 169–70; Neoplatonism and, 170; Nike swoosh and, 172–73; relation of text and image and, 171, 173–74, 260; relay and, 171; as ritual device, 170, 173; ritualization of, 229; the sacred and, 169; technology and, 171–72; TV advertising and, 176–78

embodiment: desire for virtual, 44; experience of, 12, 18

Enlightenment, 22, 66, 82, 138, 147, 177; public sphere, 165, 271 n. 2

Eribon, Didier, 59, 246

eternal return of the same, 95–96, 122,

223–24; information machines and, 226–27

exchange value, 2, 85; automata and, 183; as autonomous power, 18; display and, 36; fetishism and, 80, 86, 275 n. 3; graphical chat/MUVEs and, 166; image and, 17; metaphysics and, 31; rituals of divestment and exchange and, 245; of sign/body, 91; of signification, 117; Tantalus and, 245; the trace and, 253; use and sign values and, 117; virtual forms of, 18; Web and, 181; webcam operators and, 230, 238

Feenberg, Andrew, 32, 57, 191–92, 263

fetish: digital, 95; history of, 83–86; moving image and, 178; as object, 41; of the new, 93–94, 253–54; psychoanalytic theory and, 82; theory compared to ritual theory, 81–82; as virtual object, 79, 86–90, 114. *See also* telefetish

fetishism: allegory and, 19; archaic, 45, 215; commodity, 30, 45, 82–83, 184, 200, 203; digital surface and, 157; identity and, 253–55; of image, 247; information machines and, 15–16, 65, 79, 94, 135–36, 260; mediated resignation and agency and, 231; mobility and, 181; reiterative qualities and, 246; as relation, 88; as spatial strategy, 99–100; temporality and, 250; theories of, 15, 41; the trace and, 12, 231–32; use value and, 30; virtual objects and, 42; virtual space and, 64; Web and, 78. *See also* telefetishism

first principle, 104, 120, 122, 214; *arche* and, 94; information machines as, 191; questions of, 34, 118; sign world as, 119; virtual space as, 123. *See also* metaphysics

Flaubert, Gustave, 150–59, 190, 201, 255

flexibility, 2, 11, 16, 22, 29, 49, 156–57, 235; of image, 72; mobility and, 73; neoliberal value of, 6, 187, 197, 264; of online performances, 264–65; personal, 40, 71, 178, 196; promise of, 16; telepresence and, 166; Web and, 62, 200

flow, 2, 3, 49, 218, 225; computerization of everyday life and, 10; definition of (Williams), 269 n. 14; digital, 181; global, 161; image and, 200; information machines and, 31; metaphysics and, 122; as modular, 234; as network, 194; optic, 174; queer theory and, 211; space of, 91, 157, 184, 224–25, 265

Foucault, Michel, 32, 42, 71, 230; as gay/queer academic, 98

Four Fundamental Concepts of Psycho-analysis, The, 220

free indirect discourse, 43, 137, 148–58; as anticipating telepresence, 166; as conditional technical strategy, 146; Derridean trace and, 153, 156; digital avatar and, 195; experience without a subject and, 147, 152–54, 160, 180, 255; fantasy and, 155; fiction of unitary subject and, 156; flexibility and, 157; as form of speculative theory, 146; free indirect subjectivity and (Pasolini), 160–61; graphical chat/MUVEs and, 145–46, 161; hybrid identity formation and, 151, 154–55; ineffable and, 152–53; interorientation of author and, 154; IRC, MOOs, and MUDs and, 163–67; as outline of emergent future, 146; parallels to cinematography, 161; parallels to ritual dynamics, 152; persona and, 152, 158–59; politics of, 153–56; psychology of for readers, 151; photography and, 160; rise of nation state

and, 151; as screen, 151; space and time and, 159–63; ventriloquism and, 147, 158. *See also* middle voice

Freud, Sigmund, 81, 84, 236

friction-free capitalism, 29; Neoplatonism and, 66; virtual space and, 98

future, 15, 60, 68, 76, 87, 93, 96, 98, 142, 180, 183, 198, 226, 240, 244, 252, 255; of avatars, 117; as dystopian, 96; emergent, 42, 146, 158; fetishism and, 88, 95, 275 n. 3; loss of faith in, 95–96; as metaphor for identity, 97; as repetition, 224; Second Life and, 74; virtual, 10, 64–65, 193, 223–25, 227, 248, 280 n. 20. *See also* eternal return of the same

gay/queer men, 11, 33; bodies and, 75, 91, 216; claims to visibility and, 36, 124; commodity fetishism and, 203; diaspora and, 101; fetishism online and, 93; the future and, 97; history, 36; identity politics and, 59; IRC and, 93–94; lifecasting and, 204; living in art and, 236–41; mobility and, 224–25, 253; moving images and, 124; networked, 241; personal webcams and, 44–45, 56, 92, 207–211, 215, 217–18, 227–31, 235; premodern fetish and, 95; self-pornographization and, 210, 223, 282 n. 13; social marginalization and the Web and, 101; visibility and, 36, 56, 99. *See also* As You Gaze Upon Me, SeanPatrickLive.com

gaze, 101; as component of webcam pleasure, 218; impersonal technological, 249; male (Mulvey), 218; networked, 221; persona and, 247; personal webcams and, 219–22; as two-way process, 217

Geertz, Clifford, 44, 216, 274 n. 9

Genet, Jean, 254

Gennep, Arnold van, 54, 60, 66, 70, 78

Gibson, William, 96, 142

Gilder, George (telecosm), 113

globalization, 157, 198, 235; cosmopolitanism and, 199; information machines and, 236

Gluckman, Max, 52–54

Gnosticism, 19, 184, 198

Goffman, Erving, 116, 128

Gonzáles, Jennifer, 29, 55, 134, 135, 155, 163, 190, 221

Google, 58, 77, 204

Google Earth, 28, 58

graphical chat, 17, 18, 36; automata and, 193; dematerialization of commodity form and, 193; exchange value as use value and, 166; fetishization of mobility and, 181; as simulation of mobility, 181; and subject as circulating image, 193; as synthesis of MUDs and IRC, 141; time and, 200; as 2-D, 142; as World of Forms, 142; as zone of communicability, 272 n. 3. *See also* digital avatar; MUVEs

graphical chat/MUVEs. *See* graphical chat; MUVEs

Graphical User Interface (GUI), 27, 141; graphical chat/MUVEs as, 268 n. 4

graphing: experience of as codeless and direct, 126; forms of in relation to ritual, 124–26; as trace or index of the real, 17; relation to the trace, 115–16

Guattari, Félix, 42, 146, 242

Halperin, David, 212

Harvey, David, 30, 63

Hegel, Georg, 80–81, 84, 95

hegemony: defined, 73; lived, 52, 73–75, 116, 120–21; never complete, 78; ritual and, 73; ritualized, 71–75; ritual participants and, 56; the trace and, 121–22

Hieroglyphica, The, 169

HIV/AIDS, 223–224

Hive Mind, 64, 122, 273 n. 6. *See also* metaphysics; noosphere

Hobbes, Thomas, 21, 187–95, 265

Hoffmann, E. T. A., 181

l'Homme machine, 182

homo ludens, 68

homunculus, 237–38

Huizinga, Johan, 68–69, 70

Hume, David, 84

Hydra, 226

image: as experience itself, 250, 255; as natural language, 177, 187; not fully under human control, 121, 177, 191; relation to index and trace, 37, 67, 74, 87, 121, 132, 191, 215; ritualized, 247; as social relation, 17, 23–24, 95, 137–38, 241, 247; tension with text and, 137–38, 147–48, 167, 174, 260; as virtual object, 178, 252. *See also* moving image

l'image-mouvement, 13

index, 87, 276 n. 1; avatar as, 129; Emma Bovary as, 158; as distinct from signification, 114, 128; graphing as, 17; Peircian theory of, 103–8; temporality and, 277 n. 7; truth and, 246–47. *See also* trace

indexicality: allegory and, 179–80; avatars and, 179–80; body and, 21, 70; digital, 87; display and, 108, 126, 128; free indirect discourse, 156–59; graphical chat/MUVEs and, 263; icon and, 108; information machines and, 74; IRC/MUDs/MOOs and, 161, 164; mendacity and, 124; moving images and, 23, 37, 109; Nike swoosh and, 173; online experience and, 45; photography and, 110–20; pictures and, 108; pull-down menus and, 31; ritual and, 116, 179, 275 n. 10; Second Life and, 123, 135; sign/body and,

networks, 16, 19, 28, 70–71, 91, 99, 127, 130, 157, 164, 166–67, 192, 194, 201, 230, 233, 253, 257, 264, 267 n. 1, 269 n. 14, 277 n. 7; basic unit of economic organization, 7; culture of, 2; display and, 127; as first principle, 122; flow and, 123; information machines and, 59, 81, 197, 226, 251; noosphere and, 198, 273 n. 6; of signs, 130, 189, 191; as territory, 2; the trace and, 120; Web as, 12, 24, 215

Neuromancer, 96, 142

nominalism, 108; Cartesianism and, 113; defined, 276 n. 3; rise of photography and, 110

noosphere, 64, 113; as planetary thinking network, 198, 273 n. 6; as ritual of transmission, 198. *See also* Teilhard de Chardin; World Soul

Northanger Abbey, 151

novel, 27, 32, 36, 137, 142; characters in, 147, 162, 188, 195; dangers of (Johnson), 153; defense of (Austen), 279 n. 12; free indirect discourse and, 43, 145, 148, 152, 154, 160, 166–67, 195; graphic, 162; middle voice and, 157, 161–63; MUDs and MOOs and, 139, 163; political and, 152, 154; psychological interiority and, 150; realism and, 162; rise of, 150, 284 n. 20; telepresence and, 166–67; the trace and, 165; virtualization of the subject and, 167. *See also* free indirect discourse; middle voice

object: material, 87–89; performance of virtual, 70; the trace and, 119; virtual, 87–88, 251

Of Grammatology, 118

oikos, 2, 27; defined, 199. See also *ecumene*

One-Dimensional Man, 262

On Photography, 115

pantomime, 174; automata and, 183

parasocial interaction and desire, 243, 246

Pascal, Roy, 155

Pasolini, Pierre Paolo, 160–61, 279 n. 11

Peirce, Charles Sanders, 23, 103–14, 118, 129–30, 135, 185, 200

Peircian index: cosmopolitanism and, 109; participant-observer and, 109; potential for postrepresentational status, 107

Peircian semiotic: avatar and, 190; IRC and, 164–65; photography and, 110; political and, 120; as theory of objects, 105

Peircian signs: defined, 105–7, 276 n. 1; implications for research, 105

perception, 104, 107, 108, 112, 269 n. 17; autonomic, 12–14, 121, 125, 186; becoming and, 264; experience and, 33–35; fetishism and, 89–90; graphical chat/MUVEs and, 174; ideology, 13; immediacy of, 173; movement and, 12–13; moving images and, 13, 39, 67, 177, 191; never total, 160; ritual and, 7, 170; signs and, 91, 105, 108; the trace and, 67, 109, 121, 251; unity of, 22, 130; virtual space and, 24; visual, 171; Web and, 251; webcam operators and, 39, 130

performance: of allegory, 274 n. 9; bodily, 179; fetishism and, 39, 92, 250, 254; gay/queer, 94, 208, 232; graphical chat/MUVEs and, 60, 76, 166, 175, 200, 233, 264; hegemony and, 52, 71; IRC and, 140; living in art and, 247–48; mediated center and, 120; networked, 264; personal webcams and, 207–8, 229, 236–40, 250, 253, 264; the possible and, 75; ritual and, 5, 7, 39, 48, 52, 54–55, 60–61, 68–71, 76, 125, 210, 219, 266; signification and, 39, 71, 105, 274 n. 10; society

sacred, 48, 50–51, 61, 138; defined by ritual, 54; graphs and, 169; group cohesion and, 53; information machines and, 65; mind and, 113; as mutable ideal, 54, 64; online rituals and, 263; secular, 55, 63–64, 263, 266

sacred and profane binary, 51, 54, 62, 76, 200–201, 267 n. 1

sacred space and play, 68

Sand, George, 166, 190

Sandman, The, 182

Saussure, Ferdinand de, 104

Schwartz, Hillel, 266

science, 89, 261; cosmopolitanism and, 10; disenchanted world and, 185; Durkheim's theory of ritual and, 51; metaphysics and, 26, 118; mystical character of, 68; ritual and, 66; technology and, 191, 226, 266; transmission and, 67; visual and, 138

screen, 2, 6, 8, 13–14, 18, 59, 69–70, 96, 123, 144, 163, 197, 231; culture and, 110; display and, 126–29, 174, 270 n. 20; the gaze and (Lacan), 220–22; graphical chat/MUVEs and, 175, 181, 189, 200, 280 n. 18; identity and, 214, 264; image, 20, 250; landscape and, 38–39; names, 93, 163, 165–66, 275 n. 2; personal webcams and, 37, 39, 171, 205, 219, 250, 272 n. 3; projection and, 127; ritual and, 4; sign/body and, 90; signification and, 103, 108, 114, 190; size of, 25; spatial logic of, 72, 258; 2-D space of, 38, 174; ubiquity of, 25–26; Web applications and, 27–28

SeanPatrickLive.com, 206–07, 239–40, 242. *See also* Williams, Sean Patrick

Second Life, 2–4, 14, 20–21, 31, 35, 43, 50, 68, 72, 76, 88, 90, 93, 122, 128, 264; free labor and, 69–72; IRB and, 131–32; metaphor and metonymy in, 274 n. 9; as metaphysics, 123; play

and, 69; popularity of, 278 n. 5; religious rituals in, 40; as social center, 60; as stage for ritual, 180

self-pornographization, 210, 223, 282 n. 13

Senft, Teresa, 205, 282 n. 13

Sense and Sensibility, 148–49

Shepard, Matthew, 46, 98, 207, 224

Shields, Rob, 76, 77, 272 n. 3

Short, T. L., 104, 107, 108, 114, 128

sign/body, 4–5, 24, 27, 114, 117, 175, 231, 263; aura and, 239; consciousness and, 272; as digital avatar, 12, 136, 192, 197; as digital mask, 248; digital public sphere and, 265; as fetish, 250; as form of visual language, 101; as fragment of self, 101; Hobbesian actor online and, 21, 193; as indexical, 13, 14, 15; as moving image, 12; Neoplatonism and, 26; networked, 130; online signification and, 13; perception and, 91; personal webcams and, 130, 221, 227, 257; political economy of metaphysics and, 122–24; pose and, 239; telefetish and, 92, 222, 228; as trace or index, 14–15, 124, 217; use value and, 91; as virtual object, 17, 89, 101

sign value: exchange and use values, 117; fetishism and, 94; index, 111; ritual and, 111

Sloterdijk, Peter, 248–49

Snow Crash, 99, 137, 142–43, 194; influence on graphical chat/MUVEs, 144

Snyder, Donald, 207, 209, 233

social center: broadcast media as, 57–60, 120; as first principle, 120; as myth, 60

society of the spectacle (Debord), 23, 33, 121, 259

Sonesson, Göran, 108, 111, 112, 114

Sontag, Susan, 98, 104, 111, 115–16

space: backstage, 227; fetishization

Warner, Michael, 15, 170, 172

Watt, Ian, 148, 150

Web: as actual space, 234; as black box, 67; as cultural center, 59–60; as emergent center, 199; as form of experiential space, 13; as mobility, 234; performance of allegory and, 274 n. 9; practices as forms of life, 63; renovation of literary forms and social relations and, 148; sexuality and, 230; as site of movement, 225; as transcendental signifier, 215; as virtual homeland, 101

Web 2.0, 3, 35, 93, 143, 258

webcam operator, 11, 13, 17, 23, 72, 85, 101, 129, 204, 217, 231, 235, 238, 254, 261; avatar and, 18, 264; as boring product, 229–30; emergent networked culture and, 247; exchange value and, 230; image of, 45, 126, 130, 257, 272 n. 3; living in art and, 252; mastery and, 236; Narcissus myth and, 250; present to self, 240; rating system and, 72; ritual performance and, 56, 234, 255; site closure and, 244; spatial strategy and, 232–33; tantalization and, 246; truth claims and, 223; use value and, 18; as virtual object, 18. See also As You Gaze Upon Me; JenniCam; living in art; Sean-PatrickLive.com

webcams, personal, 8, 11, 18, 35; aura and, 221, 239–41; celebrity and, 229–30, 249; expense of, 252; experience of oneself as a trace and, 129; gay/queer use of, 206–8, 257–59; history of, 94–95; as indexical, 37; landscape and, 228; labor involved, 258–59; as liberation, 249; logics of, 235–36; Peirce's theory of signs and, 129; physical safety and, 228; pose and, 239–40; as representations of space, 227–28; as response to mass media invisibility, 283 n. 15; ritual and, 207, 244, 254; the trace and, 129; as virtual space, 227–28

weblogs, personal, 257–59; free indirect discourse and, 259; ritual and, 258; as shared process, 258

Webster, Frank, 69, 72

Weidemann, Jason, 217–21, 228, 236–40, 248–50, 252, 256, 258, 283 n. 16

White, Michele, 218

Whitehead, Alfred North, 113

Williams, Raymond, 52, 73, 196, 269 n. 14

Williams, Sean Patrick, 92, 94, 206–7, 209, 217, 221–22, 229, 242, 244–45, 250, 252, 258, 284 n. 20. See also Sean-PatrickLive.com

Winner, Langdon, 31, 57, 269 n. 19; information machines and, 268 n. 3

Woolf, Virginia, 159–60, 167

world, disenchanted, 19; re-enchanted through digital means, 195, 200–201

World of Forms, 136, 142, 179, 185, 253. See also metaphysics; Neoplatonism; transcendence

World of Warcraft, 88, 137, 139

World Soul, 64, 113, 122, 199, 273 n. 6; defined, 198. See also Hive Mind

Yee, Nick, 4, 268 n. 9

Žižek, Slavoj, 218–19

A preliminary version of the first sections of chapter 4 was published in *Culture, Theory and Critique* 44 (1) 2003. A preliminary set of arguments about the phenomenon of digital fetishism as developed in chapter 5 appeared in chapter 24 of *New Media, Old Media: A History and Theory Reader*, edited by Wendy Chun and Thomas Keenan (New York: Routledge, 2006).

KEN HILLIS is an associate professor of media studies in the Department of Communication Studies at the University of North Carolina, Chapel Hill. He is the author of *Digital Sensations: Space, Identity, and Embodiment in Virtual Reality* and coeditor of *Everyday eBay: Culture, Collecting, and Desire*.

Library of Congress Cataloging-in-Publication Data

Hillis, Ken.
Online a lot of the time : ritual, fetish, sign / Ken Hillis.
p. cm.
Includes bibliographical references and index.
ISBN 978-0-8223-4434-6 (cloth : alk. paper)
ISBN 978-0-8223-4448-3 (pbk. : alk. paper)
1. Web 2.0 — Social aspects.
2. Online social networks.
3. Online identities.
4. Shared virtual environments — Social aspects.
5. Internet games — Social aspects.
I. Title.
HM851.H546 2009
303.48'33 — dc22   2008055236